TOUCH

The Foundation of Experience

Clinical Infant Reports
Series of the National Center for Clinical Infant Programs

Clinical Infant Reports is a series of book length publications of the National Center for Clinical Infant Programs designed for practitioners in the multidisciplinary field of infant health, mental health, and development. Each volume presents diagnostic and therapeutic issues and methods, as well as conceptual and research material.

The Johnson & Johnson Pediatric Round Table series of publications was initiated in 1974. Its objective is to bring together the world's outstanding scientists and medical and health care specialists to explore child development research and pediatric concepts at the innovative edge of development. *Touch: The Foundation of Experience* is the first title to be published by the National Center for Clinical Infant Programs.

TOUCH

The Foundation of Experience

Editors

Kathryn E. Barnard, R.N., Ph.D.
T. Berry Brazelton, M.D.

Full Revised and Expanded Proceedings
of Johnson & Johnson Pediatric Round Table X

International Universities Press, Inc.
Madison • Connecticut

Library of Congress Cataloging-in-Publication Data

Touch: the foundation of experience / editors Kathryn E. Barnard, T. Berry Brazelton.
p. cm. — (Clinical infant reports)
Includes bibliographical references.
ISBN 0-8236-6605-0
1. Child development. 2. Touch—Psychological aspects. 3. Touch—Therapeutic use. 4. Developmental psychology. I. Barnard, Kathryn E. II. Brazelton, T. Berry, 1918– . III. Series.
[DNLM: 1. Touch. WR 102 T722]
RJ131.T68 1990
152.1′82—dc20
DNLM/DLC
for Library of Congress 89-20124
CIP

Manufactured in the United States of America

To Dr. Steven Sawchuck and Robert
B. Rock, Jr., friends of the National
Center for Clinical Infant
Programs and children all over the
world, wanting to be touched and held

The National Center for Clinical Infant Programs is a non-profit, tax-exempt corporation. It was established in 1977 by representatives from the fields of mental health, pediatrics, child development, and related fields, as well as community leaders, in order to improve and support professional initiatives in infant health, mental health, and development.

Contents

Contributors

Kathryn Barnard, R.N., Ph.D. University of Washington, Seattle.

T. Berry Brazelton, M.D. The Children's Hospital Medical Center and Harvard Medical School, Boston, Massachusetts.

Marian Cleeves Diamond, Ph.D. University of California, Berkeley.

Cathleen A. Fanslow, R.N., M.A. Visiting Nurse Service of New York.

Jack M. Fletcher, Ph.D. Texas Research Institute of Mental Sciences, Houston.

Peter A. Gorski, M.D. The Evanston Hospital, Evanston, Illinois.

Allen W. Gottfried, Ph.D. California State University, Fullerton.

William T. Greenough, Ph.D. University of Illnois at Urbana-Champaign.

Margaret Hollenbach, Ph.D. University of Washington, Seattle.

Anneliese F. Korner, Ph.D. Stanford University School of Medicine.

Carol H. Leonard, Ph.D. Mt. Zion Hospital Medical Center, San Francisco, California.

Seymour Levine, Ph.D. Stanford University School of Medicine.

Mary Main, Ph.D. University of California, Berkeley.

John A. Martin, Ph.D. California School for Professional Psychology, Berkeley.

Elizabeth R. McAnarney, M.D. The University of Rochester Medical Center.

Ruth McCorkle, R.N., Ph.D. University of Washington, Seattle.

Therese Connell Meehan, R.N., Ph.D., New York University Medical Center.

Michael M. Merzenich, Ph.D. University of California School of Medicine, San Francisco.

Robin Morris, Ph.D. Georgia State University.

Patricia B. Rausch, R.N., M.S.N. Deland, Florida.

Martin Reite, M.D. University of Colorado Health Sciences Center, Denver.

Susan A. Rose, Ph.D. Albert Einstein College of Medicine of Yeshiva University, New York City.

Paul Satz, Ph.D. University of California, Los Angeles.

Sally A. Sehring, M.D. Mt. Zion Hospital Medical Center, San Francisco.

Judith A. Smith, R.N., Ph.D. University of Pennsylvania.

Mark E. Stanton, Ph.D. Stanford University School of Medicine.

Stephen J. Suomi, Ph.D. National Institute of Child Health and Human Development, Bethesda, Maryland.

David M. Sweet, Ph.D. University of California, San Francisco.

H. Gerry Taylor, Ph.D. University of Pittsburgh.

Renée Weber, Ph.D. Rutgers University, New Brunswick, New Jersey.

Sandra J. Weiss, D.N.Sc. University of California, San Francisco.

Iris S. Wolfson, R.N., B.S., C.N.M. Philadelphia, Pennsylvania.

Introduction

Kathryn E. Barnard, R.N., Ph.D.
T. Berry Brazelton, M.D.

This book is the result of a fruitful collaboration between Johnson & Johnson Baby Products Company and the National Center for Clinical Infant Programs. In the Pediatric Round Table series, Johnson & Johnson Baby Products Company has brought together outstanding scientists and medical and health care specialists to share current research data and fresh information about new concepts and programs in child health and development. In its Clinical Infant Reports series, the National Center for Clinical Infant Programs addresses gaps in the professional literature, and relates theoretical concepts to issues of concern to practitioners in the new and growing multidisciplinary field of infant health, mental health, and development. The increasing awareness among researchers and clinicians of touch as the foundation of experience makes the joint publication of these proceedings particularly appropriate.

These papers form an exciting collection of philosophical and scientific work related to the complex and, at times, confusing role of touch in both development and well-being. That it has been difficult to study touch in isolation from other sensory systems may be the most important finding emanating from the Round Table.

The complexity of the cutaneous sensory modality makes it a fascinating focus for research. As one probes for the limits of this modality to identify critical areas for investigation, however, one must first describe the various functions served by touch. Documented functions of passive touching include arousal, comforting, quieting, communicating, and learning. Active touching is used in exploration, self-stimulation, and self-control.

The seven sections of this book explore a philosophical perspective on touch, the neuroanatomical perspective, animal studies and the impact of touch, touch as an integration and learning system for preterm infants, the role of therapeutic touch, the importance of touch throughout the lifespan, and touch as a touchstone.

In Part I, philosopher Renée Weber describes the phenomenon of touch in many different ways, each of which leads to a different conclusion. From a physical–sensory, psychologic–humanistic, or field philosophy viewpoint, Weber claims that the field model best fits both an integrative and intentionality dimension, which she feels characterizes the concept of touch. One gains the impression that touching can be an act of connectedness, both at a physical and intersensory level. Touch is hard to quantify in a strictly empirical sense. The importance of clarifying one's own philosophical perspective is demonstrated repeatedly as one reads the various chapters in this book, which range from a strictly empirical, experimental view of the physical aspects of touch, to field philosophy, where it is the "intentionality" of energy transfer through touch that is implied.

Part II examines neuroanatomical perspectives in relation to touch and brain plasticity. While study of tactile stimulation as a single modality has been limited, there are many studies of the sensory systems, particularly the visual pathway. A number of animal studies have examined the question of sensory deprivation versus complex and/or enriched environments. Drs. Merzernich, Diamond, and Greenough present work in their chapters which has confirmed the importance of somatosensory experience extending from the prenatal period to aging. Merzenich's line of investigation, in particular, supports both the development and maintenance of cortical mapping by tactile experience. His studies on injury and amputation in animal mòdels support a remapping process which involves the recovery of nerve cells and their projections. Exquisite studies by Marian Diamond have demonstrated chemical and structural changes in the nervous system relative to early experience. Diamond's studies lead to new thinking about the importance of environmental enrichment even in aging. Greenough proposes that maturational sequencing of modalities might hold consequences for sensory integration; the cutaneous modality may be the first to develop. Greenough raises two important models for considering developmental experience: the experience expectant and the experience dependent. The former is common to all normally reared members of the species; the latter involves experiences that are unique and have a large role for memory and in learning.

Part III involves developmental perspectives of touch and attachment. The three papers which comprise this section confirm the importance of the early work of Harry Harlow, who in 1959 recognized the importance of "contact comfort" for the development of normal behavior in primates. Dr. Suomi emphasizes the role of physical contact, especially ventral to ventral contact, for providing food, temperature control, and stimulation for the infant primate. "Contact comfort," as reflected in peer grooming, continues to be important in later development, illustrating the major role of infant physical contact in beginning primate socialization. Drs. Levine and Stanton expand the theoretical notion, claiming that physical contact moderates arousal through pituitary–adrenal activation. Their experiments demonstrate the "buffering" of mother–infant primate systems under stress conditions of separation. Dr. Reite, in his chapter, develops several new propositions. One involves the importance of touch or contact in forming attachments, and as a prerequisite to integrative functioning, manifested by pleasurable states and good physical health. A number of studies are reviewed which demonstrate the importance of loss or grieving on the hypothalmic regulating system, including changes in heart rate, sleep, and circadian rhythms. Reite postulates that because of the major role touch has in developing early attachments, it subsequently may exert a regulatory influence capable of reactivating a complete organismic response.

In Part IV the developmental perspective of touch is dramatically demonstrated with the preterm infant. Dr. Peter Gorski and his colleagues carefully illustrate the complexities of touch within the caregiver–infant relationship. The Gorski team presents data from monitoring of the cardiorespiratory function of the preterm infant which confirm that not all touching is therapeutic. Some forms of touching under certain infant states may promote autonomic disintegration.

Several experiments using tactile stimulation are reported in papers by Rausch and Korner. Touch in these studies was only one of the experimental variables. Other stimuli were vestibular and visual stimulation. Nevertheless the evidence presented by these investigators suggests an integrative and controlling influence of tactile stimulation for the immature organism.

In investigations of tactile sensitivity and tactile stimulation, researcher Dr. Susan Rose suggests that the preterm infant is not as responsive to tactile stimuli as is the term infant. She also demonstrates, however, that when the infant is provided with additional tactile vestibular stimulation the tactile responsiveness of the preterm infant can be improved. Dr. Rose's chapter highlights the differing features of passive and active touch, the latter involving activation of joints, muscles, and the organism in exploration. Her preliminary laboratory studies demonstrate that the preterm infant shows less responsiveness for both passive forms of touching and active touch as measured in cross-modality learning experiments.

Paul Satz moves farther into childhood, reexamining the operations involved in finger recognition performance to determine its predictive and concurrent relationships with reading readiness and achievement.

In a summary paper, Dr. Gottfried emphasizes the ontogenesis of tactile responsiveness, and highlights the potential role of this early learning sense for later development and learning.

In Section V, Meehan, Wolfson, and Smith explore the role of therapeutic touch. The concept of therapeutic touch involves the interventional use of energy transfer to facilitate normal functioning. This energy, or *prana*, is sensed by the self and others and is used to facilitate healing. Smith urges that more studies be done to aid in understanding this important human modality. Iris Wolfson describes an application of the concept of therapeutic touch in relation to management of women during pregnancy, including labor and delivery and early parenting.

Part VI deals with the importance of touch throughout the lifespan. Weiss's chapter investigates the role of touch in self-perception and body image. Through a study of the differential input and effect of parental touching on elementary school children, she finds a special quality in maternal touching, involving more arousal management. Her study, along with the findings of the investigation of touching in adolescence by Dr. McAnarney, emphasizes the importance of considering changes in touching experiences through childhood. McAnarney suggests that the decrease of parental touching and tactile contact in adolescence may influence some adolescents to seek intimate tactile contact from peers.

In her discussion, Mary Main develops a new theoretical perspective which demands that we explore not only the presence or absence of touch in mother–infant attachment systems, but also the questions of who, when, and how, which will lead to investigations addressing the intentionality of contact.

Ruth McCorkle and Margaret Hollenbach review specific therapeutic problems in psychotherapy, medicine, and nursing involving touch. They explore responses to isolation for bone marrow transplant patients, who represent a special case of touch deprivation. The final chapter by Fanslow discusses the effect of therapeutic touch treatments on the ambulation and mobility of patients in nursing homes. Unique experiences of helping dying patients develop an inner balance and harmony are also shared, illustrating the great significance of touch for those at the end of life.

As reflected in the summary statement, this series of chapters confirms our own thinking about the importance of touch as an intersensory integrator and one of the main contributors to development. Its importance can be seen in the neonatal period—touch can be a stimulator or a reducer of stimulation, depending on the situation or state of the infant. Touch is also a control system: a baby losing control will make a real effort to master his motor disorganization by bringing his hand to his mouth. As he mouths his fist, he will regain control of himself. If his own efforts are unsuccessful, a gentle touch from a caregiver can help the baby regain control. In addition, touch can provide a source of energy for development and learning.

Our goal in setting up this Round Table of experts was to attempt to define the importance of this modality and to examine the implications of tactile stimulation and deprivation for the developing organism. By mapping the areas in the brain which represent this modality, we can begin to see what a violation of the expected and even necessary tactile input might mean at an anatomical level. Animal studies of deprivation and of enrichment could contribute paradigms for studies of the developing human. In the area of high-risk premature and underweight neonates, there is increasing evidence for autonomic as well as anatomical effects. Opportunities for recovery from impairment in immature brains are increasingly recognized to be much greater than we had previously thought, thanks to the redundancy of unassigned neurological pathways in immature humans. Touch can play a major role in furthering organization and learning in an impaired infant. Tactile experiences need to be graded for their appropriateness versus their inappropriateness in providing organizing information to promote recovery from damage and functional assignment of the undamaged pathways. Cross-modal transfer from tactile to other modalities, such as motor functioning, seems to enhance this recovery and may become a way of assessing future competence in immature organisms. The use of touch as therapy in older, disorganized infants and children is beginning to be explored in more detail. With hypersensitive, hyperkinetic, and even learning disabled children, touch can be seen as therapeutic. For sick or disturbed older children and adults, especially for the elderly, the modality of touch can be of major therapeutic value. The nursing profession has become aware of "new" uses of therapeutic touch—a concept of the tactile and kinesthetic modalities in which the therapy focuses on touch as a major mode of communication and reorganization.

Part I: Philosophical Perspectives

1
A Philosophical Perspective on Touch

Renée Weber, Ph.D.

I have been asked to address the topic of touch from the philosophical perspective. To me, the unique task of humanism is an integrative one that tries to synthesize what scientists and social scientists must necessarily take apart in the course of their analyses and research. My focus is, therefore, holistic. It deals with the touch of person and person, or of person and animal—but not the touch of hand and skin, or hand and fur, nor the idea of tactile stimulation. These concepts are important and have their place, but not in a humanistic consideration of the subject, which must focus on touch as a holistic capacity.

What is the meaning of touch? What are its philosophical underpinnings and implications, its boundaries and effects? Different philosophical schools will differ in their answers. This chapter, therefore, explores touch from a theoretical and speculative point of view, and is not data based. Some of the theories I will raise are highly conjectural and should at present be regarded as proposals.

Philosophical writing on touch is rare, and hence philosophical perspectives on touch must be extracted from more general philosophical positions. Ultimately, divergent views on touch can be attributed to divergent answers to the question "What is a human being?" offered by various philosophical schools. But this is precisely the central question of the humanities, and depending on how this question is answered, touch—and other human capacities and interactions—will be explained quite differently. Moreover, the question is a far-reaching one that has cognitive, psychological, and even moral implications. To be philosophically solid, we would need to go back even one step further and ask: "On what do the various definitions of a human being in the various philosophical schools depend?" The answer is that they depend on underlying epistemological and metaphysical assumptions which, being assumptions, are held axiomatically and cannot be proven.

Research on the philosophical literature of touch yields almost nothing. It is surprising that the concept of touch, in the sense in which we are using it here, is virtually nonexistent in 2500 years of Western philosophy. Its appearance in books is rare, and it is mentioned only sporadically in the journal literature. Among forty-one articles on touch published over the last four decades, all but one or two deal with the epistemological and cognitive aspects of the subject, and a few treat it in the context of aesthetics and theories of art. Given this paucity of explicit material, I will look at some representative philosophical views and, though they may not deal with touch explicitly, extrapolate from their general position what their view on touch would most likely be.

I intend to map the concept of touch onto three divergent models of man and nature: the physical-sensory model, the psychological-humanistic model, and the field model. This latter is a bold and intriguing view and its offshoot, therapeutic touch, is the most novel philosophical framework applicable to touch, and the only one which devotes itself explicitly to the subject.

What is touch? The dictionary distinguishes three meanings that are relevant to my remarks. *Touch* can mean "to be in contact with"; it can mean "to lay the hand or hands on"; or it can mean "to reach and to communicate." These three definitions correlate roughly with the three models I have outlined. The physical–sensory model restricts its interest mainly to the contact theory of touch; the psychological–humanistic model explores touch as a way of reaching and communicating with a self or inner person. The field model draws on this explanation as well, but in addition, in therapeutic touch, for example, it makes use of a modern and more clinical version of touch as a laying on of hands.

These three models of touch can be correlated with distinct cultural and philosophical contexts. The physical–sensory model fits the aims and assumptions of Anglo-American philosophy; the psychological–humanistic model expresses the concerns of contemporary European philosophy, especially phenomenology and existentialism; and the field model and therapeutic touch best harmonize with Eastern philosophy and its holistic world view. I shall return to these frameworks in more detail, but want first to provide a brief overview of each of these three.

Touch as an interactional modality has been neglected by philosophy. Especially in the last three hundred years, since the time of Descartes, only mental and verbal exchanges have been considered important. Since the eighteenth century and the work of the British empiricists, interest shifted to the senses, as sensory input was felt, and continues to be felt, to be the dominant factor in shaping man's picture of nature, himself, and others. The Cartesian legacy of solipsism—the claim that I am trapped within my own universe without certain access to others—continues to haunt mainstream Anglo-American philosophy to this day. At the opposite end of the spectrum, Eastern philosophy depicts a theory of man and nature in which humans are inherently linked with the natural world at some deep level of their being. This view is affirmed by all Eastern systems as well as by the holistic philosophers in the West, such as Pythagoras, Plato, and

Spinoza. It has been strengthened by twentieth century science, notably relativity theory and quantum mechanics. The unity of observer and observed and the interconnectedness of all particles of matter that has been asserted in India since the *Upanishads* (ca. 800 B.C.) is one of the chief philosophical implications of contemporary physics, according to noted quantum physicist and philosopher of science, David Bohm (1980).

Touch is being considered increasingly important in human development, functioning, and communication. Touch is integrative and synthesizing, hence inherently holistic. But contemporary Anglo-American philosophy, the heir of Descartes and Hume, tends to be reductionistic, as is much of psychology. These tend to reduce touch to its constituent aspects, which in view of the holistic nature of touch seems paradoxical. To some extent, existentialism and phenomenology provide a hospitable climate for the humanistic implications of touch. But the richest source for mapping comes from the philosophies of the East, from Hindu, Buddhist, and Taoist thought.

They share the idea of universal and interpenetrating fields which connect all organisms at subtler levels of matter. Moreover, they postulate that human beings are localized expressions of these universal fields, functioning both as themselves and as an aspect of the field. By analogy with quantum mechanics, we are both particles and waves: on the one hand, localized and discrete; on the other hand, spread out and continuous with other waves. The field model is holistic, and it is the most comprehensive model of touch, since it can incorporate all three definitions of touch within itself. Like the physical–sensory model, it allows for touch as direct contact, but it also accommodates touch as a "laying on of hands" in therapeutic touch. Lastly, it assigns a unique meaning to touching as "reaching" the other at some level deeper than the visible and behavioral one.

To treat a holistic sense such as touch within a reductionistic framework seems problematic to me; to see it as an expression of a general holistic framework is more consistent and philosophically more appealing. On these grounds, as well as others, the field model of touch strikes me as the most interesting and promising one, and I will devote a large part of this chapter to it.

The field model makes intentionality the key to human interaction and communication. Intent so conceived is more than a thought, a fantasy, or even a private emotion without correlation in the public world. This model claims that intent is an energy. It has both a magnitude and a direction and thus functions like a vector force which finds its mark. This latter rationale is central to touch as a therapeutic tool, a subject to which I shall return later.

What is important to note is that under the old dualistic philosophy, touch functions in a nonholistic way. The practical application of this view is that the *source* of touch under the physical–sensory model, for example, ought to be irrelevant. For Descartes (1642), and Hume and Skinner (1739–1740), mechanical as well as human agents of touch ought to produce the same results, since we are dealing with physical masses contiguous to other physical masses, or sense-impressions impinging on sense-impressions. The inner state, the intentional disposition of either giver or recipient of touch, ought not to matter. Under the field model this would not be the case. Touch in the sense of *reaching* has occurred even before the sense-impressions have been consciously registered by the other. This is because the field model proposes a kind of harmonics of human interaction reminiscent of the views of Pythagoras, in which organisms can resonate along a similar frequency and be attuned via nonsensory means. This has both a literal and a metaphorical meaning, requiring a number of ancillary hypotheses for its support.

Among these are new theories of man and nature, that redefine space, time, energy, consciousness, self, and others in a way that fits neither dualistic nor reductionistic models.

The field model broadens the psychological model, moving beyond man's humanistic orientation to point to our relationship with nature as a whole, thereby evoking Spinoza's position. It postulates energies beyond those currently described by science, which—though not quantifiable nor at present well understood—seem to play a distinct role in human well-being.

One such idea is that *prana*, a vital energy postulated by virtually all Eastern philosophies, is a key factor in human health and well-being at all levels. It underlies the theory of therapeutic touch as well, in the claim that a healthy organism with overabundant energy can deliberately and with conscious intent direct that vital energy to someone depleted of it or low in it. As the conveyor of this energy, touch functions as the *seal* of the intent.

In fact, this idea has a Western precursor. It is the Renaissance that attributes unparalleled power to touch. In his fresco masterpiece, *The Creation of Man* (Sistine Chapel, Vatican), Michelangelo has God stretch out a dynamic hand toward the lifeless hand of Adam in order to transmit the spark of life to it. This vision of touch as the bearer of vital energy is an interesting variation on *Genesis*, where God directly breathes Adam into life. By contrast, Michelangelo's God uses touch.

The conception is notable in two ways. First, touch is seen as a creative principle inherent in nature, personalized here as God. Second, Michelangelo identifies touch with life itself, following Aristotle (*De Anima*), and carries the point one step further. Touch is needed not only for our survival but also for our becoming whole. Since Adam's body is already formed, it is clear that what touch adds is the animating principle—the soul or spirit—without which the body is an inert bundle of matter that cannot function. As God is both nonfinite and nonmaterial, he might logically have willed the vital energy into Adam. But Michelangelo chose otherwise. It is touch that bestows wholeness on the incomplete lump of clay that is to become the first human. Michelangelo's fresco may be an early and intuitive rendition of the principle of field touch. Its most arresting feature is the positioning of the hands, since they are the focal point of the composition. These hands do not touch: they nearly touch. They are aligned so that something flows from the cosmic hand to the human hand, but there is no physical contact. It is as if Michelangelo foresaw field theory space and energy and symbolized it in his work. If that is the case, therapeutic touch may rightfully claim him as one of its precursors.

Michelangelo's esteem of touch is shared by antiquity, and before returning to my three models, I want briefly to look at the views of the ancient Greeks. They held rival theories: Plato, in the fourth century B.C., espoused a nonlocalization theory; Aristotle, in the third century, a direct contact theory. Both puzzled over the same question: how does touch differ from the other senses? Both noted that all other senses can be correlated with a specific organ: sight with the eyes, hearing with the ears, and so on, and wondered what organ, if any, correlates with the sense of touch. Aristotle, in *De Anima*, says that "we are unable clearly to detect in the case of touch what the single subject is which . . . corresponds to sound in the case of hearing" (p. 25), and having gone through an account of each of the senses, he adds that "in the case of touch the obscurity remains" (p. 28). He concludes that "flesh is not the organ, but the medium of touch" (p. 30). The organ of touch is neither the skin nor the flesh but the heart; that is to say, something deep within the perceiving subject. What Aristotle may have groped for with this view was a unifying center for touch, commensurable with its special status. Unlike the other senses, which work through mediate contact, touch operates by immediate contact. By this criterion, taste according to Aristotle is also "a sort of touch." This idea is reflected in the Greek words for touch, *haphe* and *psausis*, both of which are associated with contact. Touch (and taste) is so crucial, observes Aristotle, that its absence spells doom to man and all animals. The animal that cannot make direct contact with, and perceive, its food cannot function, and Aristotle concludes that "it is evident, therefore, that the loss of this one sense alone must bring about the death of an animal" (p. 32).

Plato, by contrast, believes in the nonlocalization theory of touch as the feature that sets it apart from the other senses. In the *Timaeus* he argues that "hot and cold, hard, soft, heavy, light, smooth, and rough" all should count as objects of touch. His reasoning is not founded on any direct contact—for Plato avoids the idea, and even words connoting it like *haphe* or *psausis*—but because they are, in his words, "affections common to the body as a whole" (p. 92). They can be perceived without the use of a localized organ such as eyes, nose, ears, or tongue, through any part of the body. These remarks on Plato and Aristotle are based in part on an article by the contemporary Oxford philosopher, Richard Sorabji (1971), who has surveyed the status of touch in Greek philosophy. He writes: "It looks, then, as if the nonlocalization criterion, to be found in Plato and others, has retained its influence to the present day" (pp. 55–79).

The platonic concept of nonlocalization is a forerunner of the field theory of touch. It emphasizes that touch is something generalized, a synthesis of the functions of the body, and perhaps of the body and mind, soul, or spirit. Even Aristotle, to revert to him for a moment, is searching for some such integrative theory when he writes that "the soul is analogous to the hand; for as the hand is the tool of tools, so the mind is the form of forms" (p. 98). By this he draws our attention to the view he shares with Plato, namely that mere sensation does not produce knowledge. An integrating and ordering principle is needed in addition.

A debate about this claim runs through much of the history of philosophy, especially through seventeenth century rationalism and eighteenth century empiricism. Kant, in the nineteenth century, tries to reconcile these traditions in his doctrine that "percepts without concepts are blind, concepts without percepts empty." This is no mere epistemological dispute. What is involved is nothing less than what it means to be a human being. For both Plato and Aristotle, man is the rational animal, possessing a mind and a soul which make use of, and direct, the senses, and occupy a status that is logically superior to them. This is most clearly brought out by Plato, who rejects the idea that knowledge is only sense perception, a thesis popular in his day and argued in particular by the Sophists, against whom many of the Platonic dialogues were written. For example, in the *Theaetetus*, Plato raises the still unsolved question that is also applicable to touch: "Which is more correct, to say that we see or hear *with* the eyes and *with* the ears, or *through* the eyes and *through* the ears?" (pp. 184–185). Theaetetus dutifully replies, "I should say 'through' rather than 'with,' Socrates," whereupon Socrates (the spokesman for Plato) says: "Yes, my boy, for no one can suppose that in each of us, as in a sort of Trojan horse, there are perched a number of unconnected senses, which do not all meet in some one nature, the mind, or whatever we please to call it, of which they are the instruments, and with which, through them, we perceive objects of sense" (p. 185). This passage is typical of the many in which Plato opposes a reductionistic and physicalistic view of human functioning. The interesting question is: who or what is this "we" to which Plato refers and to whom he ascribes the awareness of touch and of other sensations? The answer depends on the philosophical framework to which we subscribe.

To Descartes, as to seventeenth century rationalists in general, the perceiver is the inner person, self, or thinker whom he describes in his *cogito* doctrine: "I think, therefore I am." This entity is distinct from sensation and, indeed, from the body. The mind–body dualism that Descartes establishes in his *Meditations* (1642) has persisted largely until our day. Descartes confesses that he cannot really account for the interaction of body and mind. Moreover, he bequeathes to philosophy a doctrine of interpersonal difficulty that borders on alienation: his Cartesian solipsism. Since I can have direct access to, and thus indubitable certainty only of, my own mind (hence, self), I can never be certain that other minds or selves (i.e., whole human beings) exist. Their existence is conjectural, inferential, and probabilistic. They cannot be proven with the same certitude with which I can prove my own existence. Touch, and other human interactions must, therefore, remain largely unexplained, since Cartesian solipsism casts doubts on touch as a tool of genuine communication among people. A second problem in connection with Descartes' view of man is that, in some respects, he treats the body as a mass among other masses. It would, therefore, be difficult to envisage an enhancing or therapeutic role for touch in the Cartesian framework. Despite the primacy of consciousness and the irreducibility of the self in the cogito, Descartes' position belongs to the physical–sensory model.

The outstanding and most consistent figure associated with these views is David Hume, the great British empiricist, whose universe is built upon the idea of sense-impressions. Nothing but these are ultimately real, and all our ideas are just modifications of sense-impressions. They are the building blocks of knowledge. Whatever ideas cannot be traced back to them is based on self-deception. Hume spells out his epistemological criterion in the celebrated passage which concludes his *Treatise of Human Nature* (1739–1740). In approaching any book, he says, we must ask ourselves two questions: "*Does it contain any abstract reasoning concerning quantity or number* [i.e., is it tautological and certain, like mathematics]?" and "*Does it contain any experimental reasoning concerning matters of fact*?" If the answer to these is "no," Hume urges, "Commit it then to the flames, for it can contain nothing but sophistries and illusion" (p. 87; italics are Hume's). Hume's influence on contemporary philosophy is vast. By this criterion touch would have to be explained as sense-impressions impinging on sense-impression, mediated perhaps by some neurologically complex mechanism for registering and encoding them. Touch does not involve the whole person, but is explained in physical terms, as one set of stimuli approaching another set. The idea of reaching an inward self, as in the other two models, is ruled out by Hume's stringent empiricism and skepticism. In fact, he dismisses any such entity in the discussion of personal identity in the *Treatise*. Since we never have a sense-impression of the self, Hume terms the notion a fiction.

The therapeutic role that intent associated with touch might play is incompatible with Hume's and other versions of reductionism. The intentional set of the agent dispensing the sensory stimulus is irrelevant to the message communicated through touch (unless it affects the delivery or quality of the touch). Feelings, whether altruistic or selfish, which are crucial to the other two models, are secondary to Hume. He handles them as "matters of taste" which have no independent moral or objective reality as they do in the field model. Their value derives from social consensus, and their status is purely utilitarian: to ensure a cohesive social order. Behavior rather than intent or mind-set shapes human interactions, and it satisfies the definition of touch as "reaching" another. The reaching, in Hume, cannot apply to an invisible "inner" person, for that is reduced to a bundle of habits for Hume (as for B.F. Skinner, his heir). Questions concerning the limitations of this approach are particularly acute when we look at some practical applications. If Hume is correct, ambivalent or conflicting feelings coexistent with touch ought not to affect the recipient. But the facts dispute this. Many people, especially children, are sensitive to contradictory messages and may experience seemingly friendly touch as negative. The physical–sensory model will have difficulty explaining this, and will have to argue its case in terms of subtle and scarcely detectable behavioral or muscle cues. The field model will take it as partial evidence for its claims. In the field model, the disparity between the quality of touch and the inner message of its sender cannot go undetected even if accompanied by gestures and language designed to reinforce the touch. It will be registered in the recipient's fields even in the absence of behavioral or kinesthetic cues. As a consequence, the person touched will feel unaccountably uneasy and will tend to withdraw from the interaction.

This is in contrast to the psychological–humanistic model, which lies somewhere between the other two in its position on touch. The psychological model is more holistic than the physical–sensory model, less so than the field model. It concerns itself with the purposive interaction of self-conscious agents, and focuses on such uniquely human feelings as sympathy, empathy, and love. Individuality, personhood, and the subjectivity and inwardness of consciousness are its building blocks. The power of human interaction derives from imaginative ways of relating to others, who are conceived as irreducible and autonomous agents like myself. Their existence cannot be proved, as Descartes rightly saw, but for existentialists like Heidegger, Sartre, and Buber such proof is redundant. It is a datum given along with my own existence. Phenomenologists like Merleau-Ponty concur. The existence of others is disclosed to us with the same certainty as is our own. To use an obvious example from Sartre's *Being and Nothingness* (1956), certain emotions such as shame cannot be understood without assuming the givenness of the other as an a priori fact. Merleau-Ponty, in *The Phenomenology of Perception* (1962), extends this a priori disclosedness to the world. In this he follows Heidegger, who argues that humans (unlike all other sorts of entities) always *already* live in a world: a world of nature, a world of culture, a world of interpersonal networks, all bound together by meaning. In short, man is not just the rational animal of the Greeks: he is the meaning-making and valuational animal who inhabits a universe composed of meanings and values more primary to our species than the sense-impressions on which Hume seeks to base our existence.

Meaning, for the psychological model, is as fundamental a datum as sense-impressions are for the empirical model; it constitutes the core of the human experience, our being-in-the-world with others, to use existentialist terms. Our ecological niche is the interpersonal world, linked by symbols, social categories, and shared cultural contexts.

In the psychological model, social exchange is considered the basic fact of existence. Communication and communion, or their breakdown in alienation and isolation, are the earmarks of the uniquely human world. They are irreducibles, and reducing them to a more primary set of explanations explains them away and loses their meaning. Not all the figures that may be grouped within this model focus on the positive aspects of human interchange. For Sartre, my subjectivity is always in jeopardy, its freedom endangered by the subjectivity of the other. In order to ensure my remaining the subject, I must turn the other into my object; he in turn will counterattack with the attempt to turn me into his object. Given this premise, it is not surprising to find Sartre's social theory based on conflict. He perceives the touch of the other as a threat to autonomy. Even touch as an expression of love and sexual intimacy is interpreted as the desire for control, a continuing struggle for dominance that borders on sadomasochism. Sartre's characters handle and manipulate one another, but rarely touch. Touch is, in any case, of subordinate interest to Sartre, who builds his theories around the sense of vision. His chief philosophical category is "the look," by means of which we fix, categorize, appropriate, and manipulate others. Conflict and competition predominate in Sartre's world, and his assessment of the human condition is summed up at the close of his best-known play, *No Exit* (1947), as "Hell is other people!"

For Sartre, touch is appropriation. In caressing another, he says in *Being and Nothingness* (1956), I am really caressing my own body "with the Other's body, rather than caressing her" (p. 506). That is because Sartre transposes the power of *the look*—his central epistemological category and the tool for appropriating others—to the domain of touch. Phenomenologist Merleau-Ponty rejects this view. Touch is not unidirectional but reciprocal. "In the very act of touching, one is touched in return" (1962, p. 322). He also rejects the dichotomy of an active and a passive member of the haptic experience. Touch, unlike the other senses, is inherently reciprocal. I can see but not be seen, and hear without being heard, but I cannot touch without being touched. "To touch or to be touched implies to be close to what is touched. . . . In touch, the distinction between touching subject and touched object blurs" (p. 323).

This reciprocity of touch can be broken by an act of will. The physician who must examine patients can, through a deliberate intentional act, "adopt a certain impenetrable attitude towards the other" (p. 325). But this is a special case that needs training and effort to break the natural tendency toward reciprocity. Merleau-Ponty's theory is timely, and may shed light on the current soul-searching in medical circles, which deplores the increasing distancing by many health professionals when dealing with patients (I shall return to this topic later). What is interesting is that Merleau-Ponty sees the reciprocity of touch as the *natural feature* which, unless it is unlearned and repressed, will lead to human empathy and sympathy.

Others within the psychological–humanistic tradition agree that sympathy and empathy are most perfectly expressed by touch. Just as touch brings us near the person physically, so empathy and sympathy are "feeling-acts" that bring us close to the inner world of the other. Touch is the paradigmatic sense expressing this closeness, for "only touch requires contact, the proximity of feeling to what is felt" (Wyschograd, 1981). In this view, the body as a whole is the tactile field, integrating "its sensitivity to pressure, temperature and surface qualities, together with its kinesthesis, its felt respiratory movements, its pulse, the hand's capacity for manipulative endeavor, its motility. . . ." (p. 26).

Following the theories of Merleau-Ponty, for whom the body is a unity which, unlike a thing or even a scientific object is to be compared "rather to a work of art," Wyschograd writes that "We can think of the living body as a tactile body. For the body as a whole is a potential haptic field" (p. 39). Like Plato, Aristotle, and Merleau-Ponty, she singles out touch and sets it apart from the other senses. "If we are right, if the primordial manner of being of the lived body is to be understood as tactile, then tactility cannot be included under a generic theory of sense but provides its ground. Thus the manner in which touch yields the world is the most primordial manner of our apprehension of it" (p. 39). Merleau-Ponty argues that the unity and identity of touch are founded on the unity and identity of the body as a "synergic totality." He notes that "the body is born towards tactile experience by all its surfaces and all its organs simultaneously, and carries with it a certain typical structure of the tactile world" (p. 316).

Wyschograd (1981) concludes that "while empathy and sympathy are ordinary feeling-acts which structurally resemble tactile encounters (bringing the other close, tracing his or her affective states, moving or reaching towards the other, etc.) not all tactile encounters resemble empathy and sympathy. The sculptor encounters the world as tactile but deploys touch for aesthetic ends. The physician palpates the patient's body to diagnose disease, etc." (p. 41). In these cases, Wyschograd points out, touch functions more like sight (i.e., cognitively). It becomes a way of mastering experience and appropriating it, distancing us from what we touch, as sight can appropriate objects even at a distance and need not entail closeness or reciprocity.

However fruitful these phenomenological perspectives are, one might argue that closeness and distancing are less a function of moving from the visual to the haptic field than they are a function of our attitude toward what we approach.

Many thinkers in the psychological–humanistic model have urged greater humanization in our encounters. They include Ashley Montagu, whose book *Touching* (1971) extols the bonding and developmental properties of touch. The same preoccupation with reciprocity and community is shared by the humanistic and transpersonal movements in psychology. Philosophically, however, the most solid foundation for a theory of touch is found in the work of Buber.

If Sartre is the pessimistic end of the humanistic spectrum, its other extreme is Martin Buber, the most humanistic example of this model and the one most directly applicable to theories of touch. In his book *I and Thou* (1923), he distinguishes between an I–It and an I–Thou mode of relating to others. Building on this distinction, one can correlate the I–It mode of physical interaction with manipulation and handling, the I–Thou mode with touch. The I–It mode is object-oriented, reductionistic, and utilitarian. It reduces the other to qualities, takes him apart into components as though he were a watch or some other machine, judges him, and treats him as external to oneself. In handling or manipulating the other, one uses him for one's own purposes, not for the other's sake. Says Buber: "*I–Thou* can only be spoken with [one's] whole being. *I–It* can never be spoken with [one's] whole being" (p. 3).

The I–Thou relationship is holistic. It perceives the other as a total gestalt within a framework of acceptance and mutuality. It is a living relationship, with its own dimensions of space and time that differ from ordinary space and from clock time. The I–Thou relationship takes place without being bounded by categories, in the timeless present. Buber elaborates: "When *Thou* is spoken, the speaker has no *thing* . . . but he takes his stand in relation. If I face a human being as my *Thou* and say the primary word *I–Thou* to him, he is not a thing among things . . . but I take my stand in relation to him. . . . What, then, do we know of *Thou*?

Just everything, for we know nothing isolated about it any-more" (pp. 4–10).

For Buber, it is part of our existential tragedy that we cannot remain exclusively in the *I–Thou* dimension but are forced through daily necessity to convert the *Thou* back into a utilitarian *It*, in which no genuine relationship (i.e., mutuality) can exist. This is Buber's concession to realism. He observes: "The particular *Thou*, after the relational event has run its course, is bound to become an *It*. . . . The particular *It*, by entering the relational event, may become a *Thou*. . . ." (p. 33). Despite the oscillations, the *I–Thou* relationship can fill a large part of our lives, transmuting manipulation and handling into genuine touching and reaching. Buber notes that children, above all, live in the *I–Thou* dimension more than they live in the *I–It*, and only gradually lose the magic of this direct and timeless mode of living. Though it is the natural gift of childhood, we need not lose it altogether. "Without *It* man cannot live. But he who lives with *It* alone is not a man" writes Buber (1923, p. 34). In touching another, I acknowledge that he is a *Thou*, like myself, not a thing at my disposal. To use the vocabulary of Kant, one of the great moral philosophers of the eighteenth century, touch treats the other as an end in itself, never merely as a means to my end (in accordance with Kant's categorical imperative). This has ethical and even spiritual implications. Buber ultimately brings in the apex of the triadic relationship in which the *I* and *Thou* merely form the corners. He speaks of an "eternal *Thou*" to whom each person stands related, for "in each *Thou* we address the eternal *Thou*" (pp. 104–109).

Although Buber's theory furnishes a framework for touch, he does not address the topic directly. We come closer to this in a philosophical novelist like Tolstoy, in whose masterpiece, *The Death of Ivan Ilych* (1886), touch becomes the dénouement of the whole work. Ivan Ilych, tormented on a lonely deathbed and wracked by pain, feels totally isolated from those around him: his cheerful, lying physician and his callous wife and daughter, to whom he is an obstacle who intrudes on their normal routine. He asks himself: "Why, and for what reason is there all this horror?" and finds no answer. As Ivan Ilych struggles to die, he suddenly becomes aware of the touch of a hand upon his own, followed by a trickle of tears. This gesture, by his schoolboy son, reverses the *I–It* status to which Ivan Ilych has been reduced and transforms his relationship with the child into an *I–Thou*. During months of illness, Ivan Ilych has been manipulated and at best handled, but never touched, and never reached. Now, two hours before his death, he experiences the gift of touch and this serves as the trigger for a transformation. It enables him to die reconciled with his family and at peace with himself. He has learned to transcend his lifelong self-centeredness and can for the first time feel love, not only for his son but even for his cold and calculating wife. This event takes place in nonordinary time, microtime or relativity time, but not in clock time. It is reminiscent of Buber's eternal present and of the nonordinary time frames of both therapeutic touch and Bohm's implicate order physics. Tolstoy suggests that Ivan Ilych's awareness of the other as a *Thou* initiates a stage of growth in which he discovers even at that late hour a new dimension of his humanity. Beyond this, Tolstoy hints that Ivan Ilych links up with a nonfinite level of being (like Buber's "eternal *Thou*") that transcends time and space, and upon whose touch his fear of death dissolves.

Tolstoy's work is one of the few examples in philosophy and literature in which touch functions therapeutically, in the original Greek sense of the word. *Therapeuein* means to take care of, and its humanistic roots are preserved in the word itself, for *therapon* meant an attendant, a living person. Thus, "*therapeutic*," which today signifies "curative, having healing qualities," derives from the care shown to one person by another, the *therapon* or healing presence. Yet despite their awareness of touch as a special therapeutic bond that could link human beings, the Greeks did little with it. The idea of the *therapon* as a factor in healing remained largely undeveloped until our own time. In the last decade, the potentialities of this idea have begun to be explored, as the *therapon* became associated with the idea of touch accompanied by compassionate intent. Thus, *therapeutic* touch was born.

Therapeutic touch is an offspring of the field model of man and human interaction. It rejects the dualistic view of Descartes and the simplified materialism of Hume as basically incorrect. In their stead, it proposes (Kunz and Peper, 1982) "that an energetic perspective, in which individuals are interconnected and local concentrations within a larger field, is a more accurate description, or working hypothesis, of reality. . . . Underlying this model is the assumption that the energies interchanged in ordinary human interactions are modulated in (via) a universal field which permeates all matter" (p. 3). The field model *redefines* the concept of touch to mean more than physical contact. It suggests that, in one sense, as interpenetrating waves of energy, we are always touching upon others. Dora Kunz, one of the originators of touch as therapy, writes (with Peper) as follows:

> Every living organism can be described both as a physical entity and as a system of energy fields that are constantly interacting with the environment, which includes all other organisms. These fields (like those known to science) permeate space. Each individual is a localization (concentration) of energy within these universal fields. Moreover, these individual local fields interact with one another, being part of one whole, dynamic, and interdependent system [1982, p. 3].

Touch, within the field model, holds a genuinely holistic status. "The perspective that each of us is interconnected offers a holistic model of how human beings affect each other" (p. 2). This applies to all our interactions, whether conscious or unconscious. If it is correct, it has distinct practical consequences that alter our interactions and our feelings about them. I again cite Kunz and Peper:

> An energetic approach to human interaction may explain how individuals unknowingly affect each other; it offers us the possibility of developing strategies to influence and change these interactions. In fact, the application of such a perspective may have outcomes that change our perception of human relationships, since every thought or emotion is an energy that may affect the energy field of others.
>
> These interactions can be positive, negative (draining), or neutral and are illustrated in the following examples: a person in a group becomes angry or hostile and immediately arouses a similar emotion in the other group members; a disturbed patient is soothed when a nurse quietly places her hand on his shoulder; a discussant becomes exhilarated during a lively discussion; a nurse becomes tired and drained after seeing one patient while calm and relaxed after treating another [p. 6].

All these interactions are interpreted as field phenomena, not as atomistic exchanges by atomistically conceived units.

> These experiential observations describe an energy exchange which is common to all human interactions whether they be thoughts, emotions, or physical actions. These energies radiate out from the body into space in wave-like patterns of motion that slowly attenuate and dissipate at a distance. . . .
>
> Each thought, action, and emotion can thus be seen as an energetic pattern with distinct characteristics—a pattern which we may unconsciously radiate or deliberately direct at another person. In fact, illness and health have characteristic patterns of energy flow within each individual. . . . Within the field, energies continuously circulate and flow outward, and sometimes, inward. The basic physical energy or vitality comes from what is called *prana* in Eastern philosophy [p. 7].

The field model, as can be seen, offers a holistic definition of our interactions. More importantly, it redefines the self. Far from being a thinker stuck in a mechanistically run body, as in Descartes, or a bundle of sense-impressions as in Hume, the field model defines the self as "local concentrations within a universal field" (p. 8). Each person is made up of the four fields presently identified by science: the gravitational, the electromagnetic, the strong and weak nuclear fields and in addition by postulated subtler fields, ranging from an emotional through a mental to an intuitional one. This latter, characterized by order and creativity, is involved in therapeutic touch, and is activated when drawn upon via compassionate intent.

Therapeutic touch is the practical outcome of these views. Since the specific technique is complex, I must confine myself to its basics. Therapeutic touch is the conscious and focused intent to enhance the well-being of another at all these levels; that is, the other fields besides the physical, postulated to make up a human being. Clinically, therapeutic touch addresses the alleviation of pain, anxiety, and other problems. Preliminary studies show it to have some promise despite the fact that its workings are not yet well understood. Beyond this, it has been found useful in a variety of interactions. Because of its calm, soothing, and noninvasive nature, therapeutic touch can be used from the moment the neonate emerges into the world and throughout the life spectrum, from infancy through maturity to old age. Since it communicates without words, it may be especially appropriate with the terminally ill and dying, whom it can envelop in an affirming atmosphere even in the absence of language.

Ideally, therapeutic touch aims, as do all health strategies, at restoring order, and it can be viewed as helping the body to speed up its innate healing powers and tendency toward homeostasis. Although much of the technique involves the physical body, with the hands placed on or near the site of the specific problem, its emphasis is on the whole person. It shares this goal with current reform in medical education, where a less fragmented and more humanistic approach to patients is now being actively sought. An article by Brian Nelson reviews a talk entitled, "Can Compassion Survive?" given by Dr. Daniel D. Federman of the Harvard Medical School, who notes that "modern medical education operates to orient you away from your compassionate instinct," and that "courses and textbooks [are] organized around medical disciplines or diseases, not around patients" (Nelson, 1983, p. C1). Dr. Richard Gorlin, Chairman of the Mt. Sinai Department of Medicine echoes this criticism: "'The teaching of compassion or humanistic medicine [has] to be incorporated in almost every part of medical education to be effective'" (Nelson, 1983, p. 2). "'You do it through role models and you do it all the time,'" said Dr. Gorlin, and a psychiatrist colleague added: "'I don't think you can teach compassion, but you can model it'" (Nelson, 1983, p. 2).

Therapeutic touch constitutes such a modeling. However, it does not claim omnipotence nor is it a panacea. Its focus differs from medicine, to which it can be an adjunct. For instance, emotional and other well-being may be as direct a consequence of therapeutic touch as physical improvement. At times, as was the case with the fictitious Ivan Ilych, it may not be possible to reverse the physical disorder, and by medical standards this intervention would be counted as a failure. Yet Ivan Ilych, though he died, was helped—and as Tolstoy implies, healed—at other levels.

The objection could be raised that this enhanced well-being in the absence of clinical concomitants can be attributed to the placebo effect. Certainly the physical–sensory model would legitimately raise this concern. It is true that if the mechanistic description of reality is correct, human field interaction would have no legitimate foundation and would be a fiction: an illusion due to the placebo effect. Those engaged in it would be self-deluded at best, fraudulent at worst. If the

Cartesian–Humean world picture is true, this objection is reasonable and valid. On the other hand, if field theory is correct, the objection does not hold. The so-called placebo effect may in that case be an instance of, and hence evidence for, field interactions that account for the changes in the person. According to this reasoning, to attribute the changes to the placebo effect is to beg the question.

The point, of course, cannot be settled at this early juncture. At most, those holding to the placebo effect account can claim to conform to Ockham's Razor, which decrees that hypotheses must not be multiplied beyond strictest need. By contrast, the complex hypotheses of field theory might be seen as a violation of Ockham's Razor.

To refute such an objection is difficult and may at present be impossible. One can note, however, that while scientific validation of therapeutic touch remains the goal and the challenge, we must be aware that we are dealing with an area in which an unmodified form of the positivist—physicalist model of proof may not be appropriate. New paradigms of explanation and proof may have to be devised, combining rigor of mind with intuitive sensitivity to subtler energies, and allowing for the human factor which is carefully factored out in traditional research. An unquestioning a priori adherence to traditional physicalist frameworks and assumptions about nature and man will tend to bar investigations into alternative forms of exchange and communication, such as those proposed by therapeutic touch. Lastly, one might invoke physicist David Bohm, who cautions against too rigid a philosophy of science and points us to a paradox: the claim that to be neutral or value-free is good, is itself a value, not a fact given in nature. Bohm's caveat coheres with that of Thomas Kuhn (1962), who, in *The Structure of Scientific Revolutions*, demonstrates how flexible paradigms are, and how closely tied to the consensus prevailing in the scientific (i.e., human) community at any given time.

Since the status of therapeutic touch will be discussed by

others, I shall concentrate my remarks on the philosophical issues which it raises. One concerns the idea that therapeutic touch can proceed without direct physical contact, by holding the hands near the body but not on it. This brings up the question: if we can affect others therapeutically without physical contact, what does touch add? Two possible answers suggest themselves. First, physical touch strengthens the effect of the intent, "sealing" it in some way. It can open up and facilitate communication on subtler levels, through the power of its initial immediacy. Second, one can argue that the other has been *already reached* at these subtler levels via intent, and, therefore, touched in them, since compassion is an outgoing energy and not merely a private feeling.

This idea is reflected in our language, although vaguely and metaphorically. We say: "I was touched by your kindness," or "I really feel for you," to convey that these emotions actually enter us in some way. This broadens the definition of "touch" beyond body touch to include field touch, a nonsensory or "touchless" variety of touch. Strictly speaking, we should say that according to field hypothesis, what is touched are the energy fields of the other, by my own energy fields. To reflect these dynamic interactions we need concepts and language reflecting the views of quantum and relativity theory, since Cartesian language is too dualistic to handle the new paradigms.

In practice, these are not mutually exclusive. Both body touch and field touch are useful and needed, depending on the context. Ideally, their combination seems to work best. However, as every physician, nurse, and parent knows, there are times when physical touch may be contraindicated. Examples that come to mind are patients in severe pain, as on burn units; acutely disturbed psychotic patients; or the intensely agitated child who initially is best soothed at a distance and only later touched physically. With such a variety of therapeutic options, we need not feel helpless even when overt sensory means are not at our disposal. The skilled *therapon*, whether a health professional or not, will use all these modalities synergistically.

If the field hypothesis is correct, we must also allow that certain individuals are therapeutically gifted. Examples of this drawn from experience are infants who stop crying when certain adults talk to them, touch them, or even draw near them. These people seem to be sensitively attuned to the child at all levels, resulting in field resonance and an immediate sense of well-being in the recipient of field touch. Such individuals, by analogy with those said to have a green thumb with plants, may be said to have an innate and unusually well-developed healing ability, which is activated when the need arises, sometimes even without conscious effort. Whatever the explanation, it is met with in experience. Such examples point to a human capacity beyond the ordinary meaning of touch that we are only gradually beginning to explore, namely the healing potential stored within our hands and minds. Dr. Dolores Krieger (1983) of New York University, one of the pioneers in this area, who coined the term *therapeutic touch* a decade ago, has recently suggested that it may be "an evolutionary emergent." This is a stimulating idea whose elaboration should be followed with interest. My own tentative conjecture is that the healing capacity of touch has been latent in our species all along, awaiting only the right cultural and intellectual climate.

This favorable climate has come from two directions, Western awareness of Eastern philosophy, and contemporary physics, with its field theory and its novel notions of space, time, matter, and energy. At the forefront of the philosophical implications of these is David Bohm of the University of London. Asked about the applications of quantum mechanics to human interaction, Bohm offers a view similar to that of Kunz and Peper's field model. He says:

> There are two views of space. One view is to say the skin is the boundary of ourselves, saying there is the space without

> and the space within. The space within is the separate self, obviously, and the space without is the space which separates the separate selves. . . . Therefore to overcome the separation you must have a process of moving through that space, which takes time. . . . Now if we took the view of [Bohm's implicate order physics], with this vast reserve of energy and empty space, saying that matter itself is that small wave on empty space, then we could better say that the space as a whole . . . is the ground of existence, and we are in it. So the space doesn't separate us, it unites us. Therefore it's like saying that there are two separate points and a certain dotted line connects them . . . or to say there is a real line and that the points are abstractions from that. . . . The line is the reality and the points are abstractions [Bohm quoted in Weber, 1978, p. 32].

Bohm carries this a step further. There is no empty space; what commonsense naive realism takes to be empty space is in fact teeming waves of energy. In that ocean of energy, as he terms it, everything is connected, unlike isolated droplets, and "every individual is in contact with the implicate order, with all that is around us" (Weber, 1978, p. 39). All humans are interconnected and interdependent, and they—together with every particle in the universe—are the outcome of the history of its unfolding and store the information of that history at some level of themselves. When pressed, Bohm insists that this is not a poetic metaphor but good physics. Although he terms his radical theories mere *proposals*, Bohm consistently reiterates that they are more compatible with quantum physics than are any other theories currently held. If that is so, field model philosophy is the logical implication of contemporary science. It has independent empirical backing and is not merely an appealing updated version of Indian philosophy. Bohm also postulates compassion as a primary principle in nature, and although an elucidation of this is beyond the scope of my remarks, it is of interest in its coherence with the central premise of therapeutic touch.

Therapeutic touch holds compassion to be the essential factor in healing. Whether its source is human or universal need not concern us here. Touch transmits the energy, coupled with the intent of help, and this somehow synchronizes our innate energies with those found in nature. As in Plato, therapeutic touch assumes that we touch *through* our hands as well as *with* our hands. Alongside the emphasis on compassion, there is equal emphasis on nonattachment. The caring must be intense but not personal. This sounds paradoxical, and admittedly is difficult in practice.

The idea of touch may appear inseparable from the idea of involvement, of ego investment, but this need not be so. A rich tradition in our heritage revolves around this very issue; it may explain our earlier reluctance to use touch as a therapeutic tool, a hangover from Puritan days, or perhaps the fear of invasive or unprofessional conduct toward those in our care. I refer to the concept of eros and agape, a distinction that flourished in the Middle Ages and in Christianity, but whose roots go back to classical Greece. Eros was identified with secular love, with the senses, desire, and self-interest. Giving was construed as inseparable from the hope of return. Agape, on the other hand, was sacred love, apart from the senses, not born of desire, and purged of self-interest. It came close to what we term *compassion.*

As touch, eros has been narrowly interpreted in Western culture, equated with romantic and sexual love and restricted to it. In the twentieth century, it has increasingly been portrayed as narcissistic and self-seeking, and treated in an *I–It* context. For this reason it may have appeared an unlikely candidate for therapeutic functions. At the other end of the scale, agape once sacralized all human relationships as expressions of God and frowned on sensory means of communication. Its effort was to purge itself of matter, which in some medieval philosophy, as in Puritan theories, held a quasi-sinful status.

The dissociation of eros from agape may account for the long delay in our awareness of the therapeutic power of touch. Far from seeing eros and agape as mutually exclusive, therapeutic touch reconciles and integrates them. Given compassionate intent, touch can become the most agapaic form of eros. But this view of the unity of love brings us back to Plato.

For Plato, eros is the physical counterpart of a universal, creative principle, much as it is in field theory, in Bohm, and in Buber. In the *Symposium*, his dialogue on love, Plato depicts it as an energy coursing throughout nature, expressing itself in different ways according to the context. His seven-step ladder of love in the *Symposium* symbolizes a force that underlies all human desire and striving. The love that originates in the touch of one person ends in the embrace of the universe. For Plato, it explains all attraction, be it for physical beauty and procreation; the attraction of the scientist for beautiful equations and models; and the drive toward integration within the whole: cosmic eros.

For Plato, what begins with the particular leads to the universal, and this outlook relates him to the field model. Field touch is the expression of the *therapon* that reaches across the boundaries by which we believe our world to be confined and links us to as yet mostly uncharted regions of nature and ourselves. Touch so construed is a resource which begins in human interaction and flows outward in widening circles to dimensions where nonordinary models of space, time, energy, and consciousness seem to apply.

In summary, let me acknowledge that all three models of touch draw our attention to valuable features of experience. The physical–sensory model, although it is the narrowest one, has contributed a sober methodology and a commitment to detail without which science could not proceed. Its careful crafting and painstaking scrutiny of endless variables have provided the most solid data concerning touch that we have to date. They are at least the necessary condition for our understanding. Whether they are also the sufficient condition remains an open question. By the criteria of the psychological model they are insufficient. Consequently, it seeks to supplement the sense-data world by the specifically human categories rehearsed earlier. The field model incorporates aspects of both these models, and therefore it is the most comprehensive one. Nevertheless, it too can only conjecture about the nature and effects of touch. It still lacks the data-based studies and replications, and even a very clear theory accounting for its beneficial effects. An ideal and rigorous explanation in terms of necessary and sufficient conditions—resembling a scientific law—seems at present to elude it. Since field theory applied to human interaction is in its infancy, it must await the results of the experimental studies being conducted, and in the meantime content itself with mapping its theories onto philosophical frameworks compatible with its workings.

It is true that even without these complex philosophical models, people have for millenia touched their children and each other in an expression of love and human concern, with beneficial results, whatever models we invoke. I conclude by confessing that I do not fully understand what touch is, nor why it should act so powerfully to enhance us. Buber's (1957) words in his article entitled "Distance and Relation" seem of special relevance here:

> The basis of man's life with man is twofold . . . the wish of every man to be affirmed as what he is, even as what he can become, by men; and the innate capacity of man to affirm his fellowmen in this way. That this capacity lies so immeasurably fallow constitutes the real weakness and questionableness of the human race: actual humanity exists only where this capacity unfolds [pp. 101–102].

Touch, whatever it may turn out to be, is one instrument of that affirmation.

Discussion: Chapter 1

Seymour Levine: Don't the philosophical models you've described apply primarily to Western medicine, which is only a small percentage of the world's medicine? They may have developed because of Western empiricism, and out of our whole set of cultural conditions. Eastern cultures have a complex of medical practices that are very aware of holistic approaches and organic medicine. These practices need to be considered in discussing the Eastern philosophical position, which may well have led to them.

Renée Weber: The third model I discussed, the field model, is the underlying assumption of Eastern thought. At some deep level in virtually all the Eastern metaphysics, we are all interdependent and interconnected. We're actually not separate entities. In contrast, Western philosophy since the time of Descartes has encouraged an atomistic and fragmentary approach in Western medicine. According to seventeenth- and eighteenth-century assumptions, people are like discrete little billiard balls. Twentieth-century physics denies this, but our ordinary language is still Cartesian and dualistic and does not reflect the new paradigm.

Seymour Levine: A new field is now trying to emerge called *psychoimmunology*. The term is bad—it illustrates your point about Cartesian language because again it implies a dualism—but the idea is good. A massive amount of information is available implicating psychologic issues in basic regulatory functions. However, there's tremendous resistance in the Western medical community to the viewpoint that there is an organism which is essentially in tune with its environment and whose environment very much affects its functions. Physicians have almost a vested interest in seeing those functions as autoregulatory rather than holistically regulatory.

T. Berry Brazelton: Is empiricism holding us back? Is it a symptom of where we were and what we are trying to break out of? Renée, I'm trying to relate Buber's I–It and I–Thou modes to what we see mothers do when they touch their babies. A mother in an I–Thou mode senses what's going on in the baby, what state the baby is in, and she adapts her touch to that. A complex unconscious regulatory system seems to be operating. The complexity of that system, it seems to me as a clinician, is what we ought to be after.

Seymour Levine: The behavior pattern you're describing is not exclusively human. If you spend enough time watching a variety of animals interact with their infants, as many of us here have, you tend to think of mother–infant behavior in terms of signals and communication. The system is tuned to the survival of the infant, and what goes into the survival of the infant is essentially a set of mutual dyadic, interaction processes.

William Greenough: What do you think it was that led Eastern cultures, which long ago were ahead of us empirically and "scientifically," to choose such a different direction from the one we chose in the West?

Renée Weber: Why did Eastern thinkers come to the almost axiomatic notion of unity and interconnectedness, and why did they stress that rather than individuality and separation? If pressed, I would say it must have been experiential. It was empiricism, but inner empiricism, and the most appropriate word to describe that is *meditation.* I think they turned within (now I'm using Cartesian language, which is wrong again), and through inner empiricism they discovered meditation and yoga. They experienced something within, and that became the supporting premise of their metaphysics and their stated ethics.

William Greenough: Western science has an inner empirical method, too—namely, introspection—but that approach developed completely differently.

Renée Weber: But introspection is not meditation. Introspection is dualistic. It sets up an object and a subject. Meditation is a state of consciousness that cuts across the dualism of subject and object. Obviously, this is very difficult to understand and to handle verbally, but that's the important distinction. But, if we go a step farther back and ask, why did they stumble upon meditation and why did we not, I cannot answer.

T. Berry Brazelton: One of the reasons for this whole conference is that we'd like to get beyond the empirical approaches that we have at our fingertips now, so that we can learn more about interconnections, complex systems, and ways of communicating via them. I feel a tremendous need for more research on the field model, partly in order to understand it better and partly to support the work of clinicians who are trying to use a more holistic approach to healing. A gifted clinician who gets some scientifically credible research back-up suddenly feels on another level in terms of what he or she can provide for people in a dyadic interaction such as nursing or medicine. As we design studies to provide that back-up, I think it's very clear we need to get beyond the stimulus–response kind of empiricism that most of us have been trained in.

References

Aristotle, *De Anima*, Bk. 2. In: *The Basic Works of Aristotle*, trans. W. D. Ross. New York: Random House, 1941.

Bohm, D. (1980), *Wholeness and the Implicate Order.* London: Routledge & Kegan Paul.

Buber, M. (1923), *I and Thou*, trans. R. G. Smith. New York: Charles Scribner's Sons, 1927.

——— (1957), Distance and relation. *Psychiatry*, 20:101–102.

Descartes, R. (1642), *Meditations on First Philosophy*, 2nd rev. ed., trans. L. J. Lafleur. New York: Liberal Arts Press, 1960.

Hume, D. (1739–1740), *A Treatise of Human Nature*, Part 2, Sceptical Philosophy. In: *The Philosophy of David Hume*, ed. V. C. Chappell. New York: Random House, 1963.

Krieger, D. (1983), Keynote address. In: *Proceedings, Therapeutic Touch:*

Advances in Nursing Research. Villanova College of Nursing: Villanova University, June 9.

Kuhn, T. S. (1962), *The Structure of Scientific Revolutions*. Chicago: University of Chicago Press.

Kunz, D., & Peper, E. (1982), *Fields and Their Clinical Implications*. Wheaton: The Theosophical Research Institute Monograph.

Merleau-Ponty, M. (1962), *The Phenomenology of Perception*, trans. C. Smith. New York: Humanities Press.

Montagu, A. (1971), *Touching*. New York: Columbia University Press.

Nelson, B. (1983), Can doctors learn warmth? *The New York Times*, September 13, p. C1.

Plato, *Timaeus*. In: *The Dialogues of Plato*, trans. B. Jowett. New York: Random House, 1937.

———*Theaetetus*. In: *The Dialogues of Plato*, trans. B Jowett. New York: Random House, 1937.

Sartre, J. P. (1956), *Being and Nothingness*, trans. H. Barnes. New York: Washington Square Press.

———(1947), *No Exit*, trans. S. Gilbert. New York: Albert A. Knopf.

Sorabji, R. (1971), Aristotle on demarcating the five senses. *Philos. Rev.*, 80:55–79.

Tolstoy, L, (1886), *The Death of Ivan Ilych*, trans. A. Mande & J. D. Duff. New York: New American Library, 1960.

The Upanishads, trans. Swami Prabharananda & F. Manchester. New York: New American Library, 1948.

Weber, R. (1978), The enfolding–unfolding universe: A conversation with David Bohm. *Revision J.*, 3/4:24–52.

Wyschograd, E. (1981), Empathy and sympathy as tactile encounter. *J. Philos.*, 6:25–43.

Part II: Touch and Neuroanatomical Considerations

2

Development and Maintenance of Cortical Somatosensory Representations: Functional "Maps" and Neuroanatomical Repertoires

Michael M. Merzenich, Ph.D.

Introduction

Recent studies conducted principally in the somatosensory nervous system have revealed that cortical maps are dynamically maintained and are alterable by experience throughout life (Merzenich, Kaas, Wall, Nelson, Sur, and Felleman, 1983; Merzenich, Kaas, Wall, Sur, Nelson and Felleman, 1983; Merzenich and Kaas, 1983; Kaas, Merzenich, and Killackey, 1983; Merzenich, Nelson, Stryker, Cynader, Schoppmann, and Zook, 1984). These studies indicate possible functional rules underlying the development of tactile skills in children and adults (Merzenich, Kaas, Wall, Sur, Nelson, and Felleman, 1983; Merzenich, Jenkins, and Middlebrooks, 1983; Merzenich, Nelson, Stryker, Cynader, Schoppmann and Zook, 1984). They bear important implica-

Acknowledgments: The studies summarized herein were conducted in collaboration with Drs. Jon Kaas, Michael Stryker, Mriganka Sur, Randolph Nelson, William Jenkins, John Wall, John Zook, Daniel Felleman, Max Cynader, and Axel Schoppmann. Work was supported by NIH Grant NS-10414 and the Coleman Fund.

tions for the probable basis of recovery from peripheral or central nervous system (CNS) injury (Jenkins, Merzenich, Zook, Fowler, and Stryker, 1982). They indicate a probable basis for differences between children and adults both in the rate of acquisition of new skills, and in their capacity for recovery from injury.

In this brief review, some of the evidence supporting these new concepts of brain organization and development will be outlined. Given this background, some implications of these studies for development and alteration of tactile skills in man will be discussed.

A New View of the Functional Organization of the Cerebral Cortex

A large part of the neocortex of adult primates is occupied by topographic maps of the skin surface, the retina, and the cochlea (Merzenich and Kaas, 1980). The formation of these maps has been examined in a number of developmental studies, with the greatest emphasis directed toward the definition of processes underlying the establishment of internal topographic order within the primary visual cortex (Hubel, Wiesel, and LeVay, 1977; Movshon and Van Sluyters, 1981; Sherman and Spear, 1982). Other especially influential studies have been conducted to determine mechanisms underlying the development of the representation of vibrissae within the somatosensory cortex in rodent species (Woolsey and Wann, 1976; Killackey and Belford, 1979; Kaas et al., 1983; Simons, Durham, and Woolsey, 1984). These two models for studying development of the forebrain gained particular attention in part because there are clear neuroanatomical features of these cortical zones in both young and adult animals (in the ocular dominance columns of the visual cortex; in the "barrels" of the somatosensory cortex, representing individual vibrissae) which have well-understood functional correlates.

These developmental studies have strongly reinforced

the general conclusion that the anatomical projections distributing information to different cortical zones are established early in life (prior to a postnatal "critical period") and are subsequently normally unalterable (Hubel et al., 1977; Killackey and Belford, 1979; Movshon and Van Sluyters, 1981; Sherman and Spear, 1982; Marr, 1982). Experience prior to this critical period is requisite for normal neuroanatomical development, but that experience need not be very specific. With the eyes open or with whiskers intact, a monkey or a rat will develop normal neuroanatomical connections in the primary visual area or in the vibrissal "barrel" field.

Such studies have led to the general conclusion that nervous system development is largely over at that stage, and in at least these cortical zones. All of the elements of the neural machine have appropriate and inflexibly assigned functions. Cortical representations (maps) are completed in detail. Our mental development arises from appropriate algorithmic treatment of information delivered to this hardwired machine. Such conclusions have arisen, in part, because with establishment of *neuroanatomical* boundaries in the cerebral cortex in the development models tested (e.g., along the lines of ocular dominance columns in the visual cortex or around barrels in the rodent somatosensory cortex), *functional* boundaries between these cortical map subdivisions are also created.

Studies of the somatosensory cortex in primates have revealed that at least in that system there is a hitherto unappreciated second stage of cerebral map development (Merzenich, Kaas, Wall, Sur, Nelson, and Felleman, 1983; Merzenich, Nelson, Stryker, Cynader, Schoppmann, and Zook, 1984). Specifically, these studies have shown that *functional* cortical maps are *not* static, but to the contrary are continuously altered by experience throughout life. The initial stage of development by which neuroanatomical connections are established prior to a critical period in early life establishes the limits of the repertoires of information from which later use-dependent shaping of functional map detail might be effected. We hypothesize that: (1) When the structure of cortical maps is considered in detail, there are a nearly infinite number of possible forms. (2) Correlations of inputs underlie the lifelong dynamic shaping of cortical maps. (3) A process of input "selection" underlies map dynamism; changes in synaptic effectiveness resulting from input correlations control this process. (4) Map alteration by use constitutes the general physiological basis for the acquisition of skills. (5) It possibly also manifests the adaptive process(es) underlying recognition and memory. (6) The same map dynamism would appear to account at least in part for the recovery of function after brain injury. (7) In such a self-organizing system, common or repetitive idiosyncratic experiences would result in common or idiosyncratic directions of map alterations, and experience would gradually stabilize cortical maps. (8) In such a system, there can be no static isomorphism between the skin surface and the cortical representation of that skin surface. (9) Changes in maps at any level necessitate downstream changes in effective addressing of map-to-map projections to other cortical and subcortical zones. Map instabilities and possibly hyperstabilization might be expected to occur under special circumstances: if so, they should result in mental instabilities (errors of association) and limitations in the acquisition of new information, respectively.

These conclusions and logical extensions of our studies have not, in the main, been unequivocally established by directed experiments. At the same time, studies conducted to date reveal strategies by which these important hypotheses can now be directly tested.

Some Experimental Evidence

One simple method of determining the alterability of cortical maps resulting from differential changes in inputs from the skin is to determine the consequences for such maps of peripheral nerve transection or amputation. These common injuries in man, and the neurological consequences of such injuries, are well known (Trotter and Davies, 1915; Head, 1920; Henderson and Smyth, 1948; Haber, 1958; Dellon, 1981). They constitute an exaggerated example of deprivation, because the central projection axons of transected peripheral cutaneous nerves survive the injury (Carmel and Stein, 1969; Knyihar and Csillik, 1976). Thus, any changes in orderly cortical representations of the skin surfaces would likely reflect the consequences of the severe deprivation of the cortical zone formerly representing the now transected nerve.

Our detailed cortical mapping studies (Figs. 2.1, 2.2) have shown that the cortical zones representing the skin field of the large nerves innervating the glabrous hand surfaces of the monkey (the median nerve or ulnar nerve), or of the skin field of an amputated digit, are very rapidly occupied after nerve transection or amputation by inputs from surrounding skin surfaces (Figs. 2.1, 2.3); that is, the central cortical map reorganizes; and the nondeprived surrounding skin is represented, in time, over a larger and larger cortical territory, while the transected nerve(s) lose their central representational territory.

In such studies, the sites of representation of specific skin surfaces commonly shift hundreds of microns across the cortical surface (Fig. 2.4). That has been demonstrated directly, for example, in studies in which cortical maps were derived at different times in the same animals. Any given skin site can be represented at different times anywhere over a cortical zone roughly 1200 to 1400 microns in diameter. As a consequence, cortical sites of representation commonly move from their "normal" (predeprivation) zones to a territory which had clearly earlier represented the now denervated or amputated skin field. No errors in localization result from stimulation of skin fields surrounding such small hand lesions in man (Trotter and Davies, 1915; Head 1920). This consti-

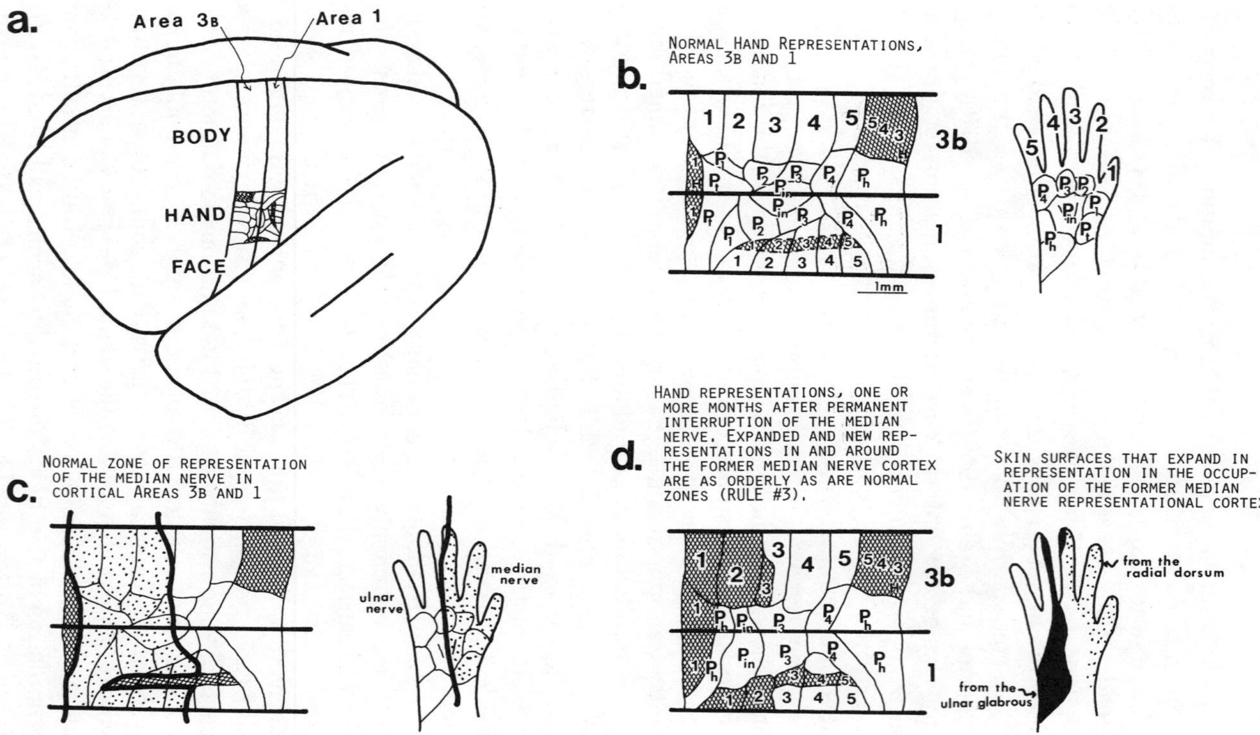
a.
Area 3B
Area 1
BODY
HAND
FACE
b.
NORMAL HAND REPRESENTATIONS, AREAS 3B AND 1
3b
1
1mm
c.
NORMAL ZONE OF REPRESENTATION OF THE MEDIAN NERVE IN CORTICAL AREAS 3B AND 1
ulnar nerve
median nerve
d.
HAND REPRESENTATIONS, ONE OR MORE MONTHS AFTER PERMANENT INTERRUPTION OF THE MEDIAN NERVE. EXPANDED AND NEW REPRESENTATIONS IN AND AROUND THE FORMER MEDIAN NERVE CORTEX ARE AS ORDERLY AS ARE NORMAL ZONES (RULE #3).
SKIN SURFACES THAT EXPAND IN REPRESENTATION IN THE OCCUPATION OF THE FORMER MEDIAN NERVE REPRESENTATIONAL CORTEX.
from the radial dorsum
from the ulnar glabrous

FIGURE 2.1

Summary of the consequences for the cortical representation of the hand in cytoarchitectonic Areas 3b and 1 of severe peripheral deprivation resulting from surgical transection of the median nerve. The site of the hand representations within the body surface representations in these cortical areas is shown in a diagrammatic illustration of a lateral view of the brain of an owl monkey, in *a*. There is a complete topographic representation of the surfaces of the hand in each of these cortical fields. These two representations are roughly mirror images of one another.

In *b*, the detailed pattern of representation of the hand in a representative normal monkey is illustrated. There, each labeled zone outlines the cortical area within which receptive field centers lie on the skin surface identified in the hand drawing at the right. Shaded areas are cortical zones in which the dorsal hand surfaces are represented. The face is represented in the cortical sector lateral to the hand representation (in this drawing, at the left); the wrist and arm are represented in the more medial aspect. Actually, individual cortical maps are highly idiosyncratic in detail, especially in Area 1. (For an illustration of representative normal maps, see Merzenich, Sur, Nelson, and Kaas [1981], Merzenich, Nelson, Kaas, Stryker, Jenkins, Zook, Cynader, and Schoppmann [1987].)

Methods for deriving these maps are illustrated diagrammatically in Figure 2.2.

In *c*, the normal zone of representation of the median nerve in these two cortical fields is dotted. The skin field of the median nerve is shown in the hand drawing at the right. The median nerve represents about 60 percent of the glabrous surface of the hand of the monkey. It is represented over a cortical zone roughly 15 square millimeters in the area.

In *d*, the basic form of cortical maps derived one or more months after permanent transection of the median nerve is illustrated diagrammatically. After this relatively short deprivation, neurons throughout the field of the median nerve are driven by "new" inputs from adjacent skin surfaces innervated by the ulnar and radial nerves. The cutaneous sources of these occupying inputs are indicated in the hand drawing at the right. (For a series of maps derived in monkeys after peripheral nerve transection, see Merzenich, Kaas, Wall, Sur, Nelson, and Felleman [1983], Merzenich, Kaas, Wall, Sur, Nelson, and Felleman [1983].)

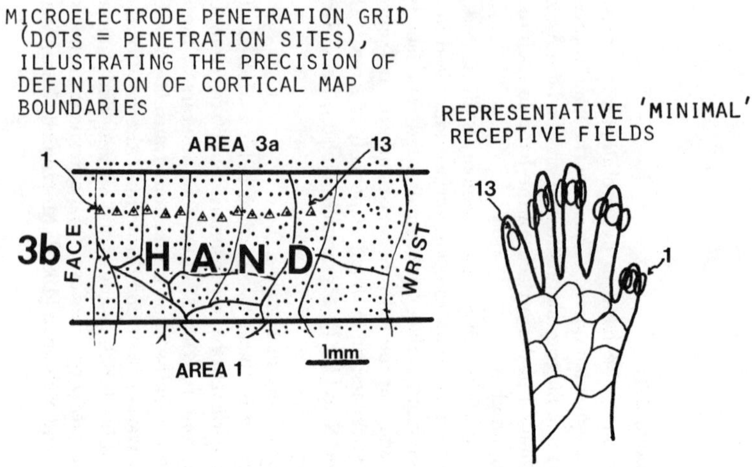

FIGURE 2.2

Diagrammatic illustration of the methods used for definition of these highly detailed cortical maps. In each experiment, several hundred parallel, vertical microelectrode penetrations are introduced into the middle cortical layers. Penetration sites are indicated by dots in the drawing. Penetrations are sited with reference to a high-magnification photograph of the cortical surface vasculature. The recording grid has an interpenetration separation from about 50 to 200 microns. In each penetration, the "minimal" receptive field is that skin zone over which the cortical neuron(s) can be driven with just-visible indentation of the skin with a fine tactile probe. Typical receptive fields are illustrated, by example, in the hand drawing at the right.

From these data, zones with receptive fields centered on given skin fields are outlined, to create a "map" of the representation of the skin surfaces in the cortex, like those shown in this and other figures of this report.

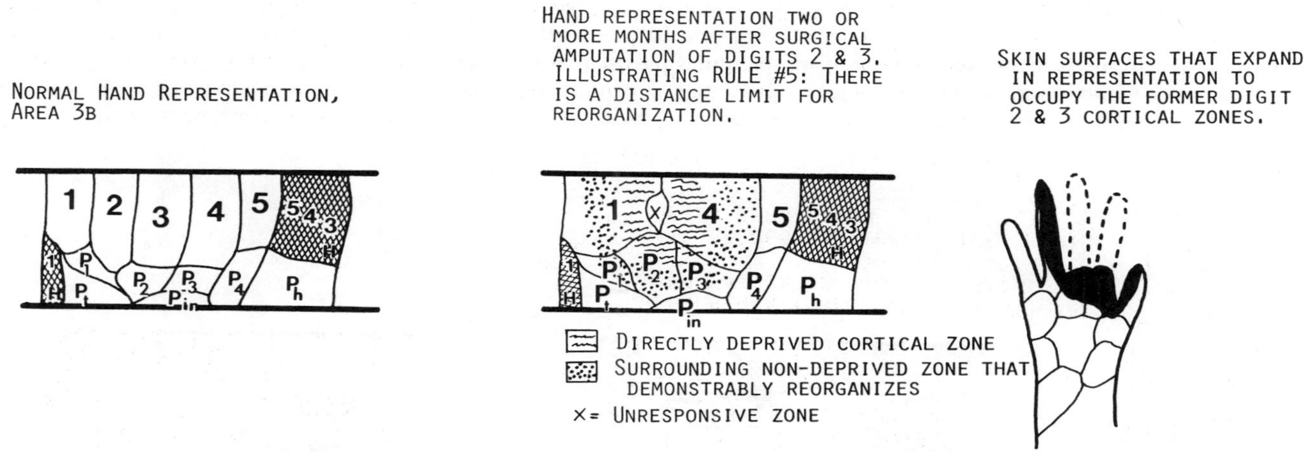

FIGURE 2.3

Diagrammatic illustration of the consequences of amputation of digits 2 and 3 for the cortical representation of the hand. This illustration is based upon two such amputation cases reported by Merzenich and colleagues (unpublished). In these monkeys, most of the cortical zone representing the missing digits was occupied by a topographic expansion of the representation of adjacent digital and palmar surfaces. The occupying skin surfaces are shown in the hand drawing at the right. A surrounding nondeprived zone also demonstrably reorganizes (i.e., all across this zone), the receptive fields for neurons, which are clearly altered from the normal.

In these and other cases, a distance limit for reorganization of roughly 600 to 700 microns was recorded; at greater distances (*s* zone in the drawing), cortical zones were never subsequently driven by cutaneous inputs.

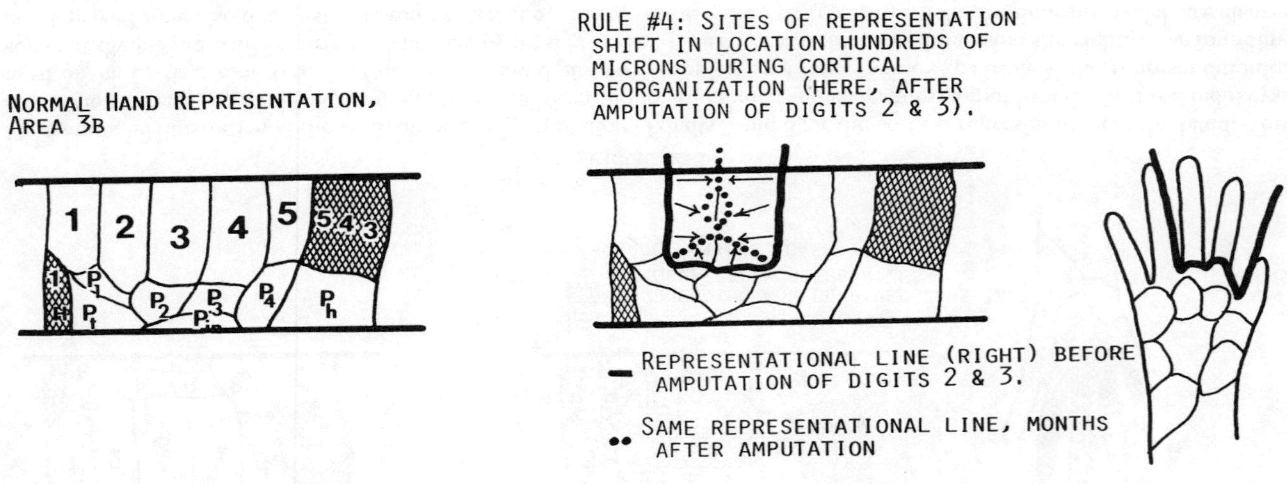
NORMAL HAND REPRESENTATION,
AREA 3B
1
2
3
4
5
543
P1
Pt
P2
P3
Pin
P4
Ph
RULE #4: SITES OF REPRESENTATION SHIFT IN LOCATION HUNDREDS OF MICRONS DURING CORTICAL REORGANIZATION (HERE, AFTER AMPUTATION OF DIGITS 2 & 3).
REPRESENTATIONAL LINE (RIGHT) BEFORE AMPUTATION OF DIGITS 2 & 3.
SAME REPRESENTATIONAL LINE, MONTHS AFTER AMPUTATION

FIGURE 2.4

Diagrammatic illustration of one important feature of cortical map reorganization. With reorganization following nerve transection or digit amputation, sites of representation commonly shift hundreds of microns in location, often to move in their entirety into a cortical zone formerly representing the deprived skin field. Such observations demonstrate that there is no static isomorphic relationship between the skin surface and cortical representational areas (Merzenich, Kaas, Wall, Sur, Nelson, and Felleman, 1983; Merzenich, Nelson, Kaas, Stryker, Jenkins, Zook, Cynader, and Schoppmann, 1987).

tutes clear evidence that the cerebral cortex is "perceptually transparent" regarding peripheral reference; that is, there is no static isomorphic relationship between the skin surface and its cortical representations.

Through the process of these dramatic remappings, a series of functional rules appear to be followed (Merzenich, Kaas, Wall, Sur, Nelson, and Felleman, 1983; Merzenich, Nelson, Stryker, Cynader, Schoppmann, and Zook, 1984). First, as skin surface representations expand, receptive field sizes are correspondingly (inversely) reduced in area (Fig. 2.5). Second, the extent (percentage) of receptive field overlap (Sur, Merzenich, and Kaas, 1980) is actively maintained throughout reorganization over at least most (not all) reorganizing zones (Fig. 2.5). Third, overall topographic order is maintained throughout reorganization, with the expanded and new representations in and around the reorganized area being as orderly as normal representations. Fourth, as outlined above, sites of representation commonly shift hundreds of microns in location during cortical reorganization. There must be a nearly infinite number of possible detailed forms of experience-derived cortical maps. Fifth, there is a distance limit for reorganization. In Area 3b, this limit is about 600 to 700 microns; it is probably somewhat greater in Area 1. These rules presumably directly reflect the neural processes underlying map establishment and alteration by experience.

Several other conclusions about the establishment and experience-dependent alteration of cortical maps have been derived from these studies (Merzenich, Kaas, Wall, Sur, Nelson, and Felleman, 1983). First, temporal correlations of inputs must underlie the establishment and maintenance of the details of map order. Second, the literature strongly suggests (as noted earlier) that the spreads of anatomical inputs are established relatively early during the development of the primary sensory areas of the forebrain. This evidence, along with the changes in map topography recorded (Merzenich, Kaas, Wall, Sur, Nelson, and Felleman,

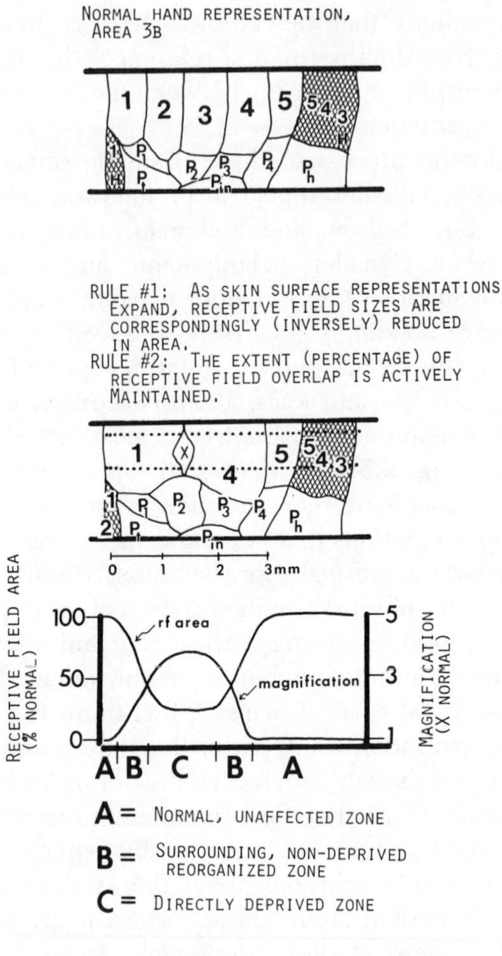

FIGURE 2.5

Illustrating another basic common consequence of map reorganization, again shown by example for the digit amputation case (Merzenich et al., 1987). As skin surface representations expand, receptive field sizes are correspondingly (inversely) reduced in area. Changes of 3–5X were recorded in these experiments. At the same time, the magnification of representation changed roughly inversely. That can only happen if the extent (percentage) of receptive field overlap is actively maintained throughout reorganization (Sur et al., 1980). Abbreviations as in Figure 2.1.

1983), indicate that map changes are due to alterations of synaptic effectivenesses, and not to growth or movement of axonal arbors or dendrites. Our general hypothesis is that at any one time, neurons respond to only a small fraction of their anatomically delivered repertoire of inputs (Merzenich, Kaas, Wall, Sur, Nelson, and Felleman, 1983; Merzenich, Jenkins, and Middlebrooks, 1983; Edelman and Finkel, 1985). Activity results in a point by point selection of effective driving inputs. This selection is always determined with an influence from surrounding sectors; that is, functionally, with preservation of shifting overlaps in representation. A model for this selective process in the cortex has recently been proposed by Edelman and Finkel (1985).

There is both neuroanatomical (Scheibel and Scheibel, 1970; Landrey and Deschenes, 1981) and physiological (Towe, Patton, and Kennedy, 1964; Zarzecki and Wiggin, 1982; Hicks, Dykes, Landrey, and Metherate, 1983) evidence that neurons at given locations in somatosensory cortical fields have significant neuroanatomically delivered inputs from skin surfaces far larger than those neurons usually evidence in (overt) receptive fields. While these "surround" inputs do not effectively drive neurons, they do generate discernible postsynaptic potentials (PSPs) on cortical neurons (Zarzecki and Wiggin, 1982). This is important, because in this dynamic system temporarily ineffective inputs must count; that is, in reference to definition of later forms of the somatosensory map.

Taken together, these studies indicate that the *details* of cortical maps are established by experience from comparatively crude neuroanatomical maps (Merzenich, Kaas, Wall, Sur, Nelson, and Felleman, 1983). By this view, then, the first stage of map development is the establishment of anatomical inputs and cortical architecture in the very young animal. The second stage is the establishment and adjustment and maintenance of the details of cortical maps by experience.

This second stage appears to be operational in monkeys throughout life.

How can this evidence for highly plastic somatosensory cortical maps be reconciled with developmental evidence for an early stabilization of cortical maps in the primary visual cortex of cats and monkeys, and within the vibrissal cortex of rodents?

These latter models were chosen in part because they represented instances in which there were coincident functional and neuroanatomical boundaries within these respective cortical zones. Movement across such boundaries, by our model, cannot occur, because the spreads of neuroanatomical inputs cannot allow it. *Alterations are possible only within the bounds of fixed neuroanatomical repertoires*. The spreads of anatomical inputs represent, by our view, the *potential* for how much experience can alter the map, and hence the potential for individual diversity. These aforementioned vibrissal and visual cortex model systems represent instances in which neuroanatomical projection boundaries strictly limit that potential (on the ocular dominance and barrel boundaries themselves). In fact, the spread of neuroanatomical inputs is much greater in most cortical zones than in Areas 3b and 1, the somatosensory zones from which our maps were derived. If the same experience-dependent map alterations occur in these other cortical fields (as we believe is almost certainly the case), there is great potential for individual map expression consequent upon differences in experience.

Some Other Relevant Studies

We have also now recorded map alteration following induction of restricted cortical lesions (Jenkins et al., 1982) (Fig. 2.6). By this process, the skin surfaces represented within the zone of a small cortical infarct come to be represented, over a period of several weeks, in the surrounding cortical zone. In the process of reorganization, the surrounding representational zone is degraded (skin surfaces

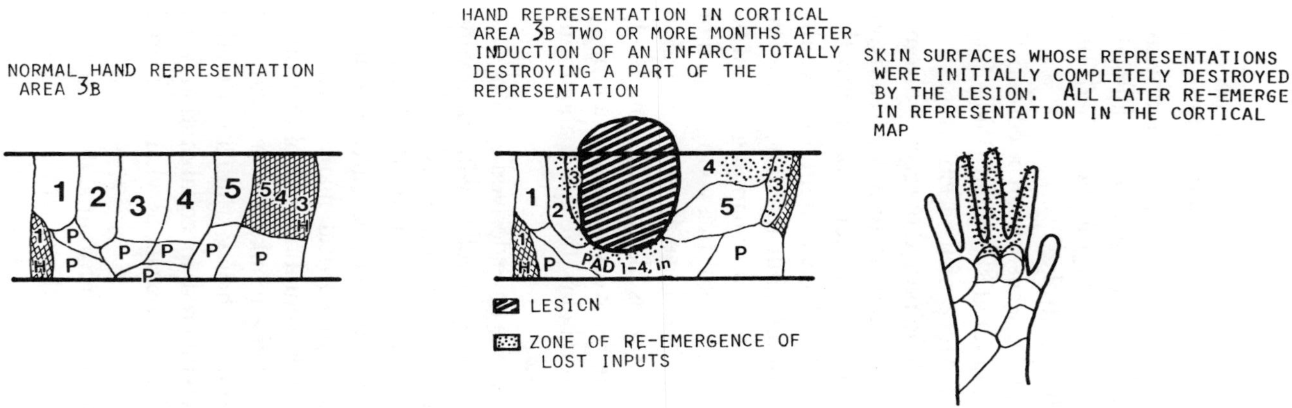

FIGURE 2.6

Diagrammatic illustration of the alteration of the cortical map of the hand surfaces within Area 3b two or more months after introduction of a small cortical infarct. The infarct, induced by electrocoagulation of surface vessels, totally destroyed the original zone of representation of the skin surfaces indicated at the right (dotted). Their representation subsequently reemerged in the surrounding region of the cortical map (dotted zones, center). Other dramatic topographic changes in the representation of the surrounding skin surfaces were also recorded in these studies. This diagrammatic figure is based on features recorded in seven such cortical lesion studies in adult owl monkeys (Jenkins et al., 1982). Abbreviations as in Fig. 2.1.

are represented over smaller territories with larger receptive fields), presumably to provide room for functionally driving inputs representing skin surface formerly represented within the infarcted zone. Cortical map reorganization following such infarcts at least roughly follows the described time course of recovery from such ministrokes.

Apparent map alterations have also been recorded following reinnervation of a denervated skin field (Wall, Kaas, Sur, Nelson, Felleman, and Merzenich, 1986) (Fig. 2.7). Studies of monkeys following a long period of recovery from a peripheral nerve injury indicate that despite the relatively random regeneration of the peripheral nerve back into the skin, the cortical map apparently effects a limited reorganizing of this disordered input. In an adult monkey, there are topographic reasons why this functional remapping cannot be completely successful (Wall et al., 1986). In a young animal or human, there is good reason to believe from neurological observations that the reorganization is likely to be completely successful, as virtually complete recovery from such an injury is commonly recorded in children below the age of about nine to ten years (Dellon, 1981).

In our most recent studies, we have derived evidence for cortical map alteration by experience evoked without involving peripheral nerve or central brain injury. Although the results of such studies are complex and studies are still incomplete, and although unequivocal changes are sometimes not recorded, clear alterations in cortical maps, including changes in cortical areas of representation and of receptive field sizes, have been seen in some monkeys wearing digital casts, and in monkeys performing a heavy stimulation tactile task (unpublished studies, conducted in collaboration with Drs. William Jenkins, John Zook, Michael Stryker, and Brad Fowler).

Finally, if experience can create substantial differences in cortical maps, then maps should be idiosyncratic in detail in different normal adult monkeys. We have recently completed

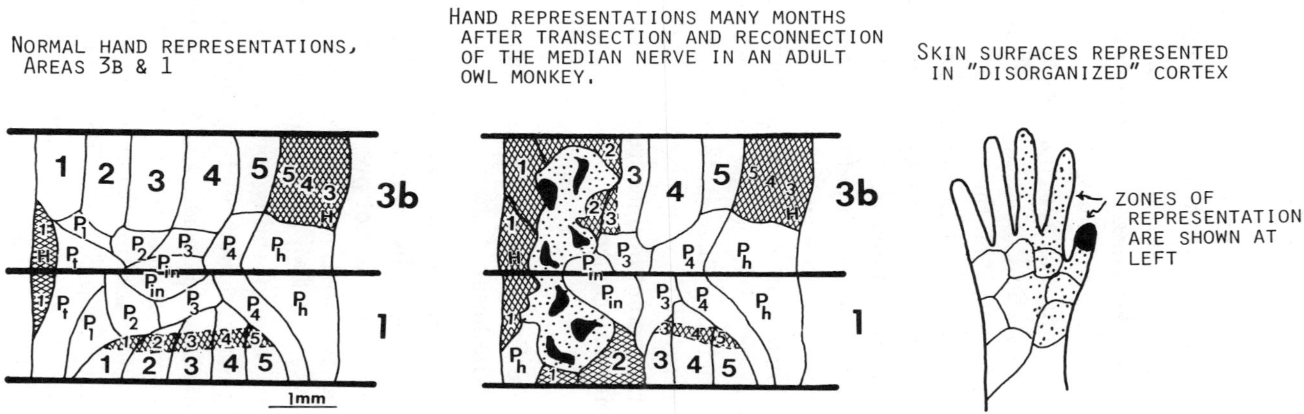

FIGURE 2.7

Diagrammatic illustration of a cortical map derived many months after successful regeneration of the median nerve in an adult monkey. Note that: (a) The regenerated nerve recovers only a fraction of its original territory (dotted; refer to the normal example in Fig. 2.1, even though at this time period all of its skin field would probably have appropriate peripheral reference, and all would be represented for light touch). (b) Any given skin surface (like the distal segment of the thumb, as illustrated in black in the drawing) comes to be represented in segregated islands of cortex. This segregation is believed to arise from a relatively randomly peripherally regenerated nerve by a functional sorting of inputs by temporal response correlation *via* a process identical to that normally establishing and maintaining the details of map topography. The map of the median nerve in an adult primate probably rarely if ever completely reorganizes for complex reasons discussed in a report by Wall and colleagues (1986).

a study of normal monkeys, and have confirmed this general conclusion. Indeed, every *detail* of cortical maps is highly variable, including: (1) the relative and absolute sizes of representation of given different skin surfaces; (2) the details of topographic relationships of adjacent skin surfaces; (3) the actual cortical surfaces falling along the four borders of the hand representational cortex in cortical Area 3b or 1; (4) the position and actual line of division of the skin of map discontinuities. The variation in representation of the dorsum of the hand in these cortical areas is especially striking in different individual adult "normal" monkeys. Glabrous surfaces commonly vary up to about two- to threefold in area in different monkeys in Area 3b; and up to seven- to eightfold in Area 1. This striking individuality in the detailed form of these cortical maps in different adult normal monkeys is consistent, again, with the conclusions that: (1) there are very many alternative possible forms of these maps; and (2) the actual overt maps defined at any point in time are principally shaped by the animal's tactile experience up to that point in time.

Some Implications of These Experimental Observations and Hypotheses

A series of implications regarding the development of tactile abilities derive from these observations. Unfortunately, studies are incomplete. They do not precisely define what it is of inputs from the skin that are most effective in altering the form of cortical maps. Given the maintenance of topographic order and shifted overlaps throughout map reorganization, it appears likely that input correlations underlie the establishment and maintenance of order, and it is likely that there is an optimal temporal sequencing of input across the skin. In this kind of system, task repetition would be a factor in generating a significant map change. The alteration of maps appears to asymptote several weeks after introduction of a differential peripheral drive. Finally, the system is competitive. Its occupation for the refinement of any particular task must bear implications for its subsequent modifiability, and must limit the potential for the development of skills directly competing for self-interested organization of the same cortical territory.

It is difficult to relate the map changes that have been recorded in our studies with any simple alteration in sensory performance or skill. One indirect relation can be drawn from studies of the changes in sensation over the stumps of amputees. Tactile acuity and sensitivity improve substantially over amputation stumps, when sensation over the stump is compared to corresponding locations on the other, intact limb (Haber, 1958). Moreover, the degree of improvement in acuity is directly related to the degree of "telescoping" of the phantom limb (Henderson and Smyth, 1948; Teuber, Krieger, and Bender, 1949; Haber, 1958). This latter observation led Teuber and colleagues to conclude that the change in acuity was a direct consequence of the representation of the stump skin enlarging its representation into the cortical zone formerly representing the now missing limb, with this expansion of representation resulting in a perceptual shortening (the "telescoping") of the phantom limb. Close neurophysiological parallels of these changes in acuity are recorded in monkeys following digital amputation. Thus: (1) The surrounding skin surfaces expand, to occupy topographically the zone representation of the now missing digit. (2) With expansion, there is an inverse change in receptive field size of up to about 5X, with the greatest changes recorded on the skin surfaces formerly bordering the now missing digit. In man, there is a corresponding skin mapping of changes in tactile acuity and sensitivity. (3) Finally, the time course of the changes are probably roughly equivalent, given the cross-species comparison. Thus, in at least this case, there is a strong inference from the neurology that changes in cortical maps have simple, direct functional consequences.

It is interesting to ask whether these map changes might

manifest *the* adaptive neural changes underlying cognitive processes. The basic features of this system are highly consistent with properties of self-organizing nerve nets hypothesized to account for recognitions, associations, learning, and memory. Indeed, Edelman (1982), and Edelman and Finkel (1985) have itemized features of a self-organizing cortex operating by Edelman's neuronal group selection theory, and the properties of the somatosensory system that we have defined are consistent in almost every detail with the hypothetical requirements of his recognition machinery. Aspects of organization of the functionally plastic somatosensory system are, indeed, consistent with most theoretical hypotheses and speculations as to the origins of higher brain functions (see Hebb [1949], Minsky and Papert [1969], Uttal [1978], and Woody [1983] for reviews of this complex issue). It is highly probable that these dynamic properties recorded in the somatosensory system are general to other sensory and motor systems. The study of this functional dynamism should rapidly provide new insights into the following areas: the development and later acquisition of skills; the mechanistic properties of neural systems underlying and accounting for the rules of cognition; understanding and possibly manipulating the basis of recovery from central brain injury; understanding the significance of recorded neural projection system organizations; understanding the functional origins of certain mental illnesses; as well as explaining other aspects of behavior and perception, hitherto largely unexplained by neuroscience.

Discussion: Chapter 2

Stephen Suomi: You mention finding differences between the cortical maps of different monkeys. Would you get variation of a similar order of magnitude if you examined the maps of the same monkey at, say, monthly or yearly intervals?

Michael Merzenich: The proportional differences might not

be as great, but we would be surprised not to see the same range of differences over a period of years.

Stephen Suomi: Suppose you could make your measurements on a macaque female before or during pregnancy, and then again after the birth, when she was holding the infant.

Michael Merzenich: We definitely believe that skin surface representations would change substantially. Recent evidence reveals that motor representations are altered as well; and that these experience-induced changes probably account for the acquisition of improved perceptual abilities and the acquisition of motor skills in young children (and in adults).

Stephen Suomi: What about behavior that stops and then reappears? Take the macaque female that's holding the infant, which changes the architecture of the representation. Then the infant goes away, and the female is doing other things. A year later, she has another infant to hold.

Michael Merzenich: Certainly relearning would take place, though not instantly. It's the equivalent (which some of you may have experienced a number of times) of relearning to smoke a cigarette. At first handling the cigarette again is foreign, and you manipulate it clumsily. But with each relearning (in my case, several of them), you are a little sooner back to a smooth performance of the task. The time course of acquisition, of loss of skill after a period without practicing it, and of reacquistion with renewed practice has been well studied by cognitive psychologists. Now, is that relearning accounted for by a representational remapping? We think so, i.e., that mapping changes parallel behavioral acquisition, loss, and reacquistion—and it's something that can be studied directly.

Seymour Levine: Are you convinced that the major differences in mapping that you've found reflect individual differences in behavior? Are these animals really using their hands in such different ways?

Michael Merzenich: That's obviously the main question. We see enormous individuality, but we have no very strong links between the details of the form of the mapped representations of skin surfaces and the behavior of the animal. That requires directed experiments in which you determine exactly what the animal is gaining or losing behaviorally as its representations are altered by experience. We are now conducting experiments of this type.

Seymour Levine: Why is it that you haven't used the word *plasticity*?

Michael Merzenich: I'm not opposed to using the word, but I think it sometimes carries the connotation that something is physically moving or changing. We have not demonstrated that any input arbors or postsynaptic processes are growing or moving.

T. Berry Brazelton: Michael, your work has exciting implications for those of us who work with premature infants. The map changes you've found that result from individuated experience suggest great potential for recovery after sensory deprivation or trauma to the CNS. I think we're on the brink of understanding recovery from trauma in neonates very differently from the way we have in the past. The opportunities for early intervention, for bringing babies toward recovery after an insult, are way beyond anything we anticipated with our old fixed-deficit model of the CNS.

I have a question, though. Did your animals show a period of hypersensitivity following the surgery? In a baby with a CNS insult, there will be an inrush of capillaries and blood vessels to the damaged area, trying to make up for the insult. Raw nerve endings are going to come into an area like that. What you see behaviorally is hypersensitivity. It may be generalized, but it is greater right around the lesion.

Michael Merzenich: Indeed, my colleague William Jenkins has recently recorded expansions of representation in zones surrounding cortical lesions that might plausibly contribute to hypersensitivity.

T. Berry Brazelton: What I'm concerned about is that babies who've been through an insult may be hypersensitive to the very experiences they need to organize their nervous systems around. Unless we respect that hypersensitivity, the information we give these infants is going to overload them and our therapeutic efforts will go astray. In other words, the input preterm infants receive may have to be adjusted to their hypersensitivity in order to bring about appropriate function. Infants try to show us their threshold for receiving information behaviorally; the challenge for clinicians, which we'll be discussing later, is to learn to interpret and respond to these behavioral signals appropriately.

References

Carmel, P. W., & Stein, B. M. (1969), Cell changes in sensory ganglia following proximal and distal nerve section in the monkey. *J. Comp. Neurol.* 135:145–166.

Dellon, A. L. (1981), *Evaluation of Sensibility and Reduction of Sensation in the Hand*. Baltimore: Williams & Wilkins.

Edelman, G. M. (1982), Group selection as a basis for higher brain function. In: *The Organization of the Cerebral Cortex,* eds. F. P. Schmitt & F. G. Worden. Cambridge, MA: MIT Press, pp. 535–563.

———Finkel, L. (1985), Neuronal group selection in the cerebral cortex. In: *Dynamic Aspects of Neocortical Function,* eds. W. E. Gall & G. M. Edelman. New York: John Wiley, pp. 653–695.

Haber, W. B. (1958), Reactions to loss of limb: Physiological and psychological aspects. *Ann. NY Acad. Sci.,* 74:14–24.

Head, H. H. (1920), *Studies in Neurology,* Vol. 1. London: Oxford University Press.

Hebb, D. O. (1949), *Organization of Behavior*. New York: John Wiley.

Henderson, W. R., & Smyth, G. E. (1948), Phantom limbs. *J. Neurol. Neurosurg. Psychiat.,* 11:88–112.

Hicks, T. P., Dykes, R. W., Landrey, P., & Metherate, R. S. (1983), Inhibitory mechanisms employing GABA in the somatosensory cortex of cats. *Proc. IUPS,* 15:134.

Hubel, D. H., Wiesel, T. N., & LeVay, S. (1977), Plasticity of ocular dominance columns in monkey striate cortex. *Proc. Roy. Soc.,* (B) 278:337–409.

Jenkins, W. A., Merzenich, M. M., Zook, J. M., Fowler, B. C., & Stryker,

M. P. (1982), The area 3b representation of the hand in owl monkeys reorganizes after induction of restricted cortical lesions. *Soc. Neurosci. Abstr.*, 8:141.

Kaas, J. H., Merzenich, M. M., & Killackey, H. P. (1983), The reorganization of somatosensory cortex following peripheral nerve damage in adult and developing mammals. *Ann. Rev. Neurosci.*, 6:325–356.

Killackey, H. P., & Belford, G. R. (1979), The formation of afferent patterns in the somatosensory cortex of the neonatal rat. *J. Comp. Neurol.*, 183:285–304.

Knyihar, E., & Csillik, B. (1976), Affect of peripheral axotomy on the fine structure and histochemistry of the rolando substance. *Exp. Brain Res.*, 26:73–87.

Landrey, P., & Deschenes, M. (1981), Intracortical arborizations and receptive fields of identified ventrobasal thalamocortical afferents to the primary somatic sensory cortex in the cat. *J. Comp. Neurol.*, 199:345–371.

Marr, P. (1982), *Vision. A Computational Investigation of the Human Representation and Processing of Visual Information*. San Francisco: W. H. Freeman.

Merzenich, M. M., Jenkins, W. M., & Middlebrooks, J. C. (1983), Observations and hypotheses on special organizational features of the central auditory nervous system. In: *Dynamic Aspects of Neocortical Function,* eds. G. M. Edelman, W. M. Cowan, & W. E. Gall. New York: John Wiley.

———Kaas, J. H. (1980), Principles of organization of sensory–perceptual systems in mammals. *Prog. Psychobiol., Physiol., Psych.*, 9:1–43.

——— ———(1983), Reorganization of somatosensory cortex in mammals following peripheral nerve injury. *Trends in Neurosci.*, 5:434–436.

——— ———Wall, J. T., Nelson, R. J., Sur, M., & Felleman, D. (1983), Topographic reorganization of somatosensory cortical Areas 3b and 1 in adult monkeys following restricted deafferentation. *Neurosci.*, 8:3–55.

——— ——— ———Sur, M., Nelson, R. J., & Felleman, D. J. (1983), Progression of change following median nerve section in the cortical representation of the hand in Areas 3b and 1 in adult owl and squirrel monkeys. *Neurosci.*, 10:639–665.

———Nelson, R. J., Kaas, J. H., Stryker, M. P., Jenkins, W. M., Zook, J. M., Cynader, M. S., & Schoppmann, A. (1987), Variability in hand surface representations in areas 3b and 1 in adult owl and squirrel monkeys. *J. Comp. Neurol.*, 258:281–297.

——— ———Stryker, M. P., Cynader, M., Schoppmann, A., & Zook, J. M. (1984), Somatosensory cortical map changes following digit amputation in adult monkeys. *J. Comp. Neurol.*, 224:591–605.

———Sur, M., Nelson, R. J., & Kaas, J. H. (1981), Organization of the SI cortex. Multiple cutaneous representations in areas 3b and 1 of the owl monkey. In: *Cortical Sensory Organization*, Vol. 1, ed. C. N. Woolsey. Clifton, NJ: Humana.

Minsky, M., & Papert, S. (1969), *Perceptions. An Introduction to Computational Geometex*. Cambridge, MA: MIT Press.
Movshon, J. A., & Van Sluyters, R. C. (1981), Visual neural development. *Ann. Rev. Psychol.*, 32:477–522.
Scheibel, M. E., & Scheibel, A. B. (1970), Elementary processes in selected thalamic and cortical subsystems—The structural substrates. In: *The Neurosciences. Second Study Program*, ed. F. O. Schmitt. New York: Rockefeller University Press.
Sherman, S. M., & Spear, P. D. (1982), Organization of visual pathways in normal and visually deprived cats. *Physiol. Rev.*, 62:738–855.
Simons, P. J., Durham, D., & Woolsey, T. A. (1984), Functional organization of mouse and rat SmI barrel cortex following vibrissal damage on different postnatal days. *Somatosen. Res.*, 1:207–245.
Sur, M., Merzenich, M. M., & Kaas, J. H. (1980), Magnification, receptive field area and "hypercolumn" size in Areas 3b and 1 of somatosensory cortex in owl monkeys. *J. Comp. Neurol.*, 44:295–311.
Teuber, H. L., Krieger, H. P., & Bender, M. B. (1949), Reorganization of sensory function in amputation stumps. Two-point discrimination. *Fed. Proc.*, 8:156.
Towe, A. L., Patton, H. D., & Kennedy, T. T. (1964), Response properties of neurons in pericruciate cortex of the cat following electrical stimulation of the appendages. *Exp. Neurol.*, 20:235–344.
Trotter, W., & Davies, W. M. (1915), Experimental studies in the innervation of the skin. *J. Physiol. (Lond.)*, 38:134–236.
Uttal, W. R. (1978), *The Psychobiology of Mind*. New York: John Wiley.
Wall, J. T., Kaas, J. H., Sur, M., Nelson, R. J., Felleman, D. J., & Merzenich, M. M. (1986), Functional reorganization in somatosensory areas 3b and 1 of adult monkeys after median nerve repair: Possible relationships to sensory recovery in humans. *J. Neurosci.*, 6 1:218–233.
Woody, C. D. (1983), *Memory, Learning and Higher Function. A Cellular View*. New York: Springer Verlag.
Woolsey, T. A., & Wann, J. R. (1976), Areal changes in mouse cortical barrels following vibrissal damage at different postnatal ages. *J. Comp. Neurol.*, 170:48–66.
Zarzecki, P., & Wiggin, D. M. (1982), Convergence of sensory inputs upon projection neurons of somatosensory cortex. *Exp. Brain Res.*, 48:28–32.

3
Evidence for Tactile Stimulation Improving CNS Function

Marian Cleeves Diamond, Ph.D.

Over the past twenty years the evidence supporting the ability of nerve cells in the mammalian forebrain to change in response to varied environmental conditions is extremely exciting. Most heartening of all are the chemical and structural modifications, especially the positive ones, which can occur at *any* age. The nerve cell appears to retain its adaptive capacity throughout a lifetime, not just maintaining a status quo, but continually responding to challenges.

I will discuss some of the evidence of cerebral cortical plasticity caused by multiple sensory modalities, including touch. In the experimental paradigm we use, composed of enriched or impoverished environments, the functional components of the environmental stimuli have not been thoroughly teased apart. For example, touch does indeed play a role, but it, by itself, has not been quantitatively measured. The somatosensory cortex does change its dimension due to the stimulation, or lack of, from these environmental conditions, but it is not clear if the cortical changes are due to touch, pressure, temperature, or some factors not yet explored. All of these modalities can be involved together when animals huddle together or investigate new surroundings and objects. In contrast to studying the effects of enriched conditions, we have examined the brains from animals living in impoverished or isolated conditions. It is very possible that the lack of touch in this environmental situation is important in producing the less well-developed sensory cortex. There is no doubt that touch plays some role in our experimental conditions.

For studying the effects of the environment on the brains of *preweaned*, male rats, the following living conditions were established (Malkasian and Diamond, 1971). All litters of male, Long-Evans rats were reduced to three pups per mother at birth. At six days of age, the pups were separated into one of three conditions: (1) One mother with three pups remained in the standard colony cage (20 × 20 × 32 cm)—The Unifamily Environment. (2) Three mothers with three pups each were placed together in a large single cage (70 × 70 × 46 cm)—the Multifamily Environment. (3) Three mothers and three pups each were placed together in a single large cage (as in No. 2) with "toys" or objects with which they could interact. These toys included swings, ladders, small maze wheels—Multifamily Enriched Condition (Fig. 3.1). The Unifamily animals and the Multifamily Enriched animals were accordingly sacrificed together as groups: one group (7 pairs) at fourteen days of age, the second group (7 pairs) at nineteen days of age, and the third group (19 pairs) at twenty-eight days of age. The Unifamily versus Multifamily (no toys) (19 pairs) groups were sacrificed at twenty-eight days of age.

At least four behavioral parameters were observed: (1) Gregariousness amongst pups; (2) General exploring of pups; (3) Responsiveness to person cleaning cage; (4) Docility at time of autopsy (the animals were handled as infrequently as possible to eliminate this variable).

Ether anesthetized animals were perfused with normal saline followed by 10 percent formol in normal saline. Paraffin

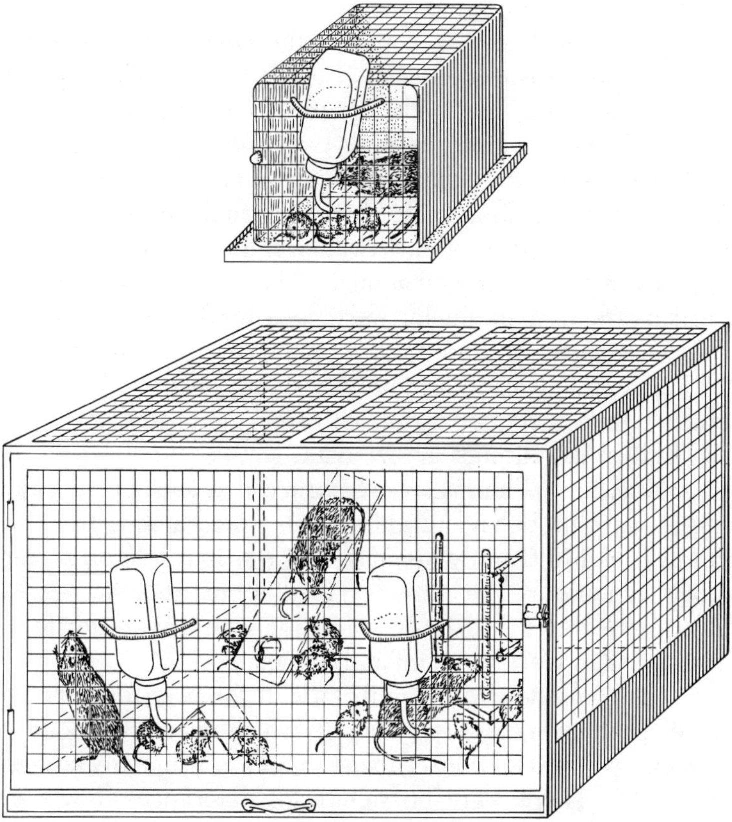

FIGURE 3.1

In the lower half of the page the Enriched Multifamily Condition is shown with three mothers each with three pups and "toys," all in one large cage. In the top half of the page is the Impoverished Unifamily Condition with one mother and three pups in a small cage with no "toys."

embedded brains were cut transversely at 10 micra, utilizing subcortical landmarks to insure uniform sampling. The crossing of the anterior commissure was used for the somatosensory samples and the habenular nucleus, for the anterior portion of the occipital cortex. On microslide projected images the thickness or depth of the cortex was measured from the dorsal aspect of Layer II to the corpus callosum (Fig. 3.2). In addition, we made camera lucida drawings of 950 neuronal nuclei (approximately twenty-five per brain from both right and left cortices). The areas of these nuclei were measured from cells in Layers II and III in the occipital cortex from nineteen pairs of the twenty-eight-day-old Unifamily and Multifamily Enriched animals. The areas of 760 neuronal perikarya and their nuclei were measured from the somatosensory cortex of these same animals. The standard student "t" was applied to determine the significance of the differences between the means of both the cortical thickness and the perikarya and nuclear size data.

All groups of animals were observed at least twice a day. There were no behavioral differences noted among the Unifamily and Multifamily animals in gregariousness or exploratory activity at the time of feeding or cleaning cages. However, the Multifamily animals were more docile at autospy than were the Unifamily animals.

The Enriched Multifamily rats at fourteen days of age developed a somatosensory cortex which averaged about 10 percent ($p < 0.001$) thicker than that of the Unifamily animals (Fig. 3.3). There were no significant differences, however, between the cortices from the Unifamily rats and the Multifamily rats with no toys. Therefore, it appears that the stimulating interaction with the toys was the important factor in increasing the cortical dimensions.

The medial occipital cortex did not respond at this age; undoubtedly, because the eyes had not opened as yet (rats' eyes usually open on day 14). Area 39, the most lateral region of the occipital cortical section, showed a 16 percent increase

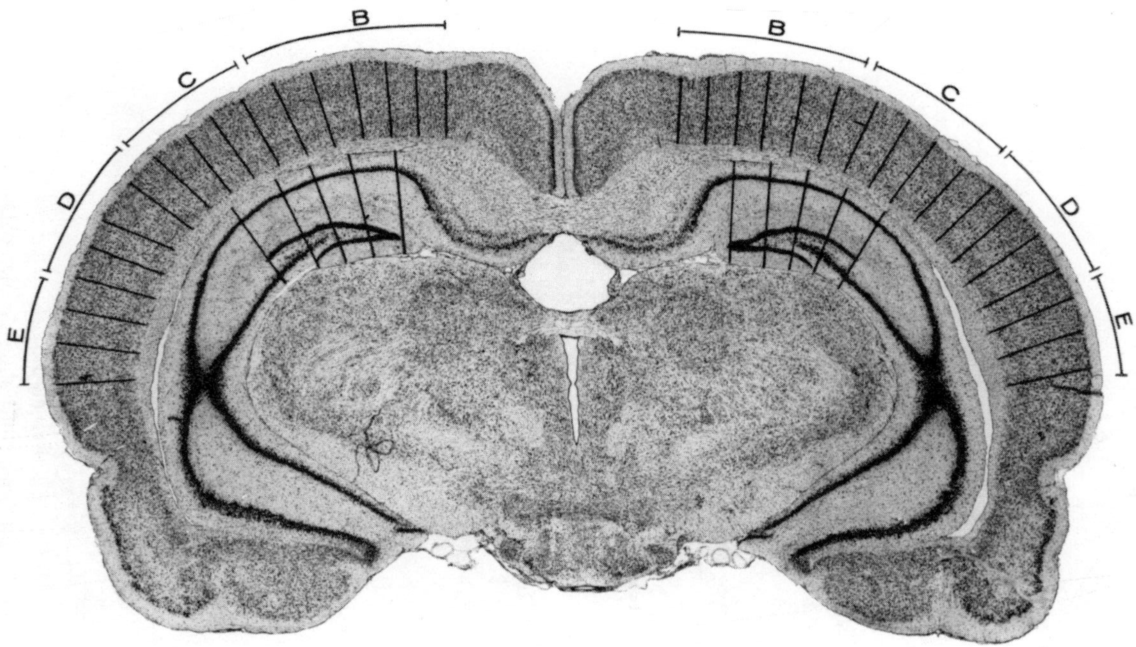

FIGURE 3.2
An illustration of cortical thickness measurements on a transverse section through the rat brain, showing the lines extending through Layer II through Layer VI down to the corpus callosum (B, C, D, E).

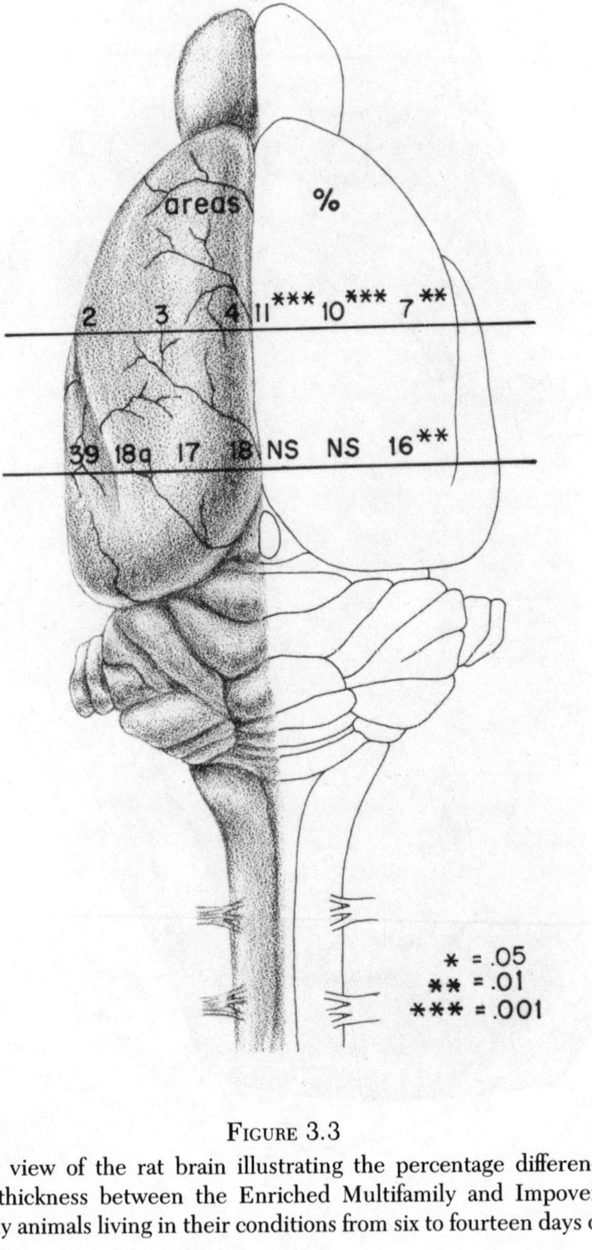

FIGURE 3.3

A dorsal view of the rat brain illustrating the percentage differences in cortical thickness between the Enriched Multifamily and Impoverished Unifamily animals living in their conditions from six to fourteen days of age.

($p < 0.01$), the largest increase seen to date with this experimental design. Evidently, a fair amount of sensory integration is taking place in this area and at this state of development.

At nineteen days of age, again the somatosensory cortex displayed an increase in cortical thickness in the Enriched Multifamily rats compared to the Unifamily rats, but at this time the occipital cortex also showed significant increases from medial to lateral, 7 to 14 percent ($p < 0.025$ to $p < 0.005$) respectively (Fig. 3.4).

By twenty-eight days of age all areas measured showed a thicker cortex in the Enriched Multifamily animals compared to the Unifamily rats. The occipital cortex appeared to be more responsive in the twenty-eight-day-old group than in any of the earlier groups.

The area of the neurons and their nuclei in Layers II and III in the somatosensory cortex showed increases by as much as 19 percent ($p < 0.05$) and 16 percent ($p < 0.05$) respectively, in the Enriched Multifamily rats compared to those in the Unifamily environment. The increase in nuclear area in the occipital cortex reached as much as 25 percent ($p < 0.01$).

Thus, it has been amply demonstrated that the enriched environment increased the dimensions of the preweaned cerebral cortex, different areas at different ages. In a previous study mapping the growth of the cortex from birth to twenty-six days of age (Diamond, Johnson, and Ingham, 1975), we learned that the cortex is growing most rapidly during this period. The present results indicate that the rate of growth can be accelerated with the enriched environment. The true cause of these brain changes is not clear, for both intrinsic and extrinsic variables have been present. That the enriched environment brought about significant increases in the thickness of the cortex and in the area of its neuronal constituents is striking. A possible step in teasing out the individual components of the environment responsible for these changes might be to remove the whiskers of the rats. By removing this

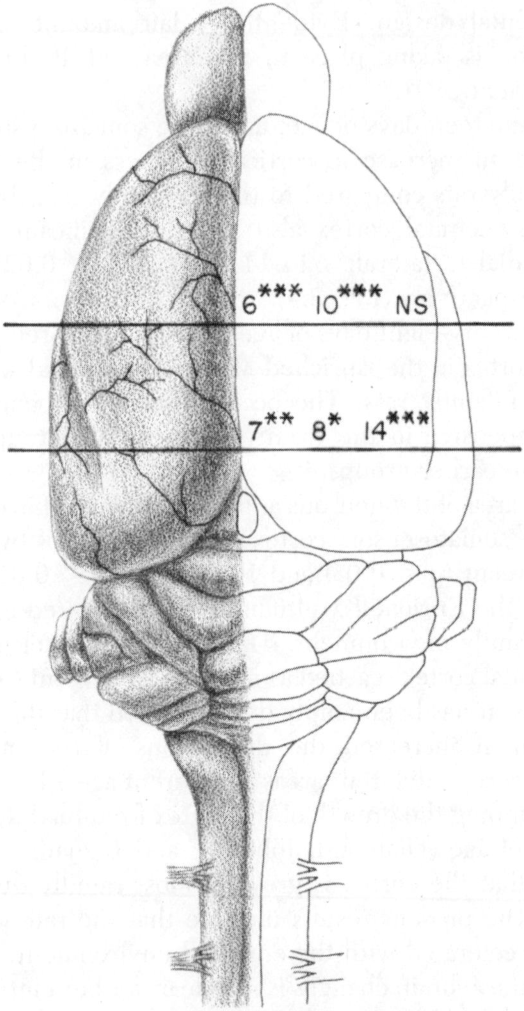

6-19 days of age
6-19 days of age

FIGURE 3.4

A dorsal view of the rat brain illustrating the percentage differences in cortical thickness between the Enriched Multifamily and Impoverished Unifamily animals living in their conditions from six to nineteen days of age.

source of tactile stimulation we might have a better idea of what parameters are causing the somatosensory changes. It is true that adult blind rats exposed to environmental complexity developed a greater cortical weight and cholinesterase concentration than did isolated controls, so some nonvisual pathways are functional in affecting the occipital cortex (Krech, Rosenzweig, and Bennett, 1963; Rosenzweig, Bennett, Diamond, Wu, Slagle, and Saffran, 1969). Handling alone for five minutes each day between two and twenty days of age is not sufficient to change cortical thickness when compared with nonhandled controls (Hoover and Diamond, unpublished). Undoubtedly, cortical responses to environmental complexity are as multidimensional as the environment itself. To date no one has thoroughly pursued the findings to understand their basis.

The basic design of the environmental conditions for the *postweaned* rats has been modified since the beginning of this investigation in our laboratory (Diamond, Ingham, Johnson, Bennett, and Rosenzweig, 1976). At first only enriched and impoverished conditions were used. After several studies were completed, it was apparent that we were dealing with two experimental conditions; there were no controls. Since then, a third group has been included, the standard colony condition, so enrichment and impoverishment could be compared with a standard (Fig. 3.5).

For the postweaned animals, the enriched condition consisted on the average of twelve rats living together in a large cage (70 × 70 × 46 cm). Several times each week stimulus objects from a common pool were placed into the cage. These objects included small ladders, wheels, mazes, swings, and a climbing apparatus; in other words, objects which provided novel stimuli as the rats explored them, very similar to those used for the preweaned animals. It was important to change the toys frequently or the brain alterations were not as marked. The standard colony conditions consisted of three rats living together in a small cage (20 × 20

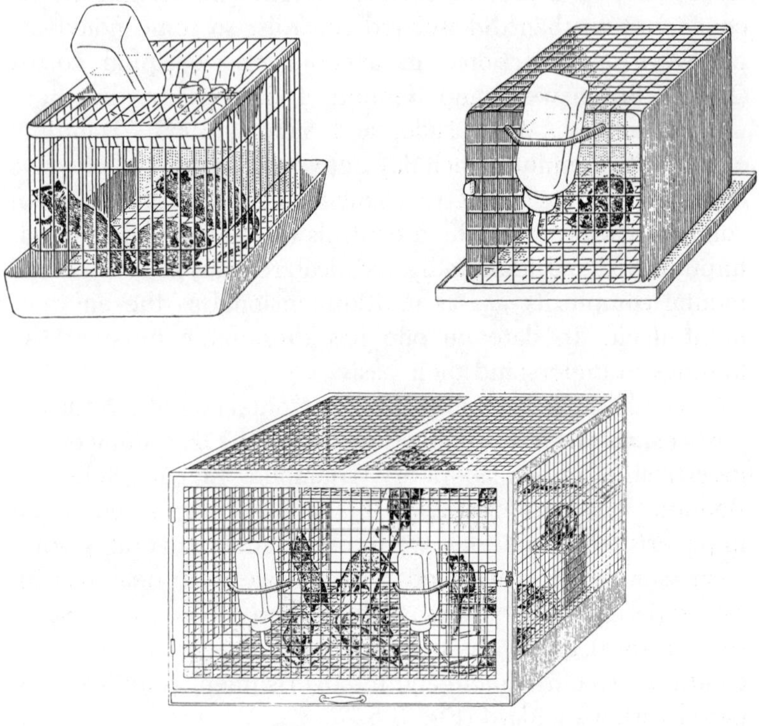

FIGURE 3.5
These three cages illustrate the postweaned living conditions. In the lower half of the page is seen the Enriched Condition, twelve rats with "toys" all within a large cage. In the upper left is the Standard Condition with three rats in a small cage with no "toys." The Impoverished Condition with but one rat in a small cage with no "toys" is shown in the upper right.

× 32 cm) with no toys. The impoverished condition consisted of one rat living by him or herself in a single small cage (same as standard colony). The single animal could see, hear, and smell other rats but did not directly interact with them or with toys. There was no opportunity to touch or "cuddle" close to fellow companions. The satisfaction of warm, intimate relationships was not available. This stands in contrast to the enriched environment, where, even though there was excess space, the rats, for the most part, did touch each other and huddle close during the day when they were least active. As new toys were introduced into the cage, the animals came to the front of the cage to investigate them.

They sniffed, approached carefully, and climbed over the toys, thoroughly exploring the objects. The whiskers were the first part of the body which touched the toys, thus conveying information to the receptive barrels in the somatosensory cortex. Apparently, the running about over the toys and around the cage was not sufficient stimulation to cause the cortex to change, for Zolman and Morimoto (1965) examined the brains of rats which had been running excessively in running wheels for an extended period of time. No changes in cortical weight were noted.

The animals were exposed to these conditions for various periods of time. Initially, it was an eighty-day period, then thirty, reduced to fifteen, and next to seven. During each of these periods, brain changes were noted. The shortest exposure which brought about significant changes was four days. One day was not sufficient to detect a change.

Sodium pentobarbitone-anesthetized, male rats were perfused with normal saline followed by 10 percent formol in normal saline. Either frozen or celloidin embedded sections were cut at either 6 or 20 micra, depending upon whether the sections were from celloidin or frozen material. The same landmarks and methods for measuring cortical thickness were used for the postweaned rats as for the preweaned animals. Cell dimensions similar to those in the preweaned animals have only been completed on the postweaned animals exposed to their environmental conditions for 80 days, from 25 to 105 days of age.

The shortest exposure which stimulated cortical differences was four days, from sixty to sixty-four days. The medial occipital cortex, area 18, showed a 4 percent ($p < 0.001$) increase when the enriched brains were compared with the standard colony brains. It appears that in the adult rat, the occipital cortex is most responsive to the enriched environment. No effects of impoverishment were noted in these animals. However, if the young postweaned rat is placed in the three conditions from twenty-six to thirty days, again just a four-day period, the effects of impoverishment were marked. Areas 4, 18, 17, and 18a all showed significant decreases when the brains from the standard colony animals were compared with those from the impoverished animals. The decreases were more striking in the occipital cortex than in the somatosensory cortex.

It is apparent from these data that depriving an animal of stimulation, either of its companions or from stimulating objects, is more detrimental to the young animal than to the adult animal. Also the occipital cortex is more susceptible to such deprivation than is the somatosensory cortex.

Soon after we learned the effects of the environment on brains of male rats, we were asked to determine the effect on the brains of offspring of rats exposed to these environments (Diamond, Johnson, and Ingham, 1971). We then mated enriched males with enriched females and impoverished males with impoverished females. The cortical thickness was measured on the brains from parents and pups immediately after birth.

The brains were collected and analyzed in the same manner as with the adults mentioned previously. Admittedly, it was much more difficult working with the newborn brains than with older ones.

No significant cortical thickness differences were noted

between the pups from the enriched or the impoverished parents (although the former showed a trend toward a thicker cortex). However, the body weights of the pups from the enriched parents were significantly greater than those of pups from impoverished parents. Upon measuring the cortical thickness of the parents, we found that the brains from the enriched males showed the usual 7 percent differences in cortical thickness compared to the impoverished (Fig. 3.6), but no such changes were seen between the postpartum enriched and impoverished females (Fig. 3.7). With closer examination of the data, it became apparent that the cortex of the impoverished, pregnant female had reached the same thickness as that of the enriched, pregnant female. This was why no significant differences were seen between their brains. Also, these data alerted us to the importance of looking at the brains of nonpregnant females exposed to these environmental conditions, something we had not done previously.

A new set of experiments was arranged, using sixty-day nonpregnant females in the different environmental conditions until 116 days of age to replicate the duration during the pregnancy experiments.

The brains were prepared for histological examination in a manner similar to that of the previous experiments. Also, the cortical thickness measurements were identical to those used previously.

The results indicated that the pattern of change in cortical thickness in the nonpregnant female was different from that in either the pregnant female or in the male of comparable age and condition. In the 116-day-old, sexually mature female, the somatosensory cortex showed a greater, more significant change than in the male of the same age and condition (Fig. 3.8). In addition, though the occipital cortex responded to the environmental conditions, it did not show as great a change in the female as in the male, and the difference between the male and female was statistically significant.

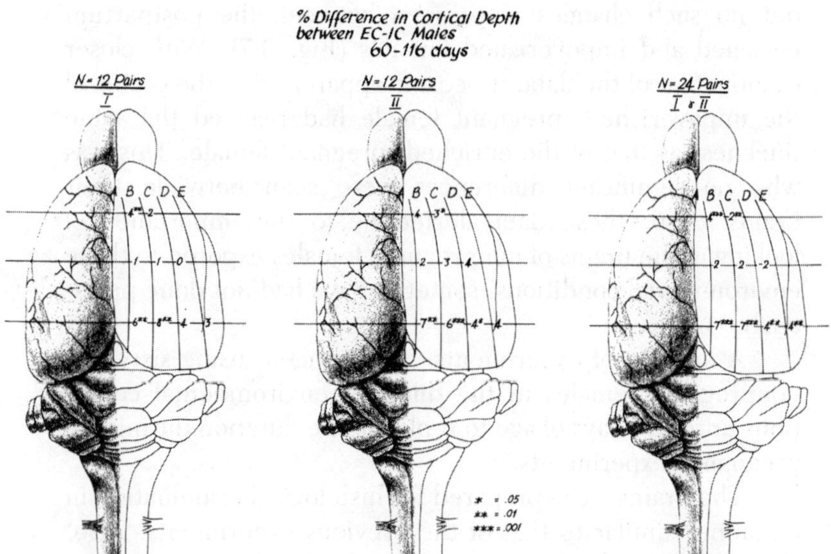

FIGURE 3.6

Three dorsal views of brains from male rats are illustrating the percent differences in cortical thickness between enriched and impoverished animals that lived in their respective conditions from 60 to 116 days of age. I is the original, II the replication, and I + II the two experiments combined.

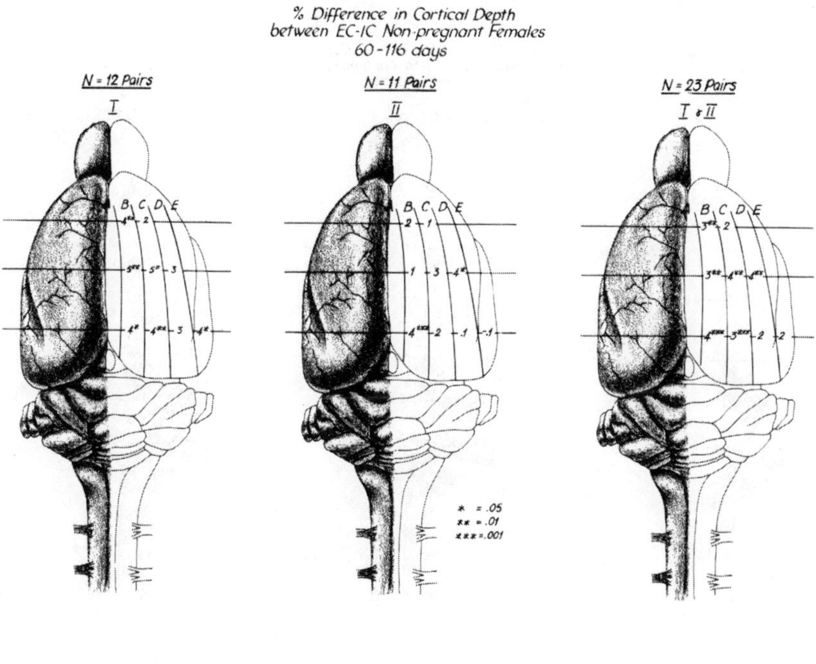

FIGURE 3.7
Three dorsal views of brains from nonpregnant female rats are illustrating the percent differences in cortical thickness between enriched and impoverished animals that lived in their respective conditions from 60 to 116 days of age. I is the original, II the replication, and I + II the two experiments combined.

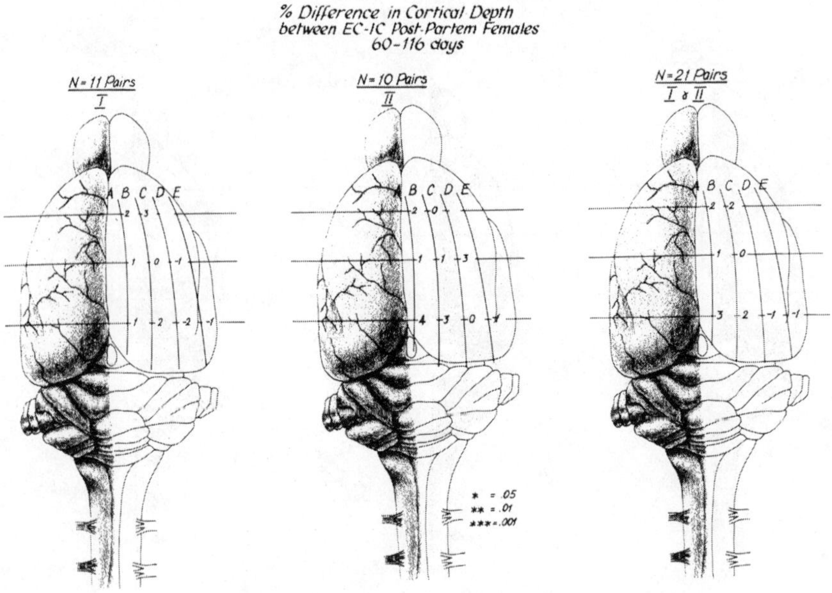

FIGURE 3.8

Three dorsal views of brains from postpartum female rats are illustrating the percent differences in cortical thickness between enriched and impoverished animals that lived in their respective conditions from 60 to 116 days of age. I is the original, II the replication, and I+II the two experiments combined.

This experiment opened new doors. One, it showed that the female somatosensory cortex was more responsive than the male's to similar environmental conditions. Two, it gave some indication that altering the environment during pregnancy could affect the body weights of the offspring. This was an encouraging finding. In this experiment, the brains were taken immediately at birth to avoid any postnatal environmental influences. Now, if we could plan another experiment and allow the animals to reach maturity and then measure the brains, would we see differences? In other words, we were posing the following question: would bigger body weight at birth provide a greater advantage in interacting with the environment, and in turn bring in more stimulation to the brain, thus creating a greater cortical mass? With this type of thinking, we then designed the latest experiments. In this set of experiments, we repeated the design of the previous one, but this time we did not sacrifice the pups at birth but allowed them to reach sixty days of age. At this time, one set of 12 F_1 rats, which had been living three to a small cage ($20 \times 20 \times 32$ cm) since weaning, was sacrificed as baseline. Another set of the sixty-day F_1 rats was placed in the usual enriched condition with twelve rats per large cage, and the third group of twelve F_1 animals was placed in the standard colony condition, three rats to a small cage. After thirty days in these respective conditions, the enriched males were mated with the enriched females and the impoverished males with the impoverished females before replacing the rats in their conditions to await birth. Twenty-one days later we had a new set of F_2 generation pups. Once again we repeated the procedure by allowing the pups to grow to sixty days of age, living three to a cage after weaning. At sixty days of age, we sacrificed twelve males and twelve females to serve as baseline for the F_2 generation. Another group of F_2 males and females was placed in the enriched and impoverished conditions and sacrificed at ninety days, after the usual thirty days of enrichment. The experiment was repeated through the F_3

generation. All of the brains from the F_1, F_2, F_3 enriched and nonenriched rats are being studied. Only one area from the occipital cortex is completed in male pups and it does demonstrate incremental changes with enrichment.

One design which had not been attempted previously was to place both males and females together in enrichment. Since we had an excessive number of F_2 pups we continued as follows. We rightly believed that pregnancy would be an additional consideration, so we placed six F_2 males and six F_2 nonpregnant females together in the enriched cage for fifteen days. At this time, we removed the first group of F_2 females which had become pregnant and replaced them with another group of six nonpregnant females. These females continued to live with the males until the males had been exposed to the conditions for thirty days, at which time all animals were sacrificed.

Conclusion

The results clearly indicate the plasticity of the cerebral cortex in response to stimulating or deprived environments. One might ask what changes are occurring in the cortex to account for thickness differences? The cortex consists of nerve cells, glial cells, and blood vessels. Any or all of these structures can respond to increased or decreased stimulation. Over the past twenty years investigators associated with our laboratory have measured: (1) the area of the perikarya and of nuclei of neurons in the medial occipital cortex, area 18 (Diamond, 1967; Diamond, Johnson, Ingham, Rosenzweig, and Bennett, 1975); (2) the dendritic branching (Holloway, Jr., 1966); (3) the dendritic spines (Globus, Rosenzweig, Bennett, and Diamond, 1973) (Fig. 3.9); (4) the length of the postsynaptic thickening (Diamond, Lindner, Johnson, Bennett, and Rosenzweig, 1975); (5) the diameters of the capillaries (Diamond, Krech, and Rosenzweig, 1964); and (6) the glial numbers (Diamond, Law, Rhodes, Lindner, Rosenzweig, Krech, and Bennett, 1966). These early studies on

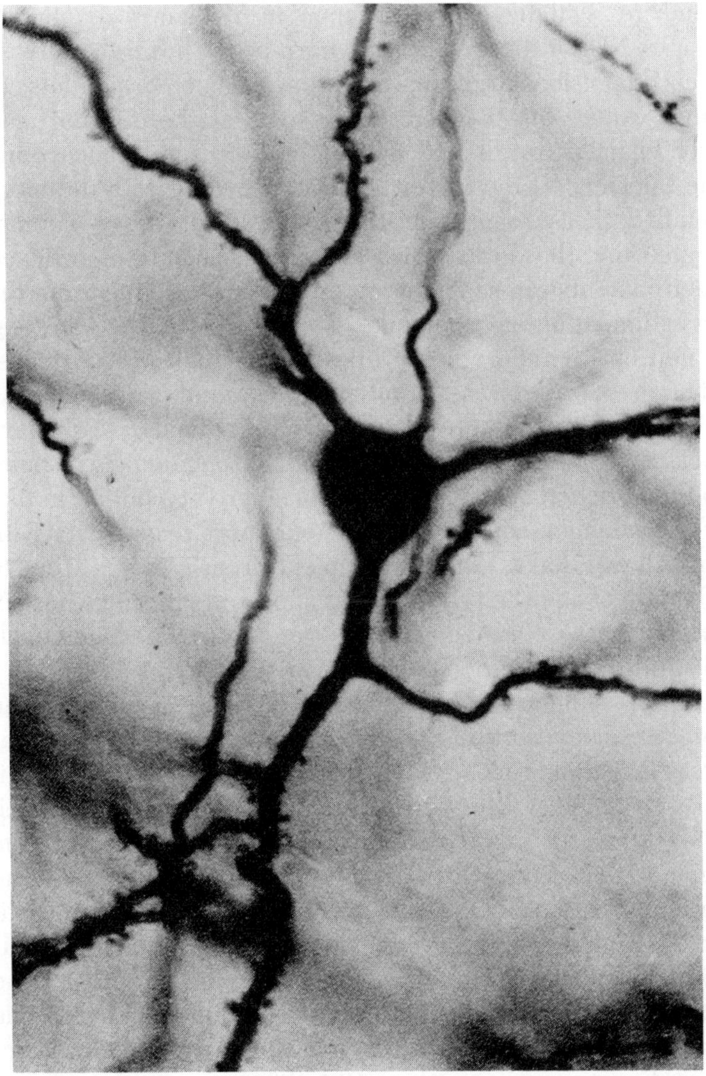

FIGURE 3.9
A photomicrograph of a nerve cell with its dendritic branches and dendritic spines is shown here. Because the section is 150 micra thick, it is not possible to have all of the branches in focus at one time.

dendrites will be expanded upon in William Greenough's chapter. All of these structures have been shown to increase their dimensions in response to stimulating environments. In other words, the tissue responds to meet the demand, and such changes can first be encountered by simply measuring the thickness of the cortex before proceeding with the more detailed measurements. Other investigators have demonstrated that those rats which have experienced the enriched environments can run a maze better than those rats from the less stimulating environments (Nyman, 1967). The increases in neuronal structure support the enhanced maze experience. Though our emphasis is on pediatrics and we should be dealing only with the results from young animals, we are very pleased to learn that the brains from our old animals respond to the enriched environment in a manner very similar to that of the younger animals. In fact, our most recent data with animals exposed to their environments from 776 days of age to 904 days of age showed increases almost identical to those of the young, postweaned animals, even though the old animals lived in their conditions for a longer period.

The significance of these results are manifold. The somatosensory cortex, the general sensory cortex, does increase its dimensions with our experimental design, and it does so at every age we have studied. Undoubtedly, touch plays a role in this somatosensory response. However, the amount of touch, which accounts for the changes in the structure of the brain, has not yet been thoroughly investigated. There is no indication that the amount of touch our animals receive is excessive or disturbing to them. The adrenals do not show any significant difference between the groups (Rosenzweig et al., 1969), whereas experiments designed to stress rats do show such differences in the adrenal weights (Theissen, Zolman, and Rogers, 1962). With the present evidence, one can conclude that touch and exploration of toys is beneficial to the individual as measured by brain and behavioral changes.

Discussion: Chapter 3

Allen Gottfried: Have you applied vestibular stimulation in any of your studies, Marian?

Marian Diamond: No, we have not specifically studied vestibular input, though undoubtedly it plays a role as the animals climb and balance in the cage and on the toys.

Allen Gottfried: So at present you define an enriched environment basically as more space and more objects?

Marian Diamond: Yes, definitely more objects. We have to change the objects at least twice a week because the animals get bored with the same ones. If the same toys are left in the cage, the cortical dimensions will decrease with time. The minute new toys are offered, the animals become alert and climb on, and explore them. We have not yet placed toys in the standard colony cage to determine if space is definitely a factor or not.

Allen Gottfried: It's interesting that toys are so important. Several longitudinal studies in North America show that one of the most potent factors relating to human mental development is play materials. But perhaps it's not just toys. Perhaps crowding plays a role, or general activity?

Marian Diamond: General activity per se, no. This was studied some twenty years ago, when Rosenzweig and his colleagues put animals in running wheels for several hours a day to see if their cortexes would change. No cortical differences were found.

Stephen Suomi: Does the brain of an animal in the enriched condition actually change shape?

Marian Diamond: Yes. The soma increases, as does the nucleus. A nerve cell is shaped like a hand with dendrites comparable to fingers, and the dimensions of the dendrites change. Some increase in number and some in length. The postsynaptic thickening length changes, and so does spine number. In other words, all parts of the cell measured to date change size in relation to environmental input.

T. Berry Brazelton: When infants come into the "enriched environment" of the hospital, their head size increases rather rapidly. We've wondered why: is it nutrition, stimulation, or what? Have you looked at fluid intake and diet in your animals to see whether they're correlated with changes in brain size?

William Greenough: We have measured food consumption in animals that grow up from weaning in these sorts of environments. The isolates consume more food than the animals in the complex environment, and they also weigh more. But their brains are smaller, so I don't think a simple nutritional answer is appropriate.

Marian Diamond: We've found that the weight gain depends on the amount of time the animals spend in the enriched and impoverished environments. After eighty days, the animals in the impoverished environment definitely weigh more, but their brains are smaller. After only thirty days, the body weights of the animals in the two environments are the same, but the brains of the animals from the enriched environment are still larger.

Paul Satz: These are group effects you're getting, Marian, and they're very predictable and lawful, but I'd love to see the distributions. There must be some animals that are not showing the effect. Have you studied them?

Marian Diamond: That's a beautiful question. Our results are statistically significant, so the majority of brains do show the differences. Why some do not, I do not know. Some of the rats may not interact with the objects in the cages. Some rats may not be good at playing, just as some are not good at mothering. We would need to mark the animals clearly, videotape their behavior, and then correlate behavior with cortical dimensions.

Peter Gorski: You really allow the rat to determine the best use of the enriched environment, don't you? So the effect you get is different from the one you might obtain by actively employing touch or handling in order to enrich.

Marian Diamond: Yes, though we did have an experiment on touch per se. The animals were held for around five or ten minutes a day (admittedly this was a small amount); after thirty days, there was no change in cortical thickness compared to untouched littermates.

T. Berry Brazelton: A finding that fascinated me, with my bias, was that the size of the female cortex goes up during pregnancy. Might it continue to increase during nurturing?

Marian Diamond: This we have yet to examine, but we now have the brains of mothers who nursed their pups for twenty-three to twenty-five days after birth. It will be many months before we have the results from this experiment, but they will indeed prove interesting.

Kathryn Barnard: Some very interesting new data from the University of Oklahoma (Ramsy is the principal investigator) show that a major contributor to prematurity or low birth weight is a condition called family enmeshment. It isn't hard to see a parallel between the impoverished environment in your studies and the enmeshment of families that are socially isolated and closed off rather than being open systems.

T. Berry Brazelton: The environment of newborn premature infants may also resemble your deprived environment. Our problem as clinicians is to differentiate between stimulation that is appropriate and enriching and stimulation that is inappropriate and perhaps overwhelming.

References

Diamond, M. C. (1967), Extensive cortical depth measurements and neuron size increases in the cortex of environmentally enriched rats. *J. Comp. Neurol.*, 131:357–364.

———Ingham, C. A., Johnson, R. E., Bennett, E. L., & Rosenszweig, M. R. (1976), Effects of environment on morphology of rat cerebral cortex and hippocampus. *J. Neurobiol.*, 7:75–86.

———Johnson, R. E., & Ingham, C. (1971), Brain plasticity induced by environment and pregnancy. *Internat. J. Neurosci.*, 2:171–178.

——— ——— ———(1975), Morphological changes in the young, adult and aging rat cerebral cortex, hippocampus and diencephalon. *Behav. Biol.*, 14:163–174.

——— ——— ———Rosenzweig, M. R., & Bennett, E. L. (1975), Effects of differential experience on neuronal nuclear and perikarya dimensions in the rat cerebral cortex. *Behav. Biol.*, 15:107–111.

———Krech, D., & Rosenzweig, M. R. (1964), The effects of an enriched environment on the histology of the rat cerebral cortex. *J. Comp. Neurol.*, 123:111–120.

———Law, R., Rhodes, H., Lindner, B., Rosenzweig, M. R., Krech, D., & Bennett, E. L. (1966), Increases in cortical depth and glial numbers. *J. Comp Neurol.*, 128:117–126.

———Lindner, B., Johnson, R., Bennett, E. L., & Rosenzweig, M. R., (1975), Differences in occipital cortical synapses from environmentally enriched, impoverished, and standard colony rats. *J. Neurosci. Res.*, 1:109–119.

Globus, A., Rosenzweig, M. R., Bennett, E. L. & Diamond, M. C. (1973), Effects of differential experience on dendritic spine counts. *J. Comp. & Physiol. Psychol.*, 82:175–181.

Holloway, Jr., R. L. (1966), Dendritic branching: Some preliminary results of training and complexity in rat visual cortex. *Brain Res.*, 2:393–396.

Hoover, D., & Diamond, M. C. (unpublished), The effects of handling on the morphology of the cerebral cortex in preweaned rats, 1969.

Krech, D., Rosenzweig, M. R., & Bennett, E. L. (1963), Effects of complex environment and blindness on the rat brain. *Arch. Neurol.*, 8:403–412.

Malkasian, D., & Diamond, M. C. (1971), The effect of environmental manipulation on the morphology of the neonatal rat brain. *Internat. J. Neurosci.*, 2:161–170.

Nyman, A. J. (1967), Problem solving in rats as a function of experience at different ages. *J. Genet. Psychiat.*, 110:31–39.

Rosenzweig, M. R., Bennett, E., Diamond M., Wu, S. Y., Slagle, R., & Saffran, E. (1969), Influence of environmental complexity and visual stimulation on development of occipital cortex in the rat. *Brain Res.*, 14:427–445.

Thiessen, D. D., Zolman, J. F., & Rodgers, D. A. (1962), Relation between adrenal weight, brain cholinesterase activity and hole-in-wall behavior of mice under different living conditions. *J. Comp. Physiol. Psychol.*, 55:186–190.

Zolman, J. F., & Morimoto, H. (1965), Cerebral changes related to duration of environmental complexity and localized activity. *J. Comp. Physiol. Psychol.*, 60:382–387.

4

Brain Storage of Information from Cutaneous and Other Modalities in Development and Adulthood

William T. Greenough, Ph.D.

Other research presented in this volume and three decades of work have made it clear that mammalian brain function may be profoundly affected by experience, particularly during development. The majority of the evidence has come from studies of modalities other than the somatosensory, especially from vision, which is the simplest to deprive or manipulate. To the extent that other modalities have been studied, the "rules" of neural development generated thus far in visual system studies appear to apply in general to the other modalities (Doving and Pinching, 1973; Clopton and Silverman, 1977; Feng and Rogowski, 1980; Greer, Stewart, Teicher, and Shepherd, 1982). For example, some aspects of

Acknowledgments: Work described in this chapter was supported by the National Science Foundation, the National Institutes of Health, the National Institutes of Mental Health, the Retirement Research Foundation, and the Illinois Pork Producers' Association. I thank Janice M. Juraska, James Black, and Temple Grandin for helpful discussions and comments on the manuscript, Iris Shasha for library assistance, and Mabel Jones for expert manuscript preparation.

sensory system development appear to involve relatively brief *periods of sensitivity* to experience followed by stabilization of functional state, while other aspects, as the work described by Merzenich and Diamond makes clear, remain sensitive, at least to some types of experience or other manipulations. In addition, in all sensory systems in which detailed morphological measures of developmental manipulation effects have been made, there is evidence that numbers or patterns of the synaptic connections between nerve cells are affected by differential experience, such that effects of experience are, in effect, stored in the "wiring diagram" of the brain.

It is my purpose here to review some data related to somatosensory development; to focus upon these two aspects of sensory system development, transient versus lasting experience, sensitivity and associated synaptic change; and to speculate upon how they may be related. The speculations are largely based upon information derived from other sensory modalities, but, I hope, applicable to the somatosensory system. I will concentrate on studies addressing the *numbers* of synapses, although it should be acknowledged that evidence also exists for changes in the characteristics of previously existing synapses.

Methods of Study

Most of the data indicating altered synaptic numbers come from light microscopic studies, in which synapses are not directly observable, such that their numbers must be inferred from parameters visible in the light microscope. The light microscope procedures involve Golgi stains, a set of silver and mercury techniques which impregnate entire neurons—their cell bodies, dendrites and, in some techniques, axons. Because dendrites receive the bulk of synaptic input from other neurons, quantification of the dendritic field sizes of neurons allows one to determine the space available for synapses and, with some assumptions about the frequency of synapses per unit of dendritic surface, the relative number of synapses per neuron. The measures of dendritic field size most commonly used are the summed length of dendrites and their branching pattern and a count of the intersections of dendrites with a set of concentric shells centered on the cell body. These measures are illustrated in Figure 4.1.

A potential problem with Golgi stains is that they stain only a small fraction of neurons in any area (usually less than 5 percent), and the basis for their selectivity is uncertain, although some evidence indicates that the cell bodies of neurons which do stain are not different from those of neurons which do not, suggesting random impregnation (Pasternak and Woolsey, 1975). Nonetheless, not knowing the basis of selection is cause for concern that estimates of synapses per neuron might reflect a nonrepresentative subset of neurons, and confirmation by some other means is warranted. Synapses can be visualized in the electron microscope and, using stereological methodology, which corrects for variation in synapse size and other differences, the density (number per unit of volume) of synapses in neural tissue can be calculated (with some assumptions about synapse shape). Similarly, the density of neuronal cell bodies can be calculated, using stains which impregnate cell bodies or nuclei of all neurons and more efficient light microscopic procedures. The ratio of synapse density to neuronal density is a volume independent measure which can be compared with Golgi stain data. We have done this, using our version of the environmental complexity (or "enriched condition") paradigm described by Diamond. We (Greenough and Volkmar, 1973), studying three different neuron types in upper visual cortex, had previously found (see below) that rats reared in complex environments had about 20 percent larger visual cortex neuronal dendritic fields than rats reared individually in laboratory cages; while rats reared in pairs in laboratory cages were intermediate but closer to the singly housed rats. Since this effect appeared to be quite consistent across neuron types, it presented an ideal situation for determining whether

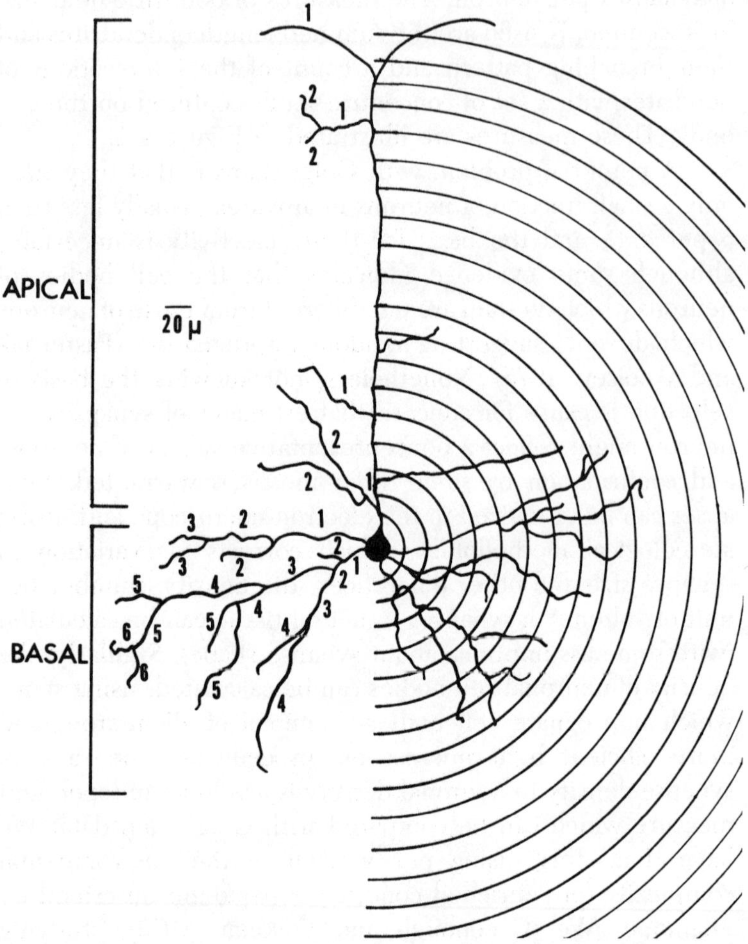

FIGURE 4.1

Scoring system for Golgi-stained neuronal dendritic fields. Branches are counted as a function of bifurcation level away from the cell body or apical dendrite, as on the left, and their length recorded. Alternatively, a more rapid approximation of dendritic length may be generated by counting intersections between dendrites and a series of concentric shells at fixed intervals around the cell body. (© 1975 by Sigma Xi. Reprinted by permission.)

synapses per neuron matched the prediction of this Golgi study. In a current electron-light microscopic stereological study (Turner and Greenough, 1985) we found comparable values for synapses per neuron (Table 4.1). Thus we feel somewhat more confident that results from quantitative Golgi stain studies accurately reflect the status at the electron microscope level.

TABLE 4.1

Synaptic and Neuronal Density and Synapse/Neuron Ratios

	Nv Neurons/mm^3	Nv Synapses/μm^3	Nn Synapses/Neuron
EC	73,807	0.6895	9,521
SC	81,698	0.6567	8,185
IC	87,610	0.6567	7,619

Note: Volume density (Nv) of synapses and neurons and number of synapses per neuron in the upper 4 layers of visual cortex of rats reared in complex (EC), social (SC), and isolated (IC) environments. *Source:* Data from Turner and Greenough (1985).

Results of Studies of Nonsomatosensory Systems

Application of these sorts of techniques to the early development of the visual systems of various mammals (with the apparent, and as yet unexplained, exception of rabbits) has revealed structural effects of sensory manipulations which, while considerably smaller in magnitude than those of environmental complexity versus individual housing, indicate the importance of experience at the time the modality first begins to function. One measure which seems particularly sensitive to very early experience manipulations is the frequency with which spines, the receiving side of the synapse on the dendrites of many types of brain neurons, occur along the dendritic membrane. Deprivation of light or patterned vision has generally been found to reduce their frequency on visual cortex neurons in rodents (Fifkova, 1970; Valverde, 1971; Rothblat and Schwartz, 1979). Visual deprivation has also been reported to reduce dendritic field size in visual cortex neurons in cats (Coleman and Riesen, 1968). When only one eye of a cat or monkey is deprived, the number of synaptic contacts associated with that eye is reduced, while those of the other eye increase (LeVay, Wiesel, and Hubel, 1980; Tieman, 1984). These effects have been confirmed in electron microscopic studies of synapses per neuron (Cragg, 1975a; Winfield, 1981). Similarly, when one ear of a rat is deprived, dendrites which receive its input are smaller than those connected to the open ear (Feng and Rogowski, 1980). Sensitivity to those forms of deprivation exists for only a brief period following the sensory system becoming functional (e.g., LeVay et al., 1980; Rothblat and Schwartz, 1979, and others). Thus these techniques have been valuable in indicating experience-produced differences in synaptic numbers in early development of the modalities in which they have been used.

As indicated above, our laboratory followed up the pioneering work of Rosenzweig, Bennett, and Diamond (1972) on the effects of environmental complexity manipulations of the sort described by Diamond in the preceding chapter. Holloway, Jr. (1966) presented, in a preliminary study, evidence indicating that some visual cortex neurons had larger dendritic fields in environmental complexity (EC) reared rats than in those reared in isolation (IC). (We prefer the term *environmental complexity* to *enriched condition* because we feel it unlikely that our laboratory environment provides significant enrichment relative to what the animal would experience in nature.) Probably the only potentially important difference between the conditions we use and those described by Diamond is that our animals receive a daily "play period" of one half to one hour in a separate environment with a new set of toys each day. All experiments described in this section have involved male littermate sets of Long-Evans hooded rats matched for body weight as well as coat color and pattern at weaning. One member of each littermate set is placed in each condition from weaning at twenty-three to twenty-five days of age until fifty-five days of age (late adolescence). The social (SC) condition is not always run. We do not consider it a "control," and, rather, tend to view the three environments as providing different degrees of opportunity for experience and associated brain information storage.

Initially we found in three upper visual cortex neuron types and one deep visual cortex neuron type that dendritic fields were more extensive in EC than in IC rats, as noted above (Volkmar and Greenough, 1972; Greenough and Volkmar, 1973). The SC rats had intermediate values, but generally were closer to the IC rats. The effects were most pronounced in the outer part of the dendritic field, suggesting that this region may be more sensitive to experience (Figure 4.2). The magnitude of the difference between EC and IC was considerably greater than the size of differences typically reported after dark-rearing. Similar effects were manifest, though to a lesser extent, in auditory cortex, suggesting that the effects were not simply due to differences in visual stimulation; however, the effects were not manifest in all cerebral cortical areas, mitigating suggestions that they might result from hormonal or metabolic differences (Greenough, Volkmar, and Juraska, 1973); additionally, we found that IC rats ate more and gained more weight than EC's (Fiala, Snow, and Greenough, 1977). Effects of differential environmental complexity were not restricted to primary sensory cortical regions. Dendritic fields of granule cells of the hippocampal dentate gyrus were similarly affected by postweaning exposure to differential environmental complexity, although the effects were smaller and less consistent across subjects (Fiala, Joyce, and Greenough, 1978). Taken with the results of Turner and Greenough (1985) described above, we conclude from these studies that the number of synapses per neuron in a variety of brain regions (maybe most, if proper conditions were employed) is determined to a significant extent by the

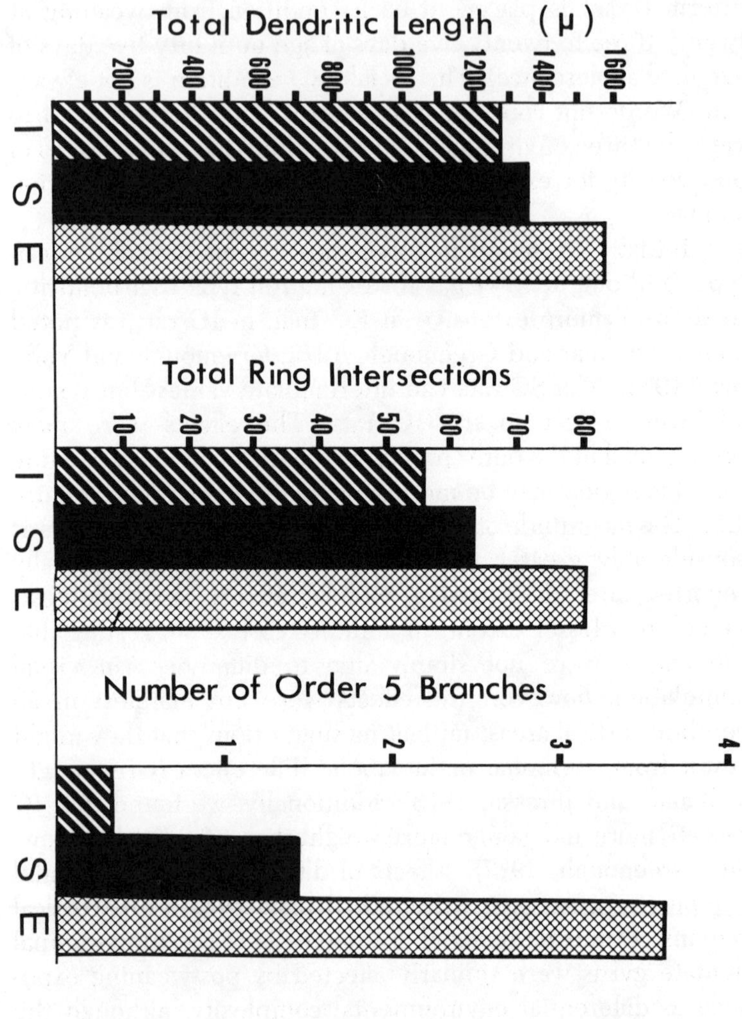

FIGURE 4.2

Three measures of the effects of isolation (I), social (S), and complex environment (E) rearing upon stellate cell dendritic fields in layer IV of visual cortex. Total (projected) dendritic length differs between E and I by approximately 20 percent. The number of branches in distal regions of the field differs by a considerably greater percentage. (© 1976 by Prentice-Hall. Reprinted by permission.)

circumstances under which the organism develops. We speculate that these changes are involved in storing information arising from experience. We will return later to evidence which bears further upon this speculation and to further speculation as to how these differences may arise.

Altering the number (or pattern) of synapses is one of the two most frequently proposed ways in which the functional circuitry of the nervous system could be changed by experience. The other is selectively altering the strength of individual connections. Both we (West and Greenough, 1972) and Diamond's group (Diamond, Lindner, Johnson, Bennett, and Rosenzweig, 1975) have reported that synaptic contacts in layer IV of the visual cortex are about 10 percent larger (diameter) in EC than in IC rats. Both laboratories measured the postsynaptic thickening, a densely staining region on the recipient neuron's intracellular membrane surface which has been termed the *active zone* (Couteaux, 1961), ignoring the small gaps, or perforations, that frequently appear in this structure. More recently we found that these perforations appeared more frequently in occipital cortex synapses of EC than IC rats, with SC rats again intermediate (Greenough, West, and DeVoogd, 1978). Recently Sirevaag and Greenough (1985) have found that at these perforations the synapse membranes are closer together than at other synapse regions. The functional significance of perforated synapses remains unclear, but the fact that they increase in frequency with functional demand in other situations (Vrensen and Cardozo, 1981; Hatton and Ellisman, 1982) suggests they may play an important role in synaptic function.

Thus there is evidence (most of it not reviewed here) for experience–dependence in both the number and the structural characteristics of synapses in nonsomatosensory brain regions, beginning as early as the time at which the regions begin to function, and extending, as Merzenich (chapter 2) and Diamond (chapter 3) also describe, well beyond traditionally conceived developmental stages. These data suggest that the brain may use more than one mechanism to alter its functional organization in response to experience.

Studies of Experience Effects Upon Somatosensory Development

As noted earlier, in contrast to other sensory modalities, studies of the role of experience in the development of the somatosensory system have been rare. The dominant developmental model using the rat's somatosensory system has involved the large snout whiskers (mystacial vibrissae) which are associated with unique structures in the somatosensory cortex, such as the cell groupings which have been termed *barrels* in mice (Woolsey and Van der Loos, 1970). The aggregation of neuronal cell bodies into barrels, one barrel for each whisker, occurs postnatally, a process which follows the organization of similar groupings of nerve cells in the brainstem sensory nucleus and somatosensory projection regions of the thalamus (Woolsey, Anderson, Wann, and Stanfield, 1979; Belford and Killackey, 1980). Barrels form by the movement of cell bodies into cell-dense walls and cell-sparse hollows. Development of barrels depends upon an intact periphery; if whisker follicles are destroyed within a few days of birth, cell aggregation into corresponding barrels is disrupted (Woolsey and Wann, 1976). However, merely removing the whiskers does not prevent cell aggregation (Van der Loos and Woolsey, 1973). The implication of this result is that mere deprivation does not affect organization of this somatosensory system—physical damage is necessary. However, two very important qualifications should be considered. First, the degree to which removing the whiskers affects the neural input from the vibrissal region in neonatal rats is not clear; the neonates' whiskers are relatively short, and the type of stimulation which would occur during this period, such as the diffuse input which may arise from nursing, might be effectively transmitted by stimulation of skin structures in the follicular region. Second, the effects of neonatal whisker removal without follicular destruction upon the fine structure of nerve cells in the somatosensory cortex have not, apparently, been studied, and it is possible that gross organization of cells into barrels occurs more or less normally, but that dendritic organization is disrupted by whisker removal.

There is some behavioral evidence that later vibrissal function may be affected by developmental functional demand. Rogowski (unpublished, cited in Burnstine, Greenough, and Tees, 1984) reared mice blind from shortly after birth along with sighted counterparts in a complex environment similar to those previously described, except that emphasisis was on elevated runways, ledges, barriers, and other structures which impeded smooth travel for those that could not see. Informal observation indicated that while both the blind and sighted animals used their vibrissae extensively, whisking them back and forth to sense objects as they moved about, the blind animals seemed to use the whiskers more, particularly in situations of apparent uncertainty about the safety (or wisdom) of the next forward step. To assess whether whisker function had been altered by this apparently increased reliance upon them for orientation in the physical environment, Rogowski examined the placing response (forelimb extension toward a surface) triggered by whisker contact. Mice were suspended by their tails in dim red light (mice have no color vision and are effectively blind in red light) and a clear plastic platform was gradually raised toward them. The distance the platform moved between the first forelimb-extension and the point at which the forelimb first touched the platform was 1.4 ± 0.4 mm for the sighted mice and $3.2 + 0.3$ mm for the blind mice ($p < 0.05$), suggesting that whisker contact with the platform was more effective in triggering placing in the blind mice. Whether the cause was a difference in peripheral sensory usage (e.g., a change in the whisking pattern) or in central processing of equivalent peripheral input, was not clear, but this study, as well as a long history of studies which suggest enhanced somatosensory function in blind humans (Burnstine et al., 1984), suggest that the somatosensory system can respond to functional demand by providing information normally available through other modalities.

One study of relative deprivation of body sensation, in which detailed brain measures were made, involved the cerebellum. In this study (Floeter and Greenough, 1979) macaque monkeys were reared (as part of a separate behavioral study) from shortly after birth in environments closely paralleling those of the rodent complex environment paradigm described by Diamond and here: (1) a complex two-room group environment containing adult, juvenile, and young monkeys and equipped with playthings (shelves, ropes, ladders, small toys, etc.); (2) in pairs in adjacent cages; and (3) in individual enclosures which prevented contact with other monkeys. The third condition produces a behavioral pattern termed the *isolation syndrome* (see Suomi, chapter 5) which has some features, if not etiology, in common with the human disorder termed *childhood autism*. Such animals exhibit extensive bouts of repeated sterotyped motor behaviors, inappropriate social behavior, and so on, the extent of which varies with the species, degree, and duration of isolation; some of these behavioral features were evident in the fascicularis macaques whose brains we examined (Sackett, Ruppenthal, Fahrenbruch, Holm, and Greenough,, 1981). We examined the cerebellum, a sensorimotor integration region involved in the coordination of movement, both because of the effects of these rearing conditions upon motor behaviors and because involvement of the cerebellum in the isolation syndrome and behaviorally related human disorders had been postulated (Prescott, 1970). We studied Purkinje cells, the only efferent neuron of the cerebellar cortex, and granule cells, the primary recipient of one of the two types of cerebellar input (the other input terminates on Purkinje cells). Purkinje cell dendritic field data collection focused upon "spiny branchlets," the part which receives granule cell input, and in some areas upon the size of Purkinje cell bodies. The results for several regions are shown in Table 4.2. Purkinje cell bodies were larger in the complex environment monkeys in both regions studied, with no statistical or apparent difference between individually and socially housed animals. A similar pattern appeared for two of the three regions in the size of spiny branchlets, while no differences were evident in granule cell dendritic fields. While some caution must be exercised in interpreting these data due to the small number of subjects involved, they suggest that the development of the cerebellum, a structure which appears to be involved in translating sensory information about body position for the coordination of movement, is sensitive to experience. There are two things the data do *not* suggest. First, they do not indicate involvement of the cerebellar regions studied in the isolation syndrome, since in no case was there a difference between the socially reared monkeys, which did not exhibit isolation syndrome behaviors, and the individually reared monkeys. Second, the data do not implicate tactile input per se in the cerebellar effects, because the structures which were affected are most closely related to vestibular input, the sensation of orientation and movement of the head in space. Moreover, preliminary studies of a lateral cerebellar region more closely tied to kinesthetic, proprioceptive, and tactile sensation revealed no statistical or apparent differences among the groups (Floeter, Casas, and Greenough, personal communication). Thus we have yet to find clear support for the view that tactile input per se affects our measures of brain development.

A study still in progress in our laboratory (Grandin, 1988) may indicate further the relative resilience of developing somatosensory regions to experience manipulations involving touch. This work involved domestic pigs (Hampshire × Yorkshire crosses), which have been noted for the large amount of somatosensory cortex devoted to the snout, which, of course, makes up a very small part of the body's surface

TABLE 4.2

Cerebellar Measures in Differentially Reared Monkeys

Area	C	S	I
	N X±S.E.M.	N X±S.E.M.	N X±S.E.M.
Spiny Branchlets			
Ventral paraflocculus	2 40.0±1.9*	4 32.9±1.1	2 36.1±1.7
Nodulus	2 26.5±1.3**	4 25.4±0.8	2 24.6±1.3
Flocculus	4 31.6±1.1	6 30.2±1.0	6 32.8±1.1
Granule cells			
Ventral paraflocculus	2 33.9±1.4	4 35.5±1.3	2 34.3±1.3
Nodulus	2 45.4±1.9	4 45.7±1.3	2 44.1±1.5
Purkinje Somas			
Nodulus	2 33.2±0.2*	3 29.8±0.2	2 30.8±0.2
Uvula	2 30.8±0.3*	4 28.8±0.5	2 28.6±0.3

Note: Means and standard errors for spiny branchlets (the parts of cerebellar Purkinje neurons which receive granule cell input) in macaque monkeys reared in large colony environments with fixed structures and play objects (C), in adjacent cages with 4 hr daily social interaction in the same cage (S), or in individual cages without view of other animals (I). Spiny branchlet and granule cell data are intersections with concentric shells; soma data are diameters in micrometers.
*$p<0.05$, **$p<0.10$ *vs* S + I (Data from Floeter and Greenough, 1979).

(Adrian, 1943). This suggests, and behavioral observation confirms, that the snout is a primary source of tactile information regarding the immediate physical environment: the typical response of a pig to a novel object in its environment is to explore it with the snout. (The second response, in our experience, is to determine the most efficient way to destroy the object.) We compared pigs reared under typical feedlot conditions (small indoor rearing pens with pairs of pigs) with pigs reared out of doors (at a temperate time of year) in a large pen in which various play objects were placed and changed at frequent intervals, and in which physical contact with a human caretaker was also occasionally offered. (One variable we did not control was that the feedlot pigs were exposed to twenty-four hour lighting, whereas the outdoor pigs were exposed to natural light.)

At this point we have completed preliminary analyses of Layers II to III of pyramidal neurons centered in the snout region of somatosensory cortex for four pigs in each condition. In this neuron type (which, in the visual cortex, is affected by complex environment experience in the rat) we can find no evidence for increased dendritic field dimensions in the more broadly experienced outdoor pigs. This could reflect either an absence of responsiveness to differential stimulation in pig somatosensory cortex or a tendency on the part of the indoor pigs to seek out tactile stimulation in their more limited environment. (It might also reflect compression or expansion of the boundaries of the snout or somatonsensory region of the type described in chapter 2 by Merzenich, but this seems unlikely.)

Limited Early Responsiveness to Cutaneous Experience?

Taken together, the above results provide only sporadic evidence that postnatal tactile stimulation affects early development of CNS regions which process tactile information. This does not mean that this aspect of the somatosensory system is somehow impervious to structural experiential influences in early development, of course. Among the reasons for the above pattern (in addition to those already mentioned) are:

1. We simply have not found the proper combination of situation and species to demonstrate structural experience effects of the sorts seen in other species (reviewed briefly in the previous section). Diamond (chapter 3), certainly suggests effects of experience on dorsal somatosensory cortex thickness in the rat, a lissencephalic (i.e., no sulci or gyri) species.

2. The effects of early deprivation in, for example, the visual system are often relatively small (except when competition within the modality is involved, as with monocular deprivation). It may seem surprising that the effects of total

visual deprivation versus exposure to patterned light are smaller than those of complex environments versus individual housing on estimates of synaptic number. What we don't know, however, is the degree to which the *pattern* of synapses differs between light- and dark-reared animals. It may be that there is a strong tendency for synapses to form and that the primary effect of early experience is to determine *which* synapses form (or survive). Some support for this view in the somatosensory system has been provided by Harris and Woolsey (1981), who studied dendritic fields of neurons in barrels following neonatal whisker follicle destruction. They found that the size of neuronal dendritic fields in the whiskers (and cell barrels) were damaged. However, in contrast to the intact controls, in which the dendrites of a barrel's cells were almost exclusively confined to that barrel, dendrites of neurons associated with damaged follicles were oriented toward the adjacent barrels of undamaged follicles.

3. Subtotal deprivation (as seems inevitable for tactile sensation) may have little effect on these basic developmental processes. If what normally occurs at this early stage is development of ability to discern basic patterns (e.g., shapes, borders, etc.) then all that may be required for normal development is the presence of those patterns in the environment.

4. In the pigs, the visual, auditory, and olfactory stimulation provided by the complex environment may actually have *detracted* from somatosensory effects. Thus, if information storage in development (and/or adulthood) requires involvement of some overriding or permissive central process, as suggested by some recent reports (e.g., Kasamatsu and Pettigrew, 1976; Mirmiran and Uylings, 1983), it may be that the complex environment takes away some attention from the somatosensory modality, whereas it would remain more dominant in the visually and auditorially bland environment of the feedlot pigs. (It is of interest in this regard that the feedlot pigs were active in manipulating the physical

environment, for example, by removing bolts from their pens, disrupting feeding and watering apparatus, and were much more physically forceful than the outdoor pigs in nuzzling the experimenter when it was necessary to reach into the pen to correct such situations.)

5. Excepting, perhaps, the whisker studies, the timing of experience manipulations may not have been appropriate to that of cutaneous sensitivity to early experience, as suggested by earlier work of Gottlieb (1971) which has been put in a more detailed theoretical context by Turkewitz and Kenny (1982). Gottlieb noted that onset of function in mammalian and avian sensory systems occurred sequentially, the cutaneous sense maturing earlier, followed sequentially by vestibular, auditory, and visual sensation. (Within the cutaneous sense, the oral or snout region was usually first to develop.) Thus the period of maximal sensitivity to tactile manipulations might occur quite early in development, relative to other modalities. Turkewitz and Kenny, following up on Gottlieb's ideas, suggested two possible reasons for this sequencing of sensory system development. First, some common resource, such as attention to the modality by other brain systems or metabolic resources (as suggested in No. 4 above), might be limited in availability, such that modalities may only develop to fullest potential if their demands upon these resources are temporally offset. Second, sequencing of maturation of sensory modalities could allow better integration among them; information acquired by one modality could be used in the development of others and in establishing relationships among them with regard to aspects of the environment (e.g., corresponding visual and tactile knowledge of the immediate physical environment). The cutaneous sense, early to develop, might thus be of great importance to the later developing modalities. It is of interest that neocortical development of somatosensory and other sensory regions is more synchronous than peripheral development, perhaps to allow for integration at this level. This view of sensory

development has considerable predictive power in relation to human data from cases in which modalities have been damaged (Burnstine et al., 1984). The Turkewitz and Kenny view suggests that the effects of tactile manipulations during development (if purely tactile manipulation could be assured) might be evident in the structure and function of other sensory or more central systems which depend upon tactile input for their development.

Later Somatosensory Plasticity

We have, of course, the evidence before us from other chapters and elsewhere that neural substrates of cutaneous sensation remain capable of reorganization in adulthood. Plasticity of intact parts of the nervous system in the face of damage appears to be widespread in the adult mammalian nervous systems. Plastic responses to experience have also been demonstrated in several regions of the adult brain in recent years (Uylings, Kuypers, and Veltman, 1978; Greenough, Juraska, and Volkmar, 1979; Juraska, Greenough, Elliott, Mack, and Berkowitz, 1980), and the somatosensory system appears to be no exception. Thus we face the possible contradiction between an apparently early maturation of cutaneous sensation, and possible associated reductions in sensitivity to postnatal experience manipulations, and evidence for continuing sensitivity of this system to experience in adulthood. While the degree to which this contradiction exists awaits further evidence in the somatosensory system, the apparent conflict between traditional views of brief periods of heightened sensitivity of sensory systems to experience in development (critical or sensitive periods) and more recent evidence for significant structural and functional responsiveness to experience later, remains for other systems. Of interest is (1) whether these early and adult phenomena are both facets of a single mechanism of CNS plasticity evident, perhaps to different degrees, throughout the life of the organism, or (2) whether they represent separate and distinct aspects of the capacity of the nervous system to respond to, or encode, information from experience at different stages of the lifespan.

One view, which has arisen from behavioral research, posits that developmental effects of experience and adultlike learning and memory are distinguished by their ability to be retrieved as memorial events (Campbell and Spear, 1972). It has been noted that developmental events which may have profound effects upon later behavior or ability are often not remembered and that adult humans rarely remember a significant number of events from the first few years of life whereas later childhood memories may be abundant. Demonstration of similar phenomena in animals (Campbell and Campbell, 1962; Nagy and Murphy, 1974) largely rules out developmental shifts to verbal encoding mechanisms or complicated psychoanalytic explanations which have been proposed. Campbell and others (Nagy and Murphy, 1974; Campbell and Coulter, 1976) have argued that adultlike learning and memory capacity emerges at a relatively specific point in development. The implication is that the neural substrates of developmental organization processes and adult memory are different.

In apparent opposition to this view, evidence is accumulating that similar neural substrates exist for developmental experience effects and adult memory phenomena. First, it has now been demonstrated that at least some kinds of specific memories can form very early in development—even before birth (Stickrod, Kimble, and Smotherman, 1982). More importantly, perhaps, it has been reported that experience manipulations in adult, even aging, animals bring about changes in the structure of neuronal dendritic fields which are remarkably similar to those produced by the same or other experience manipulations during development (Uylings et al., 1978; Juraska et al., 1980; Green, Greenough, and Schulumpf, 1983; Diamond, chapter 3). Moreover, adult animals trained on traditional psychological learning tasks, such as mazes, exhibit dendritic field changes which are qualitatively similar to those seen with developmental experience manipulations (Greenough et al., 1979; Chang and Greenough, 1982; Greenough, Larson, and Withers, 1985). This evidence would seem to suggest that the neural mechanisms of developmental information storage remain, possibly at reduced levels, a viable aspect of the capacity for functional reorganization in the adult nervous system.

Early Versus Late Plasticity: A Hypothesis

A view which allows both the development versus memory distinction and the commonality of final mechanism is suggested by the Bekoff and Fox (1972) proposal that developmental experience may be of two types. While I have taken some liberties with their definitions, they propose terms applicable to two different sorts of information that the environment can provide to the developing nervous system (similar categories were proposed by Piaget [1974]). Experience-expectant developmental interactions can be conceived as involving experiences common to all normally reared members of the species, and which can be called upon for aid in fine-tuning the nervous system by a genome limited in its capacity to precisely specify neurobehavioral organization. In contrast, experience-dependent interactions involve experiences which are unique to the individual—information about sources of food and safety, the social system, and so forth. This latter type of interaction could blend into the sort of information storage process traditionally referred to by the terms *learning* and *memory*.

It seems at least possible that the nervous system could distinguish between these two types of information on the basis of its ability to prepare for them in advance. If information is expected, then the developing nervous system could be arranged in such a way as to efficiently take advantage of it. If information is unexpected—or at least unpredictable at the individual level—it may be more difficult for the nervous system to be prepared for all possibilities.

There is evidence that can be interpreted to indicate that the nervous system recognizes this distinction, or a similar one. Early in the development of many brain systems, there is evidence for an overproduction of synaptic connections, relative to the numbers which exist in the adult system. This had been best documented structurally in the visual systems of cats and monkeys (Cragg, 1975b; Boothe, Greenough, Lund, and Wrege, 1979; LeVay et al., 1980), but is also evident in systems ranging from the spinal cord–muscle connections of the body (Brown, Jansen, and Van Essen, 1976) to brainstem sensory nuclei (Falls and Gobel, 1979), to the cerebellum (Mariani and Changeaux, 1981). Evidence also indicates excess synapse production in some pathways of developing somatosensory cortex (Ivy and Killackey, 1981). It appears that the subset of connections which survive in these systems do so because they have successfully competed with other connections for sites on, and control of, the postsynaptic cell. In cases that have been studied, the activity of the presynaptic neurons, and possibly correlated activity on the part of recipient neurons, is a key aspect of synapse survival. In the primate visual cortex, for example, adjacent patches of synapses associated with each of the two eyes are formed from an initially overlapping distribution, and if one eye is deprived of experience, synapses from the other compete more effectively for its space, rendering the deprived eye's patches smaller (LeVay et al., 1980). From such results it has been proposed that experience acts in part as a sculptor in early development, preserving the adult form while pushing away irrelevant scraps of connections.

In contrast, there is little evidence for synapse overproduction in later development and in adulthood when the number or pattern of synaptic connections is altered by experience. While a low level of synaptic turnover has been detected in some regions of the undamaged adult brain

(Sotelo and Palay, 1971), it is not clear whether this turnover is constitutively generated, with some sort of selective preservation process operating, as in development, or whether this turnover is an activity-dependent process, in which synapses are generated as a result of neural information processing and/or the need for information storage. If the latter were the case, a mechanism for postdevelopmental plasticity of a different sort from that of early development would exist—potentially one with the capacity to encode unpredicted information in nervous system organization. It may be this form of neural plasticity which is tapped by experiments indicating morphological (and possibly some aspects of physiological) change in sensory systems in later development and adulthood. And it may be that both experience-expectant and experience-dependent information storage achieve their ultimate goals of individual adaptation to the environment through different mechanisms—synapse selection versus synapse formation—but with the same ultimate end, alteration in the functional wiring diagrams of the nervous system.

Epilogue

An array of data and conjecture is presented in this volume to make the point that touch, broadly considered, may have significant value in clinical situations. (At least some of the therapeutic touch methods, however, do not involve physical contact or cutaneous sensory activation.) The point must be made, however, that there is probably nothing "magic" and possibly nothing even very special about cutaneous activation per se. The important consideration, from the clinical perspective, is to find the optimal conditions for treating patients, ranging from premature infants (whom pediatricians have decided must live, no matter how horribly) to older patients, and even those likely to die. Touch may be of value in many of these cases, as may be anything which mitigates the inhospitable environment of the hospital. We must not ignore the potential value of numerous possible types of intervention. A familiar object, or a plant or pet to care for, can have significant impact on the longevity of the dying and possibly on the survival of the critically ill. In our search for the optimal keys to individual adaptation across a range of clinical situations, we must compare and critically evaluate all forms of nontraditional intervention rather than grasping for a panacea, which implies desperation in our search.

Discussion: Chapter 4

T. Berry Brazelton: Bill, reminding us of Piaget's concepts with your terms *experience-expectant* and *experience-dependent* is an important contribution. *Experience-expectant*, as I understand it, refers to the preparation the nervous system has for experience—the basis for environmental sculpturing of the brain's organization. *Experience-dependent* refers to the building of new structures upon this species-characteristic baseline; that is, to the incorporation of individual experience. Since experience-dependent development is individual, it may be more at risk.

William Greenough: Yes and no. Individual development can be maladaptive—witness the truly crazy individuals who disrupt society—but extreme laboratory situations indicate that disruption of experience-dependent processes can be disastrous. Touch is the modality that develops first, at least in mammals. However, we know very little about it, because we can deprive an animal of most sound and all vision, but how do you deprive an animal of touch?

T. Berry Brazelton: Other kinds of experiments might give us more information. I really look forward to seeing other kinds of experiments with animals besides deprivation experiments, and I'm happy that you seem to have that in mind, too.

Peter Gorski: Bill, what happens at the opposite extreme from deprivation—if you put the animals into an overly complex environment, a chaotic, "crazy" one?

William Greenough: Presumably there is a point beyond which the rule "If a little is good, more is better" ceases to hold for our rats, but we haven't found it yet.

*Peter Gorski:*Are you sure you're getting meaningful cortical growth in the complex-environment animals rather than disorganized change?

William Greenough: Our approach is anatomical rather than physiological, and a problem when you're doing anatomy is that although you can count things, the pattern and meaning of neural connections is very hard to discern with a microscope. The questions you're asking should be answered by using physiological recording techniques. At a higher level, though, behavioral studies certainly imply positive changes in brain organization with complex environments.

Michael Merzenich: An important issue that you've raised is the relation between the kind of work you and Marian Diamond have done and the kind of work we've done. From our point of view, the real question is: Exactly what is the cortical circuitry underlying the map changes that we see? We believe that the map changes we've observed result primarily from changes of input. However, there is probably also a system in the brain that is modulating the process, and thereby controlling the rate at which things can change.

Some exciting new evidence from Dr. Evart's laboratory, in experiments done by Randall Nelson, demonstrates a powerful relationship between the motor act of the animal and the potential for organization of the somatosensory field. What they've seen specifically is that in Area 3b, during voluntary movement, the stimulation of the skin counts just as it would in a passive situation. However, Area 1 is dramatically suppressed when the animal is actually moving; only in the passive situation is Area 1 activated. We believe that these differences between the maps of Area 3b and Area 1 are due to the fact that stimulation from movement per se is not allowed to change Area 1. When you find changes in spine density or dendritic branching, then, the question is: Which process or combination of processes do they relate to?

William Greenough: New connections might be involved in longer-term changes, or in stabilizing the changes.

T. Berry Brazelton: Human newborns use state as a way of modulating and screening information. For a preterm or small-for-gestational-age (SGA) baby who has not developed the capacity to modulate appropriately, a stimulus that a full-term neonate can accept may be too much. If you say "How are you doing?" to a full-term, she'll probably search for your face and find it. But a premie might avert, go into an arched state, and perhaps spit up, have a BM, and become cyanotic. You might get more cells with that second avoidance response, but the question, I guess, would be one of appropriateness.

William Greenough: There is something about modulation and the environment of premature babies that I would like to bring up. It's my understanding, though maybe this is changing, that the intensive care nurseries in many hospitals are kept lighted twenty-four hours a day. If you did that to a rat and it happened to be an albino, you would destroy its entire retina in four days. Even more important, an infant rat needs an opportunity to track its mother's rhythms during early development. I'm concerned about the fact that all sources of natural rhythms are removed from the environment of these premature newborns. These rhythms govern very important things, such as patterns of growth hormone release.

T. Berry Brazelton: We'll be discussing the nursery environment in detail later, Bill, when we focus on the preterm infant. Many nurseries are now trying to simulate natural light rhythms, and I think this is a very constructive trend.

References

Adrian, E.D. (1943), Afferent areas in the brain of ungulates. *Brain*, 66:89–103.

Bekoff, M., & Fox, M. W. (1972), Postnatal neural ontogeny: Environment-dependent and/or environment-expectant? *Development. Psychobiol.*, 5:323–341.

Belford, G. R., & Killackey, H. P. (1980), The sensitive period in the development of the trigeminal system of the neonatal rat. *J. Compar. Neurol.*, 193:335–350.

Boothe, R. G., Greenough, W. T., Lund, J. S., & Wrege, K. (1979), A quantitative investigation of spine and dendrite development of neurons in visual cortex (area 17) of *Macaca nemestrina* monkeys. *J. Compar. Neurol.*, 186:473–490.

Brown, M. C., Jansen, J. K. S., & Van Essen, D. (1976), Polyneuronal innervation of skeletal muscle in new-born rats and its elimination during maturation. *J. Physiol.*, 261:387–422.

Burnstine, T. H., Greenough, W. T., & Tees, R. C. (1984), Intermodal compensation following brain damage or deprivation: A review of behavioral and neural evidence. In: *Early Brain Damage*, Vol. 1, eds. C. R. Almli & S. Finger. New York: Academic Press, pp. 3–34.

Campbell, B. A. & Campbell, E. H. (1962), Retention and extinction of learned fear in infant and adult rats. *J. Comp. Physiol. Psychol.*, 55:1–8.

———Coulter, X. (1976), The ontogenesis of learning and memory. In: *Neural Mechanisms of Learning and Memory*, eds. M. R. Rosenzweig & E. L. Bennett. Cambridge, MA: MIT Press, pp. 209–235.

———Spear, N. E. (1972), Ontogeny of memory. *Psychol. Rev.*, 79:215–236.

Chang, F.-L., & Greenough, W. T. (1982), Lateralized effects of nonocular training on dendritic branching in adult split-brain rats. *Brain Res.*, 232:283–292.

Clopton, B. M., & Silverman, M. S. (1977), Plasticity of inaural interaction. II. Critical periods and changes in midline response. *J. Neurophysiol.*, 40:1275–1280.

Coleman, P. D., & Riesen, A. H. (1968), Environmental effects on cortical dendritic fields. I. Rearing in the dark. *J. Anatomy*, 102:363–374.

Couteaux, R. (1961), Principaux critères morphologiques et cytochimiques utilisables aujourd'hui pour definir les divers types de synapses. In: *Actualités Neurophysiologiques, troisième serie*, ed. A. M. Monnier. Paris: Masson et Cie, pp. 145–173.

Cragg, B. G. (1975a), The development of synapses in the kitten visual cortex during visual deprivation. *Experiment. Neurol.*, 46:445–451a.

———(1975b), The development of synapses in the visual system of the cat. *J. Comp. Neurol.*, 160:147–166.

Diamond, M. C., Lindner, B., Johnson, R., Bennett, E. L., & Rosenzweig, M. R. (1975), Differences in occipital cortical synapses from environmentally enriched, impoverished, and standard colony rats. *J. Neurosci. Res.*, 1:109–119.

Doving, K. B., & Pinching, A. J. (1973), Selective degeneration of neurones in the olfactory bulb following prolonged odour exposure. *Brain Res.*, 52:115–129.

Falls, W., & Gobel, S., (1979), Golgi and EM studies of the formation of dendritic and axonal arbors: The interneurons of the substantia gelatinosa of Rolando in newborn kittens. *J. Comp. Neurol.*, 187:1–18.

Feng, A. S., & Rogowski, B. A. (1980), Effects of monaural and binaural occlusion on the morphology of neurons in the medial superior olivary nucleus of the rat. *Brain Res.*, 189:530–534.

Fiala, B. A., Joyce, J. N., & Greenough, W. T. (1978), Environmental complexity modulates growth of granule cell dendrites in developing but not adult hippocampus of rats. *Exper. Neurol.*, 59:372–383.

———Snow, F. M., & Greenough, W. T. (1977), "Impoverished" rats weigh more than "enriched" rats because they eat more. *Development. Psychobiol.*, 10:537–541.

Fifkova, E. (1970), The effect of unilateral deprivation in visual centers in rats. *J. Comp. Neurol.*, 140:432–438.

Floeter, M. K., & Greenough, W. T. (1979), Cerebellar plasticity: Modification of Purkinje cell structure by differential rearing in monkeys. *Science*, 206:227–229.

Gottlieb, G. (1971), Ontogenesis of sensory function in birds and mammals. In: *The Biopsychology of Development*, eds. E. Tobach, L. R. Aronson, & E. Shaw. New York: Academic Press.

Grandin, T. (1988), Unpublished doctoral dissertation. University of Illinois, Urbana-Champaign.

Green, E. J., Greenough, W. T., & Schlumpf, B. E. (1983), The effects of complex or isolated environments on cortical dendrites of middle-aged rats. *Brain Res.*, 264:233–240.

Greenough, W. T., Juraska, J. M., & Volkmar, F. R. (1979), Maze training effects on dendritic branching in occipital cortex of adult rats. *Behav. & Neural Biol.*, 26:287–297.

———Larson, J. R., & Withers, G. S. (1985), Effects of unilateral and bilateral training in a reaching task on dendritic branching of neurons in the rat motor-sensory forelimb cortex. *Behav. & Neural Biol.*, 44:301–314.

———Volkmar, F. R. (1973), Pattern of dendritic branching in occipital cortex of rats reared in complex environments. *Experiment. Neurol.*, 40:491–504.

——— ———Juraska, J. M. (1973), Effects of rearing complexity on dendritic branching in frontolateral and temporal cortex of the rat. *Experiment. Neurol.*, 41:371–378.

———West, R. W., & DeVoogd, T. J. (1978), Subsynaptic plate perforations: Changes with age and experince in the rat. *Science*, 202:1096–1098.

Greer, C. A., Stewart, W. B., Teicher, M. H., & Shepherd, G. M. (1982), Functional development of the olfactory bulb and a unique glomerular complex in the neonatal rat. *J. Neurosci.*, 2:1744–1759.

Harris, R. M., & Woolsey, T. A. (1981), Dendritic plasticity in mouse barrel cortex following postnatal vibrissa follicle damage. *J. Comp. Neurol.*, 196:357–376.

Hatton, J. D., & Ellisman, M. H. (1982), A restructuring of hypothalamic synapses is associated with motherhood. *J. Neurosci.*, 2:704–707.

Holloway, R. L. (1966), Dendritic branching: Some preliminary results of training and complexity in rat visual cortex. *Brain Res.*, 2:393–396.

Ivy, G. O., & Killackey, H. P. (1981), The ontogeny of the distribution of callosal projection neurons in the rat parietal cortex. *J. Compar. Neurol.*, 195:367–389.

Juraska, J. M., Greenough, W. T., Elliott, C., Mack, K. J., & Berkowitz, R. (1980), Plasticity in adult rat visual cortex: An examination of several cell populations after differential rearing. *Behav. & Neural Biol.*, 29:157–167.

Kasamatsu, T., & Pettigrew, J. D. (1976), Depletion of brain catecholamines: Failure of ocular dominance shift after monocular occlusion in kittens. *Science*, 194:206–208.

LeVay, S., Wiesel, T. N., & Hubel, D. H. (1980), The development of ocular dominance columns in normal and visually deprived monkeys. *J. Compar. Neurol.*, 191:1–51.

Mariani, J., & Changeaux, J.-P. (1981), Ontogenesis of olivocerebellar relationships. I. Studies by intracellular recordings of the multiple innervation of Purkinje cells by climbing fibers in the developing rat cerebellum. *J. Neurosci.*, 1:696–702.

Mirmiran, M., & Uylings, H. B. M. (1983), The environemental enrichment effect upon cortical growth is neutralized by concomitant pharmacological suppression of active sleep in female rats. *Brain Res.*, 261:331–334.

Nagy, Z. M., & Murphy, J. M. (1974), Learning and retention of a discriminated escape response in infant mice. *Development. Psychobiol.*, 7:185–192.

Pasternak, J. F., & Woolsey, T. A. (1975), On the "selectivity" of the Golgi–Cox method. *J. Comp. Neurol.*, 160:307–312.

Piaget, J. (1974), *Adapatation and Intelligence: Organic Selection and Phenocopy*, trans. S. Eames. Chicago: University of Chicago Press, 1980.

Prescott, J. W. (1970), Early somatosensory deprivation as an ontogenetic process in the abnormal development of brain and behavior. In:

Medical Primatology, ed. E. Goldsmith & J. Morr-Jankowski. Basel, Switzerland: S. Karger.

Rogowski, B. A. (1978), Unpublished M.S. thesis, University of Illinois, Urbana-Champaign.

Rosenzweig, M. R., Bennett, E. L., & Diamond, M. C. (1972), Chemical and anatomical plasticity of brain: Replications and extensions. In: *Macromolecules and Behavior*, 2d ed., ed. J. Gaito. New York: Appleton-Century-Crofts, pp. 205–278.

Rothblat, L. A., & Schwartz, M. L. (1979), The effect of monocular deprivation on dendritic spines in visual cortex of young and adult albino rats; evidence for a sensitive period. *Brain Res.*, 161:156–161.

Sackett, G. P., Ruppenthal, G. C., Fahrenbruch, C. E., Holm, R. A., & Greenough, W. T. (1981), Genotype determines social isolation rearing effects in monkeys. *Development. Psychol.*, 17:313–318.

Sirevaag, A. M., & Greenough, W. T. (1985), Differential rearing effects on rat visual cortex synapses. II. Synaptic morphometry. *Development. Res.*, 19:215–226.

Sotelo, C., & Palay, S. L. (1971), Altered axons and axon terminals in the lateral vestibular nucleus of the rat. Possible example of axonal remodeling. *Lab. Investig.*, 25:653–671.

Stickrod, G., Kimble, D. P., & Smotherman, W. P. (1982), In utero taste/odor aversion conditioning in the rat. *Psychol. & Behav.*, 28:5–7.

Tieman, S. B. (1984), Effects of monocular deprivation on geniculocortical synapses in the cat. *J. Comp. Neurol.*, 222:166–176.

Turkewitz, G., & Kenny, P. A. (1982), Limitations on input as a basis for neural organization and perceptual development; A preliminary theoretical statement. *Development. Psychobiol.*, 15:357–368.

Turner, A. M., & Greenough, W. T. (1985), Differential rearing effects on rat visual cortex synapses. I. Synaptic and neuronal density and synapses per neuron. *Brain Res.*, 329:195–203.

Uylings, H. B. M., Kuypers, K., & Veltman, W. A. M. (1978), Environmental influences on the neocortex in later life. In: *Maturation of the Nervous System, Progress in Brain Research*, Vol. 48, eds. M. A. Corner, R. E. Baker, N. F. van de Poll, D. F. Swaab, and H. B. M. Uylings. Amsterdam: Elsevier/North Holland, pp. 261–272.

Valverde, F. (1971), Rate and extent of recovery from dark-rearing in the visual cortex of the mouse. *Brain Res.*, 33:1–11.

Van der Loos, H., & Woolsey, T. A. (1973), Somatosensory cortex: Structural alterations following early injury to sense organs. *Science*, 179:395–398.

Volkmar, F. R., & Greenough, W. T. (1972), Rearing complexity affects branching of dendrites in the visual cortex of the rat. *Science*, 176:1445–1447.

Vrensen, G., & Cardozo, J. N. (1981), Changes in size and shape of synaptic connections after visual training: An ultrastructural approach of synaptic plasticity. *Brain Res.*, 218:79–98.

West, R. W., & Greenough, W. T. (1972), Effect of environmental complexity on cortical synapses of rats: Preliminary results. *Behav. Biol.*, 7:279–284.

Winfield, D. A. (1981), The postnatal development of synapses in the visual cortex of the cat and the effects of eyelid closure. *Brain Res.*, 206:166–171.

Woolsey, T. A., Anderson, J. R., Wann, J. R., & Stanfield, B. B. (1979), Effects of early vibrissae damage on neurons in the ventrobasal (VB) thalamus of the mouse. *J. Comp. Neurol.*, 184:363–380.

———Van der Loos, H. (1970), The structural organization of layer IV in the somatosensory region (*S1*) of mouse cerebral cortex. The description of a cortical field composed of discrete cytoarchitectonic units. *Brain Res.*, 17:205–242.

———Wann, J. R., (1976), Areal change in mouse cortical barrels following vibrissal damage at different postnatal ages. *J. Comp. Neurol.*, 170:53–66.

Part III: Animal Studies and the Impact of Touch

5
The Role of Tactile Contact in Rhesus Monkey Social Development

Stephen J. Suomi, Ph.D.

Introduction

A quarter-century ago there occurred an event that changed dramatically the degree of significance ascribed to social touch or contact by most developmental psychologists, child psychiatrists, and pediatricians. The occasion was the 1958 convention of the American Psychological Association, and the event was the Presidential Address delivered by Harry F. Harlow, Professor of Psychology at the University of Wisconsin and Director of its Primate Laboratory. In his address, entitled "The Nature of Love," Harlow presented for the first time the results of a series of experiments designed to identify those features of rhesus monkey mothers that were most important for the development of social attachments by their infants. Conventional wisdom at the time was that human infants (and probably most neonatal mammals) initially formed social attachment bonds with their mothers via association with the feeding process through nursing. Indeed, researchers and theorists representing schools of thought as diverse as behaviorism and psychoanalysis had been virtually unanimous in agreeing that the original basis for all of an individual's social relationships throughout life could be traced to hunger gratification ("drive reduction") experienced as an infant during nursing.

It was in this context that Harlow stunned his audience when he reported how he had reared rhesus monkey infants on pairs of artificial (surrogate) "mothers," one of which provided milk, the other providing no milk but instead what Harlow termed "contact comfort" via a terrycloth ventral surface (see Figure 5.1). The results were unambiguous (see Figure 5.2), and quite contrary to conventional wisdom. Harlow's infant monkeys consistently formed lasting and functionally important attachments to cloth-covered surrogates that provided no source of nourishment, and they consistently failed to develop any evidence of attachmentlike behavior toward surrogates that provided milk from a baby bottle attached to a wire mesh-covered body. For these infant monkeys the source of contact comfort was obviously far more important than the source of their nourishment in establishing and maintaining the most basic of primate social bonds (Harlow, 1958).

Harlow's presentation immediately attracted the attention of the national and international news media. Soon pictures of rhesus monkey infants cuddling cloth surrogates and avoiding wire-covered ones flashed on television screens across the country and even graced the cover of *Life* magazine. The effect on developmental theorists and researchers was immediate and widespread across several disciplines, and the change in professional perception of the early importance of social contact in the socialization process has been maintained to this day.

Ever since Harlow's pioneering surrogate experiments, most laboratory and field investigators who study the behavior of nonhuman primates have likewise been acutely aware of the important roles that social contact or touch clearly can play in the social life of their subjects. In this chapter the

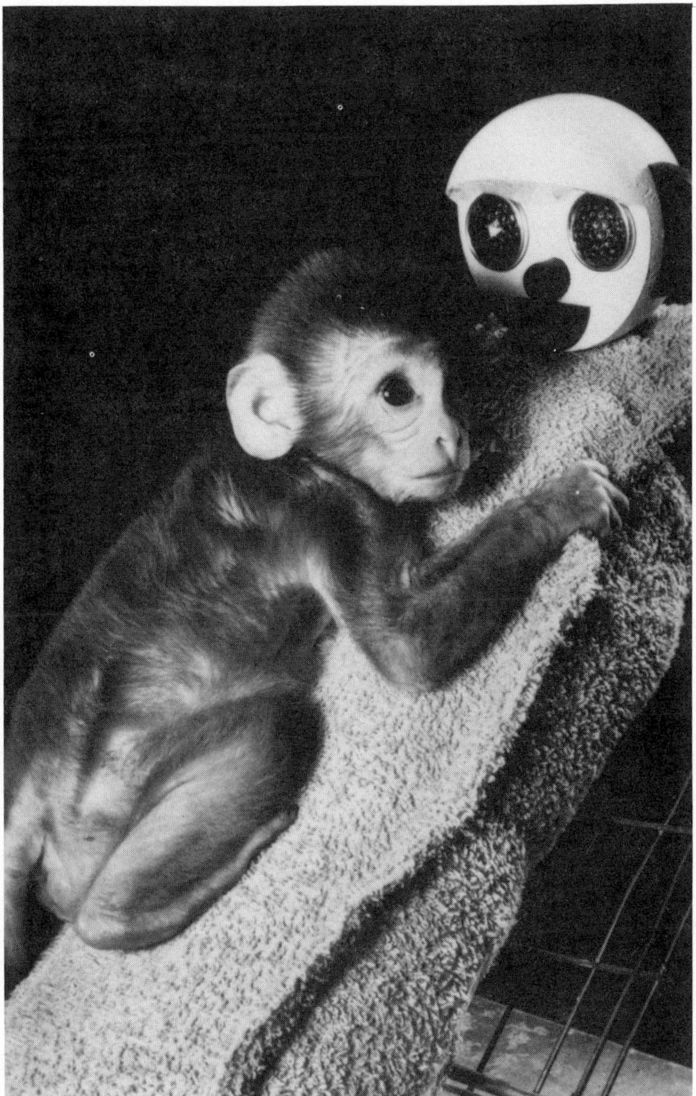

FIGURE 5.1
Rhesus monkey infant clinging to cloth-covered surrogate "mother."

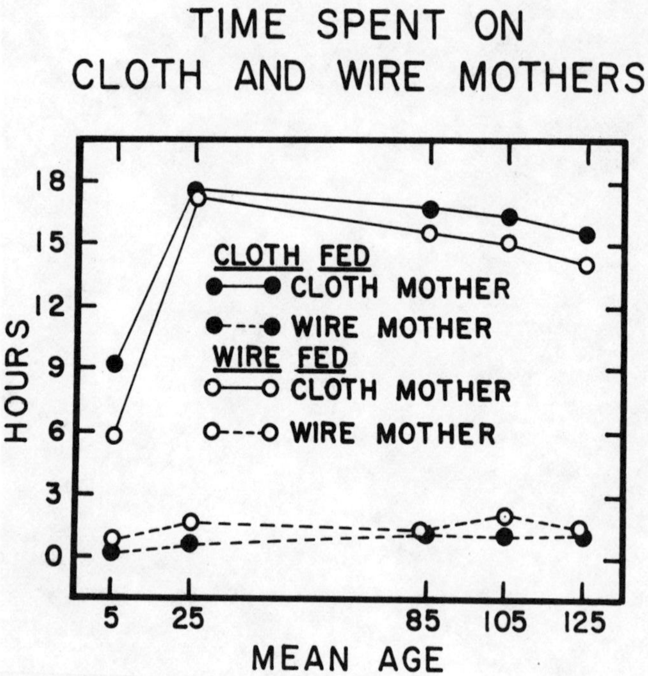

FIGURE 5.2

Relative time spent in contact with cloth and wire-covered surrogates (Harlow, 1958).

nature of these various roles in rhesus monkeys and other primates will be examined in detail.

The Preeminence of Social Contact in Rhesus Monkey Social Development

There is no question that social contact permeates most social activities in virtually all group-living advanced nonhuman primate species. Rhesus monkeys (*Macaca mulatta*) provide a prototypical example.

Of the approximately 200 primate species still in existence today, rhesus monkeys are almost certainly the second-most successful. Except for *Homo sapiens*, they have a higher worldwide population and inhabit a larger geographical area with greater climactic variability than any other species of primate. They also seem to be able to adapt to human habitation as well as any other nonhuman primates—rhesus monkeys have been living in large numbers in most of India's major cities for many centuries. In the wild, they usually live in troops numbering 15 to 100 individuals. Each of these troops represents a complex society, one that encompasses several distinct matriarchially organized kinship lineages, characterized by females who stay in their natal troop and males who typically leave their natal troop as adolescents or young adults and ultimately enter a new troop.

Even brief and casual observation of these wild-living troops reveals extensive physical contact of a variety of forms involving all of the troop members at one time or another (see, for example, Figure 5.3). We now know that specific forms of contact tend to be associated with interactions involving particular individuals in certain settings; that is, the forms, targets, and situations in which different social contacts are initiated and maintained by troop members are clearly not random (Suomi, 1979b). Instead, they appear to follow fairly specific "rules," and these rules must be learned and remembered by each member if it is to survive in the troop.

FIGURE 5.3
Typical forms of social contact seen between members of rhesus monkey social troop.

Moreover, the evidence strongly suggests that such learning begins quite early in life.

CONTACT ASSOCIATED WITH THE MOTHER–INFANT RELATIONSHIP

For rhesus monkeys, and indeed, for all species of nonhuman primates, extensive tactile contact with conspecifics begins essentially at birth. Rhesus monkey infants invariably spend the vast majority of their first days and weeks of life in intimate physical contact with their mothers. Most of the time this contact is mutually ventral (ventro–ventro) in nature, as shown by the mother–infant pair in Figure 5.4.

There is no question that mutual ventral contact with mother is highly adaptive for a rhesus monkey infant. From that position it has access to all the nourishment it needs at this stage of life, and it also can continuously experience the "contact comfort" that Harlow (1958) so dramatically described. By clinging to its mother a rhesus monkey neonate solves another basic problem of adaptation—that of maintaining its own body temperature. Macaque neonates, like most other newborn primates (including human babies), do not develop fully functioning thermoregulatory capabilities until the end of their first month of life, and until that time they need an external source of heat or they will become hypothermic in all but the warmest of climates. Thus, mutual ventral contact with mother provides an infant with thermal support in addition to any positive effects of tactile stimulation per se. Finally, an actively clinging infant permits a monkey mother relatively free locomotor activity, allowing her to keep up with her nomadic troop, as well as exposing the infant to kinesthetic stimulation it could not produce on its own at this early stage in development (Mason and Berkson, 1975). All in all, ventral contact with mother clearly serves a variety of important adaptive functions for young rhesus monkeys.

It should also be pointed out that under normal circumstances rhesus monkey infants rarely, if ever, engage in

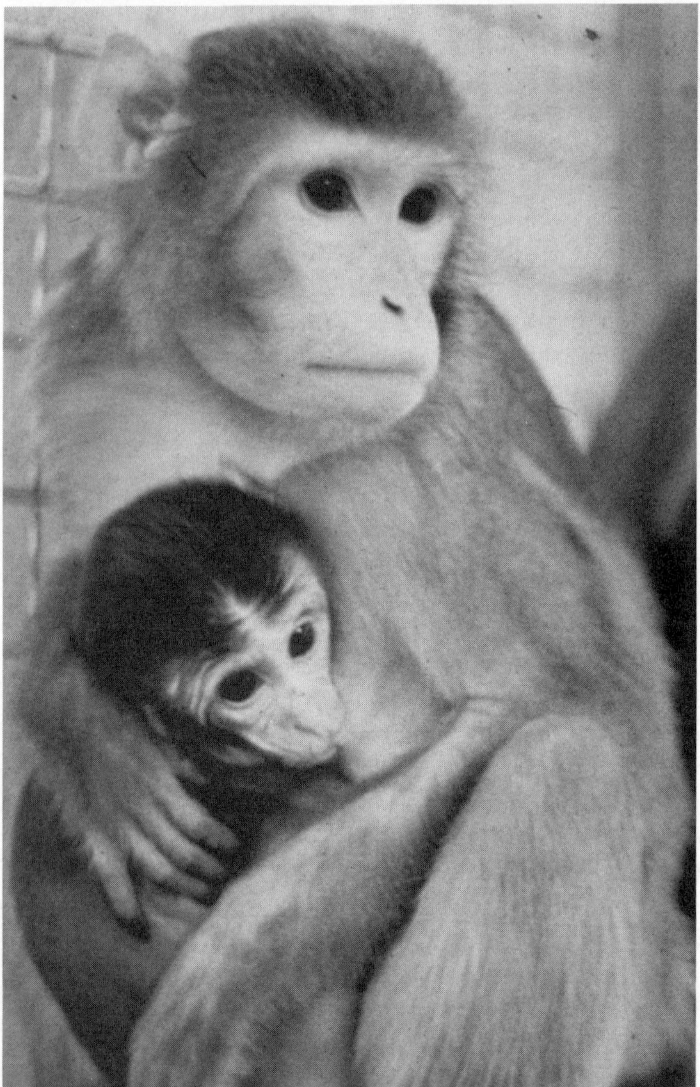

FIGURE 5.4
Mutual ventral contact between rhesus monkey mother and infant.

prolonged mutual ventral contact with anyone but their biological mother. Moreover, once past infancy relatively few rhesus monkeys are ever seen in ventral contact with any other conspecifics, with one prominent exception. The exception occurs when rhesus monkey females give birth to infants of their own. In other words, mutual ventral contact is clearly a universal characteristic of rhesus monkey mother–infant relationships, but it is also almost universally absent in most other social relationships that characterize normal rhesus monkey social life.

Nevertheless, there is considerably more to normal rhesus monkey mother–infant relationships than mutual ventral contact alone. This fact becomes increasingly obvious after an infant's first month of life, when the absolute duration of time spent in such contact with its mother begins to decline sharply (Hansen, 1966; Hinde and Spencer-Booth, 1967; Hinde and White, 1974). During this period, however, other forms of tactile contact between mother and infant emerge with increasing frequency. One of the most important of these involves *social grooming*, an example of which is illustrated in Figure 5.5. The systematic picking and spreading out of the fur of one's partner obviously serves the function of ectoparasite removal among wild-living rhesus monkeys, but social grooming also clearly serves functions beyond that of hygiene. Indeed the incidence of social grooming among rhesus monkeys living in ectoparasite-free captive environments is at least as high as that seen in feral troops. Adult and juvenile monkeys in both environments appear to use social grooming to promote affiliative relationships and to reduce social tension, especially after outbreaks of intragroup aggression.

Mothers begin grooming their infants before the end of the second postnatal week, and shortly thereafter the infants reciprocate and start to groom their mothers. In succeeding weeks and months infant-initiated grooming bouts are also directed toward other close kin and, increasingly, toward peers. Thus, an important adult behavior involving active

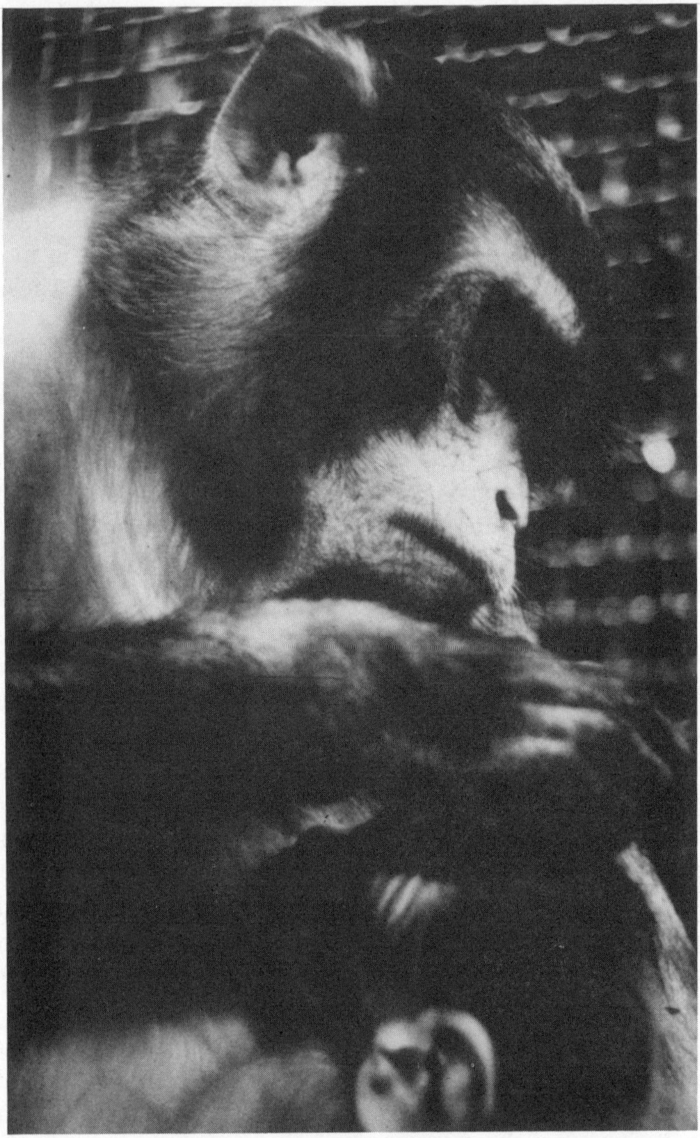

FIGURE 5.5
Social grooming of rhesus monkey infant by its mother.

tactile contact first appears in the context of the mother–infant relationship.

At the same time that rhesus monkey infants are developing grooming behavior they are also learning to use tactile contact with mother for another purpose—that of establishing and maintaining a secure base for ever-increasing exploration of their immediate physical and social environment. From their second month on, these infants venture away from their mother's immediate reach on exploratory forays that become increasingly frequent, longer in duration, and greater in distance from the mother. Each foray typically ends with the infant scurrying back to its mother for a brief period of tactile (and not necessarily mutual ventral) contact with her, and typically the infant then ventures out on another foray, often returning to the site of the immediately previous exploration. If the infant becomes frightened or tired while exploring, its return to its mother is usually marked by a longer period of contact, often in the form of mutual ventral contact. Examples of these sequences of contact-mediated exploratory behavior are presented in Figure 5.6.

The importance of the mother's role in the early exploratory behavior of her infant should not be underestimated. Indeed, when an infant is experimentally denied tactile access to its mother, all exploratory activity immediately ceases—even if she remains in visual, auditory, and olfactory contact with the infant (Seay, Hansen, and Harlow, 1962). Clearly, availability of tactile contact with mother on demand is crucial for this early exploratory behavior, even though the actual duration of contact is trivial relative to that spent in active exploration away from her immediate reach. It is in the context of this exploration that the basis for much of the infant's subsequent social behavioral repertoire becomes firmly established, especially in interactions with peers (Harlow and Harlow, 1965; Suomi and Harlow, 1975).

FIGURE 5.6

Contact-mediated exploratory behavior by rhesus monkey infants: (a) infant leaving mother for exploratory foray; (b) infant returning to mother for brief mutual ventral contact; (c) infant back on new exploratory foray away from its mother.

CONTACT ASSOCIATED WITH PEER PLAY

For young rhesus monkeys (and most likely for juveniles of most primate species), interactions with peers differ considerably from interactions with mothers. The differences are reflected in such diverse dimensions as duration of individual interaction bouts (bouts with peers tend to be shorter than those with mother), direction of developmental changes (as infants grow older, interactions with peers increase in relative frequency whereas those with mother decrease), and situations most conducive to prolonged interactions (infants are most likely to display extended interactions with peers in the absence of danger or stress, while the presence of danger or stress almost guarantees that an infant will seek out and stay with its mother). Perhaps the most obvious differences between a young monkey's interactions with its mother and interactions with peers can be seen in the nature of the tactile contact that characterizes these two sets of social relationships.

To begin, as alluded to above, the type of tactile contact most prevalent in normal mother–infant interactions—prolonged mutual ventral contact—is virtually absent in normal peer relationships. Social grooming does occur between peers, and its incidence tends to increase as the peers grow older, but in most social groups young monkeys groom their peers substantially less often than they groom virtually all maternal kin, both older and younger. The initial form of contact between peers—brief exploratory touching via hands or mouth—is fundamentally different from the extended, whole-body contact that most characterizes the mother–infant relationship. Perhaps most importantly, the type of social contact activity that comprises the bulk of peer interactions throughout the juvenile years—contact-oriented social play—rarely occurs between mothers and offspring older that four months of age (Suomi, 1979a,b).

The considerable diversity displayed in rhesus monkey

peer play, as in the peer play of human children (Hartup, 1979), is marked by comparable diversity in the range and extent of its constituent social contact, and such diversity is apparent from the very first weeks of active peer interaction. By four months of age a rhesus monkey's play repertoire encompasses both rough-and-tumble play, with its intense, wrestlinglike contact, and approach–withdrawal play, in which the primary role of one of the participants is to avoid all physical contact by the other (Harlow and Harlow, 1965; Hansen, 1966; Harlow, 1969) (see Figure 5.7). By one year of age, almost all forms of social contact that characterize social interactions between adults can be identified in an individual's normal play with its peers (Suomi and Harlow, 1975), including obvious precursors of both sex and aggression (Harlow, 1975; Suomi, 1979b). Moreover, it is in the context of peer play that sex differences in choice of both form of social contact and preferred partner in contact become most obvious (Harlow and Lauersdorf, 1974; Goldfoot, 1978), especially in comparison with the relatively minor sex differences in contact with mother among juvenile rhesus monkeys (Hinde and Spencer-Booth, 1967; Suomi, 1979a).

Contact-oriented social play remains the predominant form of peer interaction among young monkeys until they reach adolescence (Ruppenthal, Harlow, Eisele, Harlow, and Suomi, 1974), usually at about four years of age, when the incidence of both play and other interactions with peers drops precipitously. At this point, the life histories of male and female rhesus monkeys diverge, at least in natural environments. Females tend to spend more and more time in the general proximity of their mothers and increase their interactions with mother-related kin, especially older sisters and cousins. Males, on the other hand, almost always leave the entire troop in which they grew up. To what extent they leave voluntarily, as opposed to being driven out, depends on the individual male and troop. Some of these late adolescent males may join all-male gangs, while others wander off on

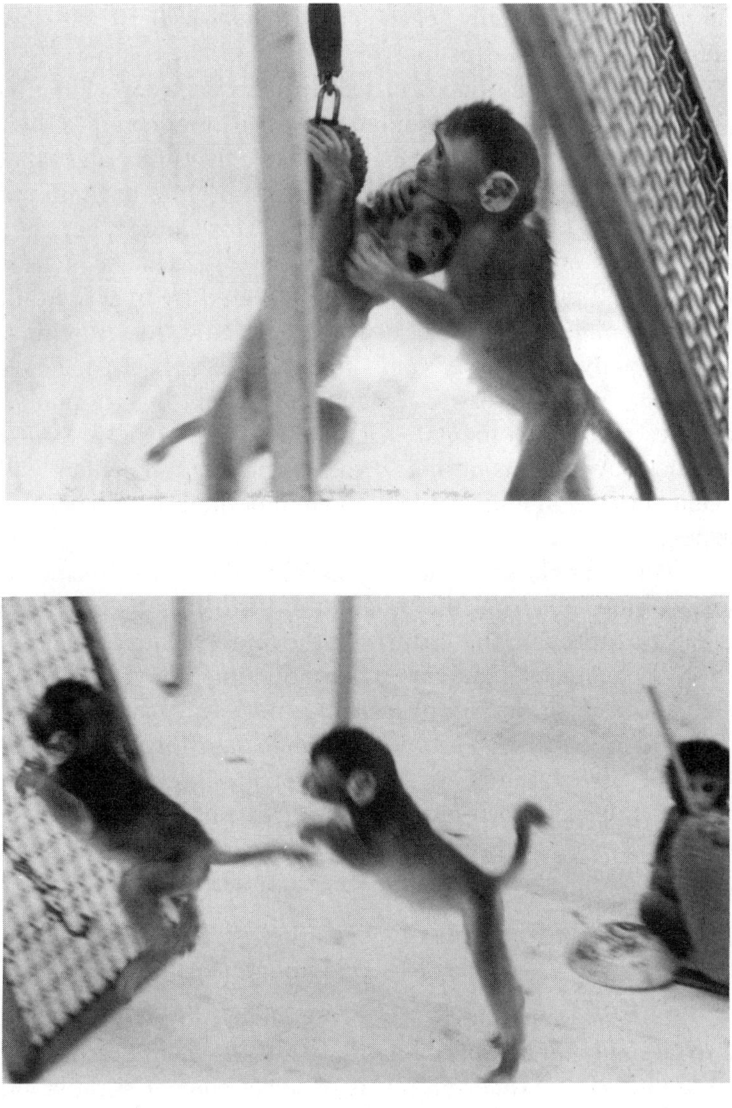

(b)

FIGURE 5.7

(a) Rough-and-tumble play, (b) approach–withdrawal play in young rhesus monkeys.

their own. Eventually, each male (if he survives) will join another troop of rhesus monkeys.

These sex differences in social roles and troop affiliation among young adult rhesus monkeys are also reflected in their use of tactile contact. Most contact between adult males takes the form of grooming, physical aggression (often to the point of wounding), and very occasional play. Most contact between adult males and females involves grooming, sex, or aggression, not all of which is necessarily initiated by males. Adult female–female contact is usually restricted to grooming, passive nonventral body contact (e.g., side-to-back, see Figure 5.8), and aggression (usually directed toward nonkin females and adolescents). Of course, when these young females have infants of their own, mutual ventral contact will again become an important component of their overall contact repertoire.

Thus, for rhesus monkeys, social contact with conspecifics is ubiquitous from the moment of birth to the end of the lifespan, although the nature of the predominant forms of contact change as a function of an individual's developmental status, sex, and identity of social partner. To what extent are the contact experiences of infants important for normal subsequent development of social behavioral repertoires and relationships in these monkeys? A large body of data, to be reviewed next, suggests that these early contact experiences are crucial for such normative development to take place.

Effects of Early Contact Deprivation on Rhesus Monkey Social Development

As reviewed above, rhesus monkey infants normally grow up in complex social environments in which there exists an abundance of different forms of social contact stimulation available almost continually throughout development. For millions of generations of rhesus monkeys, the extensive experience with contact stimulation accrued since infancy has promoted the acquisition of social skills and the learning of

FIGURE 5.8

Typical nonventral body contact between adult female rhesus monkeys. Note that each female has an infant in mutual ventral contact.

social rules that we now know are required for a biologically successful life in a typical monkey troop. We know this largely because of results from over twenty years of research in which rhesus monkeys were reared in environments that failed to provide normal contact stimulation (for a comprehensive review of this literature, see Mitchell [1970]).

EFFECTS OF SINGLE-CAGE REARING

Prior to Harlow's (1958) pioneering surrogate studies demonstrating the priority of contact comfort in the development of attachment by infant monkeys, most laboratory researchers studying nonhuman primates routinely housed their subjects in individual cages. These researchers, along with their veterinary staffs, assumed that such single-cage housing would reduce the chance of spreading disease and eliminate the risk of aggression-induced injury among their subjects without introducing any other major practical confounds or health hazards. Such assumptions were strengthened by the knowledge that adolescent and adult monkeys imported from the wild appeared to show few ill-effects from chronic single-cage housing, in that they exhibited apparently normal behavior when permitted to interact physically with other wild-born monkeys (e.g., during temporary mixed-sex pair housing for breeding purposes), and they displayed no obvious cognitive deficits in standardized learning test performances (Harlow, Harlow, and Suomi, 1971).

On the other hand, when the same single-cage housing procedures were utilized for infants born in the laboratory to females imported from the wild, it soon became apparent that something was obviously very wrong with the behavioral development of these infants. In their first few months of life they developed patterns of self-clasping and self-orality seldom seen in wild-born monkeys. In succeeding months almost all single-cage reared infants began to display idiosyncratic patterns of repetitive, stereotyped activity. Moreover, they seemed unusually fearful and reluctant to explore new toys or other objects placed in their cages. When these monkeys were finally introduced to other single-cage reared individuals or even to wild-born agemates, they did not exhibit spontaneous exploratory or play behavior. Instead, they typically would withdraw from all social contact and engage in self-directed stereotypic behavior, as depicted in Figure 5.9.

We now know that this clearly abnormal pattern of behavioral development was a direct consequence of single-cage housing initiated shortly after birth. Such housing, of course, allowed these laboratory-born rhesus monkey infants to see, hear, and smell other monkeys, including socially normal adults, on a continual basis, but it precluded any appreciable amount of tactile contact with any other monkey during early development. In retrospect, it now hardly seems surprising that these single-cage reared infants, lacking a mother (or even a surrogate) with which to cling, learned to cling to their own bodies and, in the absence of a maternal nipple, to suck their own digits. In the absence of any kinesthetic stimulation from a mother's movement or from play stimulation by peers, these infants learned to produce their own kinesthetic stimulation by developing idiosyncratic patterns of stereotypic behavior. Indeed, Mason and Berkson (1975) showed that when single-cage reared rhesus monkey infants were provided with moving surrogates, the incidence of stereotypic behavior was greatly reduced. Without any secure base, most single-cage reared infants became easily frightened, and not surprisingly they were thereafter reluctant to explore even their limited home environment.

Formal study of rhesus monkeys reared from birth in single cages or under conditions of visual as well as tactile deprivation revealed long-term deficits that seemed to persist even after the monkeys had been introduced to group living arrangements. It was consistently found that rhesus monkeys reared for at least the first six months of life in tactile isolation from conspecifics actively avoided most social contact as

FIGURE 5.9
Avoidance of social contact by newly introduced single-cage reared rhesus monkeys.

adolescents and adults, and in their infrequent social interactions they tended to be hyperaggressive (Harlow and Harlow, 1962, 1969; Sackett, 1968; Mitchell, 1970). In addition, although single-cage reared rhesus monkeys as adults were reproductively normal in the physiological sense, in that males produced viable sperm and females ovulated within normal menstrual cycles (as do socially normal rhesus monkey females), they developed gross abnormalities in their sexual behavior (Harlow, 1962; Goy, Wallen, and Goldfoot, 1974). Typically, both males and females would show severe deficits in the display and proper orientation and sequencing of the complex motor movements involved in normal copulation (see Figure 5.10). Finally, even though many single-cage reared females eventually became pregnant (often via artificial insemination techniques), approximately three-fourths of them failed to provide adequate care for their first-born offspring. Most of these single-cage reared mothers (termed *motherless mothers* by Harlow) failed to nurse their offspring, while over a third of them were physically abusive, making it necessary for the nursery staff to remove their infants for the sake of the latter's survival (Seay, Alexander, and Harlow, 1964; Ruppenthal, Arling, Harlow, Sackett, and Suomi, 1976). In summary, single-cage rearing appeared to have devastating consequences for the development of normal social behavior, and the adverse effects continued well into adulthood.

It should be pointed out that the developmental consequences of tactile isolation from conspecifics are not nearly as severe as those described above if the period of tactile isolation begins later in life. For example, Rowland (1964) found that rhesus monkey infants raised by their mothers for the first six months of life and then subjected to a six-month period of isolation (i.e., from six to twelve months of life) displayed few apparent long-term deficits, other than a tendency to be hyperaggressive, in sharp contrast to the wide range of long-term behavioral abnormalities shown by sub-

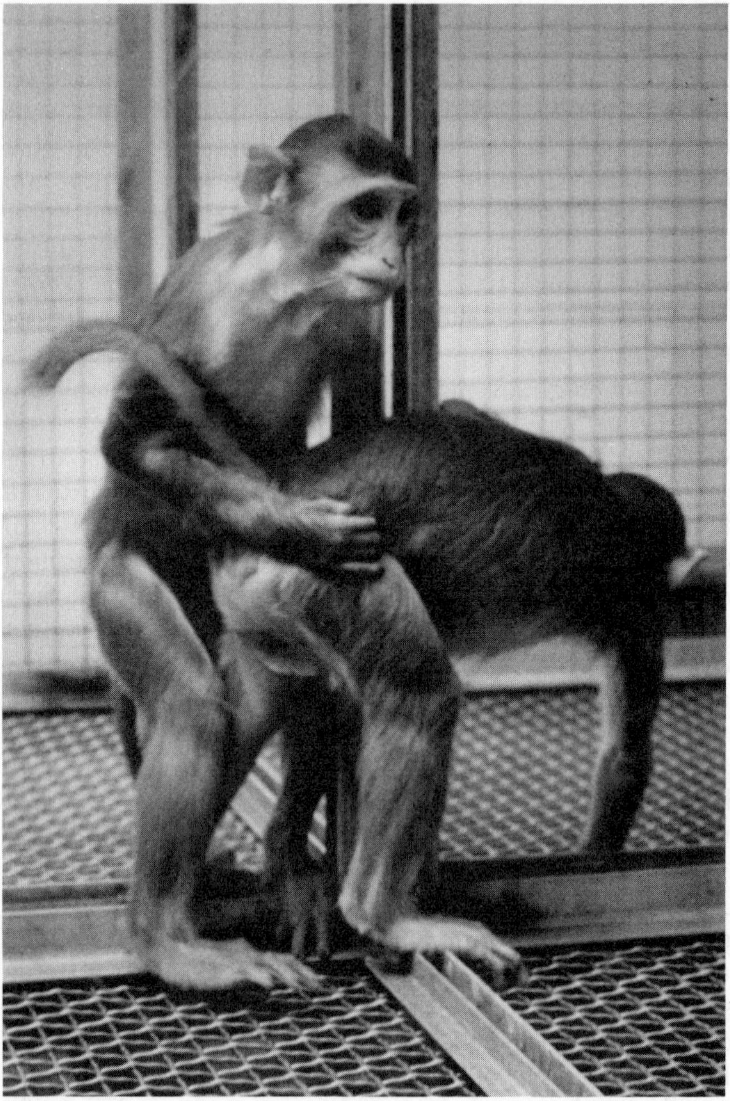

FIGURE 5.10
Inappropriate sexual posturing by single-cage reared rhesus monkey adult male–female pair.

jects isolated for their first six months of life. Thus, there may be a so-called sensitive period or phase (Scott, Stewart, and DeGhett, 1974; Immelmann and Suomi, 1981) for the basic socializing effects of tactile stimulation.

EFFECTS OF "MOTHER-ONLY" AND "PEER-ONLY" REARING

The above review should make it clear that tactile isolation from conspecifics, if initiated at, or shortly after, birth and maintained for least six months, results in profound and essentially permanent social deficits in rhesus monkey subjects, even when they have continuous visual, auditory, and olfactory contact with other monkeys during the period of tactile isolation. Fortunately, since these findings have become well known among primatologists over the past two decades, relatively few laboratory-born rhesus monkey infants are currently being reared under conditions of complete tactile isolation from conspecifics in primate facilities, at least in this country. Nevertheless, many infants continue to be reared in social environments that maintain some degree of tactile isolation from certain classes of conspecifics, while permitting unlimited contact opportunities with others. By and large, monkeys reared in these less socially barren environments exhibit much more normal patterns of social development, although the specific deficits that do appear seem to be closely related to the specific tactile stimulation that they are being denied during development. Two such environments are represented by "mother-only" and "peer-only" rearing conditions.

Under conditions of mother-only rearing, rhesus monkey infants remain with their mothers following birth, but the mother–infant dyads are then maintained in single cages that prevent all tactile contact with any other conspecifics; for example, with adult males and peers. Monkeys so reared seem to develop relatively normal relationships with their mothers, at least initially. However, these monkeys fail to leave their mother to explore as early chronologically or as frequently as do infants reared with access to peers and others besides mothers. In succeeding months mother-only reared monkeys have no opportunity to develop affectional relationships with any peers nor the chance to develop complex social play behaviors. Thus, when these monkeys are finally exposed to peers, they are not capable of normal social interactions and instead tend to be hyperaggressive. They seldom become effective playmates, and indeed may continue to be hyperaggressive throughout adolescence and into adulthood. On the other hand, most of the females turn out to be competent mothers when they have their first offspring.

Rhesus monkey infants have also been reared in laboratory environments that contain peers, but no mothers (peer-only rearing). These infants likewise develop aberrant patterns of behavior, but of a different nature than those displayed by mother-only reared monkeys. For example, peer-only reared infants readily learn to grasp one another, as shown in Figure 5.11. Clinging among together-reared peers not only is as intense as that observed between mothers and infants, but also it persists far longer chronologically. One consequence of this prolonged peer clinging is that the appearance of play in peer-only reared infants is considerably retarded. Peer-only reared monkeys, lacking a mother as a source of security, also tend to be easily frightened and reluctant to explore novel objects and new physical settings. Even as adults such monkeys tend to be abnormally timid. In other respects, however, their adult behavior appears to be relatively normal. For example, there is nothing unusual about their patterns of grooming, and female reproductive behavior seems to be unaffected. Nevertheless, there is a greater-than-normal incidence of specific social deficits in peer-only reared monkeys as adults. Some, but not all, males display incomplete mounting patterns, albeit ones that can still result in fertilization. Peer-only reared females are almost as likely to abuse their first-born offspring as are females isolated from all conspecifics during their first six months of

FIGURE 5.11
Mutual clinging among peer-reared rhesus monkey infants

life, although the relative incidence of failure to nurse their offspring is no greater than that shown by wild-born primiparous rhesus monkey females (Suomi and Ripp, 1983).

To summarize, it is clear that both short- and long-term consequences of mother-only and peer-only rearing are not nearly as severe as those associated with single-cage rearing. Nevertheless, certain social abnormalities are evident in each of these more limited forms of tactile contact deprivation early in life, and generally speaking, the longer the period of early deprivation, the greater will be the likelihood that such abnormalities will appear, and in increasingly severe forms. Moreover, there appears to be a relatively straightforward relationship between the precise nature of the early contact deprivation and the form of the subsequent social deficits. Thus, peer-only reared rhesus monkeys tend to have problems in activities that normally have their genesis in mother–infant interactions, while mother-only reared monkeys typically display deficits in activities normally originating in peer play.

EFFECTS OF BRIEF SOCIAL SEPARATIONS

Each of the rearing environments described and discussed above—single-cage rearing, mother-only rearing, and peer-only rearing—involve some degree of tactile contact deprivation initiated at or shortly after birth and maintained chronically for at least a six-month period. The effects of such long-term conditions of touch deprivation tend to be profound and prolonged, often still in evidence years after the period of deprivation has ended. Extensive study of the consequences of much shorter periods of touch deprivation has also been carried out with rhesus monkeys and other nonhuman primate species over the past twenty years (for one of many comprehensive reviews of this literature, see Mineka and Suomi [1978]). The basic design of most studies in this area has involved short-term physical separation of young subjects from conspecifics with whom they have established strong social attachments; that is to say, the studies have focused on short-term disruption of existing social relationships rather than long-term prevention of the establishment of social relationships (see Gewirtz [1961]; Harlow and Novak [1973]; and Suomi and Harlow [1977] for a more detailed discussion of the theoretical and practical distinction between these two experimental manipulations utilizing social contact deprivation).

Because chapter 6 by Levine and Stanton and chapter 7 by Reite present thorough treatments of the topic of short-term social separation effects in young primates, a comprehensive review will not be presented here. Suffice it to say, a large number of studies have convincingly demonstrated that short-term physical separation from a current attachment object typically results in immediate and often dramatic behavioral disruption and intense physiological arousal. These reactions do not appear to be moderated when subjects are able to maintain visual, auditory, and olfactory contact with their attachment object(s) during the period of physical separation—indeed, in many cases the availability of such nontactile access seems to exaggerate the intensity of the separation reaction (Seay and Harlow, 1965). On the other hand, the availability of limited tactile contact, for example, through wide-gauge wire mesh, during the period of separation appears to attenuate the separation reaction to a substantial degree (Suomi, Collins, Harlow, and Ruppenthal, 1976). Finally, it should be emphasized that investigators have detected behavioral and physiological changes induced by short-term separation manipulations that persist long after the period of separation has ended. Thus, short-term separations can clearly have major long-term consequences (Stevenson-Hinde, Zunz, and Stillwell-Barnes, 1980).

SIGNIFICANCE OF STUDIES OF CONTACT DEPRIVATION IN YOUNG NONHUMAN PRIMATES

Taken as a whole, the results of numerous studies of contact deprivation in young rhesus monkeys provide a compelling compliment to the general findings from investigation of the role of contact in normal social development in this species. In a nutshell, the stimulation provided through tactile contact with conspecifics seems crucial for such normal development to take place. It is now well established that in species-normative social environments tactile contact stimulation comes from a wide range of sources and takes a substantial number of different forms, typically changing in predictable fashion as an individual monkey is growing up. We also know that when tactile contact is prevented or restricted, certain systematic problems in social development seem to follow, many of which are clearly profound and often permanent. Seen in this light, tactile contact is obviously a very basic and necessary component of normal rhesus monkey social life.

Rhesus monkeys are not the only nonhuman primates that have served as subjects in studies of contact deprivation. For example, the consequences of single-cage rearing have been investigated in at least four other macaque species, the three species of great apes, in New World primates such as squirrel monkeys and marmosets, and even in some "primitive" prosimian primate species. In most cases, the results obtained in these deprivation studies have paralleled the findings for rhesus monkeys. However, there have also been some notable and indeed puzzling exceptions to this picture of apparent cross-species consistency of deprivation effects. Sackett, Holm, and Ruppenthal (1976) reported that pigtail macaque infants reared for their first nine months in tactile isolation from all conspecifics displayed spontaneous recovery upon removal from isolation, with low levels of self-clasping and stereotypic behavior and with relatively rapid development of sophisticated social behavioral repertoires. Similar results were obtained from deprivation studies of crab-eating macaques (Berkson, 1968; Sackett, Ruppenthal, Fahrenbruch, Holm, and Greenough, 1981).

There also appears to be substantial species differences

within the primate order in the nature and intensity of reactions to brief social separations (Rosenblum and Kaufman, 1968; Kaufman and Rosenblum, 1969; Mineka and Suomi, 1978). Finally, we now know that there are substantial individual differences between members of the same species in both long-term consequences of single-cage rearing and in reaction to separation (Suomi, 1983).

The discovery of major species and individual differences in response to single-cage rearing and brief social separation belies easy explanation or interpretation. There is some suggestive evidence that variability in contact deprivation effects are in part attributable to species differences in the complexity of normal social repertoires and natural social groupings (Suomi, 1982), but many questions regarding the origins and proximal mechanisms of these species differences clearly remain.

Discussion: Chapter 5

Seymour Levine: How do you explain the comparative data showing relatively transient effects of long-term social isolation in some species?

Stephen Suomi: Some species, such as pigtails, appear to show essentially spontaneous recovery after isolation when they are introduced to a social group. This is a very puzzling finding. My hunch is that it may be explained in part by the reception isolates get from their conspecifics when they're first put into the group. By macaque standards, rhesus monkeys are unusually aggressive; pigtails are less so. So it may be that pigtail isolates get more appropriate social stimulation when they enter a group than rhesus monkeys do.

William Greenough: Are there sex differences in the profundity of isolation effects?

Stephen Suomi: For rhesus monkeys, the data suggest that social deficits are more pronounced for males reared in isolation than for females, perhaps because the normal adult role requires the male to leave his troop of birth, operate independently for a while, and then join a new troop, which usually isn't eager to have him.

T. Berry Brazelton: Have you found ways to reverse the effects of long-term tactile isolation—to rehabilitate monkey infants that were reared alone?

Stephen Suomi: About ten years ago, Harry Harlow and I did a study in which we attempted to rehabilitate animals reared for the first six months in tactile and visual isolation. We let our isolates, when they came out of isolation, interact with socially competent individuals only three months old, that is, much younger than the isolates themselves. The three-month-olds were socially normal, but still small and too young to be aggressive, so they didn't pose a physical threat to the isolates. Even more important, they were still at an age when ventral contact with a mother monkey was a major part of their behavioral repertoire.

When the isolates were first introduced to the three-month-old "therapists," they would retreat to the corner of the playroom or test cage and roll up into a ball. And the first thing the younger therapists would do was run over and start clinging to the isolates, interacting in essentially the same way they would have with other, normal three-month-olds. We noticed very quickly that with this sort of activity the incidence of abnormal, self-directed behaviors on the part of the isolates began to decline. They began reciprocating, and sometimes even initiated contact.

As the therapists grew older, ventral-oriented behaviors began to disappear and were replaced by simple play patterns. During the time they spent with the isolates each day, the therapists would use these play patterns in social interactions. After four or five months of this, there were essentially no statistical differences between the isolates and their younger therapists on any behavior. We had seen what seemed to be pretty complete recovery.

T. Berry Brazelton: What about the "motherless mothers" that abuse or neglect their first infants? Can you rehabilitate them—teach them to be better mothers?

Stephen Suomi: In looking back over the data, one finds that the best predictor of whether a female that abused or neglected one infant was going to be a good mother to another was the amount of time the female spent with the first infant. Specifically, females that spent at least two days, forty-eight hours, with their infants, no matter what the quality of care, virtually always became good mothers to the next infant.

My speculation is that what is missing from the early experience of the inadequate mothers may be ventral contact with another individual. An inadequate mother that spent forty-eight hours with her infant, even if she rejected the infant and pushed it away, did experience some ventro–ventro contact. This little bit of experience, even later in life, may be sufficient to make such contact acceptable to the female after subsequent births. It may be like a priming mechanism.

We've instituted some therapeutic approaches based on this idea. In one approach, we give motherless females access to females with infants when they themselves are adolescents or young adults. Another approach uses foster grandparents: male–female pairs that are past reproductive age. These individuals, even though they're too old to reproduce, turn out to be excellent parents. When the motherless infants get frightened, they can run to the older female, who gives ventral contact; the older male often breaks up fights among peers, especially as the isolates grow older. When infant females reared in this way become mothers, the incidence of inadequate mothering is no greater than with females reared by their biological mothers.

Elizabeth McAnarney: Despite the importance of ventro–ventro contact, monkey mothers and infants don't seem to look at each other's faces much. Do you have any comments about that?

Stephen Suomi: To the best of my knowledge, both eye contact and vocal communication are exceedingly common in normal human mother–infant interactions but very rare in rhesus monkeys and other Old World monkeys. Chimpanzees, being great apes, spend a lot more time in eye contact with their infants.

Susan Rose: I'm curious about the differences between the monkey mothers whose infants were taken away right after birth and the mothers who spent at least forty-eight hours with their infants. Were the monkeys in the latter group less abusive? In other words, is their improved performance with the next infant really a matter of time and ventral contact, or is something else involved?

Stephen Suomi: That's a good question; the data aren't broken down that way. I can tell you, though, that some females have been separated from their infants immediately after the birth because the infants were to be reared in peer-only groups—that is, for experimental reasons having nothing to do with the adequacy of the female's maternal behavior—and these females do not show improvement with subsequent offspring. If a female's first two infants are both taken away at birth, not because of any improper care on her part, there is still a fairly high probability that she'll be a poor mother to the third infant.

T. Berry Brazelton: Steve, do you ever see the biological grandmother prohibit certain maternal behavior toward the infant, or give her daughter directions about it?

Stephen Suomi: It's a complicated issue. There's plenty of evidence for a biological basis for some sex-typed behavior differences, but there's also evidence that the differences can be exaggerated by the behavior of those around, especially adults. For example, rhesus adult males ordinarily take little part in caretaking activity and interact very little with infants or youngsters, except that they seem to encourage, if you will, sex-appropriate behavior. These animals will encourage young males, especially those not their own, to engage in rough-and-tumble play, and they'll play back. If a young female tries to initiate rough-and-tumble play, many times the male will swat it or otherwise discourage it. Similarly, you see males intervening when some of the juveniles are engaging in precursors of reproductive behavior, especially if the mix is not right. So I think there's clear evidence of social influence, even though you may be starting off with a biological difference.

Patricia Rausch: Do the females involve themselves in rough-and-tumble play as infants?

Stephen Suomi: Some do at first, but after a few months females tend to avoid that sort of interaction, and if a male tries to initiate it they won't reciprocate. On the other hand, in experimental situations in which a single female is growing up with a group of male peers, this female's play will be rough-and-tumble, for the most part. So it depends on the social situation.

Michael Merzenich: In the unusual case in which a female engages in rough-and-tumble play for several years of life, is she as solid maternally as other females?

Stephen Suomi: Every one that I've seen has turned out to be a perfectly fine mother.

References

Berkson, G. (1968), Development of abnormal stereotyped behaviors. *Development. Psychobiol.*, 1:118–132.

Gerwirtz, J. L. (1961), A learning analysis of the effects of normal stimulation, privation, and deprivation on the acquisition of social motivation and attachment. In: *Determinants of Infant Behaviour*, Vol. 1, ed. B. M. Foss. London: Methuen.

Goldfoot, D. A. (1978), Development of gender role behaviors in heterosexual and isosexual groups of infant rhesus monkeys. In: *Recent Advances in Primatology*, Vol. 1, eds. D. Chivers & J. Herbert. London: Academic Press.

Goy, R. W., Wallen, K., & Goldfoot, D. A. (1974), Social factors affecting the development of mounting behavior in male rhesus monkeys. In: *Reproductive Behavior*, eds. W. Montagna & W. Sadler. New York: Plenum Press.

Hansen, E. W. (1966), The development of maternal and infant behavior in the rhesus monkey. *Behaviour*, 27:107–149.

Harlow, H. F. (1958), The nature of love. *Amer. Psychol*, 13:673–685.

———(1962), The heterosexual affectional system in monkeys. *Amer. Psychol.*, 17:1–9.

———(1969), Age-mate or peer affectional system. In: *Advances in the Study of Behavior* Vol. 2, eds. D. Lehrman, R. Hinde, & E. Shaw. New York: Academic Press.

———(1975), Love and aggression. Kittay Scientific Foundation Annual Award Address, New York City.

———Harlow, M. K. (1962), The effects of rearing conditions on behavior. *Bull. Menn. Clinic*, 26:213–224.

——— ———(1965), The affectional systems. In: *Behavior of Nonhuman Primates* Vol. 2, eds. A. M. Schrier, H. F. Harlow, & F. Stollnitz. New York: Academic Press.

——— ———(1969), Effects of various mother–infant relationships on rhesus monkey behaviors. In: *Determinants of Infant Behaviour* Vol. 4, ed. B. Foss. London: Methuen.

——— ———Suomi, S. J. (1971), From thought to therapy. *Amer. Scientist*, 59:538–549.

———Lauersdorf, H. E. (1974), Sex differences in passion and play. *Perspect. in Biol. & Med.*, 17:348–360.

———Novak, M. A. (1973), Psychopathological perspectives. *Perspect. in Biol. & Med.*, 16:461–478.

Hartup, W. W. (1979), Peer relations and the growth of social competence. In: *The Primary Prevention of Psychopathology*, Vol. 3, eds. M. Kent & J. Rolf. Hanover, NH: The University Press of New England.

Hinde, R. A., & Spencer-Booth, Y. (1967), The behaviour of socially living rhesus monkeys in their first two and a half years. *Animal Behav.*, 15:169–196.

———White, L. (1974), Dynamics of a relationship: Rhesus mother–infant ventro-ventro contact. *J. Comp. Physiolog. Psychol.*, 86:8–23.

Immelmann, K., & Suomi, S. J. (1981), Sensitive phases in development. In: *Behavioral Development: The Bielefeld Interdisciplinary Project*, eds. K. Immelmann, G. Barlow, L. Petrinovich, & M. Main. New York: Cambridge University Press.

Kaufman, I. C., & Rosenblum, L. A. (1969), The waning of the mother—infant bond in two species of macaque. In: *Determinants of Infant Behaviour* Vol. 4, ed. B. M. Foss. London: Methuen.

Mason, W. A., & Berkson, G. (1975), Effects of maternal mobility on the development of rocking and other behaviors in rhesus monkeys: A study with artificial mothers. *Develop. Psychol.*, 8:197–211.

Mineka, S., & Suomi, S. J. (1978), Social separation in monkeys. *Psychol. Bull.*, 85:1376–1400.

Mitchell, G. D. (1970), Abnormal behavior in primates. In: *Primate Behavior,* ed. L. A. Rosenblum. New York: Academic Press.

Rosenblum, L. A., & Kaufman, I. C. (1968), Variations in infant development and response to maternal loss in monkeys. *Amer. J. Orthopsychiat.*, 38:418–426.

Rowland, G. L. (1964), *The Effects of Total Social Isolation Upon Learning and Social Behavior in Rhesus Monkeys*. Unpublished doctoral dissertation. University of Wisconsin, Madison, Wi.

Ruppenthal, G. C., Arling, G. L., Harlow, H. F., Sackett, G. P., & Suomi, S. J. (1976), A 10-year perspective of motherless mother monkey behavior. *J. Abnorm. Psychol.*, 85:341–349.

———Harlow, M. K., Eisele, C. D., Harlow, H. F., & Suomi, S. J. (1974), Development of peer interactions of monkeys reared in a nuclear family environment. *Child Develop.*, 45:670–682.

Sackett, G. P. (1968), Abnormal behavior in laboratory reared rhesus monkeys. In: *Abnormal Behavior in Animals,* ed. M. Fox. Philadelphia: Saunders.

———Holm, R., & Ruppenthal, G. C. (1976), Social isolation rearing: Species differences in behavior of macaque monkeys. *Develop. Psychol.*, 10:283–288.

———Ruppenthal, G. C., Fahrenbruch, C., Holm, R. A., & Greenough, W. T. (1981), Social isolation rearing effects in monkeys vary with genotype. *Develop. Psychobiol.*, 17:313–318.

Scott, J. P., Stewart, J. M., & DeGhett, V. J. (1974), Critical periods in the organization of systems. *Develop. Psychobiol.*, 7:489–513.

Seay, B. M., Alexander, B. K., & Harlow, H. F. (1964), Maternal behavior of socially deprived rhesus monkeys. *J. Abnorm. & Soc. Psychol.*, 69:345–354.

———Hansen, E. W., & Harlow, H. F. (1962), Mother–infant separation in monkeys. *J. Child Psychol. Psychiat.*, 3:123–132.

———Harlow, H. F. (1965), Maternal separation in the rhesus monkey. *J. Nerv. & Ment. Dis.*, 140:434–441.

Stevenson-Hinde, J., Zunz, M., & Stillwell-Barnes, R. (1980), Behavior of one-year-old rhesus monkeys in a strange situation. *Animal Behav.*, 28:266–277.

Suomi, S. J. (1979a), Peers, play, and primary prevention in primates. In:

Primary Prevention of Psychopathology, Vol. 3, eds. M. Kent & J. Rolf. Hanover, NH: Press of New England.

———(1979b), Differential development of various social relationships by rhesus monkey infants. In: *Genesis of Behavior*, Vol. 2, eds. M. Lewis & L. A. Rosenblum. New York: Plenum Press.

———(1982), Animal models of human psychopathology: Relevance for clinical psychology. In: *Handbook of Research Methods in Clinical Psychology*, eds. P. Kendall & J. Butcher. New York: John Wiley.

———(1983), Social development in rhesus monkeys: Consideration of individual differences. In: *The Behavior of Human Infants*, eds. A. Oliverio & M. Zappella. New York: Plenum Press.

———Collins, M. L., Harlow, H. F., & Ruppenthal, G. C. (1976), Effects of maternal and peer separations on young monkeys. *J. Child Psychol. Psychiat.*, 17:101–112.

———Harlow, H. F. (1975), The role and reason of peer friendships in rhesus monkeys. In: *Friendship and Peer Relations*, eds. M. Lewis & L. A. Rosenblum. New York: John Wiley.

———Harlow, H. F. (1977), Early separation and behavioral maturation. In: *Genetics, Environment, and Intelligence*, ed. A. Oliverio. Amsterdam: Elsevier/North-Holland Press.

———Ripp, C. (1983), A history of motherless mother monkey mothering at the University of Wisconsin Primate Laboratory. In: *Child Abuse: The Nonhuman Primate Data*, eds. M. Reite & N. Caine. New York: Alan R. Liss.

6
The Hormonal Consequences of Mother–Infant Contact

Seymour Levine, Ph.D., and Mark E. Stanton, Ph.D.

When one observes the behavior of mammalian females and their offspring, with very few exceptions there is an initial period of time where mother and infant are in constant contact. Aside from reproductive behavior, perhaps no other pattern of behavior has been studied more thoroughly in a variety of species, and few have revealed as universal a pattern. During the initial phases of mother–infant contact, there is a period of time (varying, dependent upon the species) where the mother and infant are almost constantly together. For the rodent (e.g., the rat), this period of time is approximately eight to fourteen days, at which time the mother begins to leave the infant for longer periods. In the case of primates, the length of time varies dramatically according to the species. For example, the period of constant contact for the squirrel monkey is approximately one month; for the chimpanzee, mother and infant dyads are in almost

Acknowledgments: This research was supported by HD-02881 from NICH&HD; MH-23645 from NIMH; and Research Scientist Award MH-19936 from NIMH to Seymour Levine. Mark Stanton was supported by Postdoctoral Training Grant MH-15147 from NIMH.

continuous contact during the first six months. The data we will present suggest that such contact has important functional consequences during development. We will argue that contact may be a crucial mechanism whereby infants can modulate their level of arousal.

Primate Studies

The squirrel monkey is an arboreal South American primate that breeds seasonally under natural conditions. As a result, the year is divided approximately into a mating–gestation phase and a birth–rearing phase. The infants are born precocially after a gestation of 160 to 170 days. At birth the infant climbs onto the mother's back with minimal assistance, and remains in continuous contact with the mother until the onset of independent activities. Nursing is accomplished by the infant shifting to the mother's ventrum and rooting for the nipple. This technique is usually mastered by the second day of life. As in most primate species, the biological mother is normally the primary caretaker, and specific attachment relationships appear to develop within the first days after birth. After the first day, the mother exhibits a specific recognition of her own offspring and usually will not accept another infant, although some females will transfer their maternal behavior to another infant following the death of their own infant. Infant selectivity of attachment does not develop as rapidly, but experimental observations indicate a clear ability to discriminate the maternal figure by several weeks of age (Kaplan and Russell, 1974). The rapid formation of an attachment relationship appears to occur through the performance of caregiving behavior by the mother and complementary expression of behavioral reflexes on the part of the infant. These reflexes, which include clinging, rooting, and suckling, are first expressed nonspecifically toward any object with appropriate stimulus characteristics (e.g., claspability, warmth). The expression of these reflexes appears to be reinforcing and, when directed toward the same object repeatedly, can cause the object to become a specific focus of attachment. The nature of the mother–infant relationship in the squirrel monkey begins to change rapidly, however, as the infant becomes attracted to other aspects of the environment. This outward seeking behavior, described as curiosity, affectance, motivation, or exploratory behavior, leads to a fairly rapid decline in affiliative behavior between mother and infant. A general developmental profile is illustrated in Figure 6.1 which shows the average progression of four males and four females across seven months of life (Coe and Rosenblum, 1974). It should be noted that although the infant begins to spend more time away from the mother after the first month of life, one very characteristic behavior following even mild environmental perturbations is the infant's immediate seeking of proximity and reestablishment of contact with the mother. Thus, even as late as six and seven months of age, when a disturbance occurs in the environment (e.g., strangers, strange conspecifics), the infant can be observed on the mother's back.

A number of years ago, the Laboratory of Developmental Psychobiology began a systematic series of investigations on mother–infant relationships in the squirrel monkey. We were particularly concerned with both the behavioral and hormonal sequelae that occurred following brief periods of separation. There were two major reasons for adding the variable of pituitary–adrenal system activity to our behavioral measurements when studying mother–infant relationships. First, there was compelling evidence that the pituitary–adrenal response is an extremely sensitive indicator of the organism's detection of a variety of environmental changes. In contrast to previously held beliefs, pituitary–adrenal activity has been shown to be very sensitive to minor changes in novelty (Hennessy and Levine, 1977; Hennessy, Heybach, Vernikos, and Levine, 1979); appears to be able to act bidirectionally (Levine, Weinberg, and Brett, 1979); and often provides evidence concerning the state of the organism which is

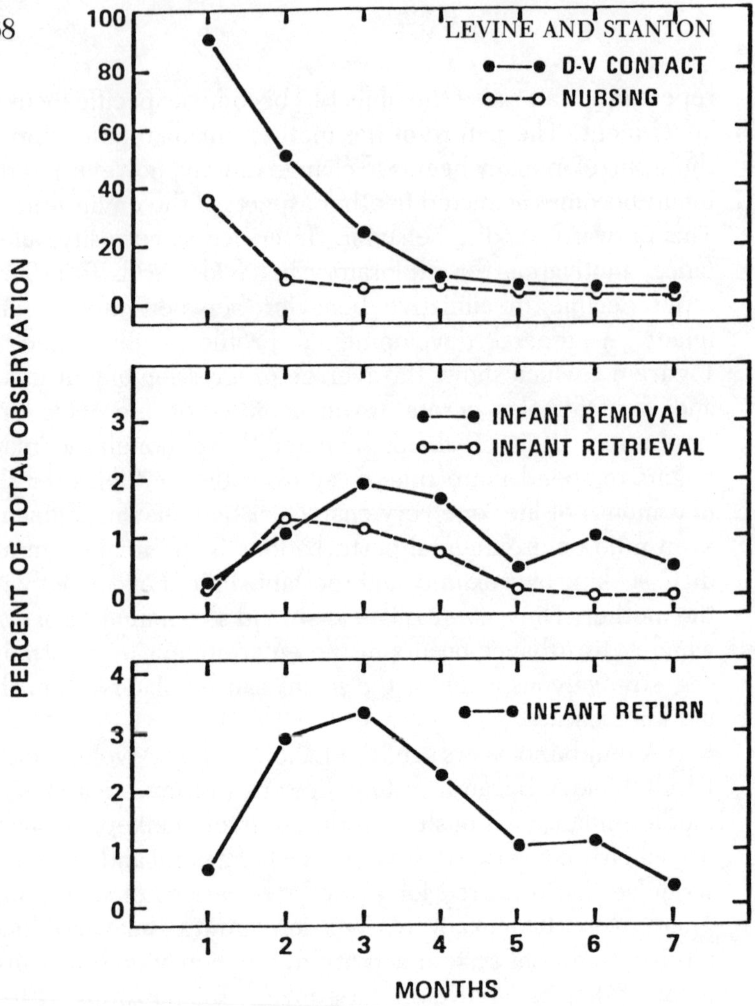

FIGURE 6.1
Developmental changes in the occurence of various mother–infant behaviors in the squirrel monkey: (top) physical contact and nursing; (middle) retrieval and removal of the infant: and (bottom) reunion initiated by the infant (Coe and Levine, 1981). (Reprinted with permission: *Anxiety: New Research and Changing Concepts*, © 1981 by Raven Press.)

difficult to obtain strictly by behavioral measurements (Hennessy and Levine, 1979). Using this system as an independent biological index of the response to separation has enhanced considerably the interpretation of overt behavior. Second, when examining the mother–infant relationship, the focus has been predominantly on the infant. If we accept the basic tenets of theories of attachment which discuss bonding between two members of a dyad, then one would expect that various perturbations in the mother–infant relationship should affect both mother and infant. However, the literature on primates indicates that it is difficult to determine any gross behavioral change on the part of the mother following the loss of her infant. We introduced measurement of the hormonal response to alterations in the mother–infant relationship with the hope that we could detect a physiological response on the part of the mother which was not clearly demonstrable by gross behavioral changes.

The data we have obtained by using both the behavioral and hormonal responses to separation have not only proved to be valuable, but in fact, have led to an interpretation of the separation process which is different from the traditional view relating the separation response to protest, agitation, and despair (Mineka and Suomi, 1978). Our view of separation, and the responses which accompany it, has been presented in numerous other reviews (Levine, 1983). This view basically interprets the infant's behavior during separation as a set of coping responses that seek to establish reunion with the mother. The basic proposition underlying much of our work is that the infant utilizes the mother as its primary mechanism for arousal reduction, and that contact with the mother can eliminate or attenuate both the behavioral and endocrine responses to arousal-inducing stimuli. It is in the context of reunion that the mechanisms of contact (and therefore, touch) may prove to be a crucial variable with regard to the infant's capacity to modulate its own level of arousal.

Of the many stimuli which can induce arousal in the

infant, perhaps the most potent one is separation from the mother. In what is now a large number of investigations, we have found that under most circumstances, the infant shows a dramatic elevation of plasma cortisol when separated from its mother. There are many variables which affect the magnitude of this response, including length of separation, conditions of separation, and whether the infant is separated and left in its home cage or separated and placed into a novel cage. However, even though there are numerous variables affecting the cortisol response, it tends to be a much more reliable and invariant response to separation than are behavioral responses.

Given the potent arousal-inducing effect of separating mother and infant, we investigated the arousal modulating properties of maternal contact and touch in a series of studies which employed a separation–reunion condition (Mendoza, Smotherman, Miner, Kaplan, and Levine, 1978). The separation–reunion condition involves removing the mother and infant from the home cage, separating them (which, in view of the excessive vocalizations emitted by both members of the pair clearly appears to be disturbing), and immediately reuniting the pair and returning them to their home cage for a period of thirty minutes. This is consistent with the use of handling by some investigators (Ader, Friedman, Grota, and Schaefer, 1968) as a standard procedure for activating the pituitary–adrenal system. Under these conditions, which intuitively appear to be very distressing, we observed no change in plasma cortisol after thirty minutes of reunion in either the mother or the infant (Figure 6.2). These data were somewhat surprising, since we had previously demonstrated that removing a nonlactating female from her cage and immediately returning her to the home cage does lead to a significant elevation of plasma cortisol thirty minutes later. Two hypotheses were offered to account for these data. The first was that the mother and infant have the capacity to "buffer" each other from stress; that is, under some conditions

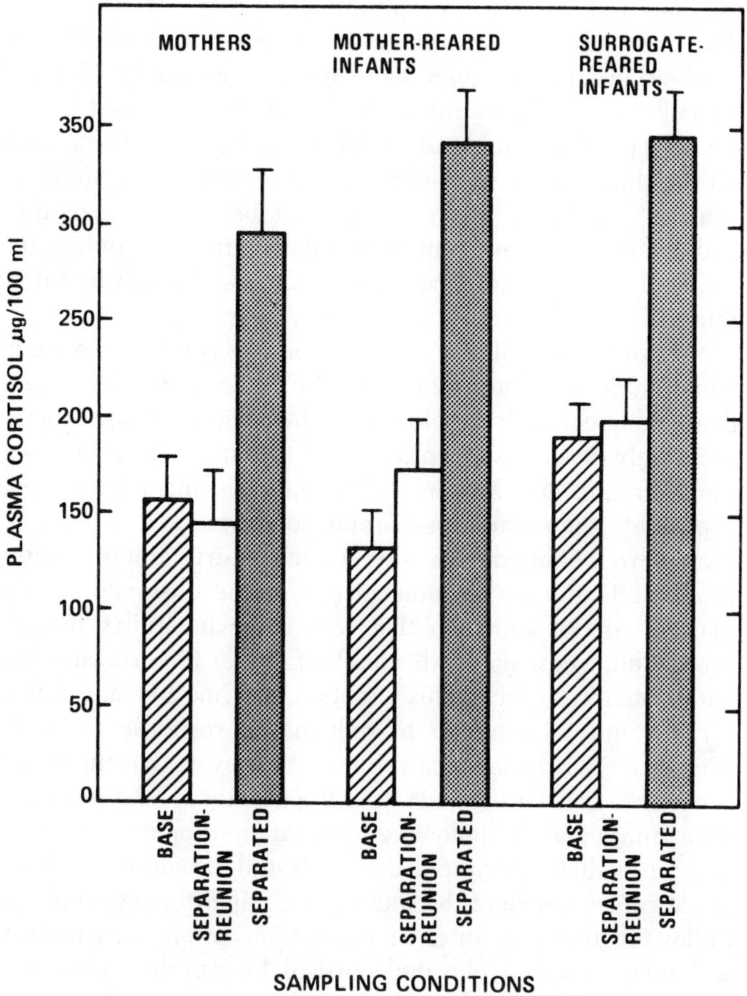

FIGURE 6.2

Mean (±S.E.) plasma cortisol concentrations for mothers and infants for each experimental condition (Mendoza et al., 1978). (Reprinted with permission: *Developmental Psychobiology,* Vol. 11, pp. 169–175. ©1978 by John Wiley and Sons.)

contact between the mother and infant prevents an increase in arousal as measured by pituitary–adrenal system activity. The alternative explanation was that cortisol levels of both mother and infant could have been significantly elevated initially, but by thirty minutes had returned to basal levels. Thus, separation could indeed have constituted a stress, both for the thirty-minute separation condition and the separation–reunion condition. However, contact between the mother and infant in the immediate reunion paradigm could have reduced the stress to permit a return to basal levels by thirty minutes.

In order to evaluate this question, we conducted a study which indicates that the first hypothesis—that mother–infant contact buffers each member from the stress response—more accurately describes the process. In this study (Levine, Coe, Smotherman, and Kaplan, 1978), mothers and infants were exposed to the separation–reunion condition, and blood samples were obtained five, fifteen, and thirty minutes after reunion. Under no circumstances did the observed rise in plasma cortisol approach that seen following thirty minute separation. These data indicated that, under the experimental circumstances used in this situation, the mother and infant serve a mutual function to reduce the response to stress (Figure 6.3). It is important to note, however, that the infant remains in constant contact with the mother for the period of time immediately following separation–reunion. Another finding in this experiment demonstrated an additional functional consequence of the mother and infant being reunited. Following thirty minutes of separation, when both mother and infant showed elevated cortisol levels, the infant was reunited with the mother; thirty minutes later another blood sample was taken. These data indicated that the infant continued to show elevated cortisol values as high as those observed after the thirty-minute separation, but that the mother's cortisol levels actually showed a reduction (Figure 6.4). These data were difficult to interpret until the results

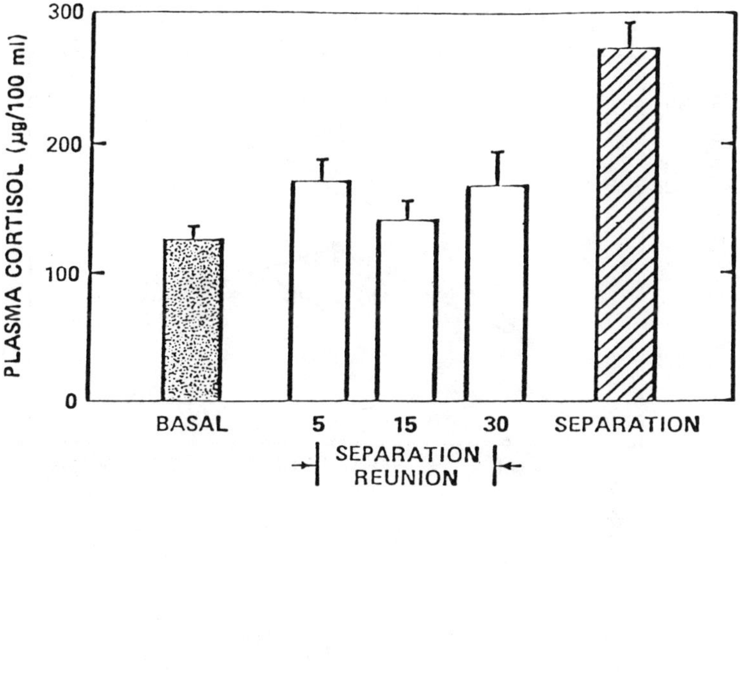

Figure 6.3
Mean (±S.E.) plasma cortisol values for each experimental condition (Levine et al., 1978). (Reprinted with permission: *Physiology & Behavior*, Vol. 20, pp. 7–10, ©1978 by Pergamon Press.)

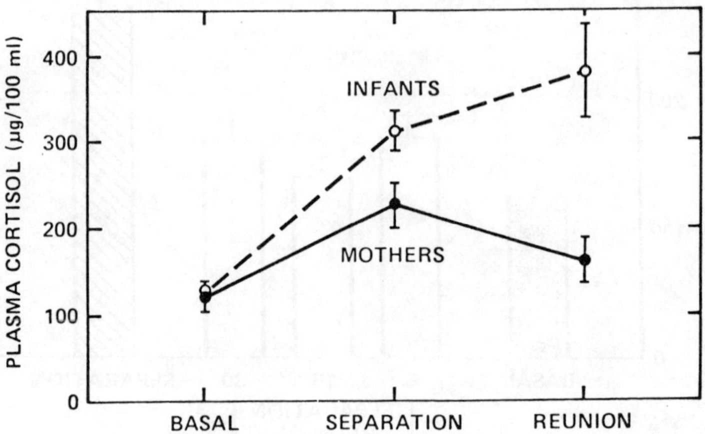

FIGURE 6.4
Mean (±S.E.) plasma cortisol concentrations for mothers and infants for each experimental condition (Levine et al., 1978). (Reprinted with permission: *Physiology & Behavior*, Vol. 20, pp. 7–10, ©1978 by Pergamon Press.)

from conditions of prolonged separation were obtained, indicating that cortisol rises in a linear relationship to the length of separation (Coe, Wiener, Rosenberg, and Levine, 1985b; Figure 6.5). Although the infant's cortisol levels do not appear to quickly return to basal levels following reunion, they are modulated in the sense that they do not show the continued elevations observed following prolonged separation. An analogous (if somewhat different) effect occurs in the mother, who shows a significant drop following reunion, whereas following prolonged separation she tends to maintain elevated levels of cortisol. It therefore appears that even following a brief separation, being reunited once again can reduce the responses of both mother and infant that were observed as a consequence of separation.

Thus far, all of the evidence indicates that maternal contact modulates the activation of the pituitary–adrenal system, either by buffering the response, or by facilitating the return of the hormonal system to homeostasis following a period of separation which has led to elevated plasma cortisol values. This latter form of modulation was again demonstrated in a recent experiment involving longer periods of reunion. When animals were subjected to separation, we observed a linear increase in plasma cortisol levels as a function of the duration of separation. However, if plasma cortisol values were elevated by a brief period of separation (30 min), these values tended to begin to return to basal levels within one hour following reunion with the mother (Coe, Wiener, Rosenberg, and Levine, 1985a; Figure 6.6). Therefore, under conditions of separation stress it appears that proximity, and particularly contact with the mother, results in a reduction of both the infant's and the mother's arousal levels.

Control is one of the most important aspects of the organism's behavior necessary for modifying and reducing the response to stressful events (Levine, 1983). The concept of control plays a central role within the framework of coping theory. The capacity of an organism to exert control over

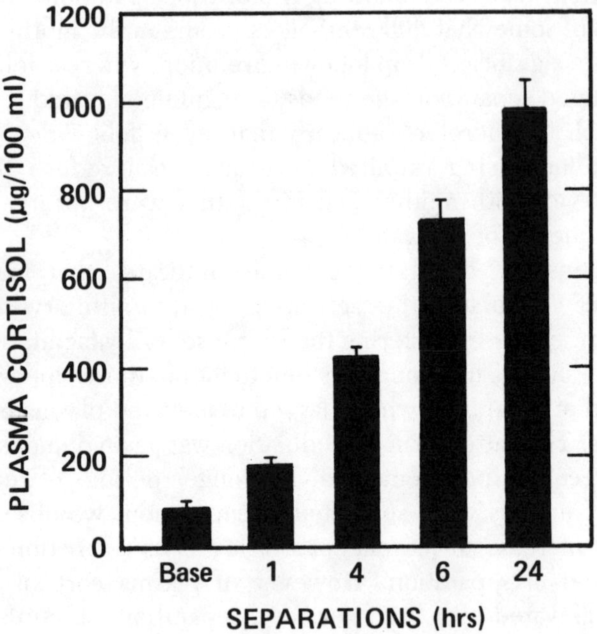

FIGURE 6.5
Plasma cortisol responses at different times following separations (Coe et al., 1985b). (Reprinted with permission: *Handbook of Squirrel Monkey Research*, pp. 127–148, ©1985 by Plenum Press.)

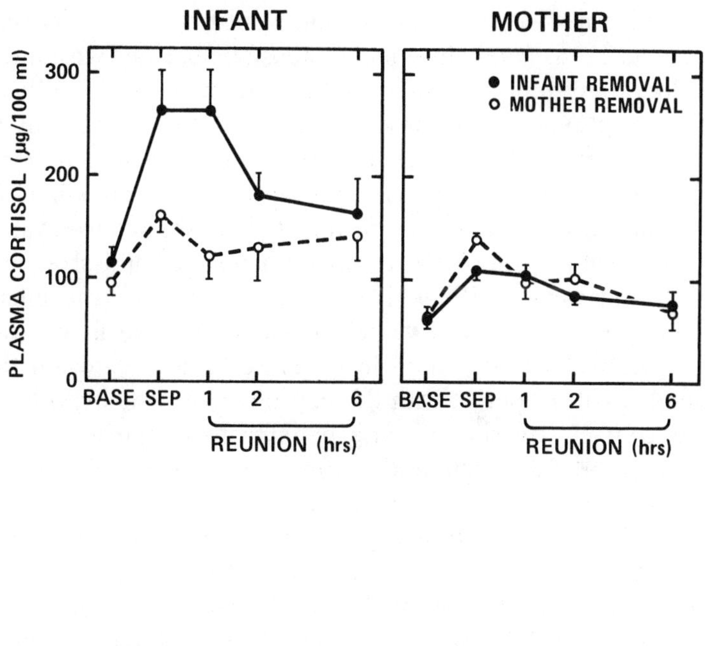

FIGURE 6.6
Plasma cortisol responses following reunion (Coe et al., 1985a). (Reprinted with permission: *The Psychobiology of Attachment and Separation*, pp. 163–199, ©1985 by Academic Press.)

stressful stimuli results in either an attenuation or an absence of the usual behavioral and hormonal responses. We have proposed that very early in development the infant learns to control its environment by making use of contingent relationships between its responses and outcomes—outcomes which at this early stage usually involve the modification of maternal behavior. Thus, the infant's responses to stress, either vocalization to facilitate contact, or high activity levels leading to even more rapid contact, represent mechanisms whereby the infant learns that it can exert some control over its environment and thus maintain some homeostatic balance within the endocrine system. It is important to note, however, that there are exceptions to this process, and that the attainment of contact and proximity does not always result in the amelioration of the stress response. For example, even when in contact with the mother, the infant does show an elevated cortisol value when exposed to both novelty and strangers (Vogt and Levine, 1980). However, even though the infant shows elevated cortisol values, these values are in no way comparable to those found in response to novelty when the infant is not in contact with the mother. Thus, the hypothesis that contact still serves some beneficial functional role remains valid, although under these circumstances, the response is attenuated rather than eliminated.

It is impossible to address comprehensively the subject of contact and touch without discussing the classic studies on contact comfort. The original paper by Harlow and Zimmerman (1959), which has proved to be a landmark in experimental psychology, disproved the prevailing hypothesis that attachment in infant rhesus macaques was based solely on the pleasures of feeding. The findings of this experiment indicated that the overriding factor in such attachment was contact comfort. This argument was based on the finding that young monkeys formed a clear preference for cloth surrogates over wire surrogates, regardless of which surrogate was involved with feeding. Mason (1971) has developed an elaborate theory based on contact comfort as the predominant factor in the establishment of attachment relationships. To quote Mason, "We know from Harlow's celebrated experiments that contact is a significant factor in the development of filial attachment. We have reason to conclude that the affected mechanism is reduction in emotional arousal" (p. 249). Thus, Mason's theory of development of filial attachment in monkeys is based primarily on the phenomenon of clinging, and therefore, touch. The data indicate that the presence of a surrogate in an unfamiliar environment can, indeed, ameliorate the behavioral and physiological responses of the surrogate-reared infant when placed in a novel condition. Increased vocalization is usually observed in surrogate-reared macaques following removal of the surrogate. However, Mason, Hill, and Thomsen (1971) reported that either its own surrogate or a totally novel surrogate was capable of reducing the response to this removal. Thus, behavioral agitation and the physiological response of increased cortisol levels were ameliorated. Hennessy (personal communication) has reported similar findings in squirrel monkeys. Surrogate-reared squirrel monkeys were observed across a four-hour session at the end of which a blood sample was collected for analysis of plasma cortisol levels. In all cases, distress vocalizations and plasma cortisol levels resulting from placement in a novel room were reduced in the presence of a surrogate. However, there is one important difference between surrogate-reared infants and mother-reared infants. In a mother-reared infant, only the mother appears to be capable of reducing the infant's cortisol response, whereas in a surrogate-reared infant, almost any object to which the animal can cling will reduce the infant's cortisol response. These data emphasize the importance of clinging in surrogate-reared infants, but also raise issues concerning the attachment process. Thus, for the mother-reared infant, in which a primary attachment is established, only contact with the primary attachment figure appears to be capable of performing the functional role of reducing arousal levels.

Rodent Studies

Whereas the primate represents an example of the effects of maternal contact in a precocial species, the rodent is an example of an altricial species; that is, an organism that is born in a highly underdeveloped and helpless state. The response characteristics of the neonatal rat pup are, at best, restricted. These pups are able to vocalize and emit ultrasonic signals which are important in facilitating maternal behavior, but locomotion is disorganized and requires much effort. The motor responses that neonatal pups do show are limited to writhing, rooting, and suckling. Interestingly, it has been argued that suckling is not only a consummatory act for the neonatal rat, but also the primary means by which it maintains contact with the mother (Blass, Hall, and Teicher, 1979). The sensory capacities of these infants are also immature at birth. The eyes and ears are closed; taste buds are not fully developed; and the rat pup therefore relies primarily on information from tactile and olfactory sensory modalities (Rosenblatt, 1979). Nipple attachment and suckling, for example, are under olfactory control (Singh and Toback, 1975; Teicher and Blass, 1977). These rat pups also follow a thermal gradient when returning ("homing") toward the nest (Rosenblatt, 1979).

Physiologically, the neonatal rat pup is by no means fully developed in the adult sense. Instead, many physiological functions are regulated by the mother. For example, newborn rats are unable to thermoregulate. Only the presence of the mother prevents their core body temperature from mirroring temperature changes in the external environment. Gastrointestinal function is another example. Urination and defecation do not occur in the absence of stimulation (anogenital licking) by the mother. Specific gut hormones, such as cholycystikinin (CCK), fail to suppress intake of nutrients, again with the result that the mother largely determines how much milk the neonatal pup consumes. Clearly then, the newborn rat lacks the sensory acuity and mobility of the adult, and is extremely dependent physiologically upon the mother.

For the most part, these conditions prevail during the first ten to fourteen days of the neonatal rat pup's life. During this period, the mother determines when, and for how long, bouts of mother–infant contact occur. For approximately the first week of life, the mother spends a greater portion of her day in contact with the pup in either active or passive suckling (Leon, 1979). Between the ages of ten and twenty days, however, there appears to be a dramatic developmental change. The pups become increasingly able to regulate their own body temperature between twelve and sixteen days. Eyes and ears open around fifteen days of age. Pups become capable of more adultlike locomotion between twelve and sixteen days. Beginning at fifteen to sixteen days of age, the pups begin to eat and drink independently, although mother's milk continues to be the primary food source well into the fourth week of life. Coincidental with the onset of independent consumption of nutrients, there is a change in the physiological control of nipple attachment and detachment. Prior to ten to fourteen days, nipple attachment occurs regardless of the pup's deprivational state or of the nutritive value of the stomach contents. After this ten to fourteen day developmental period, however, nipple attachment occurs only in food-deprived pups, and can be suppressed by gastric preloading of nutrients or by injection of specific hormones, such as cholycystikinin (Blass et al., 1979). During the third and fourth weeks of life, there is also a dramatic change in the mother–infant interaction. The mother spends increasingly less time with the pups, who are now the primary initiators of mother–infant contact. However, it is important to note that suckling and maternal contact remain important to pups as old as twenty days of age. At this age, pups that have been deprived of suckling, but not of food, attach to the nipple and suckle as readily as do food-deprived pups (Williams, Hall, and Rosenblatt, 1980). Thus, although many aspects of development in the infant rat pup are clearly different from those of the more precocial primates, a pattern of intensive continued mother–infant contact and subsequent maintenance of that contact (even after a period of independence) appears to be a common feature of both species throughout the period of development.

There is now a large body of literature dealing with the ontogeny of arousal and pituitary–adrenal system activity in the rat. The ability of the pituitary–adrenal system to be activated by specific stimuli appears to follow a developmental course not unlike that of many other regulatory functions in the rat pup. The ability of the pup to exhibit a pituitary–adrenal response when exposed to a variety of environmental disturbances is not observed during the first two weeks of life. Almost all of the research investigating maturation of the neuroendocrine systems regulating adrenal output has been concerned with the processes whereby organisms increase their output of the pituitary–adrenal system. However, in recent years, it has been demonstrated that there is also a central inhibitory process whereby, in adults, certain consummatory behaviors appear to have a rapid and pronounced suppressive effect on pituitary–adrenal activity. This inhibitory effect can take at least two forms. First, consummatory responses (such as drinking and eating) bring about dramatic reductions in circulating adrenocorticoids that have already been elevated by conditions of stress. Second, engaging in consummatory activities can, under some circumstances, prevent stress-induced elevations of plasma corticosterone from occurring. When viewing the behavior of the mother and infant, and in particular, the amount of time that the infant is in contact with the mother and suckling, it appeared that this would be an interesting model for examining two aspects of pituitary–adrenal activity during development. First, one could examine the maturation of the inhibitory process, which has not been previously examined. Second, one could use this model as a way of attempting to demonstrate the generality of the role of contact, with or without suckling, in modulating the infant's arousal response.

To examine the ontogeny of this psychoendocrine inhibitory process, we tested rat pups that were not yet weaned but that were capable of showing a stress-induced adrenal response (Stanton, Wallstrom, and Levine, 1987). Thus, the subjects in our experiments were twelve, sixteen, and twenty days of age at the time of testing. In the first experiment, pups were taken from the nest, fitted with oral cannulas which would permit infusion of milk into the mouth (Hall and Rosenblatt, 1977), and, after twenty-four hours of isolation in a heated incubator, were tested for their hormonal response to thirty minutes of exposure to novelty. This was done by simply placing the pups individually in a small heated test chamber that they had never encountered before. Four experimental groups were tested. Pups in two groups spent the test period suckling an anesthetized dam, one group receiving periodic milk infusions (Dam/Milk), the other not (Dam/No Milk). Pups in two other groups were placed alone in a test chamber not containing an anesthetized dam, again one group receiving milk infusions (No Dam/Milk), the other not (No Dam/No Milk). At the end of the thirty-minute test period, blood was collected for subsequent assay of plasma corticosterone. For comparison, two basal groups were also included, one comprised of pups that were left undisturbed in the nest (Nondeprived), the other comprised of pups that were treated like the four experimental groups above, but were sampled immediately prior to the test period (Nontested).

The results of the first experiment appear in Figure 6.7. Inspection of the four experimental groups (right four bars in each panel) indicates that at all ages the opportunity to contact and suckle an anesthetized dam markedly lowers levels of plasma corticosterone relative to the levels shown by pups

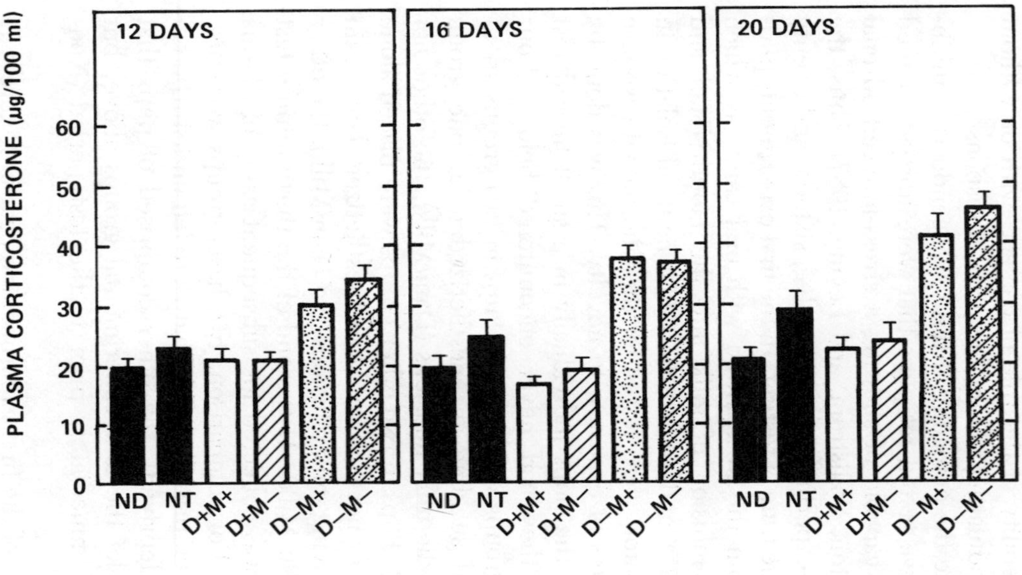

FIGURE 6.7

Mean plasma corticosterone values of rat pups assigned to six treatment conditions at each of three ages postpartum (age and treatment factors are both between-groups). The treatment conditions are: ND, Nondeprived Base; NT, deprived but non-tested base; D + M +, Dam/Milk; D + M-, Dam/No Milk; D-M +, No Dam/Milk; D-M-, No Dam/No Milk (see text for further explanation). Vertical bar markers denote one standard error of the mean (Stanton et al., 1986). (Reprinted by permission of John Wiley & Sons, Inc.: *Developmental Psychobiology*, copyright ©1986 by John Wiley & Sons, Inc.)

placed alone in the novel chamber. In contrast, consumption of milk delivered through an oral cannula had no significant effect, regardless of whether or not this consumption occurred in conjunction with suckling. Considering this effect of suckling–contact in reference to the two basal conditions (left two bars of each panel) raises three points. First, thirty minutes of suckling–contact brought the level of plasma corticosterone in the experimental pups down to that shown by pups left undisturbed in the nest. Second, these levels represented a reduction from pretest levels (compare the Nontested group, NT in Figure 6.7) at sixteen and twenty days, but not at twelve days of age. This reflects the fact that twenty-four hours of deprivation failed to elevate corticosterone as much at twelve days as it did at the older ages. This probably reflects a maturational delay of the pituitary–adrenal stress response (Levine, 1970). Finally, the corticosterone levels shown by the two basal groups reveal that exposure to the novel chamber in the absence of the mother led to further elevations in corticoids at all three ages, although the elevations were more pronounced at the older ages. Thus, the inhibitory influence of suckling and maternal contact on pituitary–adrenal activity consisted largely of blocking the novelty-induced elevations that occurred in the absence of the mother. It should be emphasized that milk consumption was of little influence in producing pituitary–adrenal inhibition and that all of the effect could be accounted for by suckling–contact.

These results show that pituitary–adrenal activity in infant rats can be inhibited by maternal reunion and suckling. They do not, however, show whether the infant consummatory response of suckling is necessary for this inhibitory effect or whether maternal contact is sufficient. We therefore performed a second experiment (Stanton et al., 1986) which examined the role of these factors under the experimental conditions that were used in the previous experiment. Figure 6.8 shows the corticosterone levels of a deprived but non-

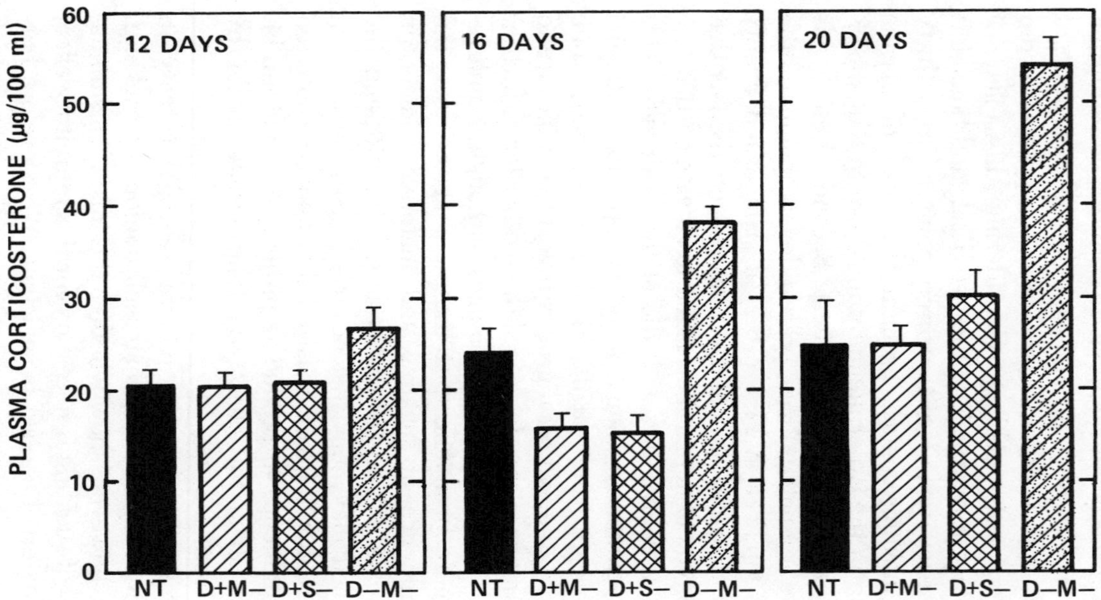

FIGURE 6.8

Mean plasma corticosterone values of rat pups assigned to four treatment conditions at each of three ages. Treatment conditions are as described in Figure 6.7 except for: D + S-, maternal contact without suckling or milk. Vertical bar markers denote one standard error of the mean (Stanton et al., 1986). (Reprinted by permission of John Wiley & Sons, Inc.: *Developmental Psychobiology*, copyright ©1986 by John Wiley & Sons, Inc.)

tested group (NT in Figure 6.8), a group (D + M-) comprised of pups which suckled an anesthetized dam; a group (D + S-) comprised of pups which contacted an anesthetized dam but were prevented from suckling by a physical barrier (adhesive tape) over the nipples (the group which was allowed to suckle also encountered a dam with adhesive tape on its ventrum, but with the nipples exposed); and a group (D-M-) comprised of pups which were placed alone in the novel test chamber. Again, the results show that maternal contact and suckling prevents the increase in corticosterone that normally occurs when rat pups are exposed to a novel environment. More importantly, however, this experiment shows that maternal contact per se is sufficient to produce this effect, at least at the younger ages studied.

Conclusion

Although the data presented from both the primate and rodent models do implicate contact and touch as significant concomitants of the infant's ability to regulate its own responses to stress, these studies were clearly not designed specifically to examine touch. They are confounded by a number of other potentially important variables, particularly the simple proximity of a familiar conspecific—the mother. What is impressive, however, is that contact seems to be an invariant response to the presence of novel or environmentally disturbing conditions. This has been demonstrated most clearly in the monkey, but there is also evidence indicating that when arousal is increased by electric shock or injecting amphetamine, the infant rat increases its time in contact with the mother (see discussion by Randall and Campbell [1976], p. 457). Thus, for the squirrel monkey, disturbing environmental conditions invariably cause the infant to return to the mother, even at an age when it has ceased to spend a major portion of its day in contact with its mother. For the rat, even at twenty days of age, when the infant is close to weaning and clearly spending a greater portion of its life in independent activities, suckling–contact can still markedly diminish the evinced response to a stressful condition—in this case, exposure to novelty.

There is a major difference between the squirrel monkey and the rat. For the squirrel monkey, it appears that once an attachment relationship has been established, only contact with the mother appears to be able to buffer the response to stress. In the rat, there appears to be no evidence of attachment in the traditional sense, and thus, like the surrogate-reared primate infant, almost any lactating dam which the infant rat can contact and suckle has the capacity to reduce the infant's pituitary-adrenal output. Nevertheless, contact with a maternal object, or with an object to which an infant can cling, plays an important role in the infant's capacity to modulate its response to stress.

We have hypothesized that the infant actively participates in the processes that lead to a reduction of the stress response. It has been well documented that control is an important determinant in reducing the physiological response to aversive stimuli. Control is defined here as the capacity to make active responses during the presence of an aversive event. For the infant, one such response is that of contact and/or clinging. This may be the predominant response of the infant when the mother is present. Therefore, the infant's earliest experience with control that results in an effective coping response is focused around contact and clinging. Thus, the infant is functioning in a contingent environment in which it can control outcome through the specific responses of contact and clinging. For the infant these responses may establish the basic patterns that result in effective coping into adulthood.

Discussion: Chapter 6

T. Berry Brazelton: Your work really brings out the importance of tactile contact as a control system. Touch helps one learn how to deal with inner stress responses as well as outer ones. It's fascinating to me that contact regulates the mother's responses as well as the infant's. Of course, in parent–child work like mine, we can't just look at the baby and ignore the mother's intentions and actions and feedback systems.

Seymour Levine: The very concept of mother–infant interaction, of a mutual relationship, requires that one look at both members of the pair. The mother–infant relationship is the primordial social system. This is where the infant begins the whole process of being able to utilize the elements of its environment to become a socialized organism, and touch is vital to that process.

William Greenough: As Renée pointed out, touch is always reciprocal. You don't have to look at someone who's looking at you, but it's impossible not to touch someone who is touching you.

T. Berry Brazelton: We often see a grieflike reaction in mothers who give their babies to day care in early infancy. Do you think they experience a rise in cortisol that they habituate to over time?

Seymour Levine: My interpretation emphasizes coping rather than habituation. Coping involves an active set of mechanisms—psychological defenses that appear to be effective in reducing the cortisol response. Essentially, the mother develops a set of skills to deal with the new situation.

Susan Rose: Do you think uncertainty plays a role in elevating cortisol?

Seymour Levine: Cortisol levels are very sensitive to specific psychological events that seem to have an element of uncertainty, such as loss of control, novelty, exams, impending surgery.

Susan Rose: Has anyone looked at cortisol levels in human infants?

Seymour Levine: No. Technically it could be done, but practically there are a lot of problems. It is known, though, that adult women show a dramatic cortisol elevation as a function of the birth process itself. It would be very nice to determine how rapidly cortisol returns to a basal level, with and without contact with the infant. How effective the infant is in modulating the mother's response is a very important question.

Michael Merzenich: I'd like to make a couple of physiological points that relate to your paper and to Steve Suomi's. One is that there are differences in the distribution of receptors on the body surface, and a mammal—a primate, like a rhesus monkey or an owl monkey—has a very high proportional representation of what are called slowly adapting afferents on the belly skin. These receptors are excited continuously when the belly skin is depressed, as during ventral contact between mother and infant. An increase in these slowly adapting afferents on the breast is one of the secondary sex characteristic changes of female primates.

Second, I think it's obvious that there are differences of affect when different forms of stimulation are applied to the skin. Touch can be calming or irritating; tickling the feet has different results from stroking the belly. We think of the qualitative aspects of sensation as being among the highest aspects of our behavior, but from a neurological point of view I don't think they're hard to understand. There is a unique mix of tactile inputs, with unique qualitative sensations evoked, from different skin regions on the body. Neurologically, it's fairly easy to see how I might imagine that some kind of contact with my stomach is a good thing!

Seymour Levine: That's not quite enough, because it suggests that contact is all, which it clearly is not. As the work with surrogate monkey mothers shows, contact serves a lot of functional purposes, but contact alone will not give you an infant that develops adaptively. Something else is involved, something related to the infant's capacity to utilize what is going on in the environment.

Michael Merzenich: There are certainly differences in the feedback situations of an infant with a surrogate and an infant with its mother. With the surrogate, there are obviously some things missing from this mutual feedback.

Seymour Levine: That's one useful way of looking at things, but I don't think it gives you the whole picture.

References

Ader, R., Friedman, S. B., Grota, L. J., & Schaefer, A. (1968), Attenuation of the plasma corticosterone response to handling and electric shock stimulation in the infant rat. *Physiol. & Behav.*, 3:327–331.

Blass, E. M., Hall, W. G., & Teicher, M. H. (1979), The ontogeny of suckling and ingestive behaviors. In: *Progress in Psychobiology and Physiological Psychology*, Vol. 8, ed. J. M. Sprague & A. N. Epstein. New York: Academic Press.

Coe, C. L., & Levine, S. (1981), Normal responses to mother–infant separation in nonhuman primates. In: *Anxiety: New Research and Changing Concepts*, eds. D. F. Klein & J. G. Rabkin. New York: Raven Press, pp. 155–177.

———Rosenblum, L.A. (1974), Sexual segregation and its ontogeny in squirrel monkey social structure. *J. Hum. Evolut.*, 3:1–11.

———Wiener, S. G., Rosenberg, L. T., & Levine, S. (1985a), Endocrine and immune responses to separation and maternal loss in nonhuman primates. In: *The Psychobiology of Attachment and Separation*, eds. M. Reite & T. Field. New York: Academic Press, pp. 163–199.

———Wiener, S. G., Rosenberg L. T., & Levine, S. (1985b), Physiological consequences of maternal separation and loss in the squirrel monkey. In: *Handbook of Squirrel Monkey Research*, eds. L. A. Rosenblum & C. L. Coe. New York: Plenum Press, pp. 127–148.

Hall, W. G., & Rosenblatt, J. S. (1977), Suckling behavior and intake control in the developing rat pup. *J. Comp. Physiol. Psychol.*, 91:1232–1247.

Harlow, H. F., & Zimmerman, R. R. (1959), Affectional responses in the infant monkey. *Science*, 130:421–432.

Hennessy, J. W., & Levine, S. (1979), Stress, arousal, and the pituitary–adrenal system: A psychoendocrine hypothesis. In: *Progress in Psychobiology and Physiological Psychology*, Vol. 8, eds. J. M. Sprague & A. N. Epstein. New York: Academic Press, pp. 133–178.

Hennessy, M. B., Heybach, J P., Vernikos, J., & Levine, S. (1979), Plasma corticosterone concentrations sensitively reflect levels of stimulus intensity in the rat. *Physiol. & Behav.*, 22:821–825.

———Levine, S. (1977), Effects of various habituation procedures on pituitary-adrenal responsiveness in the mouse. *Physiol. & Behav.*, 18:799–802.

Kaplan, J., & Russell, M. (1974), Olfactory recognition in the infant squirrel monkey. *Development. Psychobiol.*, 7:15–19.

Leon, M. (1979), Mother–young reunions. In: *Progress in Psychobiology and Physiological Psychology*, Vol. 8, eds. J. M. Sprague & A. N. Epstein. New York: Academic Press.

Levine, S. (1970), The pituitary–adrenal system and the developing brain. *Prog. in Brain Res.*, 32:79–85.

———(1983), A psychobiological approach to the ontogeny of coping. In: *Stress, Coping and Development in Children*, eds. N. Garmezy & M. Rutter. New York: McGraw-Hill, pp. 107–131.

———Coe, C. L., Smotherman, W. P., & Kaplan, J. N. (1978), Prolonged cortisol elevation in the infant squirrel monkey after reunion with mother. *Physiol. & Behav.*, 20:7–10.

———Weinberg, J., & Brett, L. P. (1979), Inhibition of pituitary–adrenal activity as a consequence of consummatory behavior. *Psychoneuroendocrinol.*, 4:275–286.

Mason, W. A. (1971), Motivational factors in psychosocial development. In: *Nebraska Symposium on Motivation*, Vol. 18, eds. W. J. Arnold & M. M. Page. Lincoln: University of Nebraska Press, pp. 35–67.

———Hill, S. D., & Thomsen, C. E. (1971), Perceptual factors in the development of filial attachment. *Proceedings of the Third Congress of Primatology, Zurich, 1970*, Vol. 3. Basel: Karger, pp. 125–133.

Mendoza, S. P., Smotherman, W. P., Miner, M. T., Kaplan, J., & Levine, S. (1978), Pituitary–adrenal response to separation in mother and infant squirrel monkeys. *Development. Psychobiol.*, 11:169–175.

Mineka, S., & Suomi, S. J. (1978), Social separation in monkeys. *Psychol. Bull.*, 85:1376–1400.

Randall, P. K., & Campbell, B. A. (1976), Ontogeny of behavioral arousal in rats: Effect of maternal and sibling presence. *J. Comp. Physiol. Psychol.*, 90:453–459.

Rosenblatt, J. S. (1979), The sensorimotor and motivational bases of early behavioral development of selected altricial mammals. In: *Ontogeny of Learning and Memory*, eds. N. E. Spear & B. A. Campbell. Hillsdale, NJ: Lawrence Erlbaum.

Singh, P. J., & Toback, E. (1975), Olfactory bulbectomy and nursing behavior in rat pups. *Development. Psychobiol.*, 8:151–164.

Stanton, M. E., Wallstrom, J., & Levine S. (1987), Maternal contact inhibits pituitary–adrenal activity in preweanling rats. *Development. Psychobiol.*, 20:131–145.

Teicher, M. H., & Blass, E. M. (1977), First suckling response of the newborn albino rat: The roles of olfaction and amniotic fluid. *Science*, 198:635–636.

Vogt, J. L., & Levine, S. (1980), Response of mother and infant squirrel monkeys to separation and disturbance. *Physiol. & Behav.*, 24:829–832.

Williams, C. L., Hall, W. G., & Rosenblatt, K. S. (1980), Changing oral cues in suckling of weaning-age rats: Possible contributions to weaning. *J. Comp. Physiol. Psychol.*, 94:472–483.

7
Touch, Attachment, and Health: Is There a Relationship?

Martin Reite, M.D.

Introduction

Touch is a magic word, loaded with meanings and connotations. It can bring to mind closeness, warmth, love, being cared for, contact—for the most part comforting feelings. The connection with closeness, the reestablishment of social attachments, was recently popularized by one of our major corporations with the slogan "reach out—reach out and touch someone." Touch has, of course, the more specific scientific meanings, as verb or noun, to physically touch or to be in contact with, or the tactile sense. When used as a noun to represent the tactile sense, there is a complete anatomy and physiology, both central and peripheral, to accompany the concept. Inspection of a major dictionary of the English language will show the multiplicity of other meanings of the word. *The Oxford English Dictionary* has over 1800 lines dedicated to definitions of the word *touch*. A most important

Acknowledgments: This research was supported by USPHS Grant No. MH19514. M. Reite was supported by NIMH Research Scientist Award No. 5K02 MH46335. I thank John Capitanio for his helpful critique of the manuscript.

connotation of the word *touch* is the association with healing (e.g., the laying on of the hands to effect a cure). The Bible is replete with references to the healing powers of touch, as, for example: "When he was come down from the mountain, great multitudes followed him. And behold, there came a leper and worshipped him, saying, Lord, if thou wilt, thou canst make me clean. And Jesus put forth his hand and touched him, saying, I will; be thou clean. And immediately his leprosy was cleansed" (Matthew 8:1–3). This meaning of the word extends from early history up to, and through, the present day. It forms a significant part of the nucleus of this volume. It is the thesis of this chapter to examine a possible mechanism whereby a basis in science might be found to underly such tradition. This chapter will of necessity, therefore, depart from exclusive presentation of experimental data. It will include such data, but in ways, and with associations and connections that are as of yet not well established. While it might raise more questions than are answered, I hope in the process to place in juxtaposition concepts that might not previously have been so placed, and thus develop a set of constructs, outlined of necessity in broad brush strokes, that may have explanatory value in linking aspects of the science of touch to more loosely defined feeling (and physiological) states evoked by the word.

Touch is a fundamental, possibly necessary component of the development of the earliest social attachment bonds. Attachment bonds are central to the normal development and integrative functioning of the high primates, especially man. Their presence is associated with pleasurable states, and good physical health. Their absence, or disruption, is associated with dysphoria, and increased risk of impaired health. Their inappropriate disruption may constitute a major psychobiological insult to the organism. The strong belief that touch has healing powers may be related to the fact that, having been once a major component in the development of attachment bonds, it retains the ability to act as a releaser of certain of the physiological accompaniments of attachment—specifically those associated with good feeling states, and good health. The exhaustive treatment of this subject would require a volume of its own, and more data than are presently available. I will attempt, however, to sketch it in outline form here.

The Role of Touch in the Development of Social Attachment

In high primates, both human and nonhuman, one of the fundamental, and the earliest, attachment relationships is the bond between mother and infant. Physical contact, touch, appears central to the development of this relationship. Klaus and Kennell (1982) reviewed the important role played by touch in the development of mother–infant attachment in humans. Examining observational data from a number of investigators on the patterns and sequence of the way in which mothers touch their newborn offspring, these authors stated: "Thus we have fragmentary evidence for what we believe is a significant principle—that human mothers engage in a species-specific sequence of [touching] behaviors when first meeting their infants, even though the speed of this sequence is modified by environmental and cultural conditions" (Klaus and Kennell, 1982, p. 73).

Similar, although more detailed and definitive, evidence exists implicating the role of touch or tactile contact as central to the development of mother–infant attachment in nonhuman primates. Examining the development of the mother–infant relationship in pigtail (*Macaca nemestrina*) infants, newborn infants spend 100 percent of their time in close physical contact with their mothers. Even at five months of age, when the infants are active social creatures, and capable of living independently apart from the mother, they are spending over 50 percent of their day, and 100 percent of their night, in physical contact with their mothers (Reite and Short, 1980).

In seminal experiments reported by Harlow and Zimmerman (1959), tactile contact was described as being of central importance to the development of the attachment bond between infant rhesus monkeys and their inanimate surrogate mothers. Infants were described as preferring their terry cloth covered surrogates to wire gauze covered surrogates, even though the latter were the providers of milk and warmth. The cloth covered mother was highly preferred to the wire mother in times of stress. Infants raised on cloth covered mothers, showed less evidence of what the experimenters termed *emotionality* in response to feared objects compared to infants raised on wire mothers, and they also exhibited greater retention of affectional responses over time. In describing the development of the "first affectional system," that between mother and infant, Harlow (1962) stated: "Our researches on the first affectional system indicated that there are multiple variables operating to tie the infant monkey to the mother, and they are similar to those described and stressed by Bowlby for the human being. The most important single variable disclosed by our researches is sheer bodily contact between infant and mother . . ." (p. 210).

Other chapters in this volume present empirical data relative to this issue. Levine and Stanton (chapter 6) present evidence implicating touch as a critical variable in the ability of infant squirrel monkeys to modulate their own arousal levels vis-à-vis their mothers. Their data suggest that once an attachment relationship has formed between squirrel monkey mother and infant, physical contact with the mother appears capable of buffering the infant's response to stress. Suomi (chapter 5) presents evidence implicating tactile contact with conspecifics as a major force in the development and maintenance of social attachment in rhesus monkeys. Not only is early contact (e.g., touch) important for normal behavioral development, but in the absence of such early experience, the mothering ability of adult female monkeys appears seriously compromised (Suomi and Ripp, 1983).

Thus converging data from many sources implicate touch

as central to the development of early mother–infant attachment. The mother–infant bond is likely the prototype of future attachment bonds—peer–peer, adult–adult, and, in man, bonds to inanimate objects, concepts, and components of the sense of self. The role of touch in the establishment and maintenance of such subsequent bonds is less clear. It is clear, however, that the role of touch in modulating or influencing social bonds or relationships in monkeys is not limited to infancy, for grooming, a social behavior involving tactile contact, is very important to maintenance of social bonds in adult nonhuman primates of many species. Defler (1978), and Boccia (1982, 1983) have presented evidence supporting the hypothesis that social grooming in adult monkeys may represent a form of tactile communication.

There is as well, of course, an extensive literature on the effects of early "handling" on subsequent development in (primarily) the rat. Ranging from effects on resistance to stress (Levine, 1957) and immune function (Solomon, Levine and Kraft, 1968) to learning, growth of the brain, and brain chemistry (Tapp and Markowitz, 1963), this is an area in which results are difficult to interpret, as pointed out by Schaefer (1968). To what extent touch or tactile stimulation is involved in such phenomena is unclear, although work by Hofer (1975) has demonstrated that certain aspects of the mother rats' tactile stimulation of the infant are very important regulators of their pups' level of behavioral arousal, which has prominent physiological correlates. Similarly, Schanberg, Evoniuk, and Kuhn (1984) have demonstrated that "active tactile stimulation of preweanling [rat] pups by the mothers provides specific sensory cues that maintain normal growth and development" (p. 135). Of course such tactile stimulation as a mother rat provides her pups is multimodal and provides at least vestibular stimulation as well as touch.

With respect to man, it has been demonstrated that premature infants subject to experimentally administered tactile and kinesthetic stimulation took more formula and gained more weight, than control infants not so stimulated (White and Labarba, 1976). Perhaps also relevant is the observation that infants who are classified as "anxiously attached" (as opposed to "securely attached") frequently have mothers who demonstrate an aversion to close body contact (Ainsworth, Blehar, Waters, and Wall, 1978). Such individuals tend to show up disproportionately in samples of abused and/or neglected children (Gaensbauer and Harmon, 1982). The current situation with respect to man has perhaps best been summarized by Ashley Montagu in his volume *Touching: The Human Significance of the Skin* (1971):

> We do not have much evidence of a direct kind that tactile stimulation or its absence affects the growth and development, physical or psychological, of the human infant. Such direct evidence is largely lacking for the simple reason that it has never been sought in man. We do, however, have as we have seen, plenty of direct evidence of this sort for nonhuman animals. Also, we have a great deal of direct evidence in human infants which thoroughly supports the extrapolation that tactile stimulation is at least as important in the physical and psychological growth of the human infant as it is in the nonhuman infant [Montagu, 1971, p. 191].

Physiological Correlates of Mother–Infant Separation

One aspect of separation, although certainly not the only one, is deprivation of touch; thus it clearly is part of the equation. These data also can be seen as relevant to clinical issues, and may begin to provide a viewpoint for conceptualizing the role in touch as it applies to healing.

Early work in monkey mother–infant separation was a direct outgrowth of the description by Spitz (1946) of "anaclitic depression," and the descriptions of the protest–despair behavioral pattern seen in human infants and children who were separated from their mothers (Robertson, 1953; Bowlby,

1953, 1960). A series of monkey studies followed, performed in several laboratories during the 1960s, including those of Harlow, Hinde, and Kaufman (see Reite and Short [1983], for a review). These studies, for the most part, demonstrated that monkey infants, separated from their mothers, exhibited a "protest–despair" or "agitation–depression" behavioral reaction phenomenologically quite similar to that seen in human infants and children. While most of the altered behavior resolved following reunion with the mother, long-term effects apparently due to early maternal separation experiences could be demonstrated as long as twenty-four months after one or two six-day mother–infant separations in rhesus monkeys (Spencer-Booth and Hinde, 1971a).

During the past decade, our laboratory has been examining the physiological correlates of the agitation–depression behavioral reaction following maternal separation in young pigtailed monkeys. We have developed a totally implantable multichannel biotelemetry technology to facilitate this research (Pauley, Reite, and Walker, 1974; Pauley and Reite, 1981). Implantable telemetry permits us to record a number of different physiological variables, such as heart rate (HR), body temperature, electroencephalograph (EEG) patterns, and sleep patterns from the completely unrestrained subject living in its social group (Reite, Pauley, Kaufman, Stynes, and Marker, 1974; Reite, Pauley, Walker, Kaufman, and Stynes, 1974). In a typical experiment, infants are naturally born to social group living mothers, and are reared in their natal social groups. Extensive behavioral developmental data are collected from birth on. At about four to six months of age, the biotelemetry systems are surgically implanted in the infants, under general anesthesia. Following recovery from surgery, the telemetry systems are turned on and begin transmitting multivariable physiological data around the clock, twenty-four hours a day, for the duration of the experiment. The telemetered signal is picked up by one of several antennas located around the social group pen and led to a receiver whose output is demodulated to separate the individual physiological signals. Physiological data is processed by an on-line dedicated computer system (Reite and Short, 1983), and may also be recorded on an ink-writing polygraph for scoring sleep patterns, and so on.

After an adequate normal baseline period, nominally four to seven days, the mothers are removed from the social group, with the separated infant remaining in the familiar social group. Immediately following separation, the infants are behaviorally quite agitated and upset, search vigorously for the mothers, and exhibit frequent cooing, the distress call of the young macaque. The period of behavioral agitation is accompanied by marked increases in both HR and body temperature (BT), characteristic of generalized physiological arousal. Studies in other laboratories have shown that the initial period of protest or agitation is accompanied as well by prominent increases in serum cortisol (Gunnar, Gonzales, Goodlin, and Levine, 1981).

The period of behavioral agitation is followed in a day or two by the onset of a profoundly different behavioral reaction, distinguished by a characteristic slouched posture, diminution in, or absence of, play behavior, a slowing of motion with evidence of impaired coordination, and a characteristically sad facial expression. This period of behavioral "depression" is accompanied by decreases in both HR and BT (Reite, Seiler, and Short, 1978), increases in cardiac arrhythmias (Seiler, Cullen, Zimmerman, and Reite, 1979), disturbances in nocturnal sleep patterns including more time awake, more frequent arousals, less REM sleep, longer REM latencies, and a fragmentation and shifting of slow ease sleep to later in the night (Reite and Short, 1978), as well as other physiological changes.

For purposes of illustrating the above mentioned physiological correlates of separation, I will present in Figures 7.1 to 7.5 following, examples of behavioral and physiological data obtained from thirteen pigtail monkey infants who were separated from their mothers for a period of ten days. These thirteen infants ranged in age from 131 to 228 days (mean age 168 days) at the time of separation. Behavioral data were obtained from all thirteen; all physiological variables could not be recorded from all animals at all times, however. All data (except the behavior "slouch" in Figure 7.1) are presented as percent change from a four-day baseline mean, represented by "B," and by the horizontal dotted line through 0. The separation period is divided into four segments, S_A through S_D. S_A represents the first day (and night) of separation, beginning at the time of separation, approximately 1300 hours. S_B represents data from separation days 2 to 4, S_C days 5 to 7, and S_D days 8 to 10. Reunion data are represented by R_A, the first day and night of reunion, and R_B, days 2 to 4 of reunion.

Figure 7.1 illustrates changes in two behaviors that are characteristically prominently affected by separation: play and slouch. Play is social play with other infants or adults. Slouch is the characteristic hunched over posture frequently seen in separated and depressed infants. In Figure 7.1, play is presented as percent change from baseline, whereas slouch, since it does not occur during baseline, is presented as the raw data percent total time observed (%TTO). The measures of variance represent standard errors of the mean. Behavioral data were obtained from six five-minute behavioral observations, three in the morning and three in the afternoon, between 0800 and 1700 hours. Details of the manner in which behavioral data are obtained and scored has been presented elsewhere (Reite and Short, 1983). As can be seen in Figure 7.1, play diminishes dramatically beginning with the first day of separation, where values in the vicinity of 75 percent below baseline are common. It is noteworthy that play continues to be below baseline levels following reunion, largely due to the infants' spending a great deal more time in physical contact with the mother, and therefore not being available for play interactions.

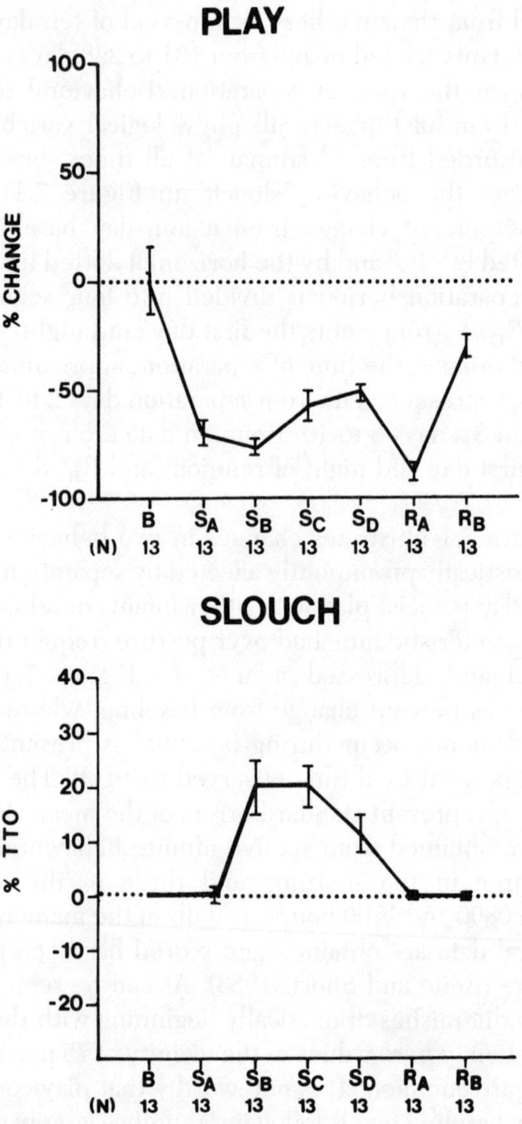

FIGURE 7.1

Changes in play and slouch behaviors for 13 pigtail infants who experienced a 10-day maternal separation.

Slouch behavior is seen to go from a baseline value of zero up to about 20 percent of total time observed during the first and middle period of a ten-day separation. Slouch diminishes almost to zero following reunion with the mother, although occasionally infants may exhibit some slouch behavior following reunion if they are not immediately accepted by their mother.

Figure 7.2 illustrates changes in mean day heart rate and mean night heart rate for the same group of infants. Mean day heart rate represents a mean of all heart rate samples obtained between 1000 and 1600 hours and mean night heart rate is the mean of all samples obtained between 2200 and 0400 hours. As seen in Figure 7.2, mean day heart rate increases above baseline levels on the first day of separation, associated with the agitated behavior exhibited by the recently separated infant. Subsequently, day heart rate remains lower than baseline throughout the period of separation and extends into reunion, although reunion values tend to be closer to baseline levels. To some extent, the decrease in heart rate seen during the daytime in separation is due to decreases in activity, especially lack of play. This is not the sole explanation, however; for when heart rate is controlled for behavioral state, it is still significantly lower during separation than during baseline. The decrease in heart rate during reunion is explained in part by the fact that the infants again remain inactive because they spend a great deal more time in close physical contact with the mother.

There is also considerable variability from animal to animal in the reunion heart rate, with some animals showing a return to normal baseline levels when they are normally active and other animals showing a persistent and sustained decrease in heart rate extending in some cases up to several weeks following reunion. The explanation for the individual variability is not known.

Mean night heart rate (Figure 7.2) shows a decrease in this group of animals beginning on the first night of separation

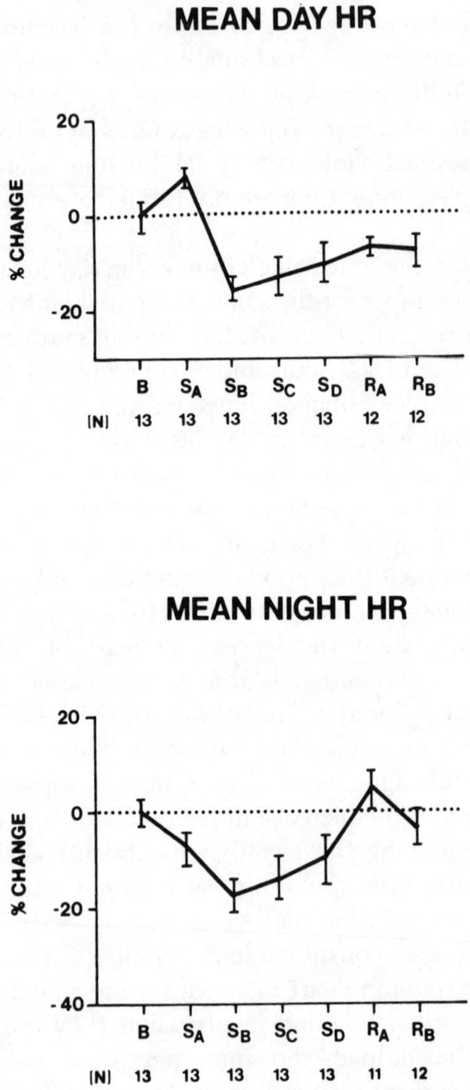

FIGURE 7.2

Changes in mean day heart rate (1000–1600 hours) and mean night heart rate (2200–0400 hours) as percent change from baseline in 13 pigtail infants separated for 10 days.

and extending through the remainder of separation. Mean night heart rate for the most part returns to baseline levels following reunion with the mother. Mean night heart rate is probably a better indicator of basal heart rate levels, as it is not as influenced by the level of daytime physical activity displayed by the infant. Not illustrated in Figure 7.2 is the marked increase in cardiac arrhythmias frequently seen in separated infants, especially during the time of maximal heart rate decreases (Seiler et al., 1979).

Figure 7.3 illustrates changes in mean day body temperature and mean night body temperature for the same group of infants. Day and night body temperatures were obtained in the same way as heart rate values. Body temperature data were missing from one animal entirely and were lost for several animals later in the experimental periods. As seen on the top panel of Figure 7.3, there is a slight increase in mean day body temperature on the S_A day, again associated with the initial agitation response to separation. Mean day body temperature varies relatively little during the period of separation, even though the animal's level of physical activity is altered. Body temperature increased following reunion with the mother. Mean night body temperature shows a pronounced decrease from baseline beginning with the first night of separation, and while nocturnal body temperature values tend to return toward baseline values as separation progresses, not until reunion are normal baseline values once again obtained.

We also have seen changes in the regulation of heart rate and body temperature circadian rhythms during maternal separation (Reite, Seiler, Crowley, Hydinger-MacDonald, and Short, 1982), including a slight phase delay of approximately one hour during the separation period, even though circadian zeitgebers, in the sense of social group activity patterns, feeding patterns, and light–dark cycles, have not changed.

Figure 7.4 illustrates changes in sleep latency, total time spent awake between initial sleep onset, and final arousal in

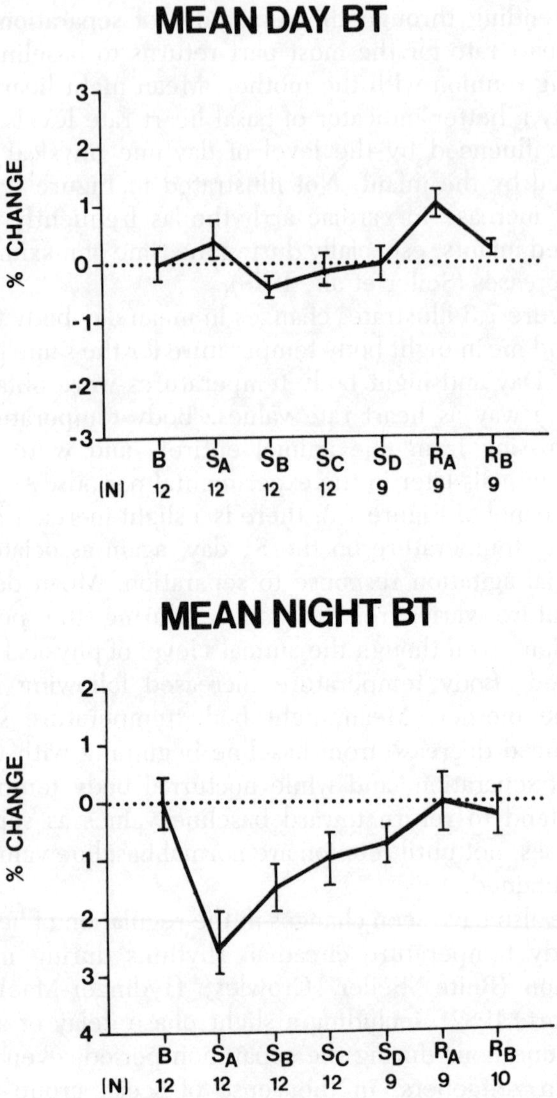

FIGURE 7.3

Changes in mean day body temperature and mean night body temperature for 10 pigtail infants during a 10-day mother–infant separation represented as percent change from baseline.

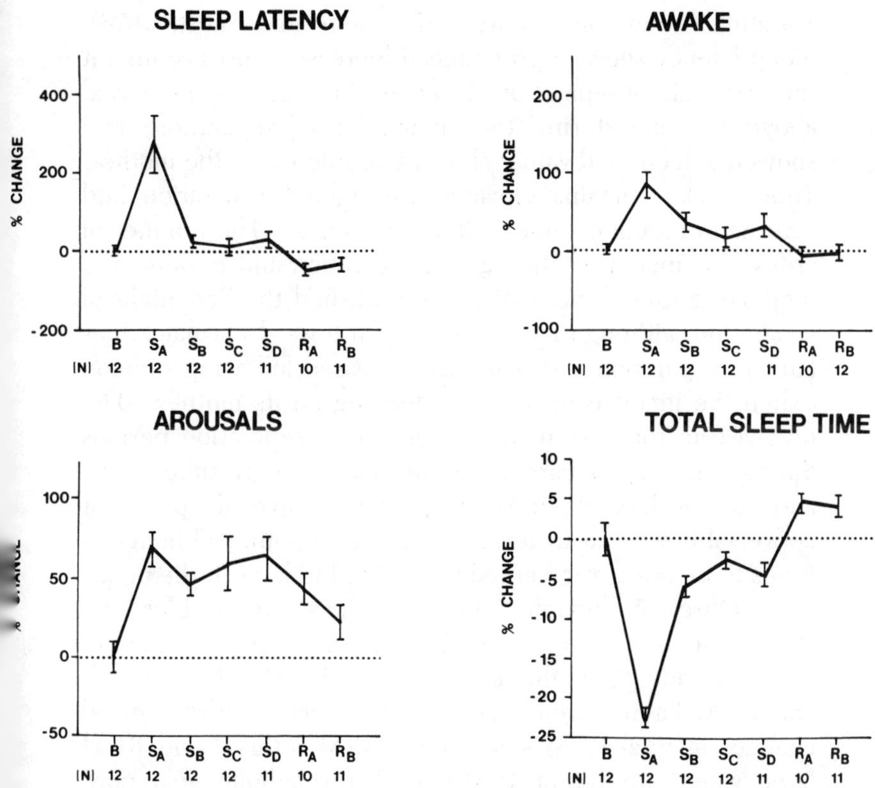

FIGURE 7.4
Changes in sleep latency, total time awake, number of arousals, and total sleep time in 12 of 13 pigtail infants during a 10-day maternal separation experiment.

the morning, the number of arousals during the night, and total sleep time for twelve of this group of thirteen animals. Sleep data could not be obtained from one animal. Sleep patterns are conventionally scored from the EEG paper record, as has been previously described (Reite, Stynes, Vaughn, Pauley, and Short, 1976; Reite and Short, 1978). Sleep latency shows a pronounced increase, most prominent the first night of separation. It remains only slightly increased above baseline during the remainder of separation, and showed a decreased value following reunion with the mother. Time awake remains elevated throughout separation and returns to baseline values following reunion. The number of arousals is increased throughout separation and reunion and total sleep time is dramatically diminished the first night of separation, although it tends to return toward normal values later in separation and is in fact increased following reunion (when the infant is once again sleeping on its mother). The decrease in total sleep time seen during separation periods S_B, S_C, and S_D appears to be due both to more time awake and to the loss of REM sleep. Slow wave sleep is not appreciably altered in terms of time or amount, although it tends to be more fragmented and shifted to later in the night.

Figure 7.5 illustrates changes in the sleep variables total REM time (in minutes), inter-REM interval (IRI), number of REM periods per night, mean length of each REM period, and REM latency from sleep onset. There are pronounced changes in total REM sleep, inter-REM interval and REM latency, and number of REM periods throughout separation, with decreases in REM, decreases in the number of REM periods, and increases in REM latency and increases in the inter-REM interval during separation. The values tend to show some rebound following a reunion with the mother, an effect not noted in four-day separations (Reite and Short, 1978).

We have also seen evidence of changes in the regulation of EEG rhythmicity associated with the depressive behavioral

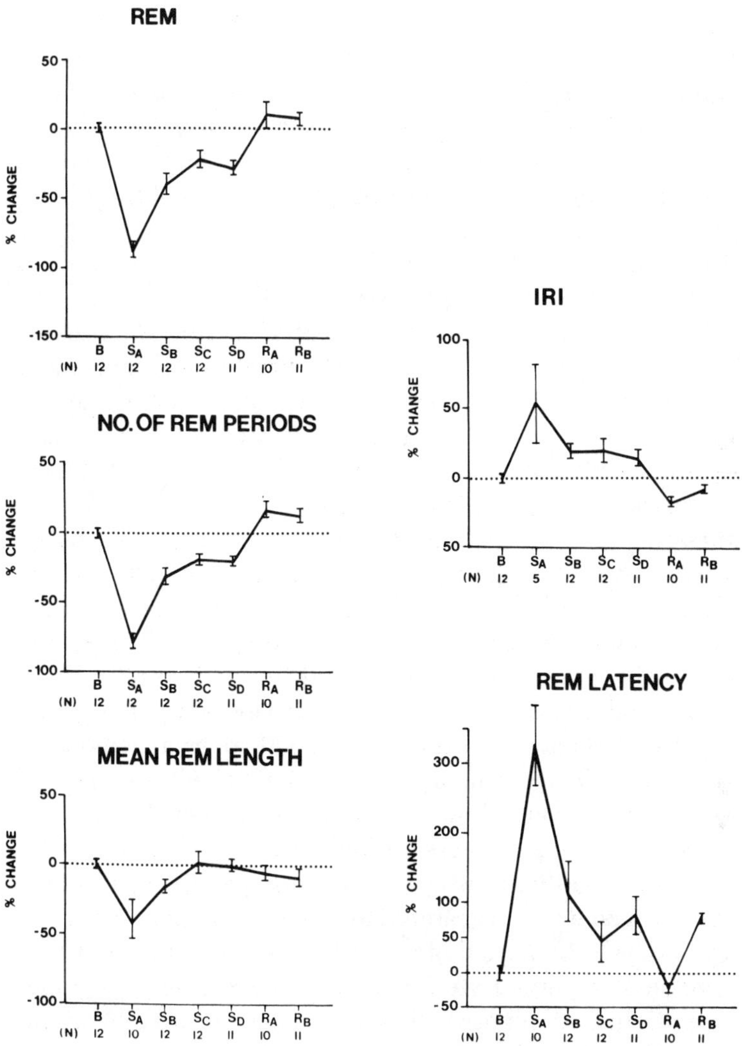

FIGURE 7.5

Changes in the sleep variables REM, number of REM periods, mean REM length, inter-REM interval (IRI), and REM latency from sleep onset in 12 of 13 pigtail infants experiencing a 10-day maternal separation presented as percent change from baseline.

response following separation (Reite, Short, Seiler, and Pauley, 1981; Short, Iwata, and Reite, 1977), as illustrated in Figures 7.6 and 7.7. Figure 7.6 illustrates an implanted infant during the baseline period prior to separation. The infant in the illustration is being enclosed by the mother and its concomitant physiology is presented at the left of the photograph. Note the rhythmical activity in the central temperal EEG lead (CT EEG) a power spectral analysis of which is included at the lower right corner of the illustration. This rhythmical activity seen over central temporal leads is thought to represent a correlate of phasic motor inhibition, and is probably homologous with the rhythme en arceau, or mu rhythm, described in humans (Gastaut, Terzian, and Gastaut, 1952). Figure 7.7 illustrates the same infant following separation, exhibiting the slouched posture and sad facial expression characteristic of depression. Once again, the simultaneous physiology is illustrated at the left. The characteristic central-temporal rhythmicity is noted to occur in the same location, but as illustrated by the spectral plot in the lower right, frequency has decreased from 7.5 to 6.25 Hz.

Several recent studies from our laboratory have suggested that separation experiences, both peer and mother–infant, may affect immunological function as well. In an initial pilot study, a pair of pigtail macaque monkey infants, removed from their mothers within forty-eight hours of birth and reared together as peers, were subsequently, at an age of twenty-seven weeks, separated from each other for a period of eleven days. The period of separation was accompanied by a depression of lymphocyte response to the mitogens phytohemagglutinin and concanavalin A, a measure of cellular immune function (Reite, Harbeck, and Hoffman, 1981). In a subsequent experiment two bonnet (*M. radiata*) monkey mother–infant pairs were separated from each other for a fourteen-day period. Again the separation produced a decrease in lymphocyte response to mitogen stimulation in both members of both pairs (Laudenslager, Reite, and Harbeck,

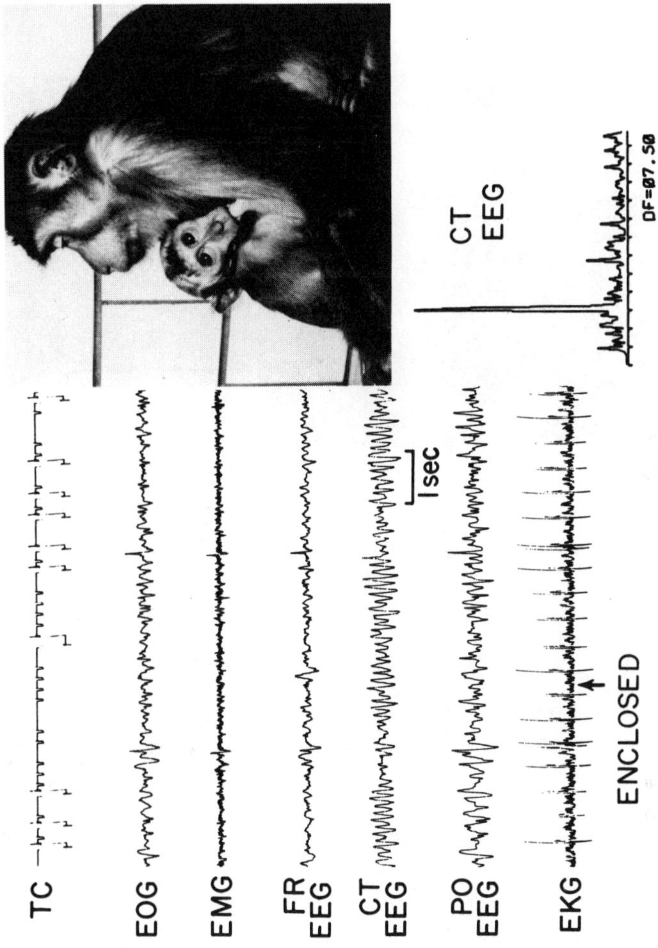

FIGURE 7.6

An illustration of a 22-week old pigtail infant enclosed by its mother with the simultaneously transmitted physiological data illustrated on the left. TC = time code; EOG = eye movement; EMG = posterior nuchal muscle activity; FR EEG = frontal EEG; CT EEG = central-temporal EEG; P-O EEG = parieto-occipital EEG; EKG = electrocardiogram. The photo was taken at the time indicated by the arrow beneath the EKG tracing. A power spectral plot based upon an FFT of the illustrated epoch of CT EEG is illustrated at the lower right. Dominant frequency was 7.5 Hz.

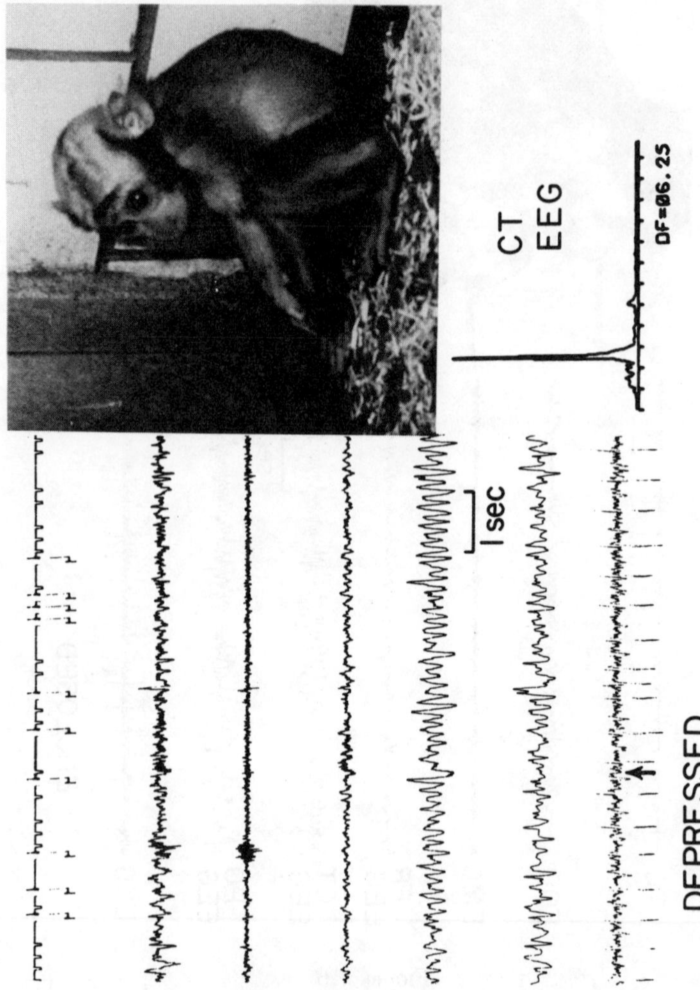

FIGURE 7.7
Infant R23.1 during the period of behavioral depression following maternal separation (see Figure 7.6 legend for details). The CT EEG activity is still present but has decreased in frequency to 6.25 Hz.

1982). A recent study has suggested that altered immunological function may persist into adulthood in monkeys who have experienced a short maternal separation in infancy (Laudenslager, Capitanio, and Reite, 1985).

It has been widely noted by many investigators that a prominent component of the mother–infant relationship during the reunion period following maternal separation is an increase in time spent in physical contact by the dyad (Kaufman and Rosenblum, 1967; Spencer-Booth and Hinde, 1971b; Hinde and Davies, 1972; Reite, Short, Seiler, and Pauley, 1981). The reasons for this increase in physical contact are in all probability overdetermined, and can be viewed from several motivational perspectives. Indisputable, however, is an increase in net time spent in close physical and tactile contact.

Thus, the response to separation appears to include both changes in autonomic physiology and impairment in cellular immune function as well. This constellation of physiological changes is compatible with an alternation and/or impairment in central autonomic homeostasis; we have suggested it may be representative of disturbance in hypothalamic regulation of autonomic activity (Reite et al., 1981).

The mechanisms underlying the observed behavioral, physiological, and immunological changes have not yet been isolated and identified. The loss of the mother, that is, the disruption of the major attachment bond, appears to be of central importance. Not yet excluded, however, are factors such as altered nutrition due to loss of mother's milk. While most of the mother–infant separation experiments have used infants old enough to be on solid food, careful examination indicates they were still spending a significant amount of time on the nipple. How much of this was nutritive versus nonnutritive sucking is not clear, although work is in progress in these areas (Reite, 1985). These caveats do not, of course, apply to peer separation paradigms, where similar protest–

despair behavioral reactions following separation have been described (Suomi, Harlow, and Domek, 1970).

Relationship of Primate Separation to Human Loss

It is interesting to examine these findings in comparison to those symptoms accompanying grief in human beings, since the monkey separation paradigms would appear to model most closely grief in response to loss. Somatic symptoms accompanying grief in human beings typically include the following: (1) changes in appetite—often anorexia and weight loss; (2) sleep disturbances—most often described as insomnia; (3) cardiac—often subjective palpitations; (4) respiratory—shortness of breath or sighing respirations; and (5) motor—often apathy and withdrawal, or restlessness and inability to sit still (Lindemann, 1944; Averill, 1968; Parkes, 1972). While we have no independent measures of appetite or respiration, young monkeys undergoing a period of maternal separation clearly show evidence of changes in the regulation of HR, sleep patterns, and motor activity, in a direction similar to the subjective symptoms accompanying grief in adult humans.

Similarly, there have been several reports of alterations in cellular immune function following bereavement in human adults. Bartrop, Lazarus, Luckhurst, Kiloh, and Penny (1977), studying twenty-six recently bereaved adults, found evidence of a decrease in lymphocyte response to mitogen stimulation in a six-week period following bereavement. Schleifer, Keller, Camerino, Thornton, and Stein (1983), studying fifteen adults for a two-month period following death of a spouse, described an impairment of lymphocyte response to mitogen stimulation. These findings are similar to the alterations in lymphocyte response to mitogen stimulation we have found in both peer separation pigtail infants and bonnet mothers and infants who have been separated from each other.

The presence of impaired physiological homeostasis,

with disturbance in immunological function, following separations and losses, may provide the beginning of an explanation for the by now well-established increase in morbidity and mortality following bereavement (Epstein, Weitz, Roback, and McKee, 1975; Jacobs and Ostfeld, 1977), and the mounting evidence implicating separations and losses as etiologically significant antecedents of a variety of nonpsychiatric medical disorders (Reite and Short, 1983).

In a similar vein, the presence of social attachments has been linked to improved health (Cassel, 1974, 1976). In a nine-year major epidemiological follow-up study of 6928 randomly selected adults in Alameda County, California, Berkman and Syme (1979) found that people who lacked social and community ties were more likely to die in the follow-up period than those with more extensive contacts. It was also reported that this relationship between the absence of social ties and increased mortality was essentially independent of self-reported physical health at the time of the original survey, the year of death, the subjects' socioeconomic status, and their health practices including smoking, consumption of alcoholic beverages, obesity, level of physical activity, and their utilization of preventive health services. Certainly, one explanation for such findings may be that those who are socially isolated are susceptible to the adverse psychological and physiological influences of isolation, or perhaps are subject to the chronic presence of those types of physiological responses described by ourselves and others as accompanying the disruption of attachment bonds. An alternative and equally plausible explanation is that those who, for whatever reason, enjoy the presence of social attachment bonds and social affiliations, also enjoy improved physiological functioning, which results in better regulation of physiological systems and improved functioning of the immunological system, the end result of which is better health.

It is illuminating in this regard to consider the notion that a major function of social attachment may be in the promotion and facilitation of psychobiological synchrony between individuals. Implicit in this notion is that such synchrony would be associated with optimal functioning of physiological systems, which could well result in improved health. This idea, expressed initially by Bowlby (1973) has recently been, reviewed with supporting evidence by Field (1985), and Reite and Capitanio (1985).

Considerable recent evidence implicates social attachment as being a behavioral system that is neurobiologically based and mediated, and that attachment behaviors may well be mediated by specific Central Nervous System (CNS) anatomical and neurochemical systems, involving especially limbic and hypothalamic regions (Reite and Capitanio, 1985; Steklis and Kling, 1985; Panksepp, Siviy, and Normansell, 1985).

A major question, then, at this point, is how might all this be related to touch? Several points need to be considered in this regard. First, separations and losses imply the disruption of attachment bonds. Second, touch appears to be an important part of the initial establishment of attachment bonds, especially in young organisms, or at least with respect to the initial mother (or parent)–infant bond. The extent to which touch contributes to the development of attachment bonds is, of course, somewhat more obvious than is the role of loss of touch in the response to separation, or the disruption of attachment bonds. Suomi (chapter 5) suggests that in young rhesus monkeys visual, olfactory, and auditory contact with the mother are not sufficient to prevent the behavioral response to separation in young rhesus monkeys. Yet touch or physical contact alone—at least from another female adult (not the mother) is also not sufficient to revive the response to maternal separation in pigtail and bonnet monkey infants. Separated infants of both species, when adopted and held in close physical contact by other adult females in the social group, nonetheless may display prominent behavioral and physiological responses to maternal separation (Reite, Seiler, and Short, 1978; Reite and Short, 1983). Thus, touch alone is not sufficient; it appears to depend on whose touch it is as well.

It is also likely that there are significant species differences in the role played by touch in the development and maintenance of social attachments. Certainly in human mother–infant dyads, it would appear that the role played by eye contact in this regard is of fundamental importance, probably to a greater degree than is the case in nonhuman primates.

Nonetheless, it seems that touch is instrumental in the development and maintenance of attachment, at least in the early life of high primates, and that subsequently the experience of touch in appropriate situations may exert a regulating or signal influence on physiological systems similar to that afforded by the process of "being attached." To the extent that this is involved with improved physiological functioning and ultimately improved health, touch could then be viewed as a signal stimulus capable of evoking and/or reactivating a more complex organismic reaction, one component of which is improved physiological functioning.

The mechanisms that might underlie such a relationship remain unclear. The evidence for behaviorally conditioned immunosuppression described by Ader and Cohen (1975) does suggest, however, that the immune system may be responsive to conditioned learning. Similarly, considerable evidence now exists suggesting that many physiological symptoms, including autonomic ones, are capable of being influenced by learning (Miller, 1978, 1981). Thus a set of data exists that would provide an explanatory basis for relating touch to altered physiological function. While empirical support for such a relationship has yet to be obtained, the construct would appear to present the opportunity for the development of a set of testable hypotheses. We hope continued work in this area will clarify our knowledge of the relationship between touch, attachment, and health.

Discussion: Chapter 7

Judith Smith: In discussing loss and human illness, what do you mean by loss?

Martin Reite: I mean loss in a comprehensive sense. I think the best illustration of loss in terms of its increasing one's susceptibility to illness was Robert Burton's *Anatomy of Melancholy*, published in 1621, in which he first related loss to the development of depression or affective disorders. He included under loss not only the loss of a person, as through bereavement, but the loss of health, a major symbolic loss, a loss of self-esteem. Loss is very stressful.

There is ample evidence that separations and losses, or the disruption of attachment bonds, can lead to impaired health. There is also evidence that the presence of attachments promotes health, and that tactile stimulation is important to the development of attachment bonds. What I'm suggesting is that perhaps on some symbolic level touch invokes mechanisms associated with attachment that ultimately can lead to optimal physiological functioning.

Kathryn Barnard: In your series of studies, did the monkey infants that were separated from their mothers recover?

Martin Reite: Some animals recover completely and others don't. They show long-term changes for some four to six weeks after reunion with the mother.

T. Berry Brazelton: Does that have anything to do with the mother's behavior?

Martin Reite: It may. We haven't studied it directly, but we have noticed that the mothers of animals that have not recovered seem less interested in the infants after reunion than they were during the baseline period.

T. Berry Brazelton: In our work, we often see a reaction that looks like grief in mothers who must put a child in the hospital or in day care. This is something that we've ignored for too long. I know from experience that when a young baby goes into day care, we can expect the child to have sleep problems, feeding problems, and immunological problems for the next few months, until the adjustment is made. And I know the same thing will happen to the mother; she too will have sleep problems, eating problems, and immunological problems for a while. Maybe we can play a preventive role and somehow aid the homeostatic system that we're dealing with.

Martin Reite: We have here a response system that we've sort of taken for granted for a number of years. We've been implicity aware of its importance, and what we're trying to do now is to work out the biology of the system. I think we're going to find out that there's a lot of biology involved, and one of our goals should be to try and took at it from both a comparative and a phylogenetic standpoint. If we can understand the biology, then the psychology will make more sense.

References

Ader, R., & Cohen, N. (1975), Behaviorally conditioned immunosuppression. *Psychosom. Med.*, 37:333–340.

Ainsworth, M. D. S., Blehar, M. L., Waters, E., & Wall, S. (1978), *Patterns of Attachment*. Hillsdale, NJ: Lawrence Erlbaum.

Averill, J. R. (1968), Grief: Its nature and significance. *Psycholog. Bull.*, 70/6:721–748.

Bartrop, R. W., Lazarus, L., Luckhurst, E., Kiloh, L. G., & Penny, R. (1977), Depressed lymphocyte function after bereavement. *Lancet*, 1/2:834–836.

Berkman, L. F., & Syme, S. L. (1979), Social networks, host resistance and mortality: A nine-year follow-up study of Alameda County residents. *Amer. J. Epidemiol.*, 109:186–204.

Boccia, M. L. (1982), Grooming site preferences as a form of tactile communication, and their role in the social relations of rhesus monkeys. *Internat. J. Primatol.*, 3:262.

———(1983), A functional analysis of social grooming patterns through direct comparison with self-grooming in Rhesus monkeys. *Internat. J. Primatol.*, 4:399–418.

Bowlby, J. (1953), Some pathological processes set in train by early mother–child separation. *J. Mental Sci.*, 99:265–272.

———(1960), Grief and mourning in infancy and early childhood. *The*

Psychoanalytic Study of the Child, 15:9–52. New York: International Universities Press.

———(1973), *Attachment and Loss*, Vol. 2. New York: Basic Books.

Cassel, J. (1974), An epidemiological perspective of psychosocial factors in disease etiology. *Amer. J. Pub. Health*, 64:1040–1043.

———(1976), The contribution of the social environment to host resistance. *Amer. J. Epidemiol.*, 104:107–123.

Defler, T. R. (1978), Allogrooming in two species of macaque (*Macaca nemestrina* and *Macaca radiata*). *Primates*, 19:153–168.

Epstein, G., Weitz, L., Roback, H., & McKee, E. (1975), Research on bereavement: A selective and critical review. *Comp. Psych.*, 16/6:537–546.

Field, T. (1985), Attachment as psychobiological attunement: Being on the same wavelength. In: *The Psychobiology of Attachment*, ed. M. Reite & T. Field. New York: Academic Press, pp. 415–454.

Gaensbauer, T. J., & Harmon, R. J. (1982), Attachment behavior in abused/neglected and premature infants. In: *The Development of Attachment and Affiliative Systems*, eds. R. N. Emde & R. J. Harmon. New York: Plenum Press, pp. 263–279.

Gastaut, H., Terzian, H., & Gastaut, Y. (1952), Etude d'une activité electroencephalographique meconnue: "le rhythme rolandique en arceau." *Marseille Med.*, 89:296–310.

Gunnar, M. R., Gonzalez, C. A., Goodlin, B. L., & Levine, S. (1981), Behavioral and pituitary–adrenal responses during a prolonged separation period in infant rhesus macaques. *Psychoneuroendocrinol.*, 6:65–75.

Harlow, H. (1962), Development of the second and third affectional systems in macaque monkeys. In: *Research Approaches to Psychiatric Problems*, ed. T. T. Tourlentes, S. L. Pollack, & H. E. Himwich. New York: Grune & Stratton.

Harlow, H. F., & Zimmerman, R. R. (1959), Affectional responses in the infant monkey. *Science*, 130:421–432.

Hinde, R. A., & Davies, L. M. (1972), Changes in mother–infant relationship after separation in rhesus monkeys. *Nature*, 239:41–42.

Hofer, M. A. (1975), Studies on how early maternal separation produces behavioral change in young rats. *Psychosom. Med.*, 37:245–264.

Jacobs, S., & Ostfeld, A. (1977), An epidemiological review of the mortality of bereavement. *Psychosom. Med.*, 39:344–357.

Kaufman, I. C., & Rosenblum, L. A. (1967), The reaction to separation in infant monkeys: Anaclitic depression and conservation–withdrawal. *Psychosom. Med.*, 29:649–675.

Klaus, M. H., & Kennell, J. H. (1982), *Parent–Infant Bonding*. St. Louis: C. V. Mosby, p. 314.

Laudenslager, M. L., Reite, M., & Harbeck, R. (1982), Suppressed immune response in infant monkeys associated with maternal separation. *Behav. & Neural Biol.*, 36:40–48.

———Capitanio, J. C., & Reite, M. (1985), Possible effects of early separation experiences on subsequent immune function in adult Macaque monkeys. *Amer. J. Psychiat.* 142:862–864.

Levine, S. (1957), Infantile experience and resistance to physiological stress. *Science*, 126:405.

Lindemann, E. (1944), Symptomatology and management of acute grief. *Amer. J. Psychiat.*, 24:141–148.

Miller, N. E. (1978), Biofeedback and visceral learning. *Ann. Rev. Psychol.*, 24:373–404.

———(1981), An overview of behavioral medicine: Opportunities and dangers. In: *Perspectives on Behavioral Medicine*, eds. S. M. Weiss, J. A. Herd, & B. H. Fox. New York: Academic Press.

Montagu, A. (1971), *Touching: The Human Significance of the Skin.* New York: Columbia University Press.

Panksepp, J., Siviy, S. M., & Normansell, L. A. (1985), Brain opioids and social emotions. In: *The Psychobiology of Attachment*, eds. M. Reite & T. Field. New York: Academic Press, pp. 3–50.

Parkes, C. M. (1972), *Bereavement.* New York: International Universities Press.

Pauley, J. D., & Reite, M. (1981), A microminiature hybrid multichannel implantable biotelemetry system. *Biotel. & Patient Monitor.*, 8:163–172.

——— ———Walker, S. D. (1974), An implantable multichannel biotelemetry system. *Electroencephalog. Clin. Neurophysiol.*, 37:153–160.

Reite, M. (1985), Implantable biotelemetry and social stress in monkeys. In: *Animal Stress*, ed. G. Moberg. Bethesda, MD: American Physiological Society.

———Capitanio, J. P. (1985), On the nature of social separation and social attachment. In: *The Psychobiology of Attachment*, ed. M. Reite & T. Field. New York: Academic Press, pp. 223–258.

———Harbeck, R., & Hoffman, A. (1981), Altered cellular immune response following peer separation. *Life Sci.*, 29:1133–1136.

———Pauley, J. D., Kaufman, I. C., Stynes, A. J., & Marker, V. (1974), Normal physiological patterns and physiological–behavioral correlations in unrestrained monkey infants. *Physiol. & Behav.*, 12:1021–1033.

——— ———Walker, S., Kaufman, I. C., & Stynes, A. J. (1974), A systems approach to studying physiology and behavior in monkey infants. *J. Appl. Physiol.*, 37:417–423.

———Seiler, C., Crowley, T. J., Hydinger-MacDonald, M., & Short, R. (1982), Circadian rhythm changes following maternal separation in monkeys. *Chronobiologia*, 9:1–11.

——— ———Short, R. (1978), Loss of your mother is more than loss of a mother. *Amer. J. Psychiat.*, 135:370–371.

———Short, R. (1978), Nocturnal sleep in separated monkey infants. *Arch. Gen. Psychiat.*, 35:1247–1253.

——— ———(1980), A biobehavioral developmental profile (BDP) for the pigtailed monkey. *Development. Psychobiol.*, 13:243–285.

——— ———(1983), Maternal separation studies: Rationale and methodological considerations. In: *Ethopharmacology: Primate Models of Neuropsychiatric Disorders*, ed. K. Miczek. New York: Alan R. Liss, pp. 219–254.

——— ———Kaufman, I. C., Stynes, A. J., & Pauley, J. D. (1978), Heart rate and body temperature in separated monkey infants. *Biol. Psychiat.*, 13:91–105.

——— ———Seiler, C., & Pauley, J. D. (1981), Attachment, loss, and depression. *J. Child Psychol. & Psychiat.* 22:141–169.

Stynes, A. J., Vaughn, L., Pauley, J. D., & Short, R. A. (1976), Sleep in infant monkeys: Normal values and behavioral correlates. *Physiol. & Behav.*, 16:245–251.

Robertson, J. (1953), Some responses of young children to loss of maternal care. *Nursing Times*, 49:382–386.

Schaefer, T. (1968), Some methodological implications of the research on "early handling" in the rat. In: *Early Experience and Behavior*, eds. G. Newton & S. Levine. Springfield IL: Charles C Thomas.

Schanberg, S. M., Evoniuk, G., & Kuhn, C. M. (1984), Tactile and nutritional aspects of maternal care: Specific regulators of neuroendocrine function and cellular development. *Proc. Soc. Experiment. Med. & Biol.*, 175/2:135–146.

Schleifer, S. J., Keller, S. E., Camerino, M., Thornton, J. C., & Stein, M. (1983), Suppression of lymphocyte stimulation following bereavement. *J. Amer. Med. Assn.*, 250/3:374–377.

Seiler, C., Cullen, J. S., Zimmerman, J., & Reite, M. (1979), Cardiac arrhythmias in infant pigtail monkeys following maternal separation. *Psychophysiol.*, 16:130–135.

Short, R., Iwata, S., & Reite, M. (1977), EEG changes during the depressive reaction following maternal separation. *Psychophysiol.*, 14:120.

Solomon, G. F., Levine, S., & Kraft, J. K. (1968), Early experiences and immunity. *Nature*, 220:821–823.

Spencer-Booth, Y., & Hinde, R. (1971a), Effects of brief separations from mothers during infancy on behavior of rhesus monkeys 6–24 months later. *J. Child Psychol. & Psychiat.*, 12:157–172.

——— ———(1971b), The effects of 13 days maternal separation on infant rhesus monkeys compared with those of shorter and repeated separation. *Animal Behav.*, 19:595–605.

Spitz, R. A. (1946), Anaclitic depression. *The Psychoanalytic Study of the Child*, 2:313–342. New York: International Universities Press.

Steklis, H., & Kling, A. (1985), Neurobiology of affiliative behavior in non-human primates. In: *The Psychobiology of Attachment*, ed. M. Reite & T. Field. New York: Academic Press, pp. 93–134.

Suomi, S. J., Harlow, H., & Domek, C. J. (1970), Effect of repetitive infant–infant separation on young monkeys. *J. Abnorm. Psychol.*, 76/2:161–172.

———Ripp, C. (1983), A history of motherless mother monkey mothering at the University of Wisconsin Primate Laboratory. In: *Child Abuse: The Nonhuman Primate Data*, eds. M. Reite & N. Caine. New York: Alan R. Liss, pp. 49–78.

Tapp, J. T., & Markowitz, H. (1963), Infant handling: Effects on avoidance learning, brain weight, and cholinesterase activity. *Science*, 140:486–487.

White, J. L., & Labarba, R. C. (1976), The effects of tactile and kinesthetic stimulation on neonatal development in the premature infant. *Development. Psychobiol.*, 9:569–577.

Part IV: Touch as an Integration and Learning System

8

Caregiver–Infant Interaction and the Immature Nervous System: A Touchy Subject

Peter A. Gorski, M.D., Carol H. Leonard, Ph. D., David M. Sweet, Ph. D., John A. Martin, Ph. D., Sally A. Sehring, M.D.

How much sensory stimulation, especially tactile, do premature infants receive in an intensive care nursery? What forms of touch do caregivers offer these fragile infants? How might such sensory events relate to physiological measures of autonomic nervous system function, thereby influencing the course of physical recovery prior to term? The Premature Behavioral Research Project at Mount Zion Hospital and Medical Center in San Francisco takes direct aim at these important questions. This chapter, drawn from work in progress, identifies our current search for the relationship early in life between sensory experience and physical health.

Clinicians and researchers differ about their perceptions of the intensive care nursery (ICN) as a source of sensory stimulation to hospitalized infants. Some believe the hospital

Acknowledgments: The authors acknowledge with deep gratitude the support and commitment of Roberta A. Ballard, M.D. and the staff of the Intensive Care Nursery of Mount Zion Hospital and Medical Center, San Francisco.

environment is depriving infants of needed sensory experiences (Scarr-Salapatek and Williams, 1973); others contend that ICNs overload the premature infant's vulnerable nervous system (Cornell and Gottfried, 1976).

Similarly, controversy exists about if, when, and how much intentional sensory stimulation might benefit the behavioral development of this population born at high risk for atypical patterns of movement, attention cognition, and communication (Gottfried, 1981). Sensitivity to the relative paucity of human handling these infants receive (relative both to healthy full-term infants and to the amount of invasive mechanical handling premature infants also endure) has prompted investigators to study the effects of a variety of forms of touching premature infants.

Several conceptual issues cloud resolution of the conflicts concerning the natural environment of the ICN or the efficacy of specific tactile intervention programs. For instance, several researchers have wondered whether the contingency of stimuli offered by the environment might be more influential than the absolute amount or type (Lawson, Daum, and Turkewitz, 1977; Gottfried, Wallace-Lande, Sherman-Brown, King, Coen, and Hodgman, 1981). Such considerations as infant sleep–wake state, position, and energy level might contribute to an individual infant's positive or negative response to any caregiver intervention.

Another important mystery concerns when an infant's neurological maturation intervention effects would continue to create lasting positive changes in behavior. Should we offer short-term intervention during hospitalization rather than support that continues after going home? Perhaps developmental facilitation should even wait until after infancy? Understanding the long-term effects awaits prospective longitudinal findings analyzing many complex interactions between infants and their care. We hope through our work to contribute to that cause in two ways: first, by tracking earliest caregiver behavior and infant responses; and second, by identifying risk factors surrounding infants and their environment at the time of a caregiving intervention that could reliably predict an individual infant's physiological response. Clinically applied, this information might direct our efforts to use touch to optimize our supportive and therapeutic aims.

Sample

This report draws from the nine premature infants studied in 1982. A total of thirty-six observation sessions averaging five hours each were analyzed. Infants ranged from 28 to 34 weeks gestational age at birth (mean = 31 weeks) (Table 8.1). The mean postmenstrual age at observation was 33.4 weeks. These infants were all selected for minimal medical complications in the neonatal period and satisfied criteria for the convalescent stage of hospitalization (Table 8.2).

TABLE 8.1
Population

Subject Number	Gestational Age (weeks)	Birth Weight (g)	Number of Bradycardias
1	29	1200	3
2	28	1000	11
3	33	1700	1
4	32	1810	1
5	30	1410	5
6	30	1260	1
7	28	960	2
8	34	1630	1
9	32	1450	25

TABLE 8.2

Convalescent Infant Observation Criteria

* Tolerating Nasogastric Tube or Nipple Feedings
* Extubated More than 24 Hours
* Breathing Room Air
* Infant Observed at Least 24 Hours Before or 48 Hours After Surgery
* Chronologic Age More Than 72 Hours
* Normal Fluid and Electrolyte Balance

Methods

DATA COLLECTION

Our observation methods have been fully described previously (Gorski, Hole, Leonard, and Martin, 1983), and include twice weekly continuous naturalistic recording of infant behavior and physiology, as well as caregiver behavior and environment. All data are collected at the infant's bedside in the intensive care nursery with an unobtrusive, cart-mounted microcomputer system. This relatively inexpensive device automatically monitors and enters physiologic data while performing all timing functions, and concurrently allows an observer to enter behavioral and other physiologic codes on a typewriterlike keyboard. For each thirty-second interval the following measurements are calculated:

1. Maximum heart rate
2. Minimum heart rate
3. Mean heart rate
4. Maximum $TcPO_2$
5. Minimum $TcPO_2$
6. Mean $TcPO_2$
7. Any sensory (auditory, tactile) stimulation (yes/no)
8. Any touching (medical or social) (yes/no)
9. Touching more than once per thirty seconds (yes/no)

10. Any auditory (yes/no)
11. Any medical touching (yes/no)
12. Any social touching (yes/no)
13. Simultaneous medical and social touching (yes/no)

Tables 8.3 and 8.4 illustrate categories of medical and social touch.

TABLE 8.3
Categories of Medical Touching

Resuscitative Stimulation	Ultrasound Testing
Bag & Mask Breathing	Chest Physical Therapy
Physical Examination	Injection
Blood Drawing	Suctioning
Applying Tape	Transfusing
Measuring Blood Pressure	Measuring Abdomen
Stethoscopic Exam	Thermometer
Weighing	Tube Adjustments
Passing/Removing Gavage Tube	Wrapping Foot For Lab Test

TABLE 8.4
Categories of Social Touching

Touching	Patting	Stroking
Kissing	Holding Close	Holding Out
Rocking	Combing	Changing
Diapering	Washing	Bottle Feeding
Burping	Covering	Enface Positioning
Placing In or Out of Infant Seat		

DATA REDUCTION

Ten consecutive thirty-second intervals were grouped into five-minute periods as follows:

1. Prebradycardic periods: five minutes prior to bradycardia
2. Postbradycardic periods: five minutes after bradycardia
3. Baseline periods: any continuous five-minute period excluding five minutes before or after bradycardia.

All five-minute periods containing data artifacts (e.g., fifteen-minute $TcPO_2$ warm-up period; $TcPO_2$ malfunction) were removed from the analysis. At this stage of the analysis there were 1200 (5-minute) baseline periods, 50 (5-minute) prebradycardic periods, and 50 (5-minute) postbradycardic periods for a total of 1300 five-minute observation periods.

For each five-minute period, the following summary statistics were generated:

Physiology

1. The maximum of thirty-second heart rate maximums
2. The mean of thirty-second heart rate maximums
3. The minimum of thirty-second heart rate minimums
4. The mean of thirty-second heart rate minimums
5. The mean of thirty-second heart rate means
6. The mean of thirty-second range in heart rate (max–mins)'s
7. The maximum of thirty-second range in heart rate (max–mins)'s
8. The minimum of thirty-second range in heart rate (max–mins)'s
9. The maximum of thirty-second $TcPO_2$ maximums
10. The mean of thirty-second range $TcPO_2$ maximums
11. The minimum of thirty-second $TcPO_2$ minimums
12. The mean of thirty-second $TcPO_2$ minimums
13. The mean of thirty-second $TcPO_2$ means
14. The mean of thirty-second range in $TcPO_2$ (max–mins)'s

15. The maximum of thirty-second range in $TcPO_2$ (max–mins)'s
16. The minimum of thirty-second range in $TcPO_2$ (max–mins)'s

Stimulation: The presence of:

17. Sensory stimulation
18. Touching
19. More than one touch per thirty seconds
20. Auditory stimulation (talk and sing)
21. Medical touching
22. Social touching
23. Simultaneous medical and social touching

Baseline means (computed for all five-minute blocks neither preceded by nor following an incident of bradycardia) were computed for each baby for each day on each of the above variables. For each five-minute period prior to an instance of bradycardia, values for each of the variables were also computed, and this value was in turn subtracted from the baseline value for that variable for that baby for that day. Differences from baseline were evaluated by nonparametric sign tests.

One baby (Baby 9) contributed half of the episodes of bradycardia to our data base; the remaining eight infants contributed approximately an equal number of bradycardia each. Therefore, it is not desirable to combine the data from all nine babies into a single analysis; a disproportionate amount of the variability among scores in a combined sample would be due to within-subject variability for a single baby, rendering any significance tests of questionable validity. Thus, where possible, two sets of analyses were conducted from the bradycardia data: (1) a within-subjects analysis for Baby 9, and (2) a mixed within-subjects/between-subjects analysis for the remainder of the sample. We combined the total sample into one analysis in a single instance, described below.

Results

Results will be presented in two parts. First, we will report ecological data about caregiver behavior toward infants, with special consideration given to forms of touch. Second, we will report associations between infant bradycardia and antecedent patterns of $TcPO_2$, heart rate, caregiver touch, and infant sleep–wake state.

ECOLOGY DATA

Because of the skewed distribution of much of our data, we present our results in terms of medians rather than means throughout this section of the chapter.

1. Nurses were present for only 20 percent of total observation time. No caregiver was present for 71 percent of the observation (Figure 8.1). Implications aside, these statistics may represent staffing patterns that assign one nurse to several infants at a time when they no longer require critical care. Physicians, parents, and all other interactors with infants were present less than 10 percent of total observation time.

The median length of time spent by nurses at the infant's care area after completing an intervention was sixty-four seconds. This raises perhaps the strongest concern of all from our data, since we have previously reported (Gorski et al., 1983) that infants can register signs of distress up to five minutes following interventions.

2. Infants spent the majority of time in the prone position. Infants were observed almost no time on their right or left sides (Table 8.5).

3. Thirteen percent of total observation time included some form of caregiver touching of infants. A nearly equal amount of medical and social touching was experienced by this group of convalescing infants. Less than 15 percent of all caregiver touching involved simultaneous medical and social tactile behavior (Figure 8.2). Roughly half of the times when touch occurred, the infant was likely to experience more than one such modality during any thirty-second epoch.

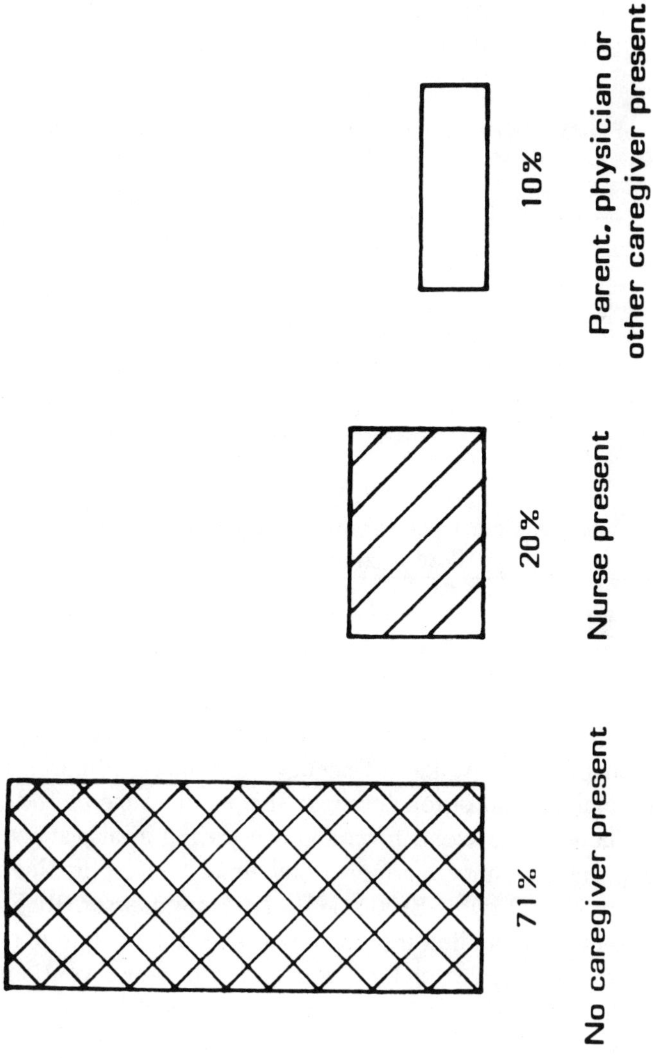

FIGURE 8.1
Percent time caregiver was present (medians).

4. Supine seemed to be the preferred position for touching babies (Table 8.6). The figures are particularly noteworthy since comparatively little total time was spent supine compared with prone (Table 8.5). This preference became even stronger for interactions when the caregiver talked to the infant during handling (Table 8.7).

TABLE 8.5

Percent of Total Observation Time Spent in Various Positions (medians)

Prone	Supine	R Side	L Side
59%	6%	1%	0

TABLE 8.6

Percent of Total Touching Time Spent in Various Positions (medians)

Prone	Supine	R Side	L Side
14%	21%	4%	0

TABLE 8.7

Percent Touching Time Concurrently Touched and Talked To By Position (medians)

Prone	Supine	R Side	L Side
3%	12%	0	0

5. Examination of the relationship between caregiver touching and infant sleep–wake revealed no significant difference between total amount of touch during sleep and awake periods. There is, however, a trend toward touch during awake states. More importantly, since far more total time is spent in sleep states at this age (Dreyfus-Brisac, 1970; High and Gorski, 1985), infants are indeed handled more when awake. Infant state does seem to influence the reason for touching. Medical interventions occurred equally often in sleep or awake states. Social categories of touch were observed to occur significantly more frequently during infants' awake states (Table 8.8).

TABLE 8.8

Percent Touching Time in Various Behavioral States (medians)

	Sleep %	Awake Nonfussing %
Total Touching	41	52
Medical Touching	40	50
Social Touching	36	53

PHYSIOLOGIC DATA

There were fifty episodes of bradycardia isolated by more than five minutes from any prior episode. As noted above, twenty-five occurred in one infant, while the remaining eight infants more or less equally contributed a combined total of twenty-five other bradycardic episodes.

TOUCH PRECEDING BRADYCARDIA

In this analysis, we combined the entire sample so as to accumulate a sufficiently large sample of touch and nontouch instances of bradycardia. We derived baseline data by tabulating episodes of touch occurring in all observation periods excluding the five minutes before, the thirty seconds during, and the five minutes following each bradycardia. The baseline condition included nearly twice as many periods without touch as periods when caregivers touched infants (X^2_1 = 87.6, $p < 0.001$) (see Table 8.9).

TABLE 8.9

Occurrence of Touch in Baseline Periods

	Touched	Not Touched
Number of Periods[a]	424	744
Percent of Periods	36.3	63.7
$X^2_{[1]} = 87.6$, $p < 0.001$		

[a] Period = block of 10, 30-second intervals.

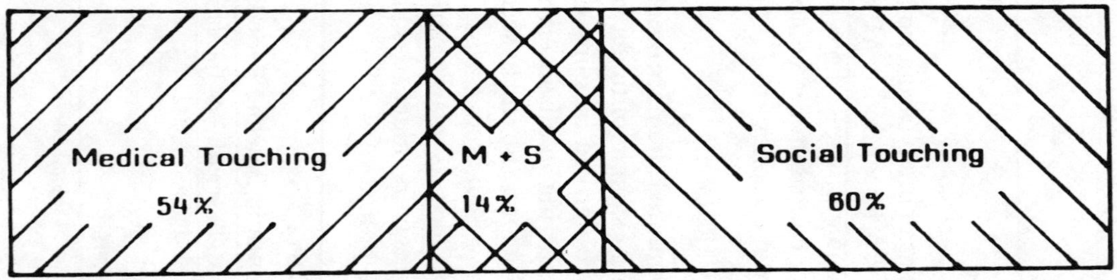

FIGURE 8.2
Quality and quantity of touching of premature infants in the intensive care nursery (medians).

In contrast, over half (29 of 50) of the prebradycardic periods registered one or more instances of touch (X^2_1 = 19.91, $p < 0.001$). This significant difference between the occurrence of touch prior to bradycardia and the baseline incidence of touch is largely attributed to one infant's extraordinary susceptibility to bradycardia (Table 8.10).

TABLE 8.10
Occurrence of Touch in Prebradycardic Periods

	Touch	No Touch
Babies 1–8	11/25	14/25
Baby 9	18/25	7/25
Total	29/50[a]	21/50

[a] $p < 0.001$.

FORM OF TOUCH AS PREDICTOR OF BRADYCARDIA

In this analysis, we examined the various kinds of touch experienced before bradycardia in order to compare these prebradycardia frequencies to baseline frequencies. We separated such conditions as any tactile or auditory stimuli, any tactile alone, two simultaneously occurring tactile stimuli, any auditory stimuli, any medical form of touch, any social form of touch, or intervals combining both medical and social touch. Furthermore, Baby 9 was tabulated independently of Babies 1 to 8.

For all infants, only auditory stimuli without touch showed significantly different frequency of occurrence prior to bradycardia when compared with baseline. The surprising direction of significance indicates that talking or singing to infants occurred significantly *less* often before bradycardia than during the rest of the day (Table 8.11). For the group of Babies 1 to 8, social forms of touch as well as simultaneous social and medical touch occurred significantly *less* often five minutes before bradycardia than during normal baseline physiologic conditions.

TABLE 8.11
Sensory Stimuli in Prebradycardic Periods

	Babies 1–8	Baby 9	Total
Sensory	15/25	9/25	24/50
Touch	16/25	9/25	25/50
Multiple Touch	14/23	16/25	30/48
Auditory	16/20[a]	16/22[b]	32/42[a]
Medical Touch	14/24	13/25	27/49
Social Touch	14/21[c]	15/25	29/46
Medical + Social	14/18[a]	13/22	27/40

[a] $p < 0.01$.

[b] $p < 0.05$.

[c] $p < 0.10$ (other values did not reach significance).

ADDING PHYSIOLOGIC VARIABLES TO TOUCH VARIABLES

Curiously, none of the the $TcPO_2$ or heart rate variables, except the mean of the mean $TcPO_2$ and the absolute minimum heart rate five minutes prior to bradycardia, significantly exceeded chance as an antecedent predicting a bradycardia event (see Tables 8.12 and 8.13). However, when presence or absence of touch in the prebradycardic period was added to the physiologic variables, several touch-physiology interactions emerged as predictors of bradycardia.

When touch occurred in the prebradycardic period, three $TcPO_2$ variables dropped below baseline significantly more often before bradycardia than at other times. These measure were: the mean of the minimum $TcPO_2$ levels five minutes prior to bradycardia; the minimum of the minimum $TcPO_2$ levels prebradycardia; and the mean of the ten mean $TcPO_2$'s in that same prebradycardic period (Table 8.12). In contrast, when no touch occurred during a prebradycardic period, only the minimum of $TcPO_2$ minimums significantly identified the prebradycardic condition. Paradoxically, the absolute minimum $TcPO_2$ was higher during the prebradycardic periods when no touch occurred than it was during the nonbradycardic baseline.

TABLE 8.12

Touch/$TCPO_2$ Interaction in Prebradycardic Periods

	Touch	No Touch	Total
Average of TC Minimums	24/29 $p < 0.01$[a]	7/21 $p < 0.10$	31/50 NS
Minimum of TC Minimums	24/29 $p < 0.01$	6/21 $p < 0.05$	30/50 NS
Average of TC Means	24/29 $p < 0.01$	9/21 NS	33/50 $p < 0.05$

[a] Number of times baseline > prebradycardia.

Heart rate variables proved peculiarly unsatisfying as markers of a prebradycardic period. Only in the absence of caregiver touch did two variables, the mean of the mean prebradycardic heart rates and the maximum heart rate variability during prebradycardic periods, show lower than baseline values with significant frequency (Table 8.13).

TABLE 8.13

Touch/Heart Rate (HR) Interaction in Prebradycardic Periods

	Touch	No Touch	Total
Maximum of HR Maximums	17/29 NS[a]	13/21 $p < 0.10$	30/50 NS
Average of HR Means	13/29 NS	14/21 $p < 0.05$	27/50 NS
Maximum of HR Max–Min	13/29 NS	14/21 $p < 0.05$	27/50 NS
Minimum of HR Minimums	21/29 $p < 0.10$	12/21 NS	33/50 $p < 0.05$

[a] Number of times baseline > prebradycardia.

BRADYCARDIA AND STATE BEHAVIOR

For the group of infants 1 to 8, 20 percent of bradycardic episodes occurred during quiet sleep, while 56 percent occurred during active sleep, 24 percent in awake nonfuss states, and never during active fuss states. This distribution roughly parallels the percent of time spent in those four state clusters on days observed when no bradycardia occurred.

Baby 9, however, became bradycardic significantly more often while in active sleep when compared to the other infants. Likewise, Babies 1 to 8 have the same distribution of state behavior prior to bradycardia as do infants who had no bradycardia throughout a day-long observation (Table 8.14). That is, prebradycardic state behavior followed a course consistent with an expected distribution of states throughout the day. Baby 9, however, again displayed much more prebradycardic time in active sleep than would be predicted on the basis of state distribution throughout a day-long observation.

TABLE 8.14

Behavioral State in Prebradycardic and Baseline Periods

	Quiet Sleep %	Active Sleep %	Awake %	Fussing %
Baseline[a]	18	46	35	2
Babies 1–8 Prebrady[b]	24	52	24	0
Baby 9 Prebrady[b]	7	76	15	2
All Babies Prebrady[b]	15.5	64	19.5	1

[a] Percent of baseline periods spent in each state.

[b] Percent of prebradycardic periods spent in each state.

Discussion

ECOLOGY DATA

The relatively brief periods of total caregiver time and care time following interventions is surprising given the nursery's impression of constant activity and stimulation. We believe the finding of such limited time spent observing after acting on infants may uncover serious preventive opportunities missed by caregivers. If clinicians rely virtually exclusively on electronic monitoring systems, they will continue to recognize and respond only to nonspecific and profound signs of distress or instability in infants. If we are to identify early signs of how infants respond to our interventions, especially any infant behavioral cues, we must spend time watching and learning about these possible communications directly from the infants.

Compared with the rich diversity of position changes in utero, the extrauterine experience of premature infants appears markedly restricted. Given the likely feedback from vestibular and proprioceptive stimuli onto the developing nervous system, we should perhaps give concerned attention to the implications of these findings on ultimate perceptual-motor and sensory integrative capacities of this preterm population. Martin, Herrell, Rubin, and Fanaroff (1979) have reported higher PaO_2 levels in the prone versus supine position. Since we found touch offered most frequently when infants lie supine, we are further concerned to study the potentially compounded risk for bradycardia from handling in positions that compromise oxygenation and/or perfusion.

We do not presume to know how much touching is beneficial to preterm infants. We are intuitively concerned, however, that a positive balance might be needed between social and medical forms of tactile experience. Indeed, our finding that social categories of touch rarely preceded bradycardia in most infants studied piqued our curiosity a step further. Returning to the original printouts of observational data, we found that in all but two instances when social touch did precede bradycardia, the infant's mother was the source of stimulation. Perhaps this proves that parents are noted to be more exciting than professional partners, even by infants too weak to handle such excitement. A different thought also occurs: parents are more limited in the time they spend with their hospitalized infants and might therefore inadvertently pack in loads of active stimulation in a shorter period of time. Less eager or more busy professional caregivers allow long rest periods during which infants might recover strength as well as social appetite.

Our data suggest that humans tend to talk to individuals when they look at them face-to-face. When one considers that healthy term infants are held and often talked to while awake, one wonders whether the comparative paucity of talk during touching is protective of premature infants or defensive psychologically for caregivers disappointed by the limited social interactive efforts of these weak infants. Again, our physiologic analyses tease us with the notion that clinicians have yet to learn to use the stabilizing power of certain human sounds in contrast to the animate and inanimate cacaphony so piercingly characteristic of intensive care nurseries.

PHYSIOLOGIC DATA

Despite the limited generalizability resultant from analyses based on a small number of instances of bradycardia in our sample, our findings point toward directions for further investigation. We believe we can already declare that all forms of human touch are not always therapeutic to all premature infants. Some infants indeed prove to be exquisitely sensitive to, and perhaps therefore often overwhelmed by, tactile intervention. Moreover, social and medical forms of touch do not appear to clearly distinguish themselves as uniquely contributing to instability expressed as bradycardia.

We were fascinated to discover that heart rate variables were largely unreliable precursors of very low heart rates. $TcPO_2$ fared better, yet it too relied on touch variables to strengthen the ability to predict bradycardia. We hope we are serving the interest of clinical neonatology through our attempt to develop fine measures of heart rate and $TcPO_2$ that might someday be easily monitored as early warning signals of autonomic disintegration or destabilization. If we could observe subtle forms of distress minutes before gross events such as bradycardia or apnea, we might then support infants in time to spare them the potentially cumulative effects of fluctuating perfusion of brain and other vital organs.

Bradycardia was frequently observed in the absence of

any preceding touch. We wonder whether such relatively spontaneous episodes have different causative mechanisms from those associated with caregiver touch. This hypothesis appears to gain support from our finding that in most pre-bradycardic periods without touch, oxygenation levels are actually higher than baseline. Perhaps those infants whose bradycardia was preceded by touch also already had border-line adequate cardiorespiratory function and were therefore more vulnerable to the added external stress from caregiving interventions. Those crises would appear to be the prevent-able ones if we could reliably predict when an infant's autonomic controls were depleted and unable to respond to further challenge from the environment.

As we accumulate larger data files, we plan to analyze more specific and complex interactions of type of touch with infant activity state and physiologic parameters. We trust our perseverance will reward our original goal to document and apply infant response signals in support of optimal neurolog-ical and behavioral outcomes following premature birth.

Discussion: Chapter 8

Susan Rose: What first made you think that the nursery environment might be responsible for problems like apnea and bradycardia?

Peter Gorski: When I was studying with Dr. Brazelton and consulting in the nursery at the Boston Hospital for Women, I was asked to see a particular baby who was having a lot of apnea and had not responded to pharmacologic intervention or physical stimulation. I simply observed the baby in the caregiving environment for a day. Then, thanks to the nurses' records of when the baby was having apneic and bradycardic episodes, I noticed that the episodes clustered around the times when the health care team made rounds at the begin-ning and end of each day. I asked them to divert rounds from that particular baby's isolette, and the number of apneic spells plummeted to near zero.

Susan Rose: What was it about rounds that caused the apnea?

Peter Gorski: There was a huge increase in the noise and activity level. The group would go right up to the isolette, and a few people might lean on it to see if the baby was really responsive. A few minutes later, there would be an apneic episode.

This time lag is very important. Babies often respond minutes after an intervention with disorganized breathing or heart rate. Because the response is not necessarily immediate, its direct relationship to prior intervention is not always obvious.

The point is not that we need to worry every time we approach or handle a premature baby. I think we can develop some predictive capacity to know when an infant can make use of our efforts.

Seymour Levine: May I ask a naive question? Is there such a thing as a healthy premature infant, or are "healthy" and "premature" mutually exclusive categories?

Peter Gorski: Some preterms, even those born two or three months before term, are phenomenally healthy, meaning that they require minimal support.

Seymour Levine: But even a "healthy" premie who requires minimal support does not have the more fully developed regulatory mechanisms that a full-term infant would use to modulate environmental events.

Peter Gorski: Absolutely. Preterm infants do show disordered regulation. They are responsive to our support efforts, but unfortunately the response may come in the form of disorganized behavior or outright catastrophic physiological events.

Seymour Levine: Your data show that a lot is happening to the infant very quickly, very intensively. A lot of caregiving goes on in a short period of time. These bursts of activity represent a dramatic change from the background stimulation level. The preterm infant may not have the autoregulatory system to deal with sudden change, sudden increases in stimulation. Gradual-onset stimulation is a very different kind of thing.

T. Berry Brazelton: If premies are already at a stress level, which I think Peter's data show us that they are, then even a small increase in stimulation might push them into disorganization.

Stephen Suomi: Peter, I'm concerned about Baby 9, the one in your sample who had so much bradycardia. Let's assume you can find some predictors of bradycardia and apnea, at least for most of your population. What about the exceptions—the babies whose reactions are different? Shouldn't we be paying attention to them?

Peter Gorski: Exactly, Steve. I think that's the opportunity available through our way of analyzing. It allows you to individualize your clinical response to the infant.

T. Berry Brazelton: Are you coming up with any behavioral indicators of individual reactions? Our nurses find that after they get to know an infant—using the four developmental lines of the Brazelton Neonatal Assessment Scale (BNAS) (autonomic, social, attentional, and motor) to guide their observations—they can predict from the baby's external behavior whether a stimulus is positive or negative. Sometimes they know just from the look on the baby's face.

Peter Gorski: The BNAS categories you mention have been very useful to us. In very immature babies, autonomic changes seem to reflect the infant's energy level and organization level. I think next we see changes in motor behavior. An infant who responds to any sensory or tactile stimulation with a long period of jerky, uncontrolled movement is wasting a huge number calories. The baby's energy is being depleted. You can see the loss of facial tone, expressing fatigue, and autonomic exhaustion is not far behind.

Much closer to term, attention capacities and the ability to sustain alert states for a relatively long time do seem to be markers of physiological stability. A preterm infant, however, is much more vulnerable autonomically at forty weeks conceptional age than is a full-term newborn, who can coordinate the physiologic, motor, state, and interactive capacities that your scale defines for us. Sometimes, when you have a preterm baby who can finally alert and watch you, you can actually cause a bradycardic or apneic episode, and I have done so on occasion. The costly effect of social interaction can easily overburden the nervous system.

T. Berry Brazelton: You seem to be on the verge of a breakthrough in finding reliable behavioral–observational indicators that we can use to back up our clinical intuitions, which to me is very exciting.

Peter Gorski: I hope that at least we are beginning to offer a systematic approach to observing the caregiving environment and the infant's simultaneous behavioral and physiological responses. Eventually, of course, we want not only to be able to observe interactive events but to anticipate the infant's response and intervene supportively.

T. Berry Brazelton: I'm especially eager for behavioral indicators of problems in these fragile babies because we are sending them home so much earlier than we used to. Sometimes the parents work to get organized, attentional behavior from the baby, and right afterward the baby collapses. We're trying to train nurses, who can then train parents, to look for the hyperalertness and other signs that precede exhaustion.

Peter Gorski: In talking with parents about this problem, we try to put things in a positive way. We explain that an exciting stimulus—pleasant as well as unpleasant—may overwhelm a baby with low energy levels. The child may be so excited by interaction with the parents that it's more than the nervous system can handle. We don't want parents to feel that they're bad for the child or that the child is rejecting them, and we don't want them to be afraid to approach the baby at all. They simply need to understand how taxing social interaction can be for a weak infant.

References

Cornell, E. H., & Gottfried, A. W. (1976), Intervention with premature human infants. *Child Develop.*, 47:32–39.

Dreyfus-Brisac, C. (1970), Ontogenesis of sleep in human prematures after 32 weeks of conceptional age. *Development. Psychobiol.* 3/2:91–121.

Gorski, P. A., Hole, W. T., Leonard, C. H., & Martin, J. A. (1983). Direct computer recording of premature infants and nursery care: Distress following two interventions. *Pediatrics* 72:198–202.

Gottfried, A. W. (1981), Environmental manipulations in the neonatal period and assessment of their effects. In: *Newborns and Parents: Parent–Infant Contact and Newborn Sensory Stimulation*, ed. V. L. Smeriglio. Hillsdale, NJ: Lawrence Erlbaum, pp. 55–61.

———Wallace-Lande, P., Sherman-Brown, S., King, J., Coen, C., & Hodgman, J. E. (1981), Physical and social environment of newborn infants in special care units. *Science*, 214/6:673–675.

High, P. C., & Gorski, P. A. (1985), Womb for improvement—Recording environmental influences on infant development in the intensive care nursery. In: *Infant Stress Under Intensive Care*, eds. A. W. Gottfried & J. L. Gaiter. Baltimore: University Park Press.

Lawson, K., Daum, C., & Turkewitz, G. (1977), Environmental characteristics of a neonatal intensive care unit. *Child Develop.*, 48:1633–1639.

Martin, R. J., Herrell, N., Rubin, D., & Fanaroff, A. (1979), Effects of supine and prone position on arterial oxygen tensions in preterm infants. *Pediatrics*, 63/4:528–531.

Scarr-Salapatek, S., & Williams, M. L. (1973), The effects of early stimulation on low-birthweight infants. *Child Develop.*, 44:94–101.

9
Effect of Tactile and Kinesthetic Stimulation on Weight Gain of Premature Infants

Patricia B. Rausch, R.N., M.S.N.

The problems of the prematurely born infant can include unstable temperature regulation due to decreased body fat, and inadequate respiration due to immature lung tissue. Feeding difficulties are frequent due to the immature gastrointestinal tract and a poor sucking reflex.

Research efforts have been focused upon these and other difficulties which are encountered by the premature neonate and which often result in death. In 1960, Kulka began extensive research to determine the effects of stimulation upon infant weight gain. Her theory states that a kinesthetic drive developmentally predates the oral drive, and is satisfied by means of stroking, fondling, cuddling, swaying motions, and rocking (Kulka, Fry, and Goldstein, 1960).

This research was conducted to determine the effect of a ten-day regimen of tactile and kinesthetic stimulation on caloric intake, stooling, and weight in small premature infants.

Method

SAMPLE

Infants selected from the study weighed 1000 to 2000 g at birth, were appropriate in birth weight for gestational age, were between twenty-four and forty-eight hours of age when the first treatments were administered, and had not been intubated with an endotracheal tube. Infants who were intubated anytime during the next twelve days postbirth were excluded from the study. Informed consent was obtained from the parents and the pediatrician of the infant.

The sample consisted of forty infants divided equally into a treatment and a control group. The first twenty infants who were admitted to the nursery after a prespecified date and who met the selection criteria were assigned to the treatment group. After the selection of the twentieth treatment infant, a historical control group was selected as follows. Hospital charts of premature infants were evaluated in reverse chronological order, beginning with the first infant born prior to the birth of the first treatment infant. The first twenty infants who matched the treatment infants on weight, gestation, sex, race, and ability to breathe spontaneously comprised the historical control group (see Tables 9.1 and 9.2).

TABLE 9.1

Distribution of Subjects Based on Race and Sex

	Control		Treatment	
	Male	Female	Male	Female
White	5	7	5	7
Black	4	4	4	4

PROCEDURE

The treatment group and the historical control group were cared for according to the nursery routine in the study

TABLE 9.2
Distribution of Subjects Based on Weight

Infants Whose Birth Weights Were From:	Control	Treatment
1900–2000 g	5	5
1800–1900 g	4	4
1700–1800 g	1	1
1500–1600 g	2	2
1400–1500 g	4	4
1300–1400 g	3	3
1000–1100 g	1	1

hospital. This routine is as follows: Feedings are given every two to three hours via nasogastric tube or bottle, depending upon the overall condition of the infant. Infants who are fed in incubators are handled during bottle feedings, but virtually no handling occurs during nasogastric tube feedings. Vital signs (temperature, pulse, and respiration) are recorded every one to two hours, again depending upon the overall condition of the infant. Bedding changes are made as needed. Parental visiting is encouraged. Parents may touch their infants as frequently as they wish. Frequency, duration, and character of parental visitation are logged on daily records.

The care of the treatment group differed as follows. The tactile kinesthetic treatment regimen was given for fifteen minutes each day for ten days beginning on the day of admission to the study. The treatment was given each morning and only when the infant was in a wakeful state and receiving no therapy or feeding. The infants remained in their radiant warmer beds or incubators during the treatments. The treatments consisted of three five-minute phases. The first and third phases consisted of five one-minute phases. The first minute consisted of gentle rubbing of the infant's neck. Each five-second period of that minute contained one gentle stroke across the infant's neck. The second minute contained gentle rubbing of the infant's back or chest, depending upon the baby's position. Each five-second period of that minute contained one gentle stroke from the neck to waist. The third minute contained gentle rubbing of the infant's legs. Each five-second period of that minute contained one gentle stroke from thigh to foot. The fourth minute contained gentle rubbing of the infant's arms. Each five-second period of that minute contained one gentle stroke from shoulder to hand. The fifth minute contained gentle rubbing of the infant's head. Each five-second period of that minute contained one gentle stroke from forehead to ear.

The second phase consisted of five one-minute parts. The first part consisted of gently flexing and extending the infant's right arm. Each five-second period contained one flexion and one extension. The second part consisted of gently flexing and extending the infant's left arm. The third part consisted of gently flexing and extending the right leg, the fourth part consisted of gently flexing and extending the left leg, and the fifth part consisted of gently flexing and extending both legs simultaneously.

The researcher maintained a daily log in which weight, stooling, and caloric intake were recorded for each infant.

Results

The Multiple Analysis of Variance (MANOVA) and Analysis of Variance (ANOVA) were performed initially and significant differences were found for each dependent measure. The Duncan's Multiple Comparisons Test was then performed. Data were separated into ten parts that represent the ten days of the study period.

The mean weight of infants in the control group was 1516 g on Day 1 and 1468 g on Day 10, a weight loss of 48 g. The mean weight of infants in the treatment group was 1561 g on Day 1 and 1586 g on Day 10, a weight gain of 25 g. The weight gain of the treatment group over the ten-day period was 73 g greater than that of the control (see Figure 9.1), but the difference was not statistically significant ($p < 0.0001$).

The mean feeding intake on Day 10 was 193 ml for infants in the control group and 282 ml for infants in the treatment group (see Figure 9.2). The mean feeding intake of infants in the treatment group on Day 10 was 89 ml greater than that of the control group. A statistically significant increase was found in the intake of the treatment group on Days 6 through 10 ($p < 0.0001$).

The mean frequency of stooling for infants in the control group on Day 1 was 2.60. The treatment group had a mean stooling frequency of 2.75 on Day 1. By Day 10 the control group had a stooling frequency of 2.95, while the treatment group had a stooling frequency of 6.20 (see Figure 9.3). Significant differences were found in the frequency of stooling in the control and treatment groups ($p>0.004$).

Conclusions

These data suggest that compensatory tactile and kinesthetic stimulation treatments improve the clinical course of premature infants. Although there was no conclusive statistical evidence of weight gain being effected by the stimulation treatments, the weight gain of infants in the treatment group was greater than that of the control group by the end of the study period. The mean weight of the treatment group on Day 1 of the study period was 46 g heavier than the mean weight of the control group on the same day. However, by Day 10 of the study period, the mean weight of the treatment group was 117 g heavier than the mean weight of the control group on the same day. These data suggest that a statistically significant difference in the weight gain of the treatment group over the control group might have been revealed had the weights been studied for longer than 10 days (see Figure 9.1).

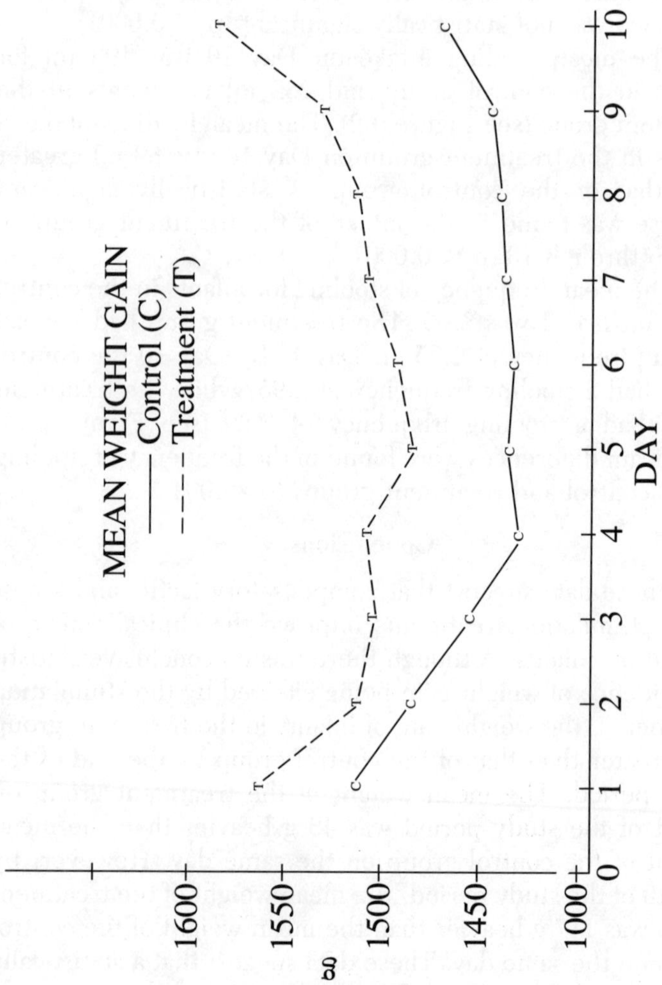

FIGURE 9.1
Mean weight gain.

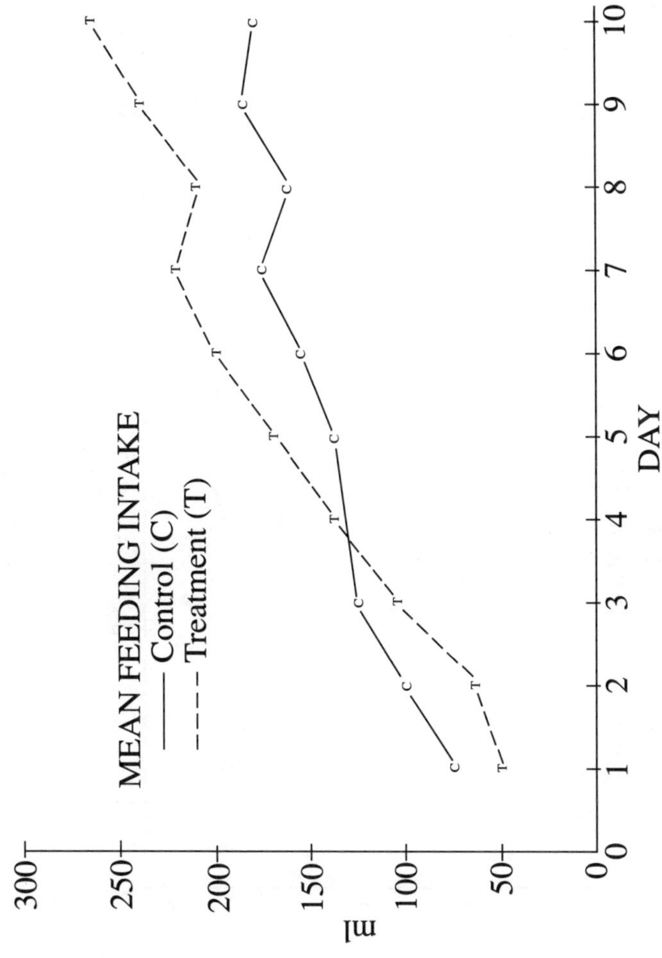

FIGURE 9.2
Mean feeding intake.

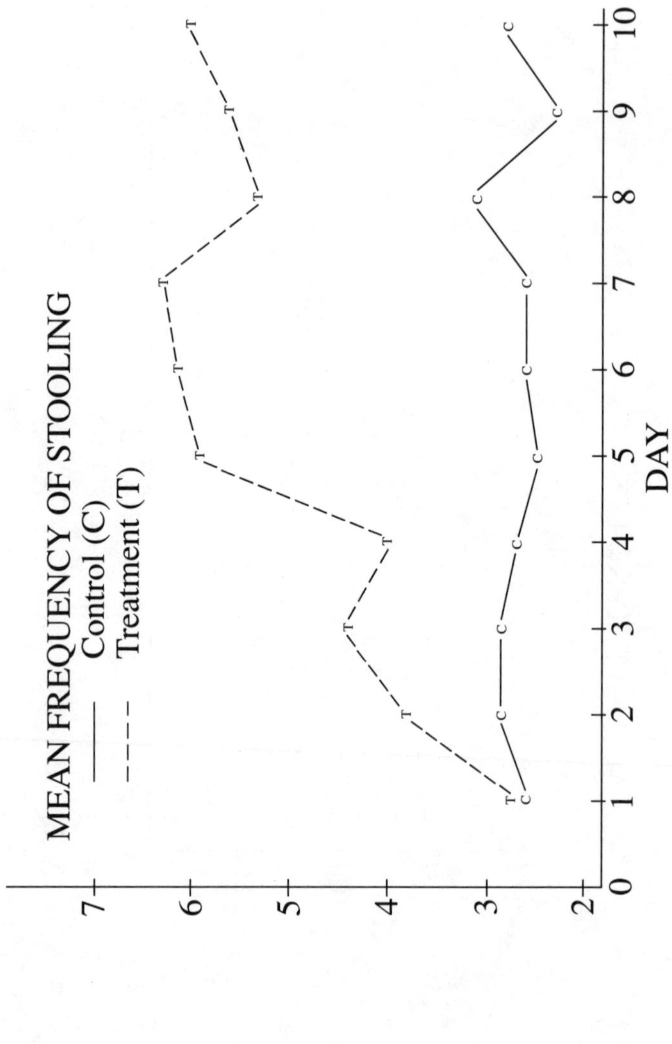

FIGURE 9.3
Mean frequency of stooling.

There was conclusive statistical evidence that the feeding intake of the premature infants was affected by the stimulation treatments. Although this effect is only statistically realized on Days 6 through 10 of the study period, it must be emphasized that by Day 2 of the study period, the treatment group had increased its mean feeding intake by 40.75 ml over the previous day, while the control group had increased its mean feeding intake by only 21.1 ml over the previous day. A statistically significant increase in the feeding intake of the treatment group was realized only on Day 6 of the treatment. By that time, the treatment group had increased its mean daily feeding intake by 158.4 ml from Day 1 of the study period, and the control group had only increased its mean daily feeding intake by 83.15 ml from Day 1 of the study period.

Logically some of this increased stooling frequency was related to the increased feeding intake. However, it is important to note that statistically significant differences occurred a day *earlier* in stooling frequency than in feeding intake. This finding supports the proposal that tactile–kinesthetic stimulation, one of the components of the stimulation inherent in maternal–newborn interaction, improves feeding ability through vagal stimulation which promotes peristalsis and expulsion of waste products, thereby decreasing gastric retention and abdominal distention. Sucking, another component of caregiver interaction, also appears to result in vagal stimulation and does result in improved gastrointestinal function and clinical course in premature infants.

Recommendations

Although this research identified areas in which a stimulation treatment has positive effects upon the clinical course of premature infants, long-term effects of the treatment have yet to be studied. The effects of treatments that are continued for longer than ten days also remain to be investigated. How this stimulation treatment may affect motor, social, or cognitive development remains to be explored. Since it is generally assumed that increased physical stimulation increases the activity of the heart and lungs, it would be advantageous to examine the morbidity and mortality of infants who have been exposed to the stimulation treatments in terms of respiratory or cardiac complications.

The stimulation procedure was explained to parents of infants in the study prior to their granting permission for their infants to participate. It would be interesting to examine whether or not this experience affected the relationships that eventually developed between parent and child.

Implications

Overall, this study identified a means by which nurses or other caregivers could positively affect the clinical course of prematurely born infants. The stimulation treatment requires a brief, daily period of time during which a nurse or other caregiver devotes attention strictly to a single infant. The stimulation treatment would ideally be administered by the infant's parents. This contact would be a positive contribution that the parent could make toward the infant's clinical course.

The sleep patterns of such young infants are not dependent upon the evening hours. Therefore, nurses or caregivers who attend the infants during the night would be able to administer the stimulation treatments at a time when there are fewer distractions from visitors and other personnel. Not only would the infant benefit in ways previously described, but the nurse or caregiver would have the special opportunity to touch and fondle each infant and become familiar with him or her as a unique individual.

The mortality and morbidity of premature infants has decreased with advanced technology. However, increased technology has caused the environment of the premature infant to become more mechanized. Continued research in the area of infant stimulation supports the importance of early parental contact. The parent can be reintroduced into his child's environment by being given the opportunity to provide stimulation that will positively affect the infant's clinical course.

Discussion: Chapter 9

Allen Gottfried: Did your touching and movement regimen seem to soothe the babies? Did it make them feel relaxed and comfortable?

Patricia Rausch: Yes, but not always at first. At the beginning of the treatment, some babies would startle and cry. It was a very individual matter—some were more sensitive than others.

Michael Merzenich: Where do premature infants seem to want to be touched, by behavioral sign? Do they seem relatively indifferent to touch in some places and more sensitive in others?

Patricia Rausch: I've found that babies tend to calm more when there is stimulation on the belly and back. It seems to be more "right now."

T. Berry Brazelton: In performing the stimulation, were you sensitive to the baby's reactions? Did you try to synchronize your own rhythm with that of the baby?

Patricia Rausch: We tried not to vary our behavior much in responses to the baby because we wanted our procedures to be repeatable. In a clinical situation, I would be much more inclined to adjust my behavior to the baby's.

Anneliese Korner: It is difficult to know whether to attribute the effects of the program to the tactile or the kinesthetic stimulation, is it not?

Patricia Rausch: Yes, it is. Frankly, the reason I included the kinesthetic procedures was that I was afraid tactile stimulation alone would not produce an effect.

Peter Gorski: Pat, I think so well of your cause that I worry about the methodological oversights in this particular study. They undercut the strength of your findings. In addition to the problem Anneliese just mentioned, some of your outcome measures are open to criticism. You need to demonstrate not just weight gain but meaningful weight gain because, as you know, premature babies are very prone to fluid overload. I think protein metabolism consumption is a much more compelling measure of utilization of intake than stooling frequency or intake volume.

Patricia Rausch: On the very last day of my study, I learned something else that will affect the outcome measures I choose next time. I had finished the last treatment on the last baby, and as I began to walk away from the bed a respiratory therapist came by and remarked, "Oh, you're all done—what a pity. This baby's going to have bradycardia now, and apnea." I said, "What?" and she said, "Yes, I've been observing that a few minutes after you do these treatments, the babies have bradycardia and apnea." Obviously, I did not look at that in this study, though I wish I had.

Kathryn Barnard: In a study by Schaffer, she put her hand on the infant's abdomen four times a day for twelve minutes each time, and one of her findings was an overall increase in apneic episodes in the infants she touched. Because of that, when one of my graduate students wanted to try gentle touch with the preterms recently, I suggested she keep track of the babies not only while she was touching them but for half an hour afterwards. Sure enough, there was absolutely no apnea while the hand was on the belly, but in the next thirty minutes there was a lot. It is as if the cutaneous stimulation serves as an organizer for the system, and when it is removed the system goes through a period of extreme disorganization.

T. Berry Brazelton: Touch is not only a cutaneous system but a sort of motor control system, too. If you have an agitated baby and you put a hand on her, she's likely to quiet.

Patricia Rausch: Yes. Touch has an encasing quality, which goes back to the uterus.

Stephen Suomi: Do conditions that simulate the intrauterine environment offer optimal stimulation for preterms, in your opinion?

Patricia Rausch: Absolutely. I wish we knew more about exactly what the infant experiences in utero, and what we can do to simulate it. We need to remember that these babies who are born early are would-be fetuses; they are prepared to live in the uterus, not the intensive care nursery. Putting a gown over the bed for one hour out of every three, as Berry said they do in his nursery, I think is wonderful (though it could also be a problem, since we need to watch skin color and things like that). If we could leave an infant in an environment that was dark all the time, there's no telling what we might accomplish.

Allen Gottfried: I'm not at all sure that's the direction intervention should take. Although some programs have tried to simulate the uterine environment (often by using sound, such as the mother's voice or heartbeat), many others have been based on the axiom that the preterm infant is sensorially deprived. They often offer multimodal stimulation and "enrichment"—a mobile in the incubator, for instance. The rationale behind this approach is that the infant is a very different organism after birth than before, and a visual environment that is dark all the time is no longer appropriate.

William Greenough: As we were saying earlier, there is an order to the development of sensory systems. Vestibular, olfactory, auditory, visual—the exact sequence depends on the species. Some central resource—maybe attention, maybe a metabolic process—may be devoted sequentially to these systems. Multimodal interventions might actually overload the central resource so that each of them would develop more poorly.

Allen Gottfried: That was the thrust of much research in the 1940s, 1950s, and 1960s. It may explain why so much emphasis is now being placed on touch.

T. Berry Brazelton: Pat, I particularly like the fact that one aim of your stimulation program was to model behavior that could be passed on to parents. I am very much in favor of involving parents with their preterm infants, and we've known for a long time in our work that parents learn a great deal from watching someone with skills like yours interact with the baby.

I have one warning, though. A long time ago, Marshall Klaus and John Kennell introduced parent rooming-in in their nursery, but Marshall told me that most parents were so anxious that they couldn't stand to spend a full twenty-four-hour period with their baby at the hospital. This made me aware that encouraging contact may not be helping parents the way we want it to. Our efforts to get parents into the premie nursery was meant to counteract some of the grief and anxiety, to give parents a chance to work through it before taking the baby home.

We began to watch parents in our own nursery. We would suggest they do something with the baby and they would do it, but they did it with their eyes closed, or squinting, or with their faces all screwed up. Our timing wasn't right for them, obviously, and they were just performing for us.

Anneliese Korner: For many parents it's very important to be encouraged to be in touch with the baby, but I think we have to be careful not to expect this of everyone. We have to respect a parent's individual response to our encouragement.

Patricia Rausch: We felt that the opportunity to give tactile stimulation helped our parents along. At least it got them to the place where they could say, "Watch what the baby does when I do this."

Pat LaGruea has done some work on touching and parental grief in parents whose preterm infants die, Berry. She's found that grieving lasts considerably longer after the death if the parents have not had the opportunity to touch the baby. Sometimes the parents never come to terms with the fact that the baby has been born and has died. When there has been tactile contact, the parents show a less extended period of disorganization.

Allen Gottfried: A study based on interviews with parents whose infants had died showed exactly the same thing. The parents said they felt they had missed out on a very valuable experience if they had not been able to touch that baby and verify its existence.

Patricia Rausch: We are even encouraging parents to make contact with the baby following death, if they have not had that opportunity earlier. We encourage them to prepare the baby for the morgue, and to go through a very ritualistic scene. It's tremendously heart-wrenching, but it has proven to make the experience a beautiful one instead of the reverse, which we're all too familiar with.

Susan Rose: Returning to your idea that the encasing quality helps quiet babies, Pat, do you know whether swaddling reduces the incidence of apnea?

Patricia Rausch: I don't know. Swaddling a high-risk preterm, who has an I.V. and perhaps is on a ventilator, would be an interesting chore.

Kathryn Barnard: I'm not sure it would be wise to swaddle a preterm who is already at risk in terms of the musculature for breathing. They may do better with full range of motion.

Anneliese Korner: Ultrasound tapes of fetuses show that they are moving a great deal, and they move very similarly to the way preterms do. To restrict that movement for any length of time might not be good—which doesn't mean one shouldn't swaddle a premie when he's very agitated, just to calm him down.

Sandra Weiss: Conceptually, there seems to be a link between swaddling infants to calm them and what we do with neuropsychiatric patients who are demonstrating uncontrolled behavior that is threatening the safety of themselves or others. The procedure of wrapping these patients firmly in sheets calms them within minutes, as if serving to reduce the irritability of the nervous system and reorganize cognitive function. The potential effects of such generalized tactile experience, even through nonhuman contact, merit further research in infant, children, and adult groups.

References

Kulka, A. C., Fry, S. T., & Goldstein, F. J. (1960), Kinesthetic needs in infancy. *Amer. J. Orthopsychiat.*, 30:562–571.

10
The Many Faces of Touch

Anneliese F. Korner, Ph. D.

Touch, contact, and the sensations associated with tactile and cutaneous stimulation are all-pervasive in everyday existence, both in interaction with the inanimate environment and in human intercourse. To study the effects of these forms of stimulation is difficult indeed, because they are rarely, if ever, experienced in pure form. Invariably, the experience of touching or being touched is associated with other forms of stimulation. Almost inseparable from touch are proprioceptive, vestibular, and/or kinesthetic stimulation. Touch often has a temporal pattern or rhythm, varying in frequency and in duration. The effects of touch or contact are frequently associated with those of warmth or coolness, softness or firmness, wetness or dryness, containment, pressure, and texture. Contact can be imparted gently or roughly. Moreover, touch or contact are frequently concurrent with, pre-

Acknowledgments: Preparation of this paper was supported by Grant MH36884, Department of Health and Human Services, Prevention Research Branch, National Institute of Mental Health. The author's research reported in this paper was supported by the William T. Grant Foundation, the Distribution Fund, the Maternal and Child Health Research Division of Clinical Services, PHSDHEW No. MC-R-060410, and Grant RR-81 from the General Clinical Research Center's Program of the Division of Human Resources, National Institutes of Health.

ceded, or followed by visual, auditory, or olfactory experiences. Because of this admixture of different forms of stimulation, it is difficult to assess reliably the effect of touch alone.

This problem is well illustrated by many intervention studies with preterm infants (see review by Cornell and Gottfried [1976] on this subject). Many of these studies purport to assess the effects of contact or of handling on the behavior and development of preterm infants, even though in most of these studies different forms of stimulation were provided simultaneously. Studies by Hasselmeyer (1964), Powell (1974), and Rice (1977) are good examples. Hasselmeyer (1964), who was one of the first to undertake an intervention study with preterm infants, assessed the effects of extra "handling" on the behavior of preterm infants. She used prescribed ways of stroking each baby's head, neck, cheeks, and chin; sat the infant up in order to rub his back, swaddled him, held him close, and rocked him for extended periods of time. Thus, the infants not only were touched, they experienced containment, vestibular and proprioceptive stimulation, and the upright. In the process, they were undoubtedly also given visual and auditory stimulation. Powell (1974) included in her handling procedure, feeding, holding, and touching imparted to one group by nurses, and to another by mothers. Rice (1977), in her study of the effects of tactile–kinesthetic stimulation on the neurophysiological development of premature infants, used stroking and massaging the infant's entire body in a caudocephalic progression, rocking, holding, cuddling, caressing, talking, and looking at the infants and attempting to get them to establish eye contact. Other investigators deliberately and explicitly set out to provide multimodal sensory stimulation to preterm infants plus a variety of other interventions. A study by Scarr-Salapatek and Williams (1973) is an excellent example. During their stay in the intensive care nursery, the infants in the experimental group were provided with tactile stimulation through extra handling and rocking. These infants were talked to, fondled, exposed to mobiles of crib birds, and to human faces. After discharge from the hospital, the experimental group was visited by a social worker at weekly intervals; the mothers were given instructions as to how to provide stimulating child care, games to play, and were given mobiles, wall posters, rattles, picture books, and other materials.

It is noteworthy that these and most other intervention studies involving extra handling seem to produce beneficial effects which include better weight gain, greater sensory responsiveness, diminished irritability, and a higher developmental status in the infants of the experimental groups. However, with the great admixture of different forms of stimulation provided, it is very difficult to attribute these benefits primarily to "handling," touch or contact. To do so is to engage in a common fallacy: we all tend to see only what we are looking at, and we tend to attribute effects primarily to those things we deliberately set out to do.

In our experimental soothing studies with full-term newborns (Korner and Thoman, 1970,1972), Evelyn Thoman and I became keenly aware of how difficult it is to separate the effects of contact from other less visible, more hidden forms of stimulation. In these studies, we wanted to find out what forms of stimulation were most effective in soothing newborns. In imitating various maternal ministrations, we found, not surprisingly, that one of the most effective interventions with crying newborns was to pick them up and hold them close to the shoulder. What we did not anticipate at all was that this intervention, in addition to promptly soothing the infants, almost invariably made them bright-eyed and alert, and led them to scan about.

The reason we got excited about this observation was that here we predictably produced a state, which many investigators of newborns feel is the one most conducive to the earliest forms of learning. While in two studies we were able to produce the state of visual alertness through this maneuver in

75 percent of all trials, it should be stressed that newborns show this state spontaneously only very infrequently (Wolff, 1966).

As a result of this unexpected finding, we became curious as to what exactly produced both the soothing effect and the visual exploratory behavior. Was it mostly the body contact provided, which, in this instance, involved cutaneous, tactile, and possibly olfactory stimulation, as well as containment and warmth? Or was it vestibular–proprioceptive stimulation and the activation of the antigravity reflexes which mostly produced the effect? To answer this question, we embarked upon an experimental study in which we tested the relative efficacy of body contact and all that is subsumed under this type of stimulation and of vestibular–proprioceptive stimulation (two forms of stimulation which can never be completely separated), with and without the upright position in soothing and in evoking visual alertness in infants. These types of stimulation were given singly and in combination in the context of what mothers commonly do with their infants. The following six interventions were made in random order with forty crying, normal newborns, equally divided into males and females, breast- and bottle-fed infants.

1. The infant was lifted from the examining table and put to the shoulder, head supported (vestibular–proprioceptive, upright, and contact stimulation).
2. The infant was lifted horizontally and cradled in arms in the nursing position (vestibular–proprioceptive and contact stimulation).
3. The infant was embraced and held close. In this position, great care was taken not to move the infant in any way (contact only).
4. The infant, who had previously been placed in a supine position in an infant seat, was raised to an upright position (upright and vestibular–proprioceptive stimulation).

5. The infant, lying supine in the infant seat, was moved to and fro horizontally as if in a perambulator (vestibular stimulation only).
6. The infant was talked to in a high-pitched voice, simulating mother-talk. The voice was used as a marker as to when to observe, after a preliminary study had shown that the voice elicited no more alerting than occurred spontaneously, without any intervention (none of the above forms of stimulation).

The results of this study clearly indicated that the interventions entailing vestibular–proprioceptive stimulation evoked significantly more alertness than did contact. Vestibular–proprioceptive stimulation combined with contact clearly produced the strongest effect. However, contact alone had no greater effect than hearing a high-pitched voice, which we previously had found not to have a greater effect on alerting than would have occurred by chance.

Very similar results were seen regarding the soothing effects of the interventions. Maneuvers that entailed vestibular–proprioceptive stimulation soothed the infants more promptly than contact alone, but contact by itself was at least a better soother than the voice.

We were struck by a number of implications of these findings. We were not aware until then that when mothers pick up their crying babies, they not only soothe them, but they provide them with a variety of visual experiences. I also was struck by the fact that in the literature, body contact has been stressed as a most fundamentally important form of stimulation for early development and that the importance of vestibular–proprioceptive stimulation, which is a by-product of almost any body contact between mother and child, had largely been overlooked.

In subsequent studies, we replicated several of these findings in different contexts (Thoman and Korner, 1971; Gregg, Haffner, and Korner, 1976). In one of these studies

(Thoman and Korner, 1971) we set out to investigate the differential effects of contact and of vestibular–proprioceptive stimulation on the *development* of rat pups. We randomly assigned nineteen litters of newborn rats into three groups:

1. reared under standard laboratory conditions;
2. swaddled snugly for ten minutes per day for the first fourteen days of life (Figure 10.1) shows how the rat pups were swaddled. As can be seen, these rat pups not only were snugly contained in cotton, they also had a good deal of contact with each other.
3. Swaddled identically as above and slowly rotated on a noiseless drum for ten minutes a day for the first fourteen days of life. To avoid habituation, the pups were rotated for forty-five seconds each minute, with fifteen seconds nonrotation interspersed at random intervals.

We used Sprague-Dawley multiparous females who, for two weeks prior to impregnation, were handled or gentled every day. This was done because Thoman and Levine (1969) had previously found that merely disturbing the nest produced a significant "early experience effect" on the pup, which, apparently was mediated through the mother. By using multiparous mothers and gentling them first, we could be more certain that the effects produced were a function of the stimulation given and not merely a product of the nest being disturbed.

The results of this study showed that contact had *some* developmental effects, but, with vestibular–proprioceptive stimulation added, the effects were much more pronounced. At fifteen days the rotated group had the highest percentage of eyes fully opened. Next was the swaddled group, with the control group having the lowest percentage. At twenty days, both the swaddled and the rotated groups showed significantly more exploratory behavior on a visual cliff test than the

FIGURE 10.1
Swaddled rat pups.

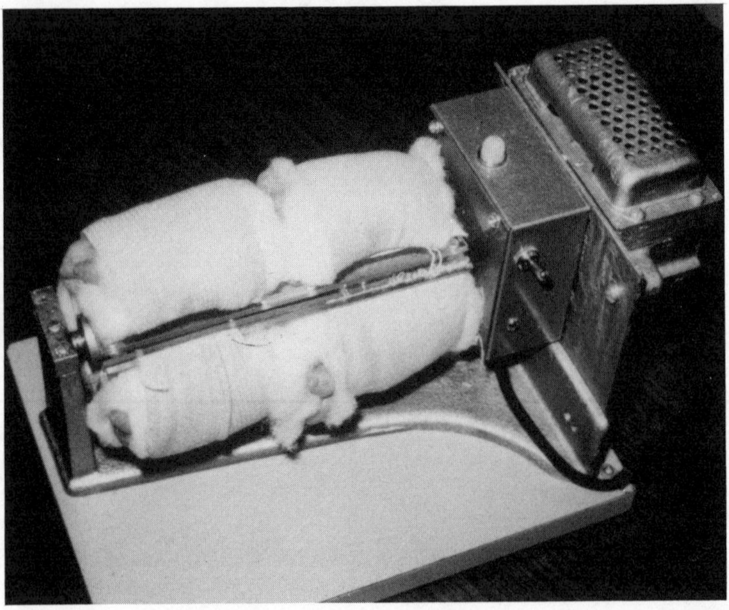

FIGURE 10.2
Swaddled and rotated rat pups.

control group. At weaning, the rotated group was significantly heavier than the swaddled and the control groups. The weight of the swaddled group was almost identical with that of the control group.

Considering the evidence from our studies, I began to feel increasingly that it might be beneficial to provide compensatory vestibular–proprioceptive stimulation to preterm infants who experience a great deal of this type of stimulation prenatally, and who are largely deprived of it when growing to term in incubators. The rationale for this type of intervention was not only based on the results of our own studies, but was underscored by different reports in the animal literature which suggested that deprivation of movement stimulation may lead to developmental deficits. For example, Erway (1975), whose work focuses on otolith functions in mice, concluded from this work that "deficiency of vestibular input either for reasons of congenital defect or for lack of motion stimulation, may impair the early development and integrating capacities of the brain, especially that of the cerebellum" (p. 20). Mason's work (1968, 1979) with primates and dogs underscores this conclusion, pointing to the fundamental importance of movement stimulation for the intactness of early development. Like Harlow, Mason isolation-reared infant monkeys on surrogate mothers. While Harlow produced highly abnormal monkeys who engaged in autisticlike, self-mutilating, and rocking behavior as a result of these rearing conditions, Mason, by providing isolation-reared monkeys with *swinging* surrogate mothers, offset the most severe developmental deficits typically seen in Harlow's monkeys. Mason also found that by providing movement stimulation to young monkeys, he produced more visual exploratory behavior in these infants than in controls. The beneficial results of intervention studies with preterm infants by Freedman, Boverman, and Freedman (1966), Neal (1967), and Barnard (1972), all of which used vestibular–proprioceptive stimulation, further supported our rationale.

The most gentle way I could think of providing compensatory vestibular–proprioceptive stimulation was through waterbed flotation. My goal of providing a flotation environment to preterm infants was not to *accelerate* their development, but to create conditions that might facilitate the natural unfolding of these infants' brain maturation, and that might enhance their physiologic, neurologic, and behavioral functioning.

In developing our infant waterbeds back in 1972, I had no illusion that we would be providing vestibular–proprioceptive stimulation in pure form. I realized that, at a minimum, we would, in addition, provide cutaneous stimulation, softness, slight containment, and in many instances warmth and exposure to the temporal pattern of maternal biological rhythms. We built waterbeds that could be used in one of three ways: A plain waterbed that is highly responsive to the infant's own movements and the movements generated by the caregiver; a waterbed that gently oscillates either continuously or intermittently. The oscillating waterbed is otherwise identical in design and consistency with the nonoscillating waterbed. Figure 10.3 shows the waterbed and the oscillator.

The waterbed was adapted to all the intensive care contingencies. Plastic flaps on the side of the waterbeds provide anchor points for restraining the infants as needed. The thermal environment created by the waterbeds has been thoroughly investigated in collaboration with the Thermal Engineering Department at Stanford. Because the waterbed is just above the incubator heater, its temperature is maintained at 2 degrees Centigrade above the ambient temperature inside the isolette. The waterbed thus helps the temperature regulation of very small preterms who are kept in very warm incubators. When used outside the isolette, or when the incubator is set at low temperatures, half an inch of foam is used to insulate the waterbed from the baby. This, according to our thermal experiments, results in a heat loss no greater than that of the incubator mattress. Between uses, the

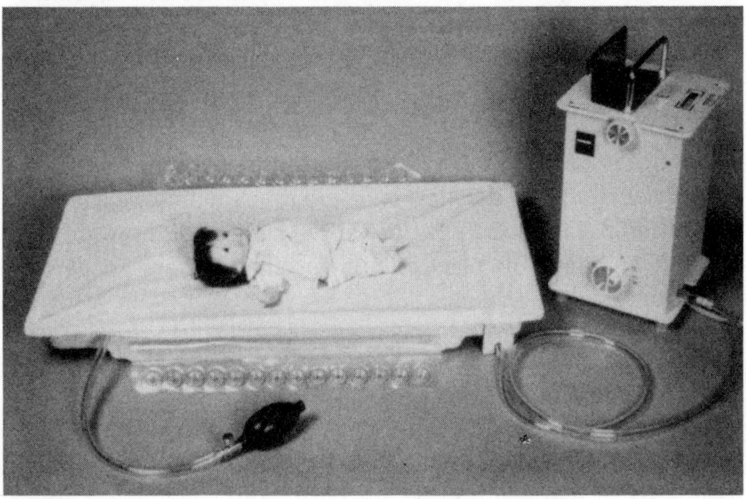

FIGURE 10.3
Preterm infant waterbed.

waterbeds are gas autoclaved. Algecide and blue dye are added to the water. The blue dye is designed to alert the caregiver in the event of a leak. This has occurred only three times in the eleven years the waterbeds have been used, and was caused by hypodermic needles which accidentally penetrated the waterbag. Blue was chosen so as not to be confused with urine, emesis, or blood. Repeated cultures of the water inside the vinyl bag have been negative even after continuous use for more than a month.

In deciding on the kinds of oscillations to be provided, I had to address all the issues one typically faces when setting up an experimental study involving stimulation. Direction, rise time, waveform, and the frequency and amplitude of oscillations all had to be decided upon. In making these decisions, I tried to avoid arbitrary choices, as is done most frequently in experimental studies. Instead, I made every effort to make choices that might have some clinical, biological, or experiential relevance.

I thus decided on head-to-foot oscillations because several studies in the literature suggested that the direction of this motion may benefit the infant's respiratory effort. Because the infant may be exposed to these oscillations for long periods of time, we decided on oscillations which measure no more than 2.4 mm in amplitude at the surface of the waterbed without an infant in place. These oscillations are so gentle, they can barely be seen.

In deciding on the frequency or the rhythm of the oscillations, I felt that it was safest to provide a temporal pattern of a maternal biological rhythm, because such a rhythm would probably not interfere with the developing organization of the infants' own biological rhythms and would expose the infants to a rhythm they would have been exposed to, had they not been born prematurely. I was influenced in this decision by Dreyfus-Brisac's (1974) hypothesis that perhaps one reason why the behavior and sleep of preterm infants is so fragmented is that these babies are deprived of the regulatory influences of maternal biological rhythms. That such influences may exist is suggested by the work of several investigators such as Sterman (1967), Jeannerod (1969), Hofer (1975, 1976), and by Bertini, Antonioli, and Gambi (1978). Sterman and Jeannerod independently showed a strong relation between maternal sleep stages and intrauterine fetal activity. In the light of this evidence in the literature, we thought that oscillations in the pattern of a maternal biological rhythm might enhance the infant's functioning. We thus chose the continuous oscillations to be slightly irregular, and to be in the rhythm of average maternal resting respirations in the third trimester of pregnancy (Goodlin, 1972). For the intermittent oscillations, we chose the rhythm of the basic rest–activity cycle as described by Klietman (1969).

Before I summarize the results of our research with the waterbeds, I would like to mention that whenever, during the last eleven years, we received requests for a waterbed from medical personnel, it was not for the potential benefits of the vestibular–proprioceptive stimulation, but for providing the infant with the *soft contact* of the fluid support system. We have had many requests for the nonoscillating waterbeds for very small preterm infants in order to preserve these babies' fragile skin. To objectively document the effects of the waterbeds on the skin of these small infants, we arranged a collaboration with a pediatrician specializing in infant dermatology. However, it soon became clear that virtually nothing was known about the skin of young preterm infants, so that objective comparisons between a treated and nontreated group could not be made. We frequently receive requests for older babies who have disseminated herpes or other severe skin diseases. The medical staff also finds the fluid support system useful for infants recovering from abdominal surgery, as these babies cannot be turned over, and for infants who are on a regimen of parenteral nutrition for severe emaciation. Waterbeds have also been requested for infants with spina bifida, hydrocephalus, and other conditions in which pressure points to the skin or to the skeletal structure are to be avoided. The most frequent requests have come from nurses concerned with the development of oblong, flat heads so commonly seen in preterm infants. It has been shown in a number of studies that the soft, fluid support of the waterbed reduces the incidence of oddly shaped heads in preterm infants (Kramer and Pierpont, 1976; Marsden, 1980; and Korner, unpublished).

And now, a brief summary of our studies which involved, in addition to contact with a soft surface, the vestibular–proprioceptive stimulation provided by the oscillations of the waterbed.

Study I

Our first study (Korner, Kraemer, Haffner, and Cosper, 1975) was designed to test whether changing the infants' environment on a twenty-four-hour basis by placing them on waterbeds was a safe procedure. Twenty-one relatively healthy preterm infants, ranging in gestational ages between twenty-seven and thirty-four weeks, were randomly assigned to experimental and control groups. The groups did not differ significantly from each other in birth weights or gestational age. The infants in the experimental group were each placed on a continuously oscillating waterbed before they were six days old, where they remained for one week. The data were collected from the nurses' and physicians' daily progress notes, from which the clinical progress of the two groups was compared. Results of this study showed that none of the infants' vital signs were significantly affected by the waterbed, nor did weight changes or the incidence of emesis differ in the two groups. However, we found one highly significant, totally unanticipated difference between the two groups: the infants in the experimental group had significantly fewer apneas as indicated by the apnea alarms.

Figure 10.4 compares descriptively the mean daily frequency of apneas starting with a baseline average for the first

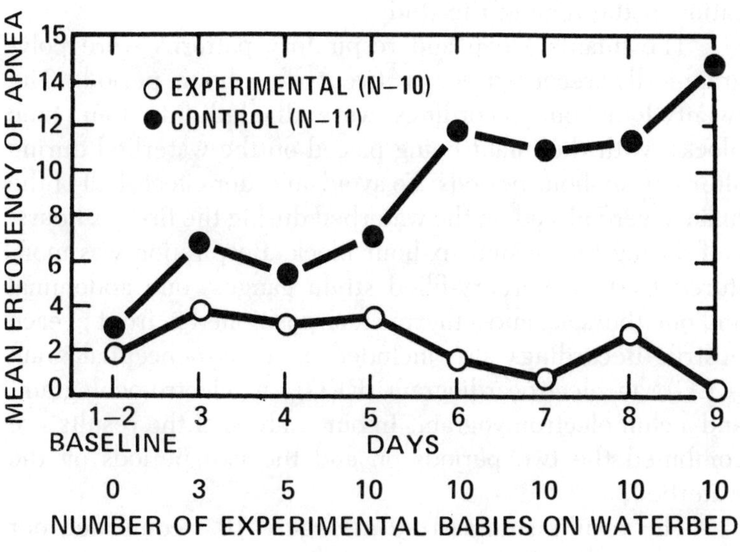

FIGURE 10.4

Comparison between experimental and control groups in mean daily apnea incidence.

two post-natal days. The difference at the start was not significant between the two groups. However, after the babies in the experimental group were put on the oscillating waterbed, the incidence of their apneas tended to drop whereas it continued to increase in the control group.

Study II

The next question was, of course, could this finding be replicated? Christian Guilleminault, with his team from the Stanford Sleep Disorder Clinic, and I decided to put this question to the test by collaborating in a polygraphic study of eight infants who were preselected for having apnea of prematurity (Korner, Guilleminault, Van den Hoed, and Baldwin, 1978). These infants' gestational ages ranged from twenty-seven to thirty-two weeks. None were on any medication at the time of the study.

The infants' sleep and respiratory patterns were polygraphically recorded for a twenty-four-hour period. The twenty-four-hour recordings were divided into four time blocks, with the infant being placed on the waterbed during alternate six-hour periods. To avoid an order effect, half of the infants were placed on the waterbed during the first six hours, half during the second six-hour block. Respiration was monitored by two mercury-filled strain gauges, one abdominal and one thoracic, and a thermisteor positioned in front of each nostril. Recordings also included an electroencephalogram (EEG), an electrocardiogram (EKG), an electro-oculogram, and a chin electromyogram. In our analysis of the results, we combined the two periods on and the two periods off the waterbed.

The results summarized in Figure 10.5 confirmed our previous finding that apneas were significantly reduced while the infants were on the oscillating waterbed. All types of apneas were reduced, short ten-second ones, long ones, central, and obstructive ones. The most consistent reduction occurred in the types of apnea which were significantly

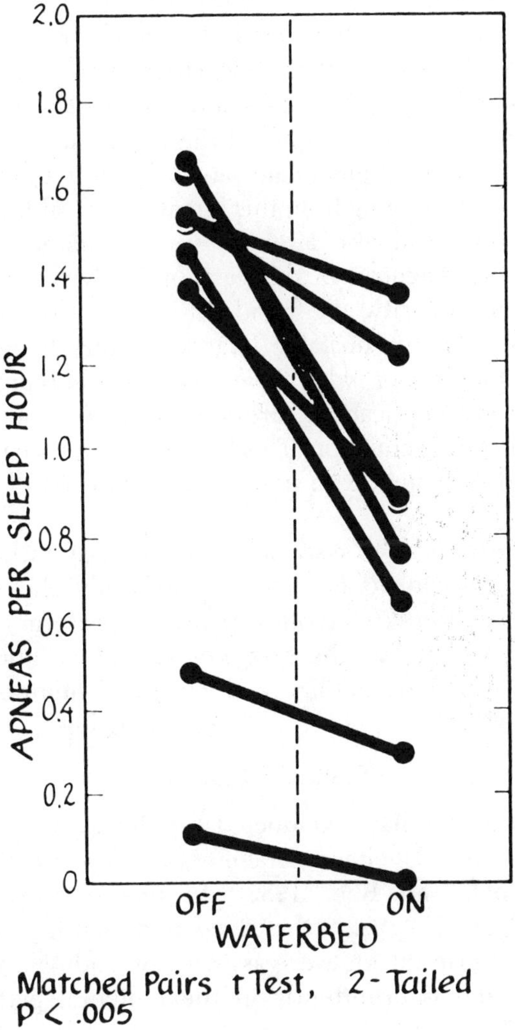

FIGURE 10.5
Apnea monitor alarms per sleep hour, off and on the oscillating waterbed.

reduced in our previous study, namely those that were sufficiently long to trip the monitor alarms.

As shown in Figure 10.6, the most severe types of apneas, as defined by their association with slowing of the heart-rate to below eighty beats per minute, also were sharply reduced, at least in seven out of the eight babies.

As can be seen, one infant ran completely counter to the general trend. Judging from this infant's medical history prior to our study, and also after he was discharged from the hospital, the diagnosis of this case probably was not one of apnea of prematurity. We found out later that this infant was not unique. Highly unstable infants who are being weaned from ventilators, or who have major cardiopulmonary or neurological complications, are not apt to respond to waterbeds with apnea reduction. This treatment approach thus may be limited to infants with uncomplicated apnea of prematurity.

We next began to systematically investigate what we had originally set out to do; namely, to study the effects of waterbeds on the *behavioral* responses of preterm infants. In particular, we studied the effects of this intervention on the infants' sleep and motility and on their neurobehavioral development.

Studies III and IV

To date, we have conducted two behavioral sleep and motility studies (Edelman, Kraemer, and Korner, 1982; Korner, Ruppel, and Rho, 1982). In one of these studies (Edelman et al., 1982), the sleep and motility of twelve healthy preterm infants were assessed on and off a waterbed that oscillated intermittently in the temporal pattern of a maternal biological rhythm, namely the adult rest–activity cycle. In the other study, seventeen theophylline-treated preterm infants were observed on and off a waterbed that provided continuous oscillations ranging between eight and ten per minute (Korner et al., 1982). That particular study

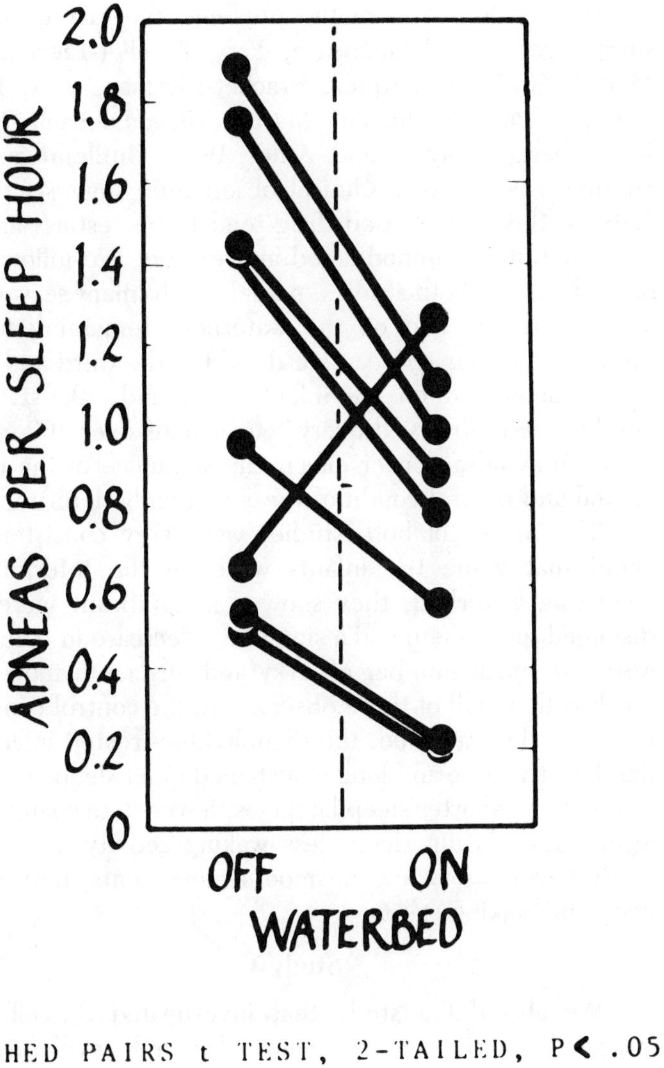

FIGURE 10.6
Apneas > 10 seconds per sleep hour with bradycardia below 80 beats per minute

was prompted by several reports in the literature that among the many side effects of theophylline, the infants' sleep is sharply reduced (Demarquez, Paty, Brachet-Lierman, and Martin, 1977; Demarquez, Brachet-Lierman, Paty, Deliac, Philippe, Paix, Babin, and Martin, 1978; Dietrich, Krauss, Reidenberg, Drayer, and Auld, 1978; Guilleminault and Souquet, 1979). Also, clinical observation suggests that infants on this widely used drug tend to be restless and that their motility is unmodulated and erratic. We followed the same design in both studies, namely each infant served as its own control on and off the waterbed, remaining in each condition for four consecutive days. On the third and fourth day in each condition, the infants' sleep and wake states and motility were observed every ten seconds over 100-minutes each. To avoid an order effect, the sequence of the experimental and control conditions was randomly determined.

The results of both studies were very consistent. We found that while the infants were on the intermittently oscillating waterbed, they showed a significant increase in sustained quiet sleep and a significant decrease in irritability. Also, the mean number of jerky and unsmooth movements was less than half of those observed in the control condition. While on the waterbed, the theophylline-treated infants had significantly more and longer sustained quiet sleep, also more active sleep, shorter sleep latencies, fewer state changes, less restlessness during sleep, less waking activity, and significantly fewer jittery and unsmooth movements, both during sleep and waking states.

Study V

We also did a study that investigated the effects of waterbed flotation on the neurobehavioral development of preterm infants (Korner, Forrest, and Schneider, 1983). The subjects, who were randomly assigned to experimental and control groups before they were four days old, consisted of infants who were all on ventilators for severe respiratory distress syndrome (RDS). To follow these infants in weekly intervals, we had to develop a longitudinal neurobehavioral assessment procedure that could be used with very small preterm infants and that had a sufficiently fine-grained scoring system to potentially discriminate between the groups. The subjects' gestational ages ranged between twenty-two and thirty-two weeks. Birth weights, gestational ages, and Apgar ratings at one and five minutes did not differ significantly between the groups.

Twenty infants were available for final evaluation when they were between thirty-four and thirty-five weeks postconceptional age. The birth characteristics of these babies were very similar to those infants who were originally randomly assigned to groups. All infants were removed from the waterbeds at least forty-eight hours prior to being evaluated. Dr. Tom Forrest, a pediatric neurologist, did not know whether the babies he examined belonged to the experimental or control group. Comparisons between the groups were made on the basis of thirteen cluster or summary scores.

The results showed that the infants in the experimental group performed significantly better in attending and pursuing inanimate and animate visual and auditory stimuli, demonstrated more mature spontaneous motor behavior, showed significantly fewer signs of irritability and/or hypertonicity, and were more than twice as often in the visually alert, inactive state. They also showed a greater number of optimal responses. In thirteen comparisons, four significant group differences and one borderline significant difference were well beyond what would be expected to occur by chance. This study, which we consider as highly preliminary because of its small sample size, composed of nothing but severely ill infants, nevertheless suggests that compensatory vestibular–proprioceptive stimulation as provided by waterbeds may enhance the neurobehavioral development of preterm infants.

Even though we are inclined to assume that it is the

compensatory vestibular–proprioceptive stimulation that is primarily responsible for benefitting the infants, we still do not know to what degree the soft contact with the waterbed contributes to the effects. Perhaps, a sleep and motility study now in progress will shed some light on this question. In that study, we will compare the sleep and motility of a large sample of healthy preterm infants on the incubator mattress, the nonoscillating and continuously oscillating waterbeds, and waterbeds that oscillate intermittently in the pattern of a maternal biological rhythm. By comparing the infants' sleep and motility on the incubator mattress with that on the plain waterbed, we may get an inkling as to whether the contact with the soft waterbed has an effect, even though the results will be confounded to some extent by the fact that the infants' movements and those generated by their caregivers will activate the waterbed from time to time. We certainly should know by the end of that study whether our waterbeds with programmed oscillations have a greater effect than the plain waterbeds, and, whether the intermittent oscillations provided in the temporal pattern of a maternal biological rhythm confer any advantage over the continuously oscillating waterbed in bringing about well-organized sleep and motility. If the latter is the case, the obvious next step would be to determine whether it is the maternal rhythm or the intermittency that conferred the advantage. This can readily be done by comparing the efficacy of the oscillations, using the maternal biological rhythm, with equally long intermittent oscillations generated at arbitrary intervals.

Intervention Studies Using Touch Alone

In concluding, I would like to briefly review three studies I have come across that have used touch in relatively pure form as an intervention with preterm infants. One of these studies is that by Kattwinkel, Nearman, Fanaroff, Katona, and Klaus (1975). Six apneic infants were first observed over a three-hour control period; during the next three hours, cutaneous stimulation consisting of rubbing the infants' extremities, was applied for five out of every fifteen minutes. Tactile stimulation produced a significant decrease in the frequency of apnea. This was true not only for the entire three hours during which the infants were stimulated, but also when the ten minutes after stimulation were compared to the corresponding ten-minute intervals during the preceding three-hour control period.

In another study by Shaeffer (1982), thirteen short gestation infants who were mechanically ventilated, received four, twelve-minute periods of touch for ten days. A nurse provided touch by placing her hands on the infants' head and abdomen. These subjects were matched with thirteen infants who had been in the nursery prior to the intervention study. The two groups were compared on eleven physiological variables. Over time, the experimental subjects had significantly higher hematocrit levels and required less oxygen (a borderline significant difference). On the other hand, these babies had more apnea than the retrospective control group. The idea behind this study is interesting indeed. However, the use of a retrospective control group makes the one significant finding of higher hematocrit levels in the experimental group somewhat questionable. There is probably no branch of medicine that is moving as fast as neonatology, so that the differences in hematocrit levels may purely be a function of differences in medical care.

One of the most promising studies using contact in relatively pure form is that of Scott and Richards (1979). Six infants served as their own control on and off lambswool pads alternating every twenty-four hours over a minimum of four days with cotton sheets. Lambswool pads not only provide softness, but also texture and, according to some New Zealand manufacturers, warmth when it is cold and coolness when it is warm. On the days when the infants were nursed on lambswool pads, they gained an extra 10 gm and they moved significantly less. Because the authors mentioned in their 1979 paper that they were conducting a study with a much larger sample, I contacted them. Unfortunately, I was unable to get any further information.

One of the most fascinating aspects of this study is how quickly its findings on a few babies have become integrated into preterm infant care. Whenever one goes into an intensive care nursery these days, one finds dozens of infants on lambswool or acrylic pads. There is a lesson to be learned from this. Ultimately, interventions that make a lot of common sense, that are not likely to do harm, but that are apt to do some good, and that can be implemented in a simple and inexpensive way, will be the ones that will find the most rapid and widespread acceptance in neonatal care.

Discussion: Chapter 10

T. Berry Brazelton: Anneliese, what comes to me out of your work is the beautiful layering of the effects you've examined. There is the improvement in state behaviors, and state is such an important control system in the baby. Increasing the baby's capacity to maintain an alert state is one of the most significant things you've done, as well as cutting off apnea at the bottom.

State organization really reflects the interaction of all the infant's sensorimotor and neurological systems. It cements them together, so to speak. I think what you've done with waterbeds is teach infants about utilizing inner state controls, which gives them a chance to build on that—to accept and learn from cognitive and social cues. When I first watched you working with the waterbeds and saw those babies you put on the beds settle down and begin to learn to manage state for themselves, and to become more effective as they gained mastery over state and motor responses in the process, it was really a breakthrough in my thinking.

Allen Gottfried: What do you think the variable facilitating the development of babies on waterbeds is? Do you think it's the soft touch or the almost imperceptible motion?

Anneliese Korner: Well, obviously I have placed my bets on vestibular stimulation. We are currently doing a sleep and motility study in which we compare the effects of the incubator mattress, a plain waterbed, a continuously oscillating waterbed, and an intermittently oscillating waterbed. If the plain waterbed has the same effect as the oscillating water bed, then the beneficial variable must be something about the soft, fluid support system. We will also try to find out whether intermittent stimulation is much more effective than continuous stimulation, as some animal researchers have suggested. If this is the case, we will do another study to find out whether it is the intermittency or the maternal biological rhythm that has the effect.

Stephen Suomi: Why does it have to be one or the other? Are we making artificial distinctions?

Allen Gottfried: Yes and no. Ecologically, it makes no difference: Stimulation of different types is confounded in nature. Scientifically, however, I think it is important to trace developmental effects to specific sources if possible.

Anneliese Korner: Perhaps I should mention that our medical personnel usually request waterbeds because of the soft contact they provide rather than for the potential benefits of vestibular–proprioceptive stimulation. They request them for tiny preterms in order to preserve these babies' fragile skin and for infants with disseminated herpes or other severe skin diseases. They also request them for infants who are recovering from abdominal surgery and cannot be turned over, and for infants with conditions such as spina bifida in which pressure points on the skin and skeletal structure are to be avoided. Most often of all, they request them because the beds seem to improve the shape of the oblong, flat heads so commonly seen in preterm infants.

T. Berry Brazelton: Our nurses ask for waterbeds for a particular kind of baby: The infant who gets severely out of control very quickly. On a waterbed, these babies begin to get contingent feedback, which is strongly reinforcing for state control and for other control systems.

Patricia Rausch: Anneliese, can you tell me how much a waterbed costs?

Anneliese Korner: Not yet. However, Browne Technology from Santa Barbara will soon produce these waterbeds and then they will become available for other investigators and for general use.

Peter Gorski: In the past, perhaps because the state of waterbed manufacturing had been so diverse, I have sometimes recommended that babies be removed from waterbeds, and they have had less apnea off the beds. Their movements improved, too.

T. Berry Brazelton: What kinds of babies were those?

Peter Gorski: The same babies you described: Babies who were having disjointed movements and were unable to inhibit their responses. I think the particular mattresses we were using gave a wave effect to the babies that enhanced their disorganization.

Anneliese Korner: We have never seen this with our types of waterbeds, probably because they cradle the baby slightly. All our controlled studies to date have shown that disjointed, tremulous movements are decreased on the waterbed. However, very unstable babies may be adversely affected by the waterbed or the oscillations with respect to apnea. It is primarily the fairly stable infants, the growing premies who still are showing some immaturity in terms of apnea, who are helped.

References

Barnard, K. E. (1972), *The Effect of Stimulation on the Duration and Amount of Sleep and Wakefulness in the Premature Infant*. Doctoral dissertation, University of Washington, Seattle. *Diss. Abstr. Internat.*, 33, 2167B. (University Microfilms No. 72–28, 573).

Bertini, M., Antonioli, M., & Gambi, D. (1978), Intrauterine mechanisms of synchronization: In search of the first dialogue. *Totus Homo*, 10/8:73–91.

Cornell, E. H., & Gottfried, A. W. (1976), Intervention with premature human infants. *Child Develop.*, 47:32–39.

Demarquez, J. L., Paty, J., Brachet-Lierman, A., & Martin, C. (1977), Traitement par la théophylline des apnées sevères du nouveau-né. Influence des taux sanguins de théophylline sur les résultats cliniques et sur le cycle veille-sommeil. Les Colloques de L'Institut National de la Santé et de la Recherche Médicale, Pharmacologie Périnatale. *Inserm*, 73:293–306.

———Brachet-Lierman, A., Paty, J., Deliac, M. M., Philippe, J. C., Paix, M., Babin, J. P., & Martin, C. (1978), Traitement préventif des apnées du prématuré par la théophylline: Etude clinique, pharmacocinétique, neurophysiologique. *Arch. Franc. Pediatr.*, 35:793–805.

Dietrich, J., Krauss, A. N., Reidenberg, M., Drayer, D. E., & Auld, P.A.M. (1978), Alterations in state in apneic pre-term infants receiving theophylline. *Clin. Pharmacol. & Therapeut.*, 24/4:474–478.

Dreyfus-Brisac, C. (1974), Organization of sleep in prematures: Implications for caretaking. In: *The Effect of the Infant on its Caregiver*, eds. M. Lewis & L. A. Rosenblum. New York: John Wiley.

Edelman, A. M., Kraemer, H. C., & Korner, A. F. (1982), Effects of compensatory movement stimulation on the sleep–wake behaviors of preterm infants. *J. Amer. Acad. Child Psychiat.*, 21/6:555–559.

Erway, L. C. (1975), Otolith formation and trace elements: A theory of schizophrenic behavior. *J. Orthomolec. Psychiat.*, 4:16–26.

Freedman, D. G., Boverman, H., & Freedman, N. (1966), Effects of kinesthetic stimulation on weight gain and on smiling in premature infants. Paper presented at the *Annual Meeting of the American Orthopsychiatric Association*, San Francisco.

Goodlin, R. C. (1972), *Handbook of Obstetrical and Gynecological Data*. Los Altos, CA: Geron-X.

Gregg, C. L., Haffner, M. E., & Korner, A. F. (1976), The relative efficacy of vestibular–proprioceptive stimulation and the upright position in enhancing visual pursuit in neonates. *Child Develop.*, 47:309–314.

Guilleminault, C., & Souquet, M. (1979), Sleep states and related pathology. In: *Advances in Perinatal Neurology*, Vol. 1, eds. R. Korobkin & C. Guilleminault. New York: Spectrum Publications, pp. 225–247.

Hasselmeyer, E. G. (1964), The premature neonate's response to handling. *Amer. Nurses Asso.*, 11:15–24.

Hofer, M. A. (1975), Infant separation responses and the maternal role. *Biolog. Psychiat.*, 10/2:149–153.

———(1976), The organization of sleep and wakefulness after maternal separation in young rats. *Develop. Psychobiol.*, 9/2:189–205.

Jeannerod, M. (1969), Les mouvements du foetus pendant le sommeil de la mère. *Com. Ren. Soc. Biol.* (Paris), 163, 8/9:1843–1847.

Kattwinkel, J., Nearman, H. S., Fanaroff, A. A., Katona, P. G., & Klaus, M. H. (1975), Apnea of prematurity. Comparative therapeutic effects of cutaneous stimulation and nasal continuous positive airway pressure. *J. Ped.*, 86/4:588–592.

Kleitman, N. (1969), Basic rest–activity cycle in relation to sleep and wakefulness. In: *Sleep Physiology and Pathology: A Symposium,* ed. A. Kales. Philadelphia: J. B. Lippincott.

Korner, A. F. (1975–1983), Unpublished observations.

———Forrest, T., & Schneider, P. (1983), Effects of vestibular–proprioceptive stimulation on the neurobehavioral development of preterm infants: A pilot study. *Neuropediat.*, 14/3:170–175.

———Guilleminault, C., Van den Hoed, J., & Baldwin, R. C. (1978), Reduction of sleep apnea and bradycardia in preterm infants on oscillating water beds: A controlled polygraphic study. *Pediatrics,* 61/4:528–533.

———Kraemer, H. C., Haffner, M. E., & Cosper, L. M. (1975), Effects of waterbed flotation on premature infants: A pilot study. *Pediatrics,* 56:361–367.

———Ruppel, E. M., & Rho, J. M. (1982), Effects of waterbeds on the sleep and motility of theophylline-treated preterm infants. *Pediatrics,* 70:864–869.

———Thoman, E. B. (1970), Visual alertness in neonates as evoked by maternal care. *J. Experim. Child Psychol.*, 10:67–78.

——— ———(1972), The relative efficacy of contact and vestibular stimulation in soothing neonates. *Child Develop.*, 43/2:443–453.

Kramer, L. I., & Pierpoint, M. E. (1976), Rocking waterbeds and auditory stimuli to enhance growth of preterm infants. *J. Ped.*, 88/2:297–299.

Marsden, D. J. (1980), Reduction of head flattening in preterm infants. *Develop. Med. & Child Neurol.*, 22:507–509.

Mason, W. A. (1968), Early social deprivation in the non-human primates: Implications for human behavior in environmental influences. In: *Environmental Influences,* ed. D. C. Glass. New York: Rockefeller University Press/Russell Sage Foundation, p. 70.

———(1979), Wanting and knowing: A biological perspective on maternal deprivation. In: *Origins of the Infant's Social Responsiveness,* ed. E. B. Thoman. Hillsdale, NJ: Lawrence Erlbaum, pp. 225–249.

Neal, M. V. (1967), The relationship between a regimen of vestibular stimulation and the developmental behavior of the premature infant. University Microfilms Inc., Ann Arbor, Michigan.

Powell, L. F. (1974), The effect of extra stimulation and maternal involvement on the development of low-birth-weight infants and on maternal behavior. *Child Develop.*, 45:106–113.

Rice, R. (1977), Neurophysiologic development in premature infants following stimulation. *Develop. Psychol.*, 13:69–76.

Scarr-Salapatek, S., & Williams, M. L. (1973), The effects of early stimulation on low-birthweight infants. *Child Develop.*, 44:94–101.

Schaeffer, J. S. (1982), The effects of gentle human touch on mechanically ventilated very-short-gestation infants. *Maternal–Child Nurs. J., Monograph 12,* 11:4.

Scott, S., & Richards, M. (1979), Nursing low-birthweight babies on lambswool. *Lancet,* 1/8124:1028.

Sterman, M. B. (1967), Relationship of intrauterine fetal activity to maternal sleep stage. *Exp. Neuro. Suppl.*, 4:98–106.

Thoman, E. B., & Korner, A. F. (1971), Effects of vestibular stimulation on the behavior and development of infant rats. *Develop. Psychol.*, 5:92–98.

———Levine, S. (1969), Role of maternal disturbance and temperature change in early experience studies. *Physiol. & Behav.*, 4:143–145.

Wolff, P. (1966), The Causes, Controls and Organization of Behavior in the Neonate. *Psychological Issues,* Monograph 17. New York: International Universities Press.

11
Perception and Cognition in Preterm Infants: The Sense of Touch

Susan A. Rose, Ph.D.

The word *touch* or its common synonyms, *feel* and *contact*, refer to a complex set of sensations which can be narrowly or broadly conceived. Although touch often refers to cutaneous sensations aroused by stimulation of receptors on the skin, sensations of the muscles and joints (proprioceptive sense) and sensations of movement (vestibular sense) are closely linked. Moreover, the unitary experience of touch is complex, encompassing as it does separate sensations of warmth, pressure, pain, weight, location, and so on (Stevens and Green, 1978).

Similarly, the roles imputed to touch encompass a broad, rich spectrum of phenomena. At the broadest level there is social touch (Kennedy, 1978) which treats the role of touch in promoting social bonds, attachment, and emotional integrity and explores the concomitant physical and physiological

Acknowledgments: Funds for the support of this work were provided by a Behavioral Sciences Research Grant from the March of Dimes Birth Defects Foundation and by Grant HD 13810 from the National Institutes of Health. The author would like to express her appreciation to Frances Goldenberg and Patricia Mellow-Carminar for their assistance.

changes induced by touch. Social touch is thus generally concerned with the effects of social deprivation and social stimulation. Since preterm infants spend their early days and weeks in the atypical environment of incubators and intensive care units, social touch may have special significance for them.

At another level, a more basic one, we can consider what touch tells us about the external world. Here, there are two aspects to distinguish, namely passive touch, which involves excitation of receptors in the skin and underlying tissue (Kenshalo, 1978) and active touch, which includes those modes of exploration in which the skin, joints, and muscles function together in obtaining information (Gibson, 1962).

Roles of Touch

Although Aristotle long ago classified touch as one of the five senses, its facets and functions remain ill-understood even to the present day. The richness and complexity of the total flow of stimulation involved in touch can perhaps best be illustrated by the roles imputed to this sense system in (1) promoting social and emotional functioning; (2) regulating physical and physiological development; and (3) guiding perception and exploration of the external world.

The characteristics of touch most thoroughly explored, at least with respect to infancy, are those related to social and emotional functioning. In recent years, the neonatal period has been considered primary in establishing appropriate social bonding between mother and infant: at both the animal and human level tactile contact with the mother has been considered to be of crucial importance in promoting normal mother–infant attachment (Spitz, 1946; Kaufman and Rosenblum, 1967; Bowlby, 1969). As is well known, infant monkeys raised by wire and cloth mothers favored the mother who provided contact comfort over the one providing simply nourishment (Harlow, 1958); moreover, separation of the infant monkey from its mother often leads to states of panic, grief, and mourning that closely resemble human reactions to loss (Kaufman and Rosenblum, 1967). It has been suggested that the provision for intimate contact between human mothers and their infants soon after birth enhances touching and cuddling and promotes a secure bond between the two; deprivation of this early interaction, as with neonatal separation, is thought to increase the incidence of inappropriate maternal behavior (Klaus and Kennell, 1976). It is interesting to note, in this context, that in many parts of the non-Western world infants are reared in extensive body contact with their caretaker. Lozoff and Brittenham (1979) noted that, among hunter–gatherers, such as the !Kung San, infants are carried or held more than half the day until the age of crawling. When carried they are kept in close body contact, being held either directly in the arms or in a sling or pouch which allows the infant to mold to the mother's body.

The preeminence of touch in many studies of behavioral, physical, and physiological development has also been notable. Animal studies by Levine (1960), Rosenzweig, Bennett, and Diamond (1971), and Denenberg (1975), among others, have demonstrated the considerable plasticity of the developing organism and indicated that lack of stimulation hinders development, whereas sensory enrichment or variation enhances development. In comparison with their nonhandled counterparts, handled rats have shown numerous anatomical changes, including heavier cerebral cortex, greater thickness of cortical tissue, and increased number of glial cells (Rosenzweig, Bennett, and Diamond, 1971). Both Levine (1960) and Denenberg (1975) have revealed a wide range of behavioral and concomitant biological effects from handling, such as increased exploratory behavior, improved learning (especially in aversive situations), reduced emotional reactivity, and various alterations in the response of the hypothalamic–pituitary–adrenal axis to stress.

Kennedy (1978) suggested that the contacts, hugs, and caresses between parents and their young offer a theme linking perceptual and social psychology. Following Montagu (1971) he noted that these contacts may exert a major influence on maturation of the central nervous system (CNS), "for the neonate of various species dies without these hugs, licks, and rubs, through failure of the autonomic system. Handling is important in gentling; grooming in social development; and a brisk toweling is standard veterinarian practice for aiding infant development in many species" (p. 295).

Research on the perceptual role of touch generally proceeds quite apart from research on its social role. As a perceptual system, touch is considered a sense system which transmits information about the external world. Traditionally, psychophysical methods of investigation have predominated in this area (Kenshalo, 1978) and, for the most part, interest has centered on detecting the causes of our rich array of sensory impressions, of isolating the mechanisms underlying our perception that we have touched or have been touched, of understanding why some sensations strike us as soft while others are rough, flexible, rigid, or sticky (Taylor, Lederman, and Gibson, 1973; Stevens and Green, 1978). Up until fifteen years ago or so, touch, along with pressure, pain, and temperature were all considered under the general rubric of cutaneous sensitivity, and tactile perception was concerned with the nature of the cutaneous sensations arising from stimulation (Gibson, 1962; Stevens and Green, 1978).

Today such perception, in which an immobile observer is stimulated by an external agent over which he has no control, is considered but one aspect of touch and has been dubbed passive touch. By way of contrast, active touch, in which sensations of the skin, joints, and muscles function together to lead to perception of object properties, is accomplished by virtue of the sensory feedback, gained through the freely exploring hand. Katz ([1925], cited in Krueger [1970]) noted that vibrations are produced when the hand is moved over a surface. He stressed the importance of movement in the perception of texture and found that perceptions of roughness and smoothness were better when the surface was felt actively rather than passively. Gibson (1962) made the same point for the perception of form and pointed out that active touch allows us to perceive corners and edges. Similar patterns of skin deformation, when imposed on a motionless individual, give rise only to rapidly changing sensations, not to a stable percept.

In conclusion, theoretical accounts of tactual perception suggest that social touch, passive touch, and active touch can be considered separately and that investigation of each will increase our knowledge of the various facets of "touch."

Passive Touch: Differences between Preterm and Full-Term Neonates

Throughout the years, there has accumulated compelling evidence that children born before term are at high risk for a host of developmental problems. They suffer significantly more handicaps in physical, emotional, social, and mental development (see review by Caputo and Mandell [1970]). Recent studies of the very young preterm have been concerned with the possibility that environmental factors may contribute to this risk. Some studies question the appropriateness of the quality and quantity of stimulation provided in the newborn intensive care unit, and indicate that the preterms' problems may be caused or exacerbated by the characteristic high intensities of light and sound present in their surroundings, or the lack of rhythmic day–night cycling, or perhaps the lack of contingent stimulation (Lawson, Daum, and Turkewitz, 1977; Gottfried, Wallace-Lande, Sherman-Brown, King, Coen, and Hodgman, 1981). Numerous other studies have sought to determine whether the preterm will benefit if changes are introduced in the quantity, quality, or patterning of stimulation present in this environment.

Somewhat less attention has been given to learning about the sensory organization and perceptual processing characteristic of the young preterm. Yet in order to understand how the environment can influence or shape the development of young organisms, it is important to understand what aspects of the environment he or she is capable of perceiving, and to what extent changes in the magnitude of that stimulation are related to changes in the magnitude of sensation (i.e., the perception of the stimulus).

It is for this reason that we decided to investigate the infant's sensitivity and responsivity to external stimuli. Our interest in using tactile stimuli stemmed from the significance imputed to this modality in development.

The first study was designed to investigate infants' responsivity to tactile stimulation and their ability to discriminate different intensities of such stimulation (Rose, Schmidt, and Bridger, 1976). These assessments were done when the preterm was close to term age (i.e., close to 40 weeks from conception). During sleep, infants were touched with plastic filaments of varying intensity while their cardiac and behavioral responsivity was monitored.

We observed twenty preterms and twenty full terms. The full-term infants were all healthy two- to three-day-old babies with five minute Apgar scores of nine to ten. All had been delivered vaginally, either by normal, spontaneous, or low forceps delivery and had had uneventful pre- and perinatal histories. The preterms had a mean gestational age at birth of around 33 weeks and a mean birth weight around 1660 g, with one-quarter of the sample weighing less than 1500 g. At testing (which took place just prior to discharge) their conceptional age averaged 38.5 weeks, their chronological age 5 weeks, and their weight 2324 g.

The tactile stimuli used were three plastic filaments of different diameters selected from the Semmes-Weinstein aesthesiometer. The filaments were those numbered 3.84, 4.56, and 5.46, the units being the logarithm of the bending force measured in milligrams. Any excess pressure exerted when pressing these filaments against the infant's skin is taken up in the bend. We followed the practice of stimulating the infants on the right side of the abdomen, applying a single filament five times in rapid succession so that the duration of the stimulation lasted for approximately 2.5 seconds; on control trials the stimulus was omitted altogether. Interstimulus intervals averaged 30 seconds, with trials beginning only when the infant was quiescent. If any spontaneous movements occurred during the intertrial interval, 30 seconds were allowed to elapse from that time. Trials were randomly arranged within blocks of five, with each block consisting of one trial with each of the three filaments and two control trials.

Infants were tested in a neonatal soundproof laboratory following the midmorning feeding. In this study, infants were tested only in the first epoch of active sleep. Sleep state was continuously monitored by behavioral observation and the infant was considered to be in active sleep during any sixty-second period with eyes closed, slow and rapid eye movements, irregular respiration, and variable motor activity (Anders, Emde, and Parmelee, 1971). In order to avoid periods of state transition, testing never began until the infant had been in active sleep for at least three minutes.

Analyses of the results revealed that preterms were considerably less responsive to tactile stimulation than were full terms. In fact, the preterms showed no significant heart rate response to any of the stimuli used here. By contrast, the full terms responded with significant heart rate acceleration to the two stronger filaments, 4.56 and 5.64 ($\bar{X} = 1.45$ bpm and $\bar{X} = 4.31$ bpm, respectively) and nearly significant acceleration to the milder 3.84 filament ($\bar{X} = 1.30$ bpm). Although the difference between the five-second prestimulus and five-second poststimulus heart rates consituted the basic measure of heart rate change used to index responsivity in this study, the striking failure of the preterm to respond was confirmed by supplementary beat-by-beat analyses of heart rate. No matter how the results were examined, there was simply no evidence of a cardiac response on the part of the preterm.

Behavioral responsivity was coded on a five-point scale (0–4) which reflected the number and vigor of limb and body movement. Although both groups gave a significant response to the strongest tactile filament (and only to that one), the preterms gave a decidedly weaker response than did the full terms ($\bar{X}=2.0$ and $\bar{X}=1.5$, respectively). Moreover, whereas full-term infants tended to respond with heart rate acceleration when they gave a behavioral response, a phenomenon reflected in a significant relationship between these two types of responsivity ($r=0.47$), preterms did not ($r=0.19$). The two types of responsivity actually seemed relatively independent in the preterm, as indicated by the low correlation obtained between motoric and cardiac responses.

In addition to the overall dampened responsiveness of preterms, the pattern of cardiac and behavioral activation that did occur appears to be different from that observed in full terms. In full terms, heart rate proved to be a more sensitive index of stimulus perception than behavior. Whereas full-term infants responded behaviorally only to the strongest stimuli, they responded with heart rate acceleration to weaker stimuli as well (Campos and Brackbill, 1973; Rose, Schmidt, and Bridger, 1978). Yet in preterms the relation was just the opposite: these infants showed no significant heart rate response to any of the stimuli, but did show a behavioral response to the strongest of the three. The heart rate response of the preterm remained smaller than that observed in full terms, even when behavioral responses were similar and involved large muscle movements. It remains unclear whether the lack of cardiac responsivity in preterm infants is related to their elevated basal (nonstimulated) cardiac rates, which tend to average thirty beats higher than those of full terms ($\bar{X}=155$ bpm and $\bar{X}=117$ bpm, respectively), threshold differences in sensitivity, or poor integration of autonomic and motor systems.

In a second study (Rose, Schmidt, Riese, and Bridger, 1980), the responsivity of full-term and preterm infants was examined over a longer period of time by continuing testing throughout the first sleep cycle, so that infants were tested in both active and quiet sleep. The infants, thirty preterms and thirty full terms, were drawn from the same subject population used in the first study and had similar medical and social backgrounds.

Several changes were introduced in the design of this study in an effort to enhance responding among the preterms. First, only the strongest stimulus (5.46) was used, since this was the only one which had evoked any response whatsoever from the preterms in the first study. Second, intertrial intervals were increased somewhat (to $\bar{X}=50$ sec). Third, control trials were interposed between successive stimulus trials, and the stimulus trials themselves were alternated between the right and left sides of the lower abdomen. These latter modifications were made to offset any possible response fatigue and to compensate for any lengthier refractory period that might exist among preterm infants.

Nonetheless, the results for the first epoch of active sleep were very similar to those found in the earlier study (Rose, Schmidt, and Bridger, 1976). Again, full-term infants responded with a significant cardiac acceleration to the stimulus, whereas preterm infants failed to respond ($\bar{X}=3.5$ bpm and $\bar{X}=1.6$ bpm, respectively). Again both groups had a significant behavioral response, but the preterm infant's response was weaker ($\bar{X}=1.3$) than the full-term infant's ($\bar{X}=1.8$), and the correlations between behavioral ratings and heart rate change scores were also weaker.

The results were quite similar in quiet sleep, that state in which eye movements are absent, respiration is more regular, and body movements are absent, except for isolated startles or jerks (Anders et al., 1971). Here too, full-term infants responded with a significant cardiac acceleration ($\bar{X}=5.0$ bpm). The response shown by preterms, although significant, was small, averaging only about one beat per minute. The behavioral responses were again significant for both groups, but significantly greater for the full term ($\bar{X}=1.5$) than the preterm ($\bar{X}=0.6$), as were the correlations between behavioral responsivity and cardiac change scores.

For the preterms, two aspects of risk, namely, birth weight and gestational age at birth, were correlated with cardiac responsiveness ($r=0.38$ and $r=0.22$, respectively, in active sleep, and $r=0.49$ and $r=0.39$ in quiet sleep). Thus, infants who were heavier and more mature at birth were more responsive during testing.

Active Touch: Differences between Preterm and Full-Term One-Year-Olds

Usually, information about the outside world does not arrive in such simple patterns of punctate tactile stimulation as those we used in our tests of passive touch. Instead, we generally experience rich and complex patterns of cutaneous stimulation, often combined with patterns of motion kinesthethically sensed. Gibson (1962) termed this type of excitation *active touch* and contrasted its exploratory nature with the merely receptive nature of passive touch. He argued that active touch is not simply a blend of two modes of sensation, kinesthesis and touch proper, but rather an exploratory movement used for isolating and enhancing "the components of stimulation which specifies the shape and other characteristics of the object being touched" (Gibson, 1962, p. 478). Whereas passive touch involves only the excitation of receptors in the skin and underlying tissue, "active touch involves the concommitant excitation of receptors in the joints and tendons along with new and changing patterns in the skin" (Gibson, 1962, p. 478).

We have carried out two studies investigating infants' use of active touch to gather information about the environment; in particular, about the shape of objects. In Study 1, we examined the ability of infants to recognize by sight objects they have experienced only by active touch (Rose et al., 1978). This ability to extract information about an object in one modality and transfer it to another is called cross-modal transfer.

In order to examine cross-modal transfer in infants, we adapted a paradigm commonly used to study visual recognition memory. In this paradigm, a stimulus is displayed for a period of visual inspection, then, the now familiar stimulus is presented simultaneously alongside a novel stimulus, for the infant to inspect them both. Typically, the infant shows a differential preference for the novel stimulus, providing evidence for recognition memory (Fagan, 1970). In adapting this paradigm, the stimuli were presented either tactually or orally during familiarization, and visually during testing. When the stimuli are presented in different modalities during familiarization and test, the occurrence of recognition memory demonstrates cross-modal transfer (Gottfried, Rose, and Bridger, 1977; Rose, Gottfried, and Bridger, 1978, 1981a, b, 1983).

We tested three groups of one-year-olds, twenty-eight preterms and sixty-six full terms, thirty-nine full terms with high socioeconomic status and twenty-seven with low socioeconomic status. The full terms had similar pre- and perinatal courses to those observed in our neonatal studies, but differed in terms of factors like parental education level, parental occupation, and living conditions. The preterm sample was also similar to those that had served in our neonatal studies and were from predominately lower socioeconomic backgrounds. Preterms were tested at twelve months "corrected age" (i.e., age estimated from expected date of birth).

Three cross-modal tasks were used in this study: one oral–visual and two tactual–visual. A different pair of objects was used in each task and members of a pair differed from one another primarily in terms of shape. In the oral–visual task, the stimulus was placed in the infant's mouth for familiarization, whereas in the tactual–visual tasks, it was placed in the infant's hand. If the infant did not spontaneously palpate the object, the experimenter moved it about in the infant's hand.

In each case, the experimenter shielded the object from the infant's view. During the familiarization period, one member of the stimulus pair was presented for thirty seconds; during the test period, the infant was shown both members of the pair, the familiar and the novel, for twenty seconds, and a comparison of the cumulative fixation to the two members of the pair served as dependent variable. At the end of the visual test period, the infant was permitted to reach for one of the paired test stimuli.

Analysis of the results revealed that preterms (and lower-class full terms as well) failed to show any evidence of cross-modal transfer whereas middle-class full terms showed significant transfer on all three tasks. In all three, the middle-class full terms looked significantly more at the novel as compared with the familiar stimulus, and reached significantly more for the novel as well. Their percentages of looking at the novel ranged from 56 to 67% (all p's < 0.05). By contrast, the scores for the other two groups ranged from 47 to 52% (all p's > 0.05).

These results indicate that middle-class full-term infants can gain knowledge about the shape of an object by feeling it and mouthing it, and they can make this information available to the visual system. They were able to do this after only thirty seconds (or less) of handling or mouthing the object.

Preterms, on the other hand, seemed not to know that the object they saw, explored with their hand or mouth and tongue is the same as the object they saw. Despite the fact that this is a period in life when infants are busily engaged in learning about the world around them by manipulating and exploring with their hands and mouth, preterms were having difficulty acquiring sufficient information in this fashion.

In Study 2 (Rose, Gottfried, and Bridger, 1979), we examined the possibility that, although unable to achieve cross-modal transfer, preterms might nonetheless be able to use the information available through active touch in learning about objects. Specifically, we were interested in the question of whether such active exploration would enhance visual recognition—whether the infant could obtain more information about the form of an object by both touching and seeing it than by seeing it alone.

The essential difference between the cross-modal procedure and this procedure is the type of familiarization or exploration the infant was permitted. In these studies we used four different familiarization conditions. In the visual condition, the infant was shown an object, and only visual inspection was permitted. In the visual–haptic condition, the infant was given the object so that he or she could see as well as actively manipulate and touch it. In the visual–haptic control condition the object was encased in a transparent box so that manipulatory activity was permitted but no tactual information about the object's shape was available. In the visual control condition the object was encased in the transparent box before being presented for visual inspection, as a check on whether such encasement compromised visual inspection. A different pair of objects was used in each task and members of the pair differed primarily in terms of shape. In all conditions, the familiarization phase lasted until the infant had accumulated twenty seconds of looking at the frontal perspective of the object.

In this study we included groups of six- as well as twelve-month-old preterm and full-term infants, and as in all our studies, preterms were tested at "corrected age."

Again, analyses revealed that preterms did not perform as well as full terms. Contrary to our expectations, manipulation turned out to impede rather than facilitate subsequent visual recognition. What is noteworthy here, however, is the finding that the negative effects of interference were accentuated in preterms. At twelve months of age, full terms achieved significant novelty scores in all conditions, ranging from 57 to 61%, even though the percentages were somewhat attenuated in conditions where manipulation was permitted during familiarization. Preterms, on the other hand, showed evidence of memory only in the two visual conditions ($\bar{X}$'s = 60 and 61%); their scores dropped to chance in the two conditions involving manipulation. In fact, at twelve months the performance of the preterm was strikingly similar to that of the younger full term. (The younger preterms had performed at chance level in all conditions.)

Overall, the preterms showed evidence of difficulty in perceiving passive touch and in effectively using active touch to explore their world. As neonates they proved relatively unresponsive to pressure exerted on their skin. At one year of age, they had difficulty using information available through active touch to visually recognize objects, and this was true whether the tactual exploratory activity was accomplished in the absence or presence of visual cues.

Social Touch: Fostering Development in the Preterm

Perhaps as a natural outgrowth of the animal studies, which seem to suggest that environmental influences can profoundly affect early development, various interventions have been introduced into the early care of the preterm. Such interventions are designed to enhance development. I do not want to review these studies in any comprehensive or exhaustive fashion since good reviews already exist (Cornell and Gottfried, 1976; Masi, 1979) but simply point out that many of the most effective interventions have involved tactual–kinesthetic–vestibular stimulation, and then briefly describe the nature and effects of our own stimulation program.

The rationale for most interventions seems to stem mainly from the view that birth before term deprives the infant of the regulatory influence of maternal biorhythms and of the tactual, vestibular, kinesthetic, and patterned auditory stimulation that characterizes the intrauterine environment (Rothchild, 1967; Dreyfus-Brisac, 1970). Thus the intervention studies have generally attempted to provide what may be considered compensatory forms of stimulation (Cornell and Gottfried, 1976). While some of the early studies have only small sample sizes and various methodological inadequacies, they nevertheless provide important leads for further research. At least temporary benefits have been noted in physical, neurobehavioral, mental, and motor development, and in the reduction of apneic episodes, with the most consistent improvements in perceptual and neurobehavioral functioning.

The majority of interventions have been initiated soon after birth and generally confined to the period before hospital discharge. Hasselmeyer (1964), who carried out one of the first such studies, found that infants who were given extra handling cried less and were more quiescent than controls. White and Labarba (1976) found that extra handling increased food consumption and weight gain, whereas Solkoff and Matuszak (1975) found that it resulted in higher scores on the Brazelton Neonatal Behavioral Assessment (BNBA). Scarr-Salapatek and Williams (1973) also reported higher scores on the Brazelton exam upon discharge, although the experimental infants in their study had been exposed to colored mobiles and talking as well as extra handling. In an earlier study, Solkoff, Yaffe, Weintraub, and Blase (1964) found that handling produced not only immediate effects, but higher scores on the Bayley test of motor development at eight months postdischarge (Powell, 1974).

Our own regimen of stimulation (Rose et al., 1980) consisted of a systematic program administered while the infants were in the intensive care unit. This program emphasized tactile, proprioceptive, and vestibular stimulation and incorporated, but to a lesser extent, some auditory and visual components as well. A regimen of gentle massaging and rocking formed the core of the intervention, which was initiated within the first two weeks after birth and was then administered daily, five days a week, for three twenty minute periods each day. In this tactual regimen the infant was massaged with the palmar surfaces and fingertips of one hand in a cephalocaudal sequence; head, shoulders, back, arms, legs, and feet. Each twenty-minute session was divided into thirds so the infant received stimulation while positioned prone, supine, and sitting. When the infant was well enough to be removed from the incubator, one of the sessions was replaced by rocking, in a rocking chair, to emphasize vestibular stimulation. All opportunities for direct visual contact and periodic talking were optimized. The regimen was terminated one or two days prior to discharge.

One of the major results of this intervention was an increase in the preterm infant's cardiac responsivity in active sleep (Rose et al., 1980). The intervened preterm, unlike the nonintervened, exhibited a significant cardiac response to tactile stimuli. In fact, the magnitude of the cardiac response actually approached that obtained from full-term infants. A second major result indicated that the effects of such early intervention may last for a long time; visual recognition memory was found to be enhanced when the infants were retested at six months of age (Rose, 1980). Whereas the control group of preterm infants failed to differentiate between novel and familiar test stimuli following brief amounts of familiarization, preterms who had received intervention during the early weeks of life showed significant novelty preferences on two of the three problems. In fact, here too, their performance was indistinguishable from that of the full terms. These results are congruent with those of several other investigators who have found that early handling affects visual exploration (White and Castle, 1964; McNichol, 1973; Siqueland, 1973).

Overall, however, the design of intervention programs is complicated by the fact that there is no compelling theoretical rationale for selecting any specific type, quantity, or patterning of stimulation. The issue is compounded by the fact that relatively little is known about the preterm's thresholds or capacities for sensory processing, a factor relevant to both designing an intervention program and assessing its effectiveness. Furthermore, with the exception of our study, I know of no study that included a full-term control group. Inclusion of such a control is of critical importance since it provides the norm against which the effects of intervention can best be assessed. And finally, we have practically no idea of the underlying mechanisms which might mediate the effect of the various interventions. While progress has been made, and there is indeed growing support for the efficacy of stimulation programs in changing behavior, the exact nature of these changes remains unspecified.

Touch: A Unique Role?

Although touch, whether passive, active, or social, clearly has important functions, it is not clear that it plays any sort of unique role in development. So, for example, deficits are reported during infancy in other facets of development as well, including neurobehavioral functioning (Kurtzberg, Vaughan, Daum, Grellong, Albin, and Rotkin, 1979); visual processing (Sigman and Parmelee, 1974; Sigman, 1976; Rose, 1980, 1983; Caron and Caron, 1981); auditory processing (Field, Dempsey, Hatch, Ting, and Clifton, 1979); and infant–caregiver interaction (Beckwith and Cohen, 1978; Goldberg, 1979). Similarly, while it has been reported that tactile intervention is effective, so are other modalities of intervention. For example, positive effects are found when the intervention is auditory (Katz, 1971; Segall, 1972), exclusively vestibular (Neal, 1968; Korner, Kraemer, Haffner, and Cosper, 1975), or a combination of both (Barnard, 1974).

In conclusion, it appears that the lags or deficits in the preterm's sensory functioning and information processing are found in various modalities; similarly, intervention in various modalities can influence the direction or path of development. Perhaps the deficits are more commonplace, pervasive, or severe in the tactual modality, but we do not know this. It may very well be that preterm infants have higher thresholds for external stimuli, slower rates of information processing, and poorer memory, and that these deficits are not modality specific; that is, do not depend upon the channel by which the information arrives. Only more research will tell us whether touch has a unique role in development.

Discussion: Chapter 11

T. Berry Brazelton: Susan, I especially like the idea of distinguishing between active and passive touch because to me it relates to the concept of state. In extreme states, such as crying or deep sleep, passive touch may add to an infant's ability to initiate and maintain control. Active touch, in contrast, acts as an alerter and as information. It helps the infant come to a receptive alert state and begin to process information.

The idea of differences in organization between preterms and full terms is also critical, I think. It takes preterms longer to develop organizational systems. They may get there, but the cost to them of reaching out for something complex like cross-modal transfer is very great. The fact that these problems are not modality-specific is important, too. Your intervention seemed to point out that perhaps any modality can provide fuel for organization, so to speak.

Susan Rose: I agree with you, Berry, that perhaps intervention in any modality can provide the "fuel for organization." That is a tantalizing idea, and one that is compatible with the results of many intervention studies. I'd also like to emphasize a point made in my chapter, that intervention studies should routinely begin to include full-term control groups for comparison.

Anneliese Korner: May I add to that? I think if we want to make comparisons with full-term infants, they should be older than the ones we usually study in the hospital. Recent evidence suggests that while two- to three-day-old full-term neonates differ greatly from preterm infants tested at term, the full terms begin to look more like the preterms when they are five days old. Behaviorally, the just-born full terms have a good deal more flexion and tone than they have at five days. In using just-born full terms as controls for preterms at term, we tend to forget that the full terms have just emerged from a very crowded environment and have gone through the birth process, with all its attendant physiological adaptations. Thus, five-day-old full terms may be more appropriate controls for preterm infants at term than the younger ones we usually study.

Susan Rose: That's a cautionary note. It suggests that the most valid comparisons may depend on our obtaining more knowledge about developmental processes in both preterms and full terms.

William Greenough: Gottlieb's idea that modalities develop better if they develop in sequence, might help explain the results of your intervention study, Susan—both the increased responsiveness to passive touch, which you expected, and the enhanced visual recognition skills at six months, which you didn't. Perhaps, at the time when cutaneous or somatosensory development would normally have been occurring in utero, your intervention helped the infant focus on that. Then later, with that development as a base, attention could be fully devoted to the visual modality.

Susan Rose: You mean the infants could more readily or efficiently devote their attention to exploring the visual world because our intervention had already facilitated development of the earlier-maturing somatosensory system?

William Greenough: The idea is based on the Turkewitz and Kenney notion of sequential development of modalities that I sketched out in my chapter.

Susan Rose: Although to my knowledge there is no evidence that fetuses can see, or that there is much to enchant them visually in utero, a lot of visual development goes on before birth. Turkewitz's work comes from a school that said infants are sensitive to proximal stimulation before they are sensitive to distal stimulation, such as vision or audition. While there is no doubt that the proximal systems develop before the distal ones, or that the somasthetic system becomes functional before the visual system prenatally, it is also clear that preterm infants are exquisitely sensitive to their auditory and visual world.

Allen Gottfried: Should intervention follow the same sequence as sensory system development?

Susan Rose: That's a very important empirical question. So many different types of intervention seem to bring about some sort of improvement, it is hard to know. Since many of these interventions do have a strong vestibular or tactile component, we may in effect be providing intervention in such a sequential manner.

William Greenough: Yes, that is my point.

Susan Rose: Alternatively, infants may self-select the stimulation that fits their stage of development. I think that some, like Turkewitz, might argue that preterms lack the multimodal contingencies available to normal infants, and that these are especially critical. For example, the preterm infant in the incubator often hears speech when no one is in sight. In this case, a good intervention would be one that built in the proper contingencies between modalities, so that if you're talking to a baby in the ICU, you're looking at her or touching her as well.

T. Berry Brazelton: Susan, you may be putting your finger on the biggest problem preterm infants have. There is a kind of disorganization at the base of their systems that interferes with learning and with adaptation to the environment. We have found essentially the same thing in our study of the face-to-face rhythms that mothers and babies develop when the babies are between three and five months old. At the age of five months plus forty weeks, preterms are very much like three-month-old full terms in the ways they interact and communicate with their mothers.

Susan Rose: I think you're describing something very similar to what we're seeing. At six and twelve months, preterms are slow, but if you give them more time to process the stimuli, they often perform like full terms. We've done some recent work on visual recognition memory that shows preterms can take in information, store it in memory, and retrieve it from memory, but they seem to need much more time to process and encode the original information.

T. Berry Brazelton: If you see the tactile modality as an organizer rather than just an information source, it would make a certain amount of sense to say that infants are learning by the tactile modality to organize themselves and then to pay attention. I think it's a very big job for preterm infants to get their systems working together—to establish basic rhythms of attention and withdrawal, sort of homeostatic systems. And it is very hard for people in the environment to learn those systems of the premie, because the keys we depend on in more organized infants just are not available.

Susan Rose: Studies that have used tactile, kinesthetic, or vestibular stimuli seem to have the most pronounced effect on development, but many other effective interventions have also been used—a heartbeat sound, for instance. I would like to suggest that these various interventions may be working through a common mechanism, perhaps having to do with improved state organization or greater regularity of state.

T. Berry Brazelton: Stability of state is one of the best markers of optimal development in prematures that we have.

Susan Rose: Many infants are discharged from the hospital while they are still unable to maintain stable states. I'm concerned about these babies. My hunch is that they are not in very good shape when they go home, and that follow-up studies will keep finding deficits.

T. Berry Brazelton: One reason we like to send them home is that our nurseries don't give them much opportunity to develop stable states. We certainly are not reinforcing them in any natural sort of way.

We ought to all have in our minds that prematurity, immaturity, central nervous system (CNS) insult, or any of the things that make for difficulties in getting going, do not stop costing a baby. Disorganization doesn't stop costing the baby after it's over. It costs for a long time afterward, and the fact that the baby can overcome it is what's remarkable. But a great deal of energy goes into the overcoming.

However, children beyond infancy who are growing up with state problems, cross-modal transfer problems, learning disabilities, and the like are dogged less by their deficits than by their poor self-image and expectation of failing. We need to provide an environment that reinforces their self-image and sense of competence. In the long run, deficits in these areas may be a lot more important than any organic problems.

References

Anders, T., Emde, R., & Parmelee, A., eds. (1971), *A Manual of Standardized Terminology, Techniques and Criteria for Scoring of States of Sleep and Wakefulness in Newborn Infants.* Los Angeles: University of California Los Angeles, Brain Information Service.

Barnard, K. (1974), The effect of stimulaton on the sleep behavior of the premature infant. *Communic. Nurs. Res.*, 6: 12–33.

Beckwith, L., & Cohen, S.E. (1978), Preterm birth: Hazardous obstetrical and postnatal events as related to caregiver–infant behavior. *Inf. Behav. & Develop.*, 1:403–411.

Bowlby, J. (1969), *Attachment and Loss*, Vol. 1. New York: Basic Books.

Campos, J., & Brackbill, Y. (1973), Infant state: Relationship to heart rate, behavioral responses and response decrement. *Development. Psychobiol.*, 6:9–19.

Caputo, D. V., & Mandell, W. (1970), Consequences of low birth weight. *Development. Psychol.*, 3:363–383.

Caron, A. J., & Caron, R. F. (1981), Processing of relational information as an index of infant risk. In: *Preterm Birth and Psychological Development*, eds. S.L. Friedman & M. Sigman. New York: Academic Press.

Cornell, E.H., & Gottfried, A.W. (1976), Intervention with premature human infants. *Child Develop.*, 47:32–39.

Denenberg, V.H. (1975), Effects of exposure to stressors in early life upon later behavioral and biological processes. In: *Society, Stress and Disease*, Vol. 2, ed. L. Levi. New York: Oxford University Press.

Dreyfus-Brisac, C. (1970), Ontogenesis of sleep in human prematures after 32 weeks of conceptional age. *Development. Psychobiol.*, 3:91–121.

Fagan, J.F. (1970), Memory in the infant. *J. Exp. Child Psychol.*, 9:217–226.

Field, T.M., Dempsey, J.R., Hatch, J., Ting, G., & Clifton, R.K. (1979), Cardiac and behavioral responses to repeated tactile and auditory stimulation by preterm and term neonates. *Development. Psychol.*, 15:406–416.

Gibson, J.J. (1962), Observations on active touch. *Psychol. Rev.*, 69:477–491.

Goldberg, S. (1979), Premature birth: Consequences for the parent–infant relationship. *Amer. Sci.*, 67:214–220.

Gottfried, A.W., Rose, S.A., & Bridger, W.H. (1977). Cross-modal transfer in human infants. *Child Develop.*, 48:118–123.

———Wallace-Lande, P., Sherman-Brown, S., King, J., Coen, C., & Hodgman, J. E. (1981), Physical and social environment of newborn infants in special care units. *Science*, 214:673–675.

Harlow, H. (1958), The nature of love. *Amer. Psychol.*, 13:673–685.

Hasselmeyer, E. (1964), The premature neonate's response to handling. *Amer. Nurs. Assn.*, 11:15–24.

Katz, V. (1971), Auditory stimulation and developmental behavior of the premature infant. *Amer. Nurses Assn.*, 20:196–201.

Kaufman, I.C., & Rosenblum, L.A. (1967), The reaction to separation in infant monkeys: Anaclitic depression and conservation–withdrawal. *Psychosom. Med.*, 29:648–675.

Kennedy, J.M. (1978), Haptics. In: *Handbook of Perception*, Vol. 8, eds., E.R. Carterette & M.P. Friedman. New York: Academic Press.

Kenshalo, Sr., D.R. (1978), Biophysics and psychophysics of feeling. In: *Handbook of Perception*, Vol. 6B, eds. E.R Carterette & M.P. Friedman. New York: Academic Press.

Klaus, M., & Kennell, J. (1976), *Mother–Infant Bonding: The Impact of Early Separation or Loss on Family Development*. St. Louis: C.V. Mosby.

Korner, A., Kraemer, H., Haffner, E., & Cosper, L. (1975), Effects of waterbed flotation on premature infants: A pilot study. *Ped.*, 56:361–367.

Krueger, L. (1970), David Katz' Der Aufbau Der Tastwelt (The World of Touch): A synopsis. *Percept. & Psychophys.*, 7:337–341.

Kurtzberg, D., Vaughan, H.G., Daum, C., Grellong, B.A., Albin, S., &

Rotkin, L. (1979), Neurobehavioral performance of low-birthweight infants at 40 weeks conceptional age: Comparison with normal fullterm infants. *Development. Med. & Child Neurol.*, 21:590–607.

Lawson, K., Daum, C., & Turkewitz, G. (1977), Environmental characteristics of a neonatal intensive care unit. *Child Develop.*, 48:1633–1639.

Levine, S. (1960), Stimulation in infancy. *Sci. Amer.*, 202:81–85.

Lozoff, B., & Brittenham, G. (1979), Infant care: Cache or carry. *J. Ped.*, 95:478–483.

Masi, W. (1979), Supplemental stimulation of the premature infant. In: *Infants Born at Risk*, eds. T. M. Field, A.M. Sostek, S. Goldberg, & H.H. Shuman. New York: S.P. Medical & Scientific Books.

McNichol, T. (1973), *Some Effects of Different Programs of Enrichment on the Development of Premature Infants in the Hospital Nursery.* Unpublished doctoral dissertation, Purdue University, W. Lafayette, Indiana.

Montagu, A. (1971), *Touching: The Human Significance of the Skin.* New York: Columbia University Press.

Neal, M. (1968), Vestibular stimulation and developmental behavior of the small premature infant. *Nurs. Res. Rep.*, 3:2–5.

Powell, L.F. (1974), The effect of extra stimulation and maternal involvement on the development of low birthweight infants and on maternal behavior. *Child Develop.*, 45:106–113.

Rose, S.A. (1980), Enhancing visual recognition memory in preterm infants. *Development. Psychol.*, 16:85–92.

———(1983), Differential rates of visual information processing in full-term and preterm infants. *Child Develop.*, 54:1189–1198.

———Gottfried, A.W., & Bridger, W.H. (1978), Cross-modal transfer in infants: Relationship to prematurity and socio-economic background. *Development. Psychol.*, 14:643–652.

——— ——— ———(1979), Effects of haptic cues on visual recognition memory in full-term and preterm infants. *Inf. Behav. & Develop.*, 2:55–67.

——— ——— ———(1981a), Cross-modal transfer and information processing by the sense of touch in infancy. *Development. Psychol.*, 17:90–98.

——— ——— ———(1981b), Cross-modal transfer in 6-month-old infants. *Development. Psychol.*, 17:661–669.

——— ——— ———(1983), Infant's cross-modal transfer from solid objects to their graphic representations. *Child Develop.*, 54:686–694.

———Schmidt, K., & Bridger, W.H. (1976), Cardiac and behavioral responsivity to tactile stimulation in premature and full-term infants. *Development. Psychol.*, 12:311–320.

——— ——— ———(1978), Changes in tactile responsivity during sleep in the human newborn infant. *Development. Psychol.*, 14:163–172.

——— ———Riese, M. L., & Bridger, W. H. (1980), Effects of prematurity and early intervention on responsivity to tactual stimuli: A comparison of preterm and fullterm infants. *Child Develop.*, 51:416–425.

Rosenzweig, M. R., Bennett, E. L., & Diamond, M. C. (1970), Chemical and anatomical plasticity of brain: Replications and extensions. In: *Macromolecules and Behavior*, 2d ed., ed. J. Gaito. New York: Appleton-Century-Crofts.

Rothchild, B. T. (1967), Incubator isolation as a possible contributing factor to the high incidence of emotional disturbance among prematurely born persons. *J. Gen. Psychol.*, 110:287–304.

Scarr-Salapatek, S., & Williams, M. D. (1973), The effects of early stimulation on low birthweight infants. *Child Develop.*, 44:94–101.

Segall, M. (1972), Cardiac responsivity to auditory stimulation in premature infants. *Nurs. Res.*, 21:15–19.

Sigman, M. (1976), Early development of preterm and fullterm infants: Exploratory behavior in eight-month-olds. *Child Develop.*, 47:606–612.

———Parmelee, A.H. (1974), Visual preferences of four-month-old premature and fullterm infants. *Child Develop.*, 45:959–965.

Siqueland, E.R. (1973), Biological and experiential determinants of exploration in infancy. In: *The Competent Infant*, eds. L. Stone, H. Smith, & C. Murphy. New York: Basic Books, pp. 822–823.

Solkoff, N., Yaffe, S., Weintraub, D., & Blase, B. (1969), Effects of handling on the subsequent development of premature infants. *Development. Psychol.*, 1:765–768.

———Matuszak, D. (1975), Tactile stimulation and behavioral development among low birthweight infants. *Child Psychiat. & Hum. Develop.*, 6:33–37.

Spitz, R.A. (1946), Anaclitic depression. *The Psychoanalytic Study of the Child*, 2:313–347. New York: International Universities Press.

Stevens, J.C., & Green, B.G. (1978), History of research on feeling. In: *Handbook of Perception*, Vol. 6 B, eds. E. C. Carterette & M. P. Friedman. New York: Academic Press.

Taylor, M. M., Lederman, S. J., & Gibson, R. H. (1973), Tactual perception of texture. In: *Handbook of Perception*, Vol. 3, ed. E. C. Carterette & M. P. Friedman. New York: Academic Press.

White, B. L., & Castle, P. W. (1964), Visual exploratory behavior following postnatal handling of human infants. *Percep. & Motor Skills*, 18:497–502.

White, J., & Labarba, R. (1976), The effects of tactile and kinesthetic stimulation on neonatal development in the premature infant. *Development. Psychobiol.*, 9:569–577.

12

A Developmental Study of Finger Localization and Reading Achievement

Paul Satz, Ph.D., Jack M. Fletcher, Ph.D., Robin Morris, Ph.D., and H. Gerry Taylor, Ph.D.

Finger sense and related disturbances of the body scheme have long been of interest to behavioral neurologists. Spillane (1942) was one of the early proponents of this view. He wrote as follows:

> The term "body scheme" was introduced by Head and Holmes (1911) to signify the concept which a person develops of his own body. The body "scheme," "image" or "pattern" means the picture of the body which is formed in the mind. It becomes evident to those observers while studying the sensory activity of the human cortex that "one of the faculties which we owe to cortical activity is the power of relating one sensation to another, whether they arise simultaneously or consecutively." The sensory cortex becomes a storehouse of sensory experience: it receives impressions, stores them and judges new ones in the light of its experience. A standard is formed against which incoming impressions are modified and subsequent conduct determined. In the formation and maintenance of this plastic body image the importance of optical and postural impressions is therefore to be expected. An obvious corollary

is that distortion of our own postural model may be associated with loss of orientation in regard to the bodies of other people. Finally, lesions of the sensory cortex may be expected to result occasionally in disorders of the body scheme [p. 42].

Clinical Studies

Gerstmann (1940) must be credited for his efforts to link a pattern of seemingly diverse disturbances in body scheme to a specific area within the left sensory cortex—more specifically, the left angular gyrus. The pattern of behavioral deficits, defined as the Gerstmann syndrome, included impairments in finger recognition (finger agnosia), left–right orientation, writing (dysgraphia), and calculation (dyscalculia). In a critical and scholarly review of this literature, Benton (1979) states:

> Gerstmann (1940) considered that an intact and well-differentiated body image was a necessary precondition for finger recognition and he ascribed finger agnosia to a limited disintegration of the body image. Thus finger agnosia, in his view, was essentially a higher-level perceptual disorder involving the different sensory components of the body image and the spatial relations among the parts of the image. A disorder of the body schema could also explain impairment in differentiating the left and right sides of one's body. Since finger agnosia involved motoric as well as perceptive components, it could also be invoked to explain why a disorder of writing was part of the syndrome. Finally, loss of the ability to calculate could be related to the use of the fingers in counting. Our decimal system and arithmetic terminology (as reflected in the term "digit") testify to the significance of the 10 fingers in the genesis of calculation [pp. 98–99].

In Gerstmann's view, finger agnosia represented the primary construct for explaining the occurrence of the other symptoms in the syndrome. Historically this behavioral syndrome provided clinical neurologists with important information on the putative underlying neuropathological substrate before the advent of computer-based neuroradiographic methods. Unfortunately, studies in the past two decades have largely failed to support this assembly of symptoms as a naturally occurring pattern of deficits and have raised serious questions concerning the focal lesion presumed to underlie the syndrome (Benton, 1961; Heimburger, DeMeyer and Reitan, 1964; Poeck and Orgass, 1966). The syndrome has been shown to be no different from other combinations of cognitive deficits that frequently accompany it (e.g., aphasia, constructional praxis, alexia, impaired visual memory) following extensive lesions of the left hemisphere. As such, the syndrome has sometimes been referred to as an artifact of defective and biased clinical observation, although a number of distinguished neurologists continue to advocate its usefulness as a behavioral diagnosis in adults (Strub and Geschwind, 1974; Roeltgen, Sevush and Heilman, 1983).

Despite the empirical evidence against the Gerstmann syndrome, each of the elements (finger agnosia, left–right confusion, dysgraphia, and dyscalculia) represent cognitive operations that, while often lacking in definitional clarity, are known to be altered by focal and/or generalized lesions in the left cerebral hemisphere of adults, but not in a syndromatic fashion. These deficits, simply or in combination with many other cognitive operations, have also long been reported to occur in children with specific reading and learning handicaps without demonstrable brain injury (Kinsbourne, 1968; Lefford, Birch, and Green, 1974; Satz, Taylor, Friel, and Fletcher, 1978; Benton, 1979). One of the more interesting, though puzzling, deficits that has persisted in this literature concerns the disturbance in finger agnosia which Gerstmann (1940) earlier proposed as a unifying construct in adults with acquired lesions of the left parietal–occipital junction. This position may have led some neurologists to postulate an agenesis or delay in the maturation of the left parietal–occipital region in children whose learning problems and disturbance in finger sense were presumed to be neurological in origin (Spillane, 1942).

One of the major obstacles in many of these clinical reports concerns the looseness by which terms such as *finger agnosia* and the like were defined. Gerstmann defined finger agnosia as an inability to name or recognize one's own fingers or those of the examiner. As Benton (1979) noted, this was an unfortunate choice of terms because it extended the concept of agnosia beyond its defined meaning of a perceptual–associational disorder within a single sensory modality. The term unfortunately "implies the existence of a unitary finger sense or faculty of finger recognition when in fact it is only a collective term for different types of defective performance" (Benton, 1979, p. 86). Unfortunately, many clinicians continue to treat this term as a unitary construct. As such it prevents one from determining whether defective finger localization is due to a naming difficulty, an aphasia, a visuo-spatial defect, and/or a sequencing problem. Benton (1979) provided one of the most perceptive comments on this issue:

> "Finger agnosia" means very little because it means so much, covering as it does diverse performances differing in nature, scope and complexity. Uncritical use of the term has been responsible for much of the confusion and controversy surrounding the Gerstmann syndrome and its meaning. Obviously, it would serve the cause of clear thinking if the term were abandoned in favor of more specific designations. But terminology, once established, has a life of its own, and even those who do not believe in the existence of a unitary "finger agnosia" still use these terms—but only, as Critchley (1966) once wrote, "under protest" [pp. 88–89].

Developmental Studies

In contrast to the preceding clinical studies, developmental psychologists have approached the study of finger localization on a more empirical basis. Particular efforts have been more to define the specific stimulus characteristics and response requirements of the various finger localization tasks, to determine the different cognitive operations involved, and to investigate how performance on these various tasks varies with chronological and mental age. Some of the landmark studies were conducted by Wake (1957), Benton (1959), and Lefford et al., (1974). These studies identified a number of specific task operations related to "finger sense." For example, Lefford et al. (1974) administered seven tasks to children from three different age levels (3, 4, and 5 years). The tasks included tests of: (1) visual–tactile localization on self; (2) visual localization on self; (3) tactile localization on self; (4) visual–tactile localization on model; (5) visual localization on model; and (6) tactile localization on model. The authors found that the overall developmental pattern, while basically a negatively accelerating curve, was also influenced by the specific stimulus characteristics and response requirements of each task. For example, some of the tasks revealed ceiling effects by age four (visual–tactile localization on self) and some tasks revealed floor effects at age three (tactile localization on model). However, all of the tests revealed differing rates of improvement across this early age interval. Wake (1957) used a similar test battery with older children (ages 6–9 years) and found further improvement with age, particularly on tests of bilateral finger stimulation. He also noted that the rate of acquisition was slower for more complex tasks, especially where a sequential response was prompted by a bilateral mode of (finger) stimulation. Finally, tasks which involved a verbal response revealed a slower rate of acquisition than tasks which merely required a pointing response (to finger touch).

These studies, in sum, have suggested that the construct of "finger sense" involves a number of different task operations and cognitive processes that are probably tied to specific stages in development. Some of the cognitive processes postulated to mediate finger localization have been described as *sensory–discriminative*, *sensory–integrative*, *perceptual–representational*, *sequential–spatial*, and *linguistic* (i.e., naming). Unfortunately, these terms represent inferences based largely on a priori assumptions concerning task selection and interpretation. Although the developmental studies have managed to strip much of the surplus meaning associated with the construct of finger agnosia, their methods have not entailed the use of certain *quantitative* and *sampling* procedures that would permit a more objective and valid determination of the different cognitive and developmental aspects of finger recognition skill.

The following study represents an attempt to examine some of the cognitive and developmental aspects of finger localization in a longitudinal–prospective sample of kindergarten children who, in later grades (G2 & G5), became average or poor readers. This design thus afforded a rare opportunity to examine the association between finger recognition skill and reading achievement from both a *predictive* and *concurrent* validation approach. The predictive validation approach provided the first opportunity to evaluate an earlier hunch of Herbert Birch that finger recognition skill, because of its cognitive and developmental characteristics, might be of potential value in the early identification of children at risk for later school failure (Lefford et al., 1974). The concurrent validation approach provided a unique opportunity to reexamine the putative association between finger recognition skill and reading achievement from a developmental perspective, and utilizing different measures of finger recognition rather than a composite measure as reported in other studies. Finally, the use of factor analytic methods permitted a more objective assessment of the cognitive operations presumed to underlie performance on various finger localization tasks.

The study, which was conducted by the present authors (Taylor, Fletcher, and Satz, 1984) as part of the Florida

Longitudinal Project (Satz et al., 1978), will be described briefly.

SUBJECTS

A battery of tests was given to nearly all (96%) of the white boys entering kindergarten in Alachua County, Florida in 1970 and to all of the white boys attending kindergarten the following year in the five largest schools in that county. The mean age of the combined sample (N = 678) in their first year in school (Grade K) was sixty-four months. At the end of their third year (Grade 2), the kindergarten battery was readministered, and measures of reading ability were obtained for 570 of the original children. Reading measures included instructional book level (teacher specification of the reader in which the child was working) and the IOTA Word Test, a formal test of word recognition (Monroe, 1928). To provide a more comprehensive measure of reading level, the two measures were combined by converting scores into T scores, which were averaged for each child.

Disabled readers (N = 80) were those children whose averaged T scores fell more than one standard deviation below the mean for the population. Eighty *nondisabled* readers, matched on age with the disabled readers, were selected from those whose averaged T scores were above or no more than 0.4 standard deviations below the mean for the total sample. Such selection resulted in a disabled group functioning about two years behind on both reading measures and a nondisabled group with mean word recognition abilities somewhat in advance of grade standard, but with mean instructional book level that was grade appropriate. Both groups had a mean age of ninety-three months at the end of Year 3.

At the end of the sixth year in school (Grade 5), the battery was administered a third time but only to the children from the two reading groups. Due to attrition, only seventy-four of the eighty disabled readers (M age = 127 months) and sixty-nine of the eighty nondisabled readers (M age = 128 months) were available for testing. The same criterion grouping of disabled versus nondisabled readers was used in Grade 5, with follow-up reading assessments at the end of this year attesting to the stability of reading group placement across years (Satz et al., 1978).

BATTERY VARIABLES

In addition to the finger recognition tasks to be described below, the battery of developmental tests administered in Grade K consisted of one nontest variable (Socioeconomic status) and ten tests described in Fletcher, Satz, Morris, and Harris (1984). With minor alterations, this same battery was administered at the end of Grades 2 and 5. As will be seen below, however, only Grade K data for the entire battery was of interest for the present study.

FINGER RECOGNITION TASKS

The four finger recognition tasks given in Grades K, 2, and 5 were as follows:

1. In Task 1 (unilateral touch-point) the distal portion of one hand (palm up) was touched briefly with the end of a paper clip while a card shielded the subject from viewing his hand. The shield was then removed, and the child attempted to point to the finger stimulated. Five trials were provided for each hand.

2. In Task 2 (unilateral touch-diagram) the stimulation conditions were identical to those in Task 1. However, rather than pointing to his own finger, the child pointed to a finger on a pictorial representation of the hands. Five trials were again provided for each hand.

3. Tasks 3 (unilateral touch-number) and 4 (bilateral touch-number) were preceded by a training phase in which the child's fingers were verbally labeled by the examiner from one to five (thumb to little finger). Once the numbering system was mastered, fingers were touched behind the shield

as in Tasks 1 and 2. One finger on one hand was stimulated on each trial of Task 3, and one finger from each hand was simultaneously stimulated on each trial of Task 4. In both tasks, the child was required to call out the number of the finger(s) stimulated. Task 3 and 4 were not administered if the child was unable to identify fingers by number when the examiner pointed out fingers in random order in view of the child. Five trials were provided in Task 3 for each hand. In Task 4 each hand was also stimulated five times, only this time stimulation was bilateral, and hence five instead of ten identifications were required. Because of the greater difficulty of Task 4, the child was given a second chance (another bilateral trial) to identify a finger if an error was made. The child needed to identify a given finger on only one of the presentations to receive credit. (Although Tasks 3 and 4 were administered at all three probes, Task 1 and 2 were eliminated from the battery after Year 3 due to ceiling effects.)

Each task placed different cognitive demands on the child. Task 1 was the simplest, requiring only sensory discrimination of the finger stimulated. For Task 2, however, the child had to discriminate the finger and point to a pictorial representation of the hand. This latter feature had been hypothesized to require an internal representation of the body schema (Benton, 1979). Task 3 added a verbal coding dimension to Task 1, and Task 4 required both verbal coding and a more complex sensory discrimination—simultaneous stimulation on two hands instead of on one hand. Based on previous research, these different task demands were expected to lead to different developmental rates and differential associations with other developmental variables.

Results and Discussion

DEVELOPMENT OF FINGER RECOGNITION SKILLS

The development of each component skill (Tasks 1–4) is presented in Figures 12.1 to 12.4. Each figure presents the

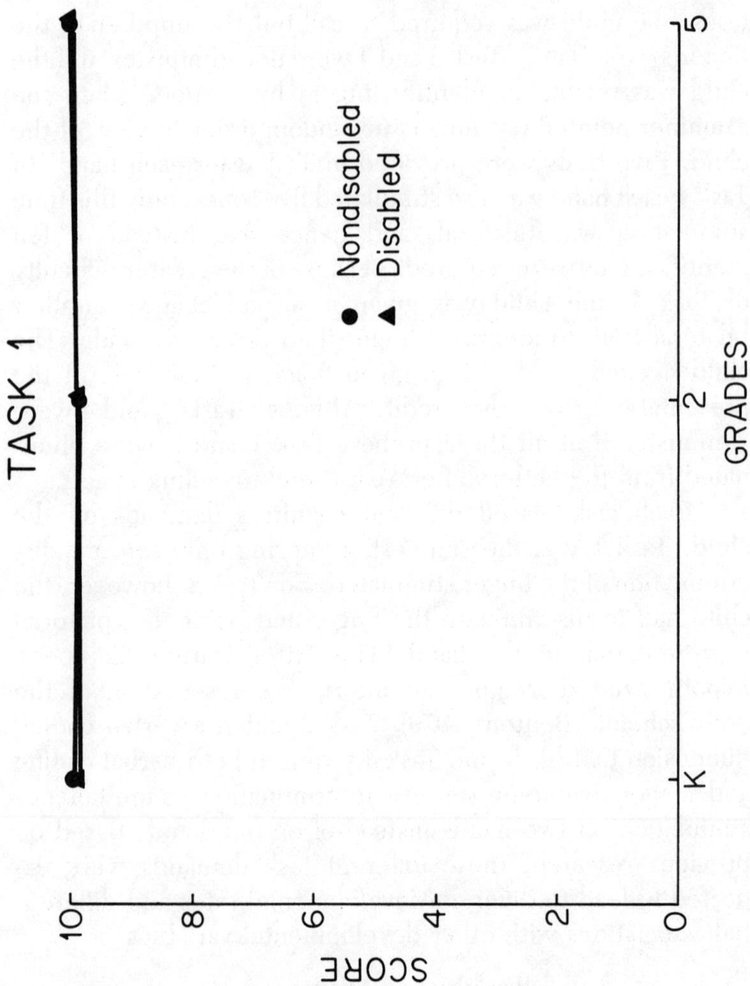

FIGURE 12.1
Task 1: Unilateral touch-point.

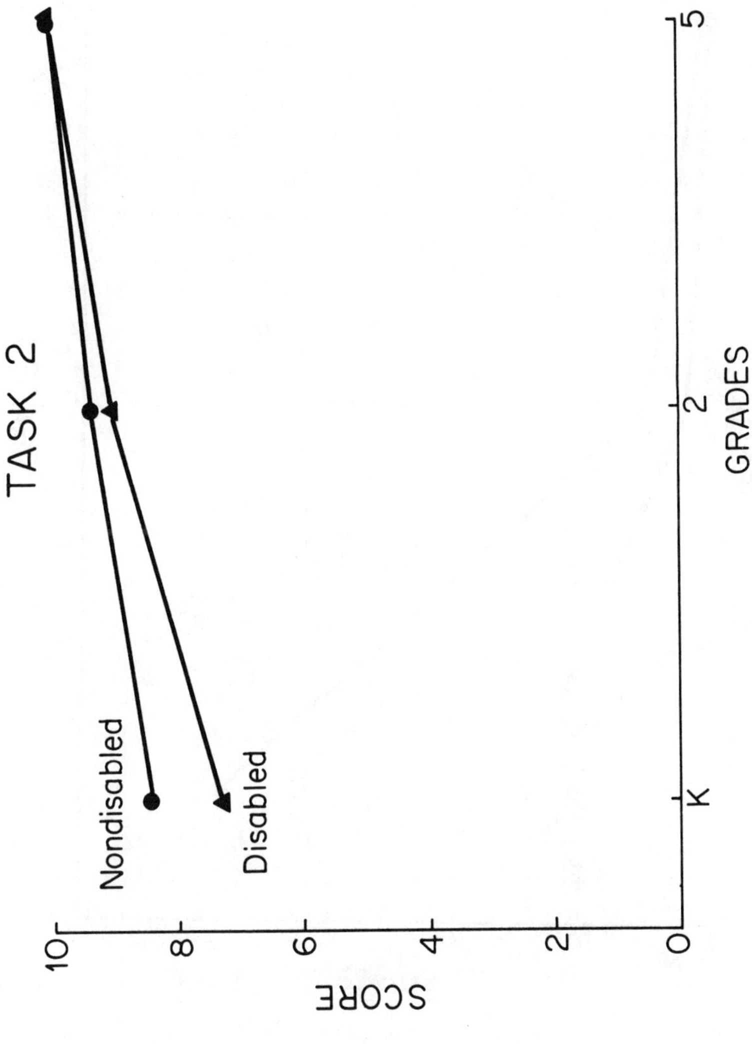

FIGURE 12.2
Task 2: Unilateral touch-diagram.

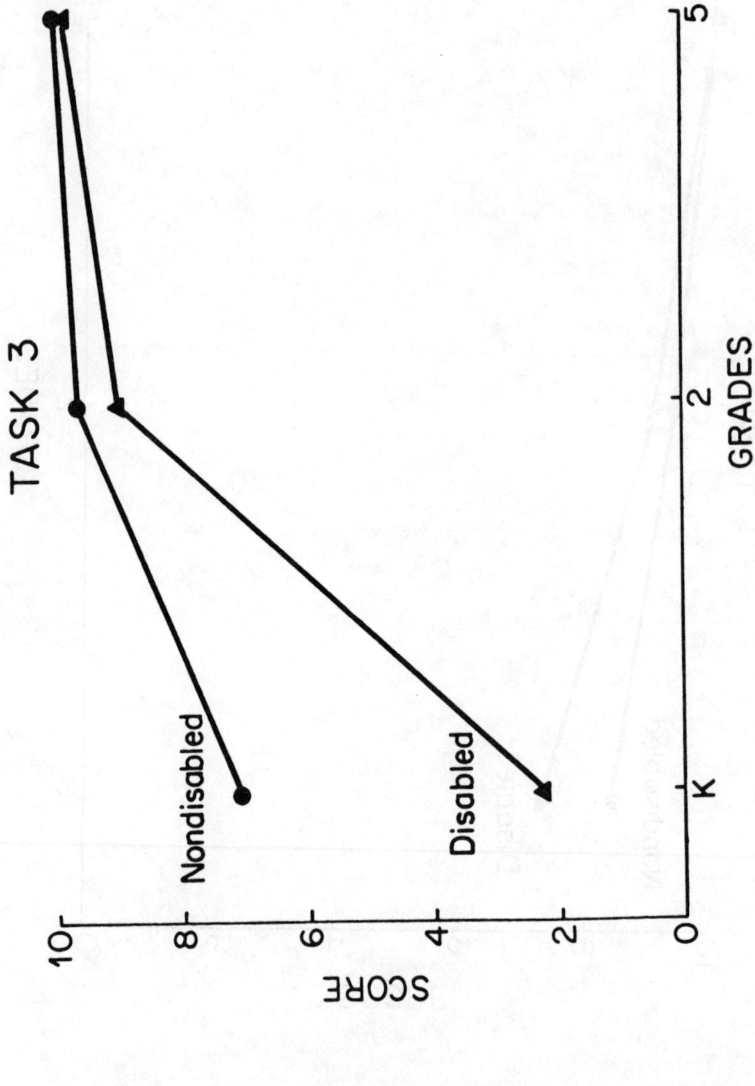

FIGURE 12.3
Task 3: Unilateral touch-number.

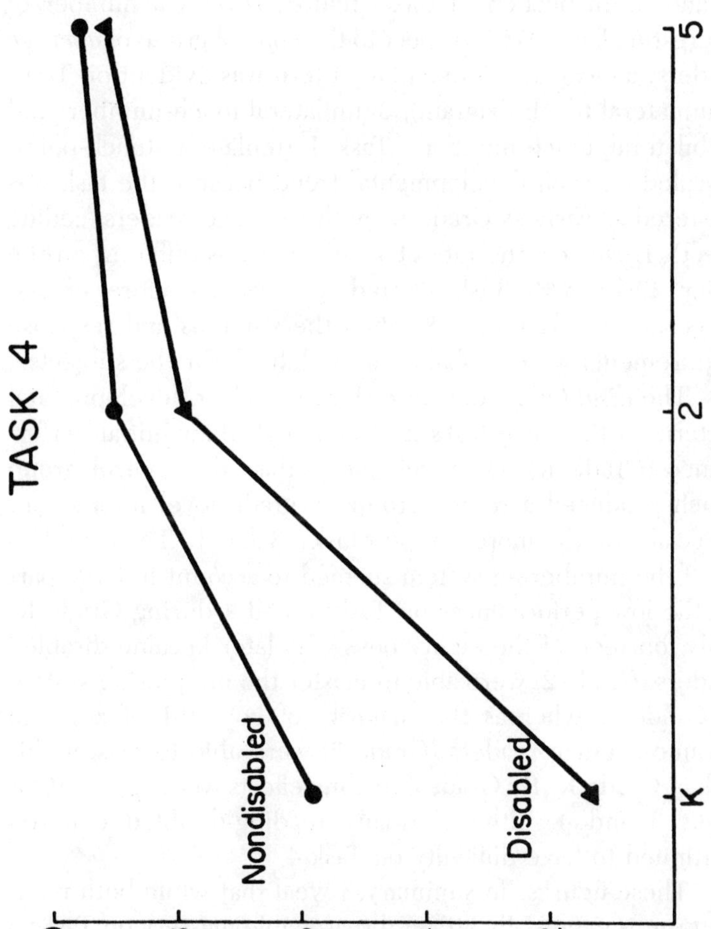

FIGURE 12.4
Task 4: Bilateral touch-number.

mean score for both hands (R & L, Range = 0–10) on each task for the reading disabled and control groups at Grades K, 2, and 5. Inspection of these figures reveals a number of interesting facts. With respect to the control group of *average* readers, a clear developmental pattern was evident on Tasks 2 (unilateral touch-diagram), 3 (unilateral touch-number) and 4 (bilateral touch-number). Task 1 (unilateral touch-point) revealed no such developmental trend because the task was mastered as early as Grade K by the average readers (ceiling effect). However, the rate of acquisition was different on the other Tasks with Tasks 3 and 4 revealing more errors, especially during Grade K when the stimulus and response requirements were probably more difficult for the subjects.

The *disabled* readers also showed a clear developmental pattern on the same tasks (2–4) although their initial performance (Grade K) was much *lower* than the control group which produced a robust group by grade level interaction, especially on the more complex tasks (3 and 4). The complexity of the numbering system seemed to account in large part for the low performances on Tasks 3 and 4 during Grade K. Only fourteen of the eighty boys who later became disabled readers (Grade 2) were able to master the numbering system in Grade K whereas the majority of boys (61 of 80) who became average readers (Grade 2) were able to master this task in Grade K. By Grade 5, ceiling effects were apparent for Tasks 3 and 4, although many reading-disabled children continued to have difficulty on Task 4.

These figures, in summary, reveal that while both reading groups eventually attained reasonable mastery on Tasks 2 to 4 between Grades K and 5, significant *delays* occurred in the children who during Grade K were *destined* to become disabled readers, especially on the more complex tasks (3 and 4). These initial delays, in fact, helped to identify those developmental precursors that, in part, were shown to predict later outcome in reading. In this framework the results confirmed the hunches earlier hypothesized by Herbert Birch and associates.

CONSTRUCT VALIDITY

To explore associations between performances on individual finger recognition tasks and other developmental measures, those finger recognition measures that were sufficiently reliable and for which there were no ceiling effects in Year 1 (Tasks 2, 3, and 4) were subjected to factor analyses involving other Year 1 measures. Such analyses were conducted only on the Year 1 battery data due to the large sample size (N = 678) and the fact that variances for the finger recognition tasks were least subject to ceiling effects in kindergarten. The three finger recognition tasks were factor analyzed individually with the other variables to avoid the clustering of finger recognition performances into a separate factor because of their moderate intercorrelations. In all factor analyses, a principal axes solution (squared multiple correlation coefficients as communalities) was used (Guertin and Bailey, 1970). Ten axes were rotated to orthogonal (varimax) and oblique (simple loadings) solutions. Only results from the oblique solutions are presented below, since these provided the best resolution of simple structure.

An initial factor analysis was computed excluding all finger recognition tasks to define the factor structure of the test battery independently of these tasks. These results, presented in Table 12.1, show that the measures loaded on three different factors.

The first, labeled Perceptual–Motor (Factor 1), received loadings primarily from Embedded Figures, Recognition–Discrimination, and Beery VMI. The first two tasks required visual matching of geometric figures, whereas the latter required visual copying of geometric figures. A second common factor, labeled Verbal–Conceptual (Factor 2), received its primary loadings from three related tasks: PPVT, WPPSI Similarities, and Word Fluency. The final factor was comprised of Alphabet Recitation, Auditory Discrimination, and

TABLE 12.1
Common Factor Analysis (Oblique Rotation) of Year 1 Battery Variables Excluding Finger Recognition Task

	Factor		
Variable	1	2	3
Beery VMI	0.66	−0.16	0.20
Recognition–Discrimination	0.70	0.10	−0.03
Embedded Figures	0.73	0.05	−0.10
WPPSI Similarities	0.05	0.61	0.08
PPVT	−0.01	0.50	0.38
Verbal Fluency	0.19	0.25	0.18
Alphabet Recitation	0.05	0.01	0.64
Auditory Discrimination	0.03	0.15	0.46
Socioeconomic status	0.02	0.02	0.46
Finger Tapping	0.24	−0.06	0.12
Right–Left Discrimination	0.22	0.13	0.04
Column sums of squared loadings	1.60	0.75	1.08

Note: VMI = visual motor integration, WPPSI = Wechsler preschool and Primary Scales of Intelligence; PPVT = Peabody Picture Vocabulary Test.

Socioeconomic status (SES). Because of the predominance of earlier developing linguistic skills and the involvement of the social variable, this factor was labeled Verbal–Cultural (Factor 3). Previous factor analyses of these measures on this and other samples (combining finger recognition tasks as a composite score) have consistently revealed this same three factor structure, even when employing different factor analytic techniques (Fletcher et al., 1984).

Individual finger recognition tasks were added separately to factor analyses to determine where these tasks loaded. Task

2 loaded with Finger Tapping and Right–Left Discrimination on a new fourth factor labeled Somatosensory Differentiation. The loading of Task 2 on Factor 4 was 0.53, with loadings on Factors 1 to 3 of −0.01, −0.03, and 0.04, respectively. Adding Tasks 3 and 4 to the factor analysis resulted in further dissociation of the various finger recognition tasks, although Factor 4 was not apparent. Task 3 loaded on Factor 3 (Verbal–Cultural). Its loadings on Factors 1 to 3 were 0.28, −0.07, and 0.51, respectively. In contrast, Task 4 loaded on Factor 1 (Perceptual–Motor). Respective loadings of this task on Factors 1 to 3 were 0.50, −0.02, and 0.29. Since Task 3 involved learning a verbal code, it was not surprising that it loaded on Factor 3 (Verbal–Cultural). Although Task 4 also required learning a verbal code, the demand for simultaneous as opposed to successive stimulation of fingers imposed relatively greater demands on sensorimotor–perceptual than on verbal skills, resulting in the loading on Factor 1 (Perceptual–Motor).

PREDICTIVE AND CONCURRENT VALIDITY

In light of the different measurement characteristics of Tasks 2, 3, and 4, we went on to examine the contribution of each of these measures to reading achievement. As a first step in this approach, two one-way multivariate analyses of variance (MANOVA) were conducted on the data at Grades K and 2. For each of these analyses, reading group assignments served as the dependent measure, and mean task scores for each probe were the predictor variables. Only those variables with sufficient reliability were included in the MANOVA. Analyses for Grade K included three (Tasks 2–4) predictor variables; for Grade 2 two (Tasks 3–4) predictor variables; for Year 6, only Task 4 had sufficient reliability, and a univariate t test was conducted.

According to the analyses, finger recognition performances significantly differentiated the two reading groups in each year. For Grade K, $F\ (1158) = 93.93$, $p < 0.01$; for

Grade 2, $F(1158) = 15.49$, $p < 0.01$; and for Grade 5, $t(1) = 6.32$, $p < 0.01$. Using techniques described by Huberty (1975) that are analogous to squared multiple correlation coefficients, we determined that about 39 percent of the variance in reading achievement could be accounted for in terms of kindergarten finger recognition skills. However, only 12 percent and 4 percent of the variance in reading achievement could be accounted for in Grades 2 and 5, respectively. This shows that the overall relationship of finger recognition tasks and reading achievement diminished over time.

In addition to verifying the predictive and concurrent validity of the finger recognition tasks for discriminating the two reading groups, the MANOVA provided a linear composite (canonical variate) of differentially weighted task scores that maximally separated disabled and nondisabled reader groups. This overall index of group separation served as a measure with which individual task scores could be correlated. The magnitude of the Pearson product-moment correlation indicated the degree to which individual scores contributed to the overall separation between reading groups due to finger recognition performance (Huberty, 1975; Fletcher, Rice, and Ray, 1978). For Grade K, Tasks 3, (0.96) and 4 (0.96) contributed equally to group discrimination, with Task 2 (0.46) contributing to a lesser degree. These correlations showed that the most uniquely neuropsychological finger recognition task (2) was less related to group discrimination than tasks (3 and 4) that were related to other developmental variables. Canonical correlations of 0.64 and 0.96 (Tasks 3 and 4) for the Grade 2 MANOVA (concurrent validity) indicated that the sensitivity of Task 3 for discriminating reading groups diminished with age. Task 4 remained related to reading achievement across all three probes, accounting entirely for the weak relationship between finger recognition performance and reading achievement in Grade 5.

Conclusion

The preceding results, in summary, shed additional light on the complex developmental and cognitive parameters of finger localization tasks, especially as they relate to reading achievement. The use of a prospective longitudinal design afforded a rare opportunity to examine the association between finger recognition skill and reading achievement from both a predictive and concurrent validation approach. The results of the predictive validation analyses confirmed an early hypothesis of Herbert Birch that components of finger recognition skill, which are intrinsically tied to cognitive and developmental operations, might be of potential value in the early identification of children at risk for later school failure (Lefford et al., 1974). In the present study, Tasks 2, 3, and 4 each contributed to the prediction of reading achievement in boys. Task 2, which most clearly required localization of fingers, was less predictive of reading achievement than Tasks 3 and 4, which were more clearly related to other developmental processes. The predictive relationship of Tasks 3 and 4 in kindergarten with later progress in reading would seem to reflect the sensitivity of the component tasks to both perceptual–discrimination and verbal processes. Both Factors 1 (Perceptual–Motor) and 3 (Verbal–Cultural) have been shown to be highly predictive of eventual reading achievement when incurred in kindergarten (Fletcher and Satz, 1980).

The results of the *concurrent* validation analyses demonstrated the effects of developmental change in the relationship between finger localization and reading. The multivariate analyses showed that the performance on these tasks was less associated with reading achievement when readministered in later grades. In other words, finger performance during Grade K accounted for more of the variance in reading predictively than it did concurrently when readministered in Grades 2 and 5. Finally, the use of a factor analytic approach permitted a more objective framework for interpreting the cognitive and developmental operations associated with finger localization and reading.

Discussion: Chapter 12

T. Berry Brazelton: Why were all your subjects boys? Because you expected a higher rate of learning problems?

Paul Satz: Yes. The rates of reading failure are four to one in favor of boys, and we wanted to increase our chances of having a substantial number of index cases in later years.

Michael Merzenich: Do you learn anything by considering the degree of the error, Paul? In other words, were there a significant number of children who made more than, say, a one-digit error on your more difficult finger recognition tasks, or were the errors usually to the adjacent digits?

Paul Satz: I don't know. We treated that as a qualitative aspect of performance.

Michael Merzenich: It's a very interesting question whether it's a qualitative error, an error of kind, or whether it's just a matter of delayed development. Although I shouldn't really try to relate our work to yours, a kind of tunnel vision that I have is that as mappings of skin surfaces are developed, the associations that can be made from them relate to the qualities of the mappings generally.

Paul Satz: I could tell you as a clinician where most of the errors occur. Most of them are when stimulation is in the middle areas. With the first and fifth fingers, there are fewer errors.

Michael Merzenich: Map-to-map associations are really important, especially when maps are changing as a function of experience. There has to be a correction of associations as maps change, and the quality of the associations that can occur relates to the quality of the mappings. That may be largely where these problems lie. If I have a poor sense of or map of my hand, it may relate to all sorts of things.

T. Berry Brazelton: I had a fourteen-year-old girl who had learned to cope with her problems but had a difficult time. When I said to her during a routine checkup, "You've really gotten over all this and you really had to work at it," she started weeping. She said, "You know how hard it's been." I think these children need to know that we know how hard it's been.

Paul Satz: There's some evidence that females with reading disabilities, though very few, suffer more. In two Canadian follow-up studies, the females had more emotional scars twenty years later. In general, though, I think it's a myth that learning disabilities leave terrible scars during adolescence and adulthood. It's also a myth that children always outgrow these disabilities.

T. Berry Brazelton: We are now picking up newborns who are hypersensitive and who we expect to be hyperactive and to have attentional disorders later. A mother told me the other day that her child had been identified as learning disabled at three years of age. When he was a small baby, this child was having trouble processing information, and the mother says she told me so. I replied that he'd outgrow it, so I missed my chance. By now, this child has an in-built expectation to fail. It's very subtle, but it's there. If we could predict these problems earlier, we could back the children up by not letting that expectation to fail get built in so early. Paul, do you have any information on prematures or SGAs in your sample?

Paul Satz: No. However, a number of people around the country have been using my test as an outcome measure in studies of high-risk pregnancies and preterm infants. Researchers are using these measures as preliminary criteria when at-risk infants reach five years of age instead of waiting until they're eight or ten to see what happens.

Peter Gorski: Jane Hunt in San Francisco, along with other investigators, now has data on school-age children who were born prematurely. Even though the children may score well on IQ tests, they are experiencing school failure at a phenomenal rate—50 percent or higher. Tests of perceptual–motor difficulties seem to pick up school-failure children much better than language tests do at ages five and six.

Susan Rose: As I understand it, the deficits in IQ are not as marked as the deficits in perceptual–motor performance.

T. Berry Brazelton: We need to have a better developmental line on these babies. Perhaps if we gave them more time at school, or taught them differently, we might have better outcomes.

Paul Satz: I looked at four longitudinal studies on preterm birth and cognitive development. Although there are too little data to be sure, infants who were selected as at risk at birth seem to look all right at four years of age. At age seven, something starts showing up which changes at eleven, and becomes something else. There are stages, and what we need are prospective studies to examine them.

References

Benton, A. L. (1959), *Right–left Discrimination and Finger Localization: Development and Pathology*. New York: Hoeber-Harper.

———(1961), The fiction of the "Gertsmann syndrome." *J. Neurol., Neurosurg. & Psychiat.*, 24:176–181.

———(1979), The neuropsychological significance of finger recognition. In: *Cognitive Growth and Development*, ed. M. Bortner, New York: Brunner/Mazel, pp. 85–105.

Critchley, M. (1966), The enigma of Gerstmann's syndrome. *Brain*, 89:183–198.

Fletcher, J. M., Rice, W. J., & Ray, R. R. (1978), Linear discriminant function analysis in neuropsychological research: Some uses and abuses. *Cortex*, 14:564–577.

———Satz, P. (1980), Developmental changes in the neuropsychological correlates of reading achievement: A six-year longitudinal follow-up. *J. Clin. Neuropsychol.*, 2:23–37.

——— ———Morris, W., & Harris, R. (1984), The Florida longitudinal project: A review. In: *Handbook of Longitudinal Research*, eds. S. Mednick, M. Harway, & K. M. Finnello. New York: Praeger, pp. 233–258.

Gerstmann, J. (1940), Syndrome of finger agnosia, disorientation for right and left, agraphia and acalculia. *Arch. Neurol. and Psychiat.*, 44:398–408.

Guertin, W. H., & Bailey, J. P. (1970), Test item dependence of several oblique factor solutions. *Ed. & Psycholog. Measure.*, 30:611–619.

Head, H., & Holmes, G. (1911), *Brain*, 34:102–111.

Heimburger, R. F., DeMeyer, W., & Reitan, R. M. (1964), Implications of Gerstmann's syndrome. *J. Neurol., Neurosurg. & Psychiat.*, 27:52–57.

Huberty, C. J. (1975), Discriminant analysis. *Rev. Ed. Res.*, 45:543–598.

Kinsbourne, K. (1968), Developmental Gerstmann syndrome. *Ped. Clin. N. Amer.*, 15:771–778.

Lefford, A., Birch, H. G., & Green, G. (1974), The perceptual and cognitive bases for finger localization and selective finger movement in pre-school children. *Child Develop.*, 45:335–343.

Monroe, R. (1928), *Monroe Diagnostic Reading Test*. Chicago: Stoelling.

Poeck, K., & Orgass, B. (1966), Gerstmann's syndrome and aphasia. *Cortex*, 2:421–437.

Roeltgen, D. P., Sevush, S., & Heilman, K. M. (1983), Pure Gerstmann's syndrome from a focal lesion. *Arch. of Neurol.*, 40:46–47.

Satz, P., Taylor, H. G., Friel, J., & Fletcher, J. M. (1978), Some developmental and predictive precursors of reading disability. In: *Dyslexia: An Appraisal of Current Knowledge*, eds. D. Pearl & A. L. Benton. New York: Oxford University Press, pp. 313–348.

Spillane, J. (1942), Disturbances of the body scheme. *Lancet*, 2:42–44.

Strub, R., & Geschwind, N. (1974), Gerstmann syndrome without aphasia. *Cortex*, 10:378–387.

Taylor, G., Fletcher, J., & Satz, P. (1984), Neuropsychological assessment of children. In: *Handbook of Psychological Assessment*, eds. L. Halparn & G. Goldstein. New York: Pergamon Press, pp. 211–234.

Wake, F. R. (1957), Finger localization scores in defective children. Paper presented at meeting of Canadian Psychological Association, Ontario.

13
Touch as an Organizer of Development and Learning

Allen W. Gottfried, Ph.D.

This chapter will focus on four issues: The origins and ontogeny of tactile responsivity in early human development; the regulatory role of touch or somesthetic stimulation in development, behavior, and medical status; the fact that touch or vestibular types of stimulation can facilitate as well as have a detrimental effect on early functioning; a comprehensive understanding of touch involves examination of the cognitive dimensions associated with it.

If we ask the question, when does behavior begin, we would in essence be addressing issues concerning the origins and ontogeny of tactile sensitivity. Prenatal behavior is rooted in the fetus's reaction to the stimulation of touch. Although observations of a living human fetus were recorded in the late 1800s and at the beginning of the twentieth century, the classic studies in human fetal activity were conducted from the 1920s to 1940s. These included the studies by Minkowski, Bolaffio, and Artom, Windle and associates, and Hooker (cited

Acknowledgment: The research presented herein was supported in part by a grant from the Thrasher Research Fund.

in Hooker, 1952; Carmichael 1954). Essentially, these researchers examined the reflexes of operatively removed fetuses. Davenport Hooker (1952) conducted the most extensive, well-controlled, and best documented studies to date.

I would like to review briefly some of Hooker's findings. Until seven and a half weeks gestational age, the human embryo shows no evidence of reflex activity. No area of the skin is sensitive to tactile stimulation. However, at seven and a half to just before the eighth week, a light touch to the lips or alae of the nose activates a reflex. Hooker describes this initial behavior as "a contralateral flexion of the neck and uppermost trunk with little or no participation of the upper extremities and none of any other portion of the body" (p. 63). Between eight and nine and a half weeks, the perioral area of sensitivity expands to include the chin and lateral parts of the mouth and nose. At ten and a half to eleven weeks, the eyelids became sensitive to tactile stimulation. By eleven and a half weeks the entire front surface of the face is sensitive in all fetuses, and by fourteen to fifteen weeks the sides of the face become sensitive. By eleven weeks, all fetuses respond to palmar stimulation and most to stimulation over arms and forearms. Responsiveness to stimulation of the sole is evident by twelve weeks, and at twelve weeks there is a response to stimulation of the thighs and legs. By thirteen and a half to fourteen weeks of gestational age, almost the entire surface of the body is sensitive to touch except for the top and back of the head, which remain insensitive until birth.

Spontaneous movement, that is, behavior in the absence of any identifiable external stimulation, occurred at nine and a half weeks. This behavior was characterized as a "vestibular righting response," a response interpreted as being caused by a disturbance of head–body relations. Also occurring at nine and a half weeks was the first evidence of proprioceptive responsiveness. Hooker (1952) described this as stretch responses, "passive extension of the fingers causes flexion at the wrist, elbow, and shoulder" (p. 67). In summary, responses to somesthetic stimulation are the first to develop in the ontogeny of human behavioral development, followed approximately two weeks later by responses to vestibular and proprioceptive stimulation. Ultrasound technology will serve to verify these initial findings.

One might now ask why there is so much emphasis on touch? The answer may reside in a general embryological principle that states "that the earlier a function develops, the more fundamental it is likely to be" (Carmichael 1954; Montagu, 1971, p. 3). Hence, an extensive amount of research has been conducted demonstrating that touch plays an important role in nonhuman as well as human development. At the infrahuman level, the plethora of experiments examining handling, gentling, cuddling, licking, and so on, revealed the significance and possible necessity of tactuality in the course of development. A number of investigators have claimed that early tactile contact influences growth rates, adaptability, learning, activity level, exploratory behavior, attachment, sociability, ability to withstand stress, and immunological development in many young mammals (Montagu, 1971). Thus, there are both bio- and psychosomesthetic functions operating here. However, it is important to emphasize that it is not entirely clear whether these outcomes are due to cutaneous, vestibular, or social communicative mechanisms. Ecologically, these factors cooccur.

A number of investigators have also examined the effects of touch stimulation in infants, in particular, premature newborns. In the past decade, we have witnessed a surge of experimental environmental intervention programs aimed directly toward at-risk newborns (Cornell and Gottfried, 1976; Gottfried, 1981, 1985b). Investigators have applied additional stimulation of various sorts to these infants. Most researchers have focused on tactile-vestibular stimulation. The studies in this volume by Rausch (chapter 9), Korner (chapter 10), and Rose (chapter 11) provide three fine examples of programs instituted. A review of intervention programs employing tactile-vestibular stimulation indicates changes in developmental and medical status. Researchers have reported increases in sensorimotor performance on a variety of scales, increase in motor development, formula intake, weight gain, head circumference, the frequency of stooling, responsitivity to tactile stimulation, muscle tone, and visual recognition memory. Changes have also been reported in state organization, behavioral indexes, and neurobehavioral functioning, reflex development, and the incidence of apnea. It is noteworthy that the means by which the tactile-vestibular stimulation has been applied has been by humans (i.e., manually), machines, and recently by the use of waterbeds. The effects have not only been found immediately but also several months subsequent to stimulation (Rose, chapter 11). Again, it is difficult to discern whether these developmental changes are due to tactile or vestibular stimulation. In any event, there is an overwhelming body of data demonstrating that stimulation associated with touch regulates behavior and development. Most of the data show positive effects.

However, the data presented by Gorski and colleagues (chapter 8) reveal that touching or handling premature infants can have a negative effect. Gorski reported that touching infants during convalescent care was associated with bradycardia. Perhaps there is "bad or unpleasant" handling, as in the case where infants are manipulated for medical and/or nursing procedures, or "good or pleasant" handling where infants receive socioemotional or tender loving care types of touching or rocking. Perhaps it is not just the type of handling, but also when handling occurs. For example, sick infants may respond negatively, whereas medically stable or healthy infants respond positively.

Clearly, these issues relate to mechanisms accounting for the effect of stimulation on developmental status. Several researchers have put forth their interpretations about the mechanisms involved. Speidel (1978) has hypothesized that crying, whether induced or spontaneous, causes PaO_2 to fall. Because crying is a common reaction to handling among sick newborns, crying may be the mediating mechanism between handling and hypoxemia. Walsh and Cummins (1975) and Cummins, Livesey, Evans, and Walsh (1977) have contended that arousal resulting from social interactions and object exploration underlies differential brain effects. The mechanism is a nonspecific activation of the cortex during arousal, which is, in turn, transduced into biosynthetic activity. Furthermore, these researchers hypothesize that in the course of ontogeny, certain neurons develop as a result of adequate sensory stimulation. Clark, Kreutzberg, and Chee (1977) have conducted studies demonstrating that vestibular stimulation, in the form of semicircular canal stimulation, facilitates reflexes and motor skills in young infants. These investigators argue that vestibular stimulation enhances maturation of vestibuloocular reflexes (which provide stable retinal images) and maturation of vestibulospinal reflexes, both of which are important for motor development. The studies by Clark, Kreutzberg, and Chee (1977) also showed that it was the vestibular stimulation associated with tactile contact that accounted for the outcomes and not tactile contact per se.

Five of the six presentations in Part IV provide data on the consequences of handling or vestibular stimulation on premature infants. However, there is a paucity of data on the amount and nature of tactile contact of premature infants in special care units. Little is known about the quantity and quality of tactile stimulation received by these infants.

I would like to summarize some data from my research program addressing this issue (Gottfried, Wallace-Lande, Sherman-Brown, King, Coen, and Hodgman, 1981; Gottfried, 1985a). My colleagues and I have conducted continuous recordings over twenty-four-hour periods to examine the contacts between caregivers and premature infants in intensive and convalescent care units in a typical day. The data revealed that infants in special care units do not lack, either in frequency or duration, contact with persons. On the average, infants in the intensive care unit (NICU) received 70 contacts per day, with one infant receiving as much as 106 contacts; infants in the convalscent care unit (NCCU) received 42 contacts per day with an upper range of 55. Virtually all contacts involved touching or handling of the infants. Contacts typically occurred two to three times per hour, were brief, with each usually lasting two to five minutes, and totaled a duration of 2.5 and 3.3 hours daily in the NICU and NCCU, respectively. There was no systematic variability across work shifts or diurnal regularity across days in the frequency and duration of contacts. Hence, infants received a considerable amount of handling with no regularity or schedule involved. The preponderance of contacts with, or handling of, infants may be appropriately described as nonsocial. Contacts in both units predominately involved medical–nursing care. In fact, virtually all of the contacts were for this purpose, and seldom did they include social activities such as social touching or rocking. It is noteworthy that approximately 97 percent of contacts involved staff members and not family. Despite the fact that infants in these units received a substantial frequency of handling, social tactile experiences hardly ever occurred. In the NICU and NCCU, the percentages of daily contacts involving social touching were 8.5 and 27.5, and for rocking were 0.5 and 10.4, respectively. The low occurrence of rocking in the NICU is understandable and recommended. However, the lack of social handling of infants in the NCCU is surprising in view of the large body of data suggesting that vestibular types of stimulation enhance development in young premature infants.

We also assessed caregivers' responses to infants' cries during contacts. Infants cried in approximately 21 percent of the contacts. The data showed that during more than half of the contacts when infants cried, caregivers did not attempt to soothe the infants. When they did attempt to soothe infants, it was done primarily by talking to the infant and seldom by social touching or by both modalities. The tendency not to attempt to soothe crying infants is interesting in view of the hypothesis of Speidel (1978) that crying may be the mediating factor in hypoxemia. The lack of responsiveness to infants' cries may also serve to delay the development of contingencies between infants' behavior and social environmental reactions.

Another series of analyses were conducted to determine the extent to which sensory experiences received by infants were coordinated during contacts, for example, the cooccurrence of handling and talking to infants, or infants being in a position when handled to see caregivers. The overall results showed that the percentages of sensory coordinated experiences were not impressively high. Although the effect of these dissociated sensory experiences is unknown, this finding is significant in view of evidence showing a deficit in the ability of premature infants up to one year of age to integrate tactual–visual–sensory information (Gottfried, Rose, and Bridger, 1977; Rose, Gottfried, and Bridger, 1978).

In summary, these observational findings show that premature infants in special care units receive a considerable amount of handling per day, both in frequency and duration. Handling or touching was primarily the result of medical–nursing care (the type of handling likely to be associated with transient hypoxemia and bradycardia, as indicated by Gorski in chapter 8), with social touching and rocking occurring infrequently (the type of handling more comparable to the stimulation described by Korner, Rausch, and Rose). There was no regularity to the occurrence of these handling experiences. Social touching was infrequently used to soothe crying infants. Furthermore, the rate of integrated social–sensory experiences involving handling was not impressively high. These data indicate that the nature of the tactile environment of infants in special care units may not be conducive to optimal development.

The last issue deals with the cognitive developmental context of tactile perception. The significance of the cognitive components of tactile perceptions was demonstrated in the presentations of Satz et al. (chapter 12) on somatosensory differentiation of finger recognition and Rose (chapter 11) on tactual–visual cross-modal transfer in infants. The issues are simply, what does touch tell about cognition and when can infants show evidence of tactile recognition? One of the most interesting descriptions concerning the cognitive aspects of touch is by Fraiberg (1977) on blind neurologically intact infants. She states:

> [B]etween five and eight months of age we have examples for all children in which the blind baby's hands explore the mother's or father's face, the fingers tracing features with familiarity and giving the viewer a sense that he was anticipating what he would find. The film record gives strong evidence that these exploring hands are discriminating and that the information from the fingers brings recognition as well as non-recognition [pp. 107–108].

This description of the manual activities of blind infants suggests that not only are manual activities the eyes of blind infants, but such differential manual activities may provide us with knowledge about cognitive capabilities of young infants. I would like to report a recent study providing the first experimental evidence of tactile recognition memory in infants (Gottfried and Rose, 1980). The experiment was conducted to determine whether infants can recognize the shapes of objects by touch alone. Infants' differential responsiveness to novel and familiar stimuli has been found to be a sensitive and reliable index of recognition memory. In this study, one-year-old infants were administered a task consisting of a familiarization stage followed by a recognition test stage. In the familiarization stage, infants were given the opportunity to examine a group of identical objects in normal lighting conditions. Immediately following this familiarization stage the lights were turned off and the infants were presented with a tray containing the familiar objects as well as a group of novel projects. Behavior in darkness was videotaped by infrared recording. Recognition memory was determined by infants' differential responsiveness to the novel and familiar objects. The results consistently showed that infants engaged in significantly more manipulation, exhibited more mouthing, and displayed more hand-to-hand transfers with novel compared to familiar objects. Hence, these data, which have been replicated, put forth evidence that infants can recognize the shapes of objects exclusively on the basis of tactile cues.

In conclusion, the somesthetic system is the initial sensory system to develop. Evidence indicates that it begins to function at seven and a half weeks following conception. Touch, or the sensory stimulation associated with touch (e.g., vestibular), does play a significant role in mammalian development. However, it must be noted that the stimulation associated with touch can have a positive as well as negative effect. We need to examine the components, correlates, and consequences of touch more critically. Although touch may be considered "the mother of the senses" as Montagu (1971, p. 1) describes it, it is of utmost importance to examine the family of senses, at least at the behavioral level, as well as the cognitive developmental context in which they reside.

Discussion: Chapter 13

T. Berry Brazelton: One thing that comes to me out of your work, Allen, is that touch versus proprioceptive versus vestibular may not be the way to look at it. Touch as an organizer might be a lot better concept.

Allen Gottfried: Our main reason for investigating intersensory stimulation was our earlier findings that premies showed deficits in tactile–visual cross-modal skills. We suspect that the environment of special care units is not facilitating the development of intersensory skills. The environment we provide for these babies, in my opinion, is very abnormal.

In some of his articles, Jerry Lucey has called the intensive care nursery an alien environment, and I think this is true. The noise level, for instance, is not only painful for the staff but probably unpleasant for the infants as well.

Judith Smith: What was the noise level in the nurseries, Allen? Can you give us a decibel level of something we're familiar with?

Allen Gottfried: We found peak levels like those in a factory, or near a large engine, or in light traffic. These peak levels lasted as long as a couple of hours sometimes, and the noise level was high the rest of the day as well. The radio was on most of the time (as in many work environments); people talked; machinery ran; phones and alarms rang. We took recordings inside operating incubators and found that the sound level in there was a little higher. Although the incubator provides temperature control, it does not in any way shelter the infant from light or sound.

Patricia Rausch: Many people who work in nurseries are aware of the noise problem, as you know. In our nursery in Orlando, we've put tape recorders in the isolettes and found that, with a great deal of effort, we can keep it almost completely silent inside.

Allen Gottfried: Some nurseries are changing. For example, Sheridan (1983) has reported a survey showing that 47 percent of nurseries now try to simulate day–night rhythms of light and dark.

Marian Diamond: I'm intrigued by Selma Fraiberg's observation that blind infants opened their mouths while they explored with their hands. The part of the brain that is associated with proprioception is just across the central gyrus from the motor area for oral function, so if you're groping for proprioceptive function, perhaps opening the mouth is not surprising.

T. Berry Brazelton: We had a couple of blind babies that we followed, and we noticed that in the two months before they started to walk they did a lot of posturing. They would hold their arms and legs wide apart and open their mouths, and we couldn't figure it out. Then when they started to walk, they never ran into anything. The radar started functioning before they got to the point of utilizing it, which was fascinating.

Peter Gorski: We should not assume that what is normal behavior toward a full-term baby is also appropriate for an infant who is neurologically at risk. However, neither should we assume that environmental conditions that are shocking to our eyes and ears are necessarily bad for babies. Intuitively I think they probably are, but we have to discover that still. Our interventions, it seems to me, should be based on developmental outcomes and on a knowledge of how specific infants respond to our efforts.

T. Berry Brazelton: If our interventions were more appropriate to the ability of the baby to incorporate them as experience, either positive or negative, they might be more effective. We set up a violation of expectancy. Going back to Bill Greenough's terms, we fail to provide the experience–expectant interactions that the baby's nervous system is programmed to accept. Judging from the work that we've been doing with expectancy, this can be a very costly thing for a preterm infant.

Allen Gottfried: Just a few years ago, we really had no knowledge about the environment of these newborns. In the last two or three years, we've collected a considerable body of evidence of the environment, both physical and social. The findings are consistent, and the information gained already forms a foundation for much more sophisticated interventions to come. Our understanding of infant responses and the neurology underlying them is expanding at a similarly rapid rate, and we hope future intervention programs will be based on findings in all these areas.

References

Carmichael, L. (1954), The onset and early development of behavior. In: *Manual of Child Psychology,* ed. L. Carmichael. New York: John Wiley, pp. 60–185.

Clark, D. L., Kreutzberg, J. R., & Chee, F. K. W. (1977), Vestibular stimulation influence on motor development in infants. *Science,* 196:1228–1229.

Cornell, E. H., & Gottfried, A. W. (1976), Intervention with premature human infants. *Child Develop.,* 47:32–39.

Cummins, R. A., Livesey, P. J., Evans, J. G. M., & Walsh, R. N. (1977), A development theory of environmental enrichment. *Science,* 197:692–694.

Fraiberg, S. (1977), *Insight from the Blind.* New York: Basic Books.

Gottfried, A. W. (1981), Environmental manipulations in the neonatal period and assessment of their effects. In: *Newborns and Parents: Parent–Infant Contact and Newborn Sensory Stimulation,* ed. V. L. Smeriglio. Hillside, NJ: Lawrence Erlbaum, pp. 55–61.

———(1985a), Environment of newborn infants in special care units. In: *Environmental Neonatalogy,* eds. A. W. Gottfried & J. L. Gaiter. Baltimore, MD: University Park Press.

———(1985b), Environmental neonatology: Implications for intervention. In: *Environmental Neonatology,* ed. A. W. Gottfried & J. L. Gaiter. Baltimore, MD: University Park Press.

———Rose, S. A. (1980), Tactile recognition memory in infants. *Child Develop.,* 51:69–74.

——— ———Bridger, W. H. (1977), Crossmodal transfer in human infants. *Child Develop.,* 48:118–123.

———Wallace-Lande, P., Sherman-Brown, S., King, J., Coen, C., & Hodgman, J. (1981), Physical and social environment of newborn infants in special care units. *Science,* 214:673–675.

Hooker, D. (1952), *The Prenatal Origins of Behavior.* Lawrence, KS: University of Kansas Press.

Montagu, A. (1971), *Touching: The Human Significance of the Skin.* New York: Columbia University Press.

Rose, S. A., Gottfried, A. W., & Bridger, W. H. (1978), Crossmodal transfer in infants: Relationship to prematurity and socioeconomic background. *Develop. Psychol.,* 14:643–652.

Sheridan, J. F. (1983) The typical perinatal center: As overview of perinatal health services in the United States. In: *Clinics in Perinatology*, Vol. 10, ed. Y. W. Brans. Philadelphia: W. B. Sanders Co., pp. 31–48.

Speidel, B. D. (1978), Adverse effects of routine procedures on preterm infants. *Lancet*, 1:864–865.

Walsh, R. N., & Cummins, R. A. (1975), Mechanisms mediating the production of environmentally induced brain changes. *Psychol. Bull.*, 82:986–1000.

Part V: A Role for Therapeutic Touch

14
A Role for Therapeutic Touch: A Review of the State of the Art

Therese Connell Meehan, Ph.D., R.N.

Therapeutic touch evolved from several years of systematic observation by Kunz and Krieger (1965–1972) of a treatment which involved a healthy person placing the hands on or close to the body of an ill person for about ten to fifteen minutes coupled with a strong intent to help or to heal that person. They were impressed with the healer's gentleness and focused intent to help, and observed that frequently this treatment did seem to help the ill person feel more relaxed, comfortable, and energetic.

This form of treatment can be dated to the beginning of recorded history. For centuries it has been referred to in the Western world as the practice of laying on of hands, and is known to have played a significant role in the community life and healing practices of many cultures. However, in recent years the rise of the dualistic and reductionist philosophies underlying modern science have precluded its description and explanation within a scientific framework. Since this form of treatment could not be accounted for by the scientific view, it was not amenable to scientific investigation, and as a result could not be considered real. It had been, therefore, relegated to the realm of faith healing and superstition.

However, as a nurse, Krieger was particularly interested in this form of treatment. Because of the centrality of touch to nursing practice she thought that this phenomenon might be important for nurses and offer potential for nursing theory development. She was faced with the formidable problem of investigating a form of treatment which historical and contemporary observation suggested had some therapeutic value, but which was frowned upon by orthodox science, and could not be explained by the predominant scientific view.

Krieger (1973, pp. 41–42) began by reviewing a number of laboratory studies, carried out by biochemists in the United States and Canada during the 1960s, which suggested that this form of treatment had the potential to increase the growth rate and chlorophyll content in plants, the rate of wound healing in mice, and affect the activity of in-vitro enzyme systems. As a conceptual rationale for her study, she used a group of concepts from Eastern philosophy. Basic to this view are the assumptions that the human being is an open system, that there is an underlying interconnectedness between the human being and the environment, and that human health is an expression of an essential energy system called *prana*, the closest translation of which in English is the concept of vitality (Krieger, 1973, p. 40). This view proposes that the healthy individual has an abundance of this energy and that the ill individual's supply is inadequate for normal functioning. Based upon this, Krieger (1973) posited an energy exchange as the underlying mode of interaction, stating that "an interchange of vitality occurs when a healthy person purposefully touches an ill person with a strong intent to help or to heal" (p. 43). Because in the Eastern view it is also assumed that this energy system is related to respiration and is intrinsic in what we would call oxygen, and because hemoglobin is concerned with transporting oxygen for cellular metabolism, Krieger reasoned that the hemoglobin value in the ill individual would be the most sensitive physiological index of this energy exchange.

The situation available for studying this treatment was an inpatient community center concerned with the investigation of holistic approaches to healing. People with chronic diseases were being treated by the laying on of hands method by a well-known healer under direct medical and nursing supervision. Under these circumstances the only ethical and practical methodology was a quasi-experimental before–after nonequivalent control group design in which individuals undergoing treatment were assigned to the experimental group and individuals not undergoing treatment, but otherwise living under the same conditions, were assigned to the control group. Building on a pilot study, Krieger (1973, p. 43) conducted a study with forty-three subjects in the experimental group and thirty-three subjects in the control group. She hypothesized that the mean hemoglobin value of the experimental group, after treatment by the laying on of hands method, would be greater than the before-treatment mean hemoglobin value, and that the mean hemoglobin value of the control group at comparable times would show no significant difference. Blood samples were drawn from all subjects before and after the course of treatment. There were no significant differences in the before-treatment mean hemoglobin values, the age range, or sex proportion in the groups. The hypothesis was confirmed at the 0.01 level of significance. Krieger (1975) replicated this study with a similar number of subjects controlling for other factors thought to influence hemoglobin values: the practice of meditation or yoga, breathing exercises, smoking, diet, and medications. The original hypothesis was again confirmed at the 0.01 level of significance. Though very limited by their quasi-experimental design, these studies lend support to the view that this treatment has the potential to induce a therapeutic effect in ill individuals.

However, Krieger's main concern with this treatment was its relationship to nursing. She believed that it was important for nurses to become more aware that close contact with a patient had the potential to have an intrinsic effect on the well-being of the patient. Kunz and Krieger (1965–1972) had found that by assuming a meditative state of consciousness and moving their hands at a distance of two to four inches from the surface of the patient's skin, over the clothes covering the patient, they could attune to the patient's condition by becoming aware of subtle sensory cues in their hands. Krieger made the assumption that this phenomenon was a function of an energy field interaction and, as it is assumed in the Eastern view of healing, that a healthy individual has an open and symmetrical flow of this energy and that in an ill individual this energy flow is in a state of asymmetry or imbalance. They found that they detected differences in the sensory cues in their hands in some areas and that they could redirect and balance these areas by moving their hands. This may sound like an improbable method for gaining information about and treating a patient. However, it has been learned and used successfully by many nurses and other health professionals in the United States and overseas. On the strength of this empirical evidence it can, for the present, be held as a possibility.

Based on these observations and under the direction of Kunz, Krieger derived a treatment she called "Therapeutic Touch." She described the individual administering therapeutic touch as assuming a meditative state of consciousness and placing her hands on or close to the body of the person she intends to help. She then "passively 'listens' with her hands as she scans the body of the patient and gently attunes to his or her condition . . . she places her hands over the areas of accumulated tension in the patient's body and redirects these energies" (Krieger, Peper, and Ancoli, 1979, p. 660).

Krieger (1975) reasoned that therapeutic touch "is a natural potential in physically healthy persons who are strongly motivated to help ill people, and that this potential can be actualized" (p. 786). In other words she reasoned that therapeutic touch can be taught and learned. Based on this reasoning Krieger and Kunz taught therapeutic touch to a group of registered nurses. Krieger then, in 1974, conducted the first investigation of the effects of therapeutic touch using patients hospitalized in metropolitan New York hospitals as subjects and professional nurses to administer the therapeutic touch treatments. Again, circumstances determined that a quasi-experimental before–after nonequivalent control group design was the most practical and feasible methodology. Hemoglobin value was chosen as the dependent variable. In the experimental group sixteen nurses included treatment by therapeutic touch while caring for patients. In the control group sixteen nurses gave nursing care to their patients without including therapeutic touch. Each nurse worked with two patients, making a total of sixty-four patients in the study. Krieger hypothesized that following treatment by therapeutic touch, the mean hemoglobin values of the patients in the experimental group would change significantly from their before-treatment values, whereas no significant change would be found in the control group. Before-treatment blood samples were drawn from all patients. Collection of blood samples and determination of hemoglobin values were done blindly using a standardized method and the same testing apparatus. Hemoglobin values were determined at comparable times for the control group patients so that there were before and after hemoglobin values available from both groups. Using the t test for difference between correlated means, the hypothesis was supported at the 0.01 level of significance.

In drawing implications from the study, the limits of the design, especially the threat to internal validity, must be kept in mind. Krieger did reduce the "selection threat" by demonstrating that there was no significant difference in the before-treatment mean hemoglobin levels between the two patient groups. Within its limitations the study does support the view that therapeutic touch can be learned and that it has the potential to have an intrinsic effect on the well-being of patients.

In order to further identify physiologic responses associated with treatment by therapeutic touch, Krieger et al. (1979) reported a case study in which they monitored electroencephlographic (EEG) and electromylographic (EMG) activity, galvanic skin response, temperature, and heart rate in three patients being treated at a pain and stress control clinic. Data collected on these patients while they were receiving treatment indicated that they became quite relaxed, and the patients reported feeling relaxed. Electroencephalographic readings demonstrated an unusually high amount of high amplitude alpha activity in the eyes-open state, an effect usually suggestive of deep relaxation. These data suggest that therapeutic touch may decrease physiologic tension and promote a state of generalized relaxation in ill people.

Building on this work, Heidt (1981) studied the effect of therapeutic touch on A-state anxiety in patients hospitalized with cardiovascular disease. She reasoned that a state of physiologic relaxation would be incompatible with A-state anxiety, that is, the acute anxiety patients experience when hospitalized with cardiovascular disease, and that if therapeutic touch could decrease physiologic tension then it could also decrease A-state anxiety. An experimental before–after single-blind control group design was used. Subjects were matched according to pretreatment A-state anxiety scores. Thirty subjects in the experimental group received a standardized therapeutic touch treatment for five minutes. One control group of thirty subjects received a treatment called casual touch (apical and peripheral pulse taking) for five minutes, and a second control group of thirty subjects received a treatment called no touch (engaged in supportive verbal interaction) for five minutes. The A-state anxiety Self-Evaluation Questionnaire X-1, developed by Speilberger, Gorsuch, and Lushene (1970) was administered before and after treatment. Comparison of pre- and posttreatment group mean scores using a correlated t ratio demonstrated that subjects who received therapeutic touch experienced a significant reduction in anxiety ($p<0.001$), and those who received casual touch and no touch experienced no significant reduction in anxiety. Also, analysis of covariance of the posttreatment scores for all three groups demonstrated that the experimental group had a significantly lower posttreatment anxiety level compared with the two control groups. These data support the hypothesis that therapeutic touch has the potential to significantly decrease acute anxiety in hospitalized patients.

Randolph (1979) studied the effect of therapeutic touch on the physiologic reactions of female college students exposed to a stressful stimulus. She reasoned that if therapeutic touch could promote a relaxation response and if relaxed individuals were less reactive in a stressful situation, then subjects being treated by therapeutic touch would be less reactive to a stressful stimulus than subjects treated by casual touch (a nurse with no knowledge of therapeutic touch imitating the hand position of the therapeutic touch treatment). An experimental before–after single-blind control group design was used. Physiologic response was measured according to skin conductance level, muscle tension, and skin temperature. Subjects viewed a film validated as a stress-producing stimulus. Thirty subjects in the experimental group were treated by therapeutic touch for thirteen minutes while viewing the film. Thirty subjects in the control group were treated by casual touch for thirteen minutes while viewing the film. Analysis of data demonstrated no significant differences between the two groups on any of the indices of physiologic response. Thus, the hypothesis that therapeutic touch can significantly affect the physiologic reactions of healthy individuals exposed to a stressful stimulus in a laboratory setting was not supported.

In 1982 Quinn, reviewing the studies investigating therapeutic touch, observed that the therapeutic touch treatments in all of the studies had involved physical contact between patient and nurse. From her knowledge and use of therapeutic touch she knew that in the ordinary practice setting the treatment was usually done without physical contact. She reasoned that if therapeutic touch is usually done without physical contact, its potential to be effective in this way should be tested.

As the theoretical rationale for her study, Quinn used a nursing conceptual model proposed in the 1960s by Martha E. Rogers (1970), a nurse theorist in the Division of Nursing at New York University. This model is based upon the philosophical assumptions of the field model, described by Dr. Weber in chapter 1, and the theories developing in contemporary science. The major premise of this model is that energy fields are the fundamental units of the human being and the environment. It is proposed that the human being extends beyond what we perceive as a physical body and is interconnected with everything in the environment. Within this context it is possible for one individual to touch another without physical contact. It is not within the scope of this chapter to describe Rogers' model. It is complex and represents a considerable shift from the generally accepted view. I mention it here because it currently provides the basis for deductive theory building about therapeutic touch as a nursing treatment.

Quinn (1982) outlined steps for a five-minute therapeutic touch treatment using the hands two and four inches from the body of the patient and called this noncontact therapeutic touch, to be done by a nurse who had at least four years experience using therapeutic touch. She also outlined steps for a five minute treatment called noncontact in which a nurse who had no knowledge of therapeutic touch mimicked the physical actions of the noncontact therapeutic touch treatment but did not include the meditative state of consciousness, intent to assist the subject, attuning to the condition of the subject, or the understanding of an energy exchange between nurse and subject. Instead, the nurse doing noncontact performed a mental operation known as "serial sevens," subtracting from 100 by 7's, to ensure that she maintained ordinary thinking consciousness. In order to determine whether or not both treatments appeared the same to the naive observer, Quinn videotaped the nurses giving their respective treatments and had the videotapes viewed by a panel of judges. The judges could not differentiate between the treatments.

An experimental before–after single-blind control group design was employed. Using patients hospitalized with cardiovascular disease and acute anxiety as measured by the A-state Self-Evaluation Questionnaire as the dependent variable (same setting, category of subjects, and dependant variable as Heidt), Quinn (1982) hypothesized that subjects receiving noncontact therapeutic touch would have a greater decrease in posttreatment anxiety scores than subjects receiving noncontact. Partial correlation analysis of the group mean posttreatment scores demonstrated support for this hypothesis at the 0.001 level of significance. This result again supports the view that therapeutic touch has the potential to significantly decrease anxiety in hospitalized patients. It also supports the view that physical contact is not necessary for therapeutic touch to be effective.

With regard to current research, two studies are in the stage of data analysis. Winstead-Fry (1983) is investigating the effectiveness of therapeutic touch as an adjunct to prepared childbirth using marital satisfaction and state anxiety as dependent variables. In an experimental group of thirty couples, the husband, who had been taught to do therapeutic touch, treated the wife while she was engaged in the Lamaze method of childbirth preparation. The control group consisted of couples who received only Lamaze childbirth preparation. This study was developed from a pilot study in which couples using therapeutic touch during childbirth preparation reported feelings of highly personalized sharing and support. This is one of several studies being done in the Division of Nursing, New York University, supported by a Public Service grant for nursing research on families and parenting.

There is a considerable amount of anecdotal and case study reporting that therapeutic touch is effective in relieving pain. My doctoral research is an experimental study investigating the effect of therapeutic touch on the experience of acute pain. This study is designed in accordance with the federal guidelines for testing analgesic drugs. The sample consists of 108 patients who have undergone elective abdominal or pelvic surgery. Acute pain experience is measured by a Visual Analogue Scale and a set of verbal descriptors. Subjects are blocked on pretreatment pain score and assigned to an experimental group receiving therapeutic touch, a single-blind control group receiving mimic treatment (similar to the noncontact treatment designed by Quinn [1982]), and a standard control group receiving a prescribed injection of analgesic medication. The effectiveness of therapeutic touch will be compared to the effectiveness of the mimic treatment and the effectiveness of the standard treatment.*

It is clear from these studies that the investigation of therapeutic touch is in its early stages. In the scientific sense, little headway has been made in describing and explaining the nature of therapeutic touch or predicting its effects, and only a small amount of confidence can be placed in the study findings. At the same time therapeutic touch research has come a long way. The studies completed to date are of particular value because they have paved the way and built a foothold for further research.

Any research intended as an experimental study assumes a causal relationship between the treatment being tested and the results obtained. In clinical studies investigating the effects of therapeutic touch the problem of causal relationships is formidable because there is no objective knowledge of how this treatment exerts effects, and dependent variables

*This study is supported by a grant from Sigma Theta Tau, the national honor society of nursing, and the Martha E. Rogers Scholarship Award for Doctoral Students for 1983, awarded by the New York University chapter of Sigma Theta Tau.

such as anxiety and pain are subjective states influenced by complex factors which are extremely difficult to assess. As experimental research continues it is necessary that studies be replicated and new studies planned using well-controlled designs. Early studies need to be replicated using randomized assignment of treatments and equivalent control groups. Special attention must be paid to single-blind control. The noncontact treatment designed by Quinn (1982) is open to question as a valid single-blind control. It can be argued that the observation of videotaped treatments is not a reasonable measure of the patient's experience of the treatments, and that in a clinical setting the nurse is likely to feel quite uncomfortable providing a treatment which she knows is not effective, and will communicate this feeling to the patient. All studies should include a double-blind technique or substitute; for example, a standard control group receiving a treatment of known effectiveness. It is only when these criteria are met that there is substantial basis for inferring a causal relationship between treatment by therapeutic touch and the results obtained. Otherwise, studies demonstrate no more than an association between therapeutic touch treatment and results obtained.

These issues raise the question of whether the experimental design is an appropriate methodology for investigating the effects of therapeutic touch. How can a humanistic treatment be examined using a methodology which is specifically designed to exclude the effect of human interaction? Obviously therapeutic touch cannot be placed in a capsule and administered blindly. This situation points to the underlying question of the relationship between therapeutic touch and the placebo effect. If compassionate and focused intent to help is a significant component of therapeutic touch treatment and the placebo effect is a function of the therapeutic intent of the individual administering a treatment, then are therapeutic touch and the placebo effect aspects of the same phenomenon? This question will be difficult to answer until we know much more about these very complex treatments.

In our attempts to discover a relationship between such hard-to-measure factors as a health professional's compassionate intent to help and a patient's experience of well-being, it seems wise not to rely on any single method of analysis or on statistical studies using aggregate data. We should approach the problem from a number of angles using different kinds of data and different methodologies. Descriptive methodology could provide more basic information about the nature of therapeutic touch treatment and the variables associated with it. The phenomenological approach could help identify aspects of the experience of therapeutic touch and their relative values and meanings in the interaction. Ethnomethodology could help identify if and how aspects of the treatment are context dependent.

Continued investigation of therapeutic touch is of particular concern to the nursing profession. In founding modern nursing, Nightingale (1859) taught that nurses were to treat the individual as a whole and place the individual in the best environment for the natural healing process to take place. Of all health professionals, nurses spend the greatest amount of time with patients. It is often assumed that a nurse's presence and therapeutic intent facilitate the comfort of a person who is ill. Most nurses would agree that touch is an integral aspect of nursing practice. Precedence for the nurse's use of hands as a focus for therapeutic intent is extensive. Hygieia, the embodiment of nursing in Greek mythology, is referred to in *The Orphic Hymns* (1977) as "Hygieia of the gentle hands." This reverence implies that the goddess's use of her hands represented an important therapeutic quality. More recently, anthropologist Margaret Mead (1956) has observed that the nurse's compassionate use of her hands is one of the unique functions of nursing in modern society. The nursing profession today is indebted to Krieger for her recognition of this potential and her work in bringing it to the forefront of our attention.

Continued investigation of treatments such as therapeutic touch is also of concern to science at large. In its 1981 survey, the United States House of Representatives Committee on Science and Technology (1981) reported that recent experiments in the physics of consciousness suggest that there exists an "interconnectiveness" of the human mind with other minds and with matter, and that this interconnectiveness appears to be functional in nature and amplified by intent and emotion. Focused intent is central to the practice of therapeutic touch, and the concept of interconnectedness is an assumption upon which the theoretical rationale of the research is based. The survey suggests that quality research on this subject has potential importance in the area of health in that the use of "mind-initiated cures" in conjunction with traditional cures could be advanced.

In many ways therapeutic touch stands at the crossroads of contemporary consciousness. It is an enigma to modern science, yet its conceptual underpinnings stem from concepts addressed by the earliest Greek philosophers and physicists at the forefront of the current scientific revolution. In some quarters it is controversial, yet it is one of the most popular subjects in nursing continuing education programs and in holistic health programs generally. It looks very simple, yet it is profoundly complex. It is an intuitive, subjective process, yet it must be subject to the scrutiny of scientific inquiry. It involves the intensely humanistic, yet nonpersonal concern of one human being for another. I hope that all those in the health care professions will join me in considering "the state of the art" and the possible directions this modality may take us in the future.

Discussion: Chapter 14

T. Berry Brazelton: I think nursing is ahead of most of the helping professions in that, for a long time, nurses have been trying to identify the forces behind caring and the transmission of caring. As Kathy Barnard explained to me while we were planning this conference, the kind of training we have had as physicians has really followed a pathological model. We've been trained to look for disease, for any kind of failure in the system, but we haven't been trained to look for strengths, for ways of energizing the system.

Therese, your exhortation to all of us to look at therapeutic touch seriously shows the opportunity for touch in health care. I really want to get on now to a field model of what you're doing. Intentionality on the part of the giver, and also intentionality or expectation on the part of the receiver, are critical ingredients. But therapeutic touch techniques should not be kept in the area of mysticism or good intent. They can be studied systematically, and they must be, in order for others to believe in the techniques and to utilize them.

Seymour Levine: In Krieger's initial studies evaluating therapeutic touch, why was hemoglobin chosen as a variable?

Therese Connell Meehan: Krieger made the assumption based on her review of Eastern literature that *prana* is associated with breathing, with what we would call oxygen. Also, some earlier studies looking at the laying on of hands had found an increase in chlorophyll in plants, and chlorophyll and hemoglobin are related. Does that clarify it?

Seymour Levine: It clarifies why Krieger looked at it, but not why it would be related in any way to the therapeutic facts.

Renée Weber: A standard yoga practice in India is to slow down breathing rates and deepen respiration. The rate of slow-down has been studied by Western medical teams, and I think it is correlated with other changes. Therefore, I think it was the easiest external indicator that Krieger could take.

Michael Merzenich: Would normal, healthy people presumably show the same hemoglobin response to therapeutic touch as people who are ill?

Therese Connell Meehan: That's an interesting question. You might find significant effects only with people who are ill or in a state of imbalance. If a person is healthy, you're assuming there's a state of balance and openness, so you might not see much effect.

Kathryn Barnard: An important issue for nursing right now is whether we should study how to comfort people who've become ill or study the comfort of people, regardless of their particular state. It's interesting to me that Krieger took patients regardless of condition. Their particular illness was not important to her.

Ruth McCorkle: Perhaps the kind of monitoring systems used in some of the newborn studies described earlier could also be used to assess therapeutic touch.

Michael Merzenich: Therese, you said at the end of your chapter that therapeutic touch is enigmatic. To my mind, nothing that's been described is not potentially understandable, nor is it contrary to our understanding of the organization of touch or the way people represent personal space. Why do you call it an enigma?

Therese Connell Meehan: I think what is difficult to understand is the human stance from which therapeutic touch is done. Something is going on, promoting the effect, that we don't understand very well. The first step in therapeutic touch is called centering, and during centering a switch in consciousness occurs that is difficult to describe. It makes you see the patient as a new person, an amazing, unique human being, even if moments before you felt overworked and angry and burned out. We don't understand how this happens or why the process of taking on a meditative state of consciousness is so important, yet it seems to make a difference in helping people.

Seymour Levine: The studies you described in your chapter didn't convince me it helps. At this point I don't care so much what the therapeutic action is; what I want to know is whether patients who receive therapeutic touch are better off in any real way. So far there really has not been a credible demonstration that the procedure works.

Paul Satz: The hope is there, but I think there's more hope than evidence right now.

Michael Merzenich: I think it can be understood exactly what the consequences of therapeutic touch are, and exactly what the therapist does to produce the positive impact. Our body surface, and the region immediately around us within reach of our limbs, represent our personal territory. This representation is not created out of nothing; it's created out of our experiences and our use of our limbs. When someone enters our territory, we either defend it or surrender to the intruder. When someone touches us or strokes us, the tendency to surrender is strong.

The importance of the meditative state may be that it requires the therapist to adopt a mental attitude that promotes the most natural kind of focus in terms of tactile contact. The closer touch comes to being what the person's nervous system wants to accept, the more therapeutic it is, presumably. In any event, it isn't magic; it's something that can be studied.

Cathleen Fanslow: I've been studying and practicing therapeutic touch since 1973, and I think I agree with you. These things are not such an enigma, because we see the results.

Therese Connell Meehan: I've been asked to help with some case study reporting at a hospital in the New York area where the nurses in the neonatal intensive care unit often use therapeutic touch with the babies. They don't touch the babies physically; they just use the technique, and it seems to promote relaxation and quieting.

Michael Merzenich: If a sense of extrapersonal space is a product of experience and development, as I've suggested, then it would be surprising if newborns had such a sense, beyond perhaps a crude awareness of contact or impending contact.

Therese Connell Meehan: My intuitive sense, from the small amount of time I spend with babies, is that they would be particularly skillful in this way.

Michael Merzenich: There is a difference between being able to detect the presence of something off the skin and having a sense of ownership of the field around you. The latter, I think it is largely believed, arises by your development of operations in the immediate area around you. Certainly you gain ownership of this space around you, and somewhere in your mind you have a highly defined construct of it. When it's invaded, there are reactions to it of a special kind, just as there are reactions to direct contact with the skin.

References

Heidt, P. (1981), Effect of therapeutic touch on anxiety level of hospitalized patients. *Nurs. Res.*, 1:32–37.

Krieger, D. (1973), The relationship of touch with intent to help or to heal, to subjects' in-vivo hemoglobin values: A study in personalized interaction. In: *Proceedings of the Ninth American Nurses' Association Nursing Research Conference.* New York: American Nurses' Association.

———(1975), Therapeutic touch: The imprimatur of nursing. *Amer. J. Nurs.*, 5:784–787.

———Peper E., & Ancoli, S. (1979), Searching for evidence of physiological change. *Amer. J. Nurs.*, 4:660–662.

Kunz, D. v. G., & Krieger, D. (1965–1972), *The Pumpkin Hollow Foundation.* Craryville, NY: Theosophical Society in America.

Mead, M. (1956), Nursing—Primitive and civilized. *Amer. J. Nurs.*, 9:1001–1004.

Nightingale, F. (1859), *Notes on Nursing: What It Is, and What It Is Not.* Philadelphia: J.B. Lippincott.

The Orphic Hymns (1977), trans. A.N. Athanassakis. Missoula, MN: Scholars Press.

Quinn, J. (1982), *An Investigation of the Effects of Therapeutic Touch Done*

Without Physical Contact on State Anxiety of Hospitalized Cardiovascular Patients. Unpublished doctoral dissertation, New York University, New York.

Randolph, G. (1979), *The Differences in Physiological Response of Female College Students Exposed to Stressful Stimulus, When Simultaneously Treated by Therapeutic Touch or Casual Touch*. Unpublished doctoral dissertation, New York University, New York.

Rogers, M. (1970), *An Introduction to the Theoretical Basis of Nursing*. Philadelphia: F.A. Davis.

Spielberger, C.D., Gorsuch, R.L., & Lushene, R.R. (1970), *STAI Manual for the State Trait Anxiety Inventory*. Palo Alto, CA: Consulting Psychologist Press.

United States House of Representatives Committee on Science and Technology (1981), *Survey of Science and Technology Issues: Present and Future*. Washington, DC: Government Printing Office.

Winstead-Fry, P. (1983), *A Report to the Profession. Nursing Research Emphasis Grant: Families and Parenting*. New York University, Division of Nursing.

15
Therapeutic Touch and Midwifery

Iris S. Wolfson, R.N., B.S., C.N.M.

Therapeutic touch has been described as the direction and transfer of energy to facilitate healing in another individual. The touch in therapeutic touch is only occasionally and incidentally touch in the narrow tactile sense of skin to skin. It is rather a part of a wider spectrum of sensations and connections between two people, as well as one's own communication with the world outside oneself. It is mainly a touch or communication of energy fields, those immediately surrounding the physical body and those beyond. The idea of energy transfer and direction, which is the underlying assumption on which therapeutic touch is based, derives from a philosophical framework which, although not at all new, has until relatively recently been confined to the realms of Eastern religious thought or antiscientific mysticism. This model has come to play an important role in health care systems such as imagery and acupuncture, and has become a dominant hypothesis of the universe in areas such as subatomic physics and quantum mechanics. This philosophy and its relation to the foundations of therapeutic touch are the subject of chapter 1, so I will give only a brief outline before discussing the process of therapeutic touch and its applications in midwifery.

Basically, this is a model which sees the world as one of total interconnectedness, a universe not of separate and distinct substances, beings, and things, which act and react in a mechanical manner, but rather one of a universal, indivisible substance, which is in fact not substance at all, but closer to movement and rhythm than matter. Because the essence of this substance is motion, it is often called energy. In acupuncture it is referred to as *chi* or life force; in Hinduism it is *prana*, breath or vital force. In subatomic physics, solid matter cannot be found. The atoms' particles yield up their particulateness to appear as energy, waves, or rays in motion—the motion itself defining the so-called particle. It is easy to understand why we have long resisted such a view; our everyday reality is in total conflict with it. The brain has an organizing aspect which makes its sense of the world in solid, separate, and immutable units. It is, however, not a completely foreign concept, as it is the stuff of transcendent thought, religious experience, and now of late, progressive science.

If we can accept the possibility that this is the universe as it exists beyond our categorizing brain, a world that exists as unity, as motion, heat, light, *prana*, or simply as energy, then life itself is part of the process of movement and flow, and health can be defined as the state of being in harmony with this flow, an integral part of the constant transfer and motion of energy in the world. Consequently disease or illness can be defined as blockage of the flow, a cutting off from the flow of universal energy. Acupuncture, for example, defines illness in just this way, as a blockage of *chi*, or life energy, at the body meridians, which are the channels or pathways of this energy.

The attempt in therapeutic touch is to organize and direct this energy for the purpose of healing. It is a process of learning and working with the rhythmic and harmonious aspects of the universe, whose pattern is apparent everywhere in nature, from the symmetry of a crystalline snowflake to the development of human consciousness. The ability to tap this energy and move in its pattern is at the core of therapeutic touch.

One other part of this conceptual framework can help explain the success of therapeutic touch, and that has to do with a way of defining substance or bodies. Consider solid matter to be slower moving and denser concentrations of energy, less susceptible to manipulation and transfer of energy than the lighter more mobile aspects. Therapeutic touch uses this idea—that the energy field of the body, which exists just beyond the physical body, is both an accurate reflection of the body, and also a more workable, mutable area than the body itself. Changes which can be wrought in the energy fields can have direct consequences in the physical body.

If illness in the body is viewed as a stoppage or diminished energy flow within and surrounding the body, the result might be described as congestion or dense areas in the energy field. Similarly, if the universal energy has a rhythm, pattern, and harmony as its nature, illness can also be described as an imbalance, an absence of this harmony, pattern, and rhythm. The task of therapeutic touch is to reestablish, by transfer or direction of this universal energy, the person's harmonious balance and vital energy flow. This realignment of the energy flow allows the individual to use her energies to activate her own recuperative powers. The healthy body is an open system—energy flows in, around, to, and from it. Therapeutic touch is an attempt to maintain and facilitate this openness, this interconnectedness.

A nearly perfect example of interconnection and transfer of energies is a pregnant woman and her unborn child. Here are two bodies which for nine months and beyond act as a unity, existing together, energies moving back and forth, indivisible. Therapeutic touch in midwifery is an attempt to draw upon the essential nature of the mother–child connections, to expand these connections to incorporate the family beyond, and to deepen and enhance them to aid the pregnancy itself. The task of a successful pregnancy is to maintain the open system, the energy flow between mother and baby, and to keep these energies harmonious and balanced prenatally, through the labor and delivery, and into the postpartum time to maintain health and to help the external bonding to be uninhibited and unblocked.

I say external bonding because there is so much communication that takes place during pregnancy which is bonding—the essence of the energy mesh between mother and child. The heartbeat of the mother, her breathing, her emotions, every aspect of her is influenced by, and influences, her child. If there is to be a bonding between them, it must be in an open system. No baby can bond by itself if the woman shuts down.

When the baby is born, it remains connected to the mother, depending on the umbilical cord to provide the transition to breathing; when the pulsing ends, the separation is hardly completed—it is barely beginning. The energy connections are still intact and operating together. In every sense the baby is not yet prepared for independent life. The mother has not broken her connection to her infant, which can be strengthened by a positive birthing experience. Neither the baby's energies nor the mother's are prepared to operate individually for some time.

What occurs after birth is the beginning of the external bonding, the connections to the mother's smells, the tactile connections, nursing, the continuation of the baby's connection to the mother's heartbeat and respirations, and most importantly the emotional attachment. Bonding as a form of energy connection, including physical, emotional, mental, and spiritual energies, can be an important extension of the family's relation to the pregnancy, the birth, and the new baby. Therapeutic touch in midwifery is a means to deepen those inherent ties between mother and baby and within the family by adding a new dimension to communication and knowing one another. It is also an excellent tool to help alleviate common discomforts and complications during the childbearing cycle.

Before moving to a discussion of the particulars of therapeutic touch in the practice of midwifery, I would like to provide a brief summary of the techniques and the basic process of therapeutic touch.

The process has as a precondition an exercise or meditation called centering. Centering, as its name implies, is an exercise aimed at finding a stable center in the swirl of everyday thought and energy, a center within oneself that allows one to touch a state of mind that transcends the ordinary reality to see the universe, as described earlier, in terms of unity rather than separateness. It allows distractions to take a background position so one can fully focus one's concentration on making an energy assessment and then on channeling energies where needed. Centering is also important to maintain one's own energy, to enable oneself to be a channel or conduit for the direction of universal energy, rather than using one's own personal energies. Our individual energy is limited and can be draining to draw upon. Centering allows us to act rather as a director and modulator of universal energy. It is crucial to remain aware of ourselves as a channel rather than a source for this energy, and centering is the primary skill needed for this awareness.

Psychic and religious healers always refer to themselves as such a channel, despite their different descriptions of the source from which they draw. It seems that they possess an instinctive ability to center themselves. Practitioners of therapeutic touch feel that this is a developable skill. The mechanics of centering will not be discussed here. I only wish to outline the process of therapeutic touch to give some background to the discussion that follows.

Intentionality is another important facet in the practice of therapeutic touch. On the surface, intentionality may seem to be nothing more than desire to heal. However, intentionality is wider ranging than mere willingness. It cannot take place without the concept of centering; it is a focus on the healing process rather than the healer, an immersion in the healing not for ego gratification, but as an open and unqualified connection with the intent to heal. I must emphasize again that the healer is a channel, a unit in the healing process. To transform oneself from a person caught up in the normal world of ego and mechanics into a healer is the central exercise of the meditation that is centering, and that is therapeutic touch. Through this centering one becomes aware of oneself as an open energy system and reaches a quiet inner place where one can be focused and attentive.

Once we have centered, the next phase is to assess the energy field. Centering and assessment are not necessarily sequential, but are actually a continuous process. It is for the purpose of this discussion that I treat them as a one-directional sequence.

Assessment is the garnering of information about the person from every available source. We try to avail ourselves of all cues regarding a person's state, with a particular expansion of our intuitive senses. We then assess the energy field around the person by moving our hands through the field, absorbing information about the sensations that are felt. The assessment is based on the idea that the healthy body's energy patterns are symmetrical, that the energy is rhythmic, mobile, and balanced. With this idea in mind one feels for areas of disturbance, asymmetrical areas on one side of the body to the other, hot or cold areas, tingling sensations, pressure, or other sensations that translate as an imbalance or blocked flow of energy. We attempt, in a centered state, to absorb this information about the pattern and organization of the client's energy field.

Once the assessment is complete, the task of therapeutic touch is to direct and move energy to adjust the field imbalances that have been assessed. This involves both the transfer of energy to the body as well as the balancing of energies within the field itself.

There is one particular sensation that often appears in an unhealthy body, that of congestion or static condition in the energy field. This congestion is described by acupuncture as a blockage in the meridians through which energy flows. It has been said that much of illness stems from this blockage. The first task then, before the direction and transfer of energy, is to free this blockage, even if only temporarily, to open up the energy field to make it more receptive to the direction of energy that follows. This process of freeing the congested, or bound energies, has been labeled by Dolores Krieger as "unruffling the field," because the dominant sensation felt by the healer is one of pressure and overlapping layers or densities like ruffles. The unruffling is accomplished by a sweeping motion of the hands, which push the energy in a smooth gesture from the area of congestion and away from the body. After this sweeping motion is done several times, the energy field begins to feel "smoothed out." This unruffling can sometimes have the effect of relieving symptoms, but its primary function is the creation of a mobile field that facilitates healing. Since energy is motion, this creation of movement puts the body in the flow of energy and therefore opens its access to receive healing energies.

The next phase of therapeutic touch is to direct and modulate energy, based on the assessment, in order to balance the energy field.

The actual direction of energy in its particulars is, like centering, outside the scope of this discussion. It is largely an intuitive process and an empirical one. We draw upon experience to guide us in using particular techniques for particular problems. It is axiomatic to say that if an area is hot, the intent is to cool it; if there is an area of pressure, to relieve it; and if one senses pulsation, to moderate it. This is accomplished by using experimentation and intuition and also by using information about the qualities of energy itself. For example, each color of the light spectrum is a wavelength of energy, and as such has been said to have its own unique properties and effects on the body: blue is calming and pain relieving, yellow is stimulating, and green is balancing. Part of therapeutic touch involves developing skill at imaging the particular form of energy felt necessary, and then projecting and directing it appropriately.

Therapeutic touch is based on the interrelatedness of all life. The use of therapeutic touch in the practice of midwifery is centered on the particular and special interconnection of a mother with her baby, and further, those special connections within the family unit. In midwifery, the use of therapeutic touch is twofold. It is used as a therapy for the treatment of anxieties, discomforts, and complications related to pregnancy and birth, and as a teaching tool to expand the skills that help to develop the interconnections that exist within the family. In this context, therapeutic touch becomes part of a philosophy that the midwife attempts to impart to the family throughout the entire pregnancy and into the birth and postpartum time.

During the prenatal phase, therapeutic touch focuses on two central issues: the development of communication between the midwife and the family and within the family itself, and the development of positive attitudes toward the birthing experience.

Therapeutic touch is a highly personalized interaction between two people. Comments by both practitioners and recipients of therapeutic touch have noted that among the outcomes of the use of therapeutic touch is a close attunement and bonding between the involved individuals. Through the warmth and concern that is engendered during therapeutic touch interaction, a close working relationship can be established between the midwife and her client as well as within the family unit. More open communication helps the pregnant couple to recognize and deal with their problems so that they do not interfere with the normal course of labor and birth. The increased bonding between midwife and client can serve to heighten the effectiveness of the counseling relationship. Further, through the use of projected energy, as an extension of traditional therapeutic touch, a lot can be communicated and accomplished without touch or language. The ability to experience and project a sense of calm to the family can decrease anxiety and facilitate the communication and birthing processes because anxiety can be a big barrier to the smooth flow of energy.

Therapeutic touch is based upon the assumption that the body is an energy field that is continually affecting and being influenced by energy fields outside itself. This, coupled with the idea that therapeutic touch creates a state of openness and increased suggestibility in its recipient, makes its use an ideal opportunity to develop positive attitudes of self-reliance, normalcy, and a belief in the basic integrity of the body and the birthing process. I believe that a positive attitude and self-confidence can go a long way in preventing problems that can arise from women's fears and lack of confidence in their ability to complete the labor and birth processes.

In order to help foster positive attitudes and basic beliefs in the body's integrity I teach a centering and visualization exercise during prenatal classes that focuses on the normal and healthy functioning of the woman's body and an active and perfectly developing fetus, and then projects forward in time to the imaged experience of the normal course of events and physiologic processes that will occur during labor and birth. The use of imagery has been shown to effect changes in the body's physiology and can be used constructively to transmit to the client an expectation for wellness and normalcy.

Imagery use can be expanded to include verbal imagery as well, and the caregiver should be sensitive to choice of words, intonation, and so forth, and particularly so after a therapeutic touch treatment.

Visualizing the fetus as healthy and normal can also be facilitated during the process of abdominal palpation, which is performed during each prenatal visit. By teaching the mother and father to reflect on the interaction of the energy fields involved and to try to develop an awareness of the subtle vibrations, the emotional connections amongst all participating can be strengthened. The palpation by the mother also gives her a new physical sensation to focus on, the feel of her baby from outside as well as inside, allowing her to better visualize a real baby rather than an abstraction and a bundle of sensations in her belly. The touching connection to the baby gives the mother someone to focus her energies toward. The abstraction of the pregnancy begins to center on a baby; its legs, buttocks, head, begin to become very real to her now. The same applies to the father and the other children. Palpation is a very good way to introduce the other family members to the baby as a real entity. When palpation is completed I often use therapeutic touch to gently smooth the energy field over the abdomen; a few brief downward strokes is usually all that is necessary.

I have taught the fathers therapeutic touch in childbirth classes, and have found that when practiced, it serves to facilitate communication and deepen the father's involvement in the pregnancy. At some point in their practice, the father can usually distinguish the energy field of the baby from that of the mother. This new way of perceiving and experiencing both mother and baby strengthens further the already existing bonds.

There are a few general suggestions that I have found helpful, from an energy perspective, for women during pregnancy. Because mother and baby are in a very open state and particularly sensitive to outside energies, the woman needs to be careful about the atmosphere with which she surrounds herself. I encourage her whenever possible to do what makes her feel happy and relaxed. I believe that these positive feelings will be transmitted to her growing baby. Listening to soothing music can be very calming, as the energy vibrations made by sound can directly affect the energy field. Listening to natural sounds, such as the ocean, helps to focus the mother's attention on a different level and rhythm, and her own rhythms are helped to harmonize and become more synchronous with the harmonious and balanced rhythms of nature. For the same reason, I encourage pregnant women to develop an attunement with nature and to try and create a symbol from nature that makes her feel peaceful and calm. She may then use this symbol to reflect back on when in labor, as an energy pattern will have developed that will enable her to remember and connect with that feeling of peace and calm to help her through her labor. One last suggestion is for women to spend some part of each day doing a relaxation and/or centering exercise. This helps to keep energy flowing harmoniously and builds daily a growing sense of inner peace. This time can also be used as a special time to be particularly attentive to any messages her body and her baby are giving her, and also for sending thoughts of love and joy to her developing baby, encouraging the inner communication process between them to grow.

Before beginning a discussion of therapeutic touch in relation to problems of pregnancy, it is important to restate that the process is an intuitive and empirical one, taking certain ideas or images, such as color being a wavelength of energy, and combining these concepts with the ability to direct and transfer energy. Therapeutic touch has had particular and notable success with creating a relaxation response, and for pain reduction—areas that have important applications to pregnancy and birth.

Rather than describe the particulars of treatment of every potential problem, I will give some examples that illustrate the general approach to problems in pregnancy as they are handled in therapeutic touch practice. It is important to note that pregnant women are very sensitive to energy transfer and the direction of energy needs to be very gentle, with particular attention to rhythmic motions. When dealing with a problem, it is important to assess the entire energy field. For example, morning sickness may have anxiety as its source and be helped by projecting a sense of calm or the color blue to the solar plexus. If the problem is from an endocrine imbalance, sometimes balancing of the field and using the color green can alleviate it. I instruct clients to breathe deeply and visualize blue light from the top of the head to the solar plexus and stomach areas. Sometimes "swallowing" blue light is helpful. Therapeutic touch treatments are used as an adjunct to traditional treatments, and many of the usual dietary, herbal, and vitamin treatments are also suggested.

Heartburn, as the name should imply, is a condition of excess heat. I project a sense of coolness and have the woman visualize blue cooling light in the area of discomfort. Physiologically, the stomach is being displaced upwards, and mental imagery can be very useful here. For example, a waterfall image with energy flowing downward is an image of coolness, blue, and flow, all of which can help counteract an upward, congested, and heated condition. I ask the woman to focus on this image as I perform therapeutic touch over the area with a gentle downward stroking.

Anemia is a common problem in pregnancy and is a particular problem for home births, where the low-risk status of the pregnancy must be impeccable. Therapeutic touch has been found to have a significant effect on raising hemoglobin levels. The use of therapeutic touch to help raise hemoglobin levels focuses on energy direction and stimulation of the spleen, liver, kidneys, and the long bones. I had one woman come to me for a therapeutic touch consultation. She was a midwife herself who had planned a home birth, but who after months of iron supplements was unable to raise her hematocrit to acceptable levels. After one session of therapeutic touch her hematocrit rose to 35.9 from 32 and she was able to consider home birth as an option again. Therapeutic touch does not always produce this dramatic effect. However, when it works it produces significant changes.

I will move along now to labor and delivery. In this

phase, it is crucial to remain aware of other aspects of birth beyond the merely physical. One must not lose sight of the total person. As an example, I had a woman in labor, who, while continuing to contract, was not dilating and whose blood pressure was rising dangerously. After therapeutic touch she began to cry and expressed some previously unrecognized fears that she had suppressed. Following this release, her blood pressure dropped and her contractions began to be effective, leading to a successful and uncomplicated delivery. It is interesting to note that a traditional medical view and treatment of this woman's blood pressure problem and lack of progress would not have addressed the true problem. Therapeutic touch sometimes has this effect of facilitating the release of emotional blocks in unexpected or unforeseen areas, a fact that one must be very sensitive to in working with birthing women.

A woman in labor is especially open and susceptible to other people's energy fields. Fearful or negative people should not be present at the birth, as these influences may adversely affect the laboring woman. I have on a number of occasions seen women's labors totally stop upon arrival at the hospital, where the surrounding environmental energy is felt by them as threatening or frightening. Because women are so vulnerable in labor, one must be very sensitive to what is said and the feelings that are projected. It is then that the imagery developed during the prenatal time proves its usefulness; images of a cervix opening, softening, becoming elastic, images of a baby's head moving downward and slipping through the cervix and into the vagina. These images of normal function and progress taught during the prenatal phase have created energy patterns that have been learned on a subconscious level, and by repeating these images verbally now, one hopes to stimulate these normal energy patterns into action.

Labor is essentially a rhythmic progression of uterine contractions leading to the birth of the baby. All efforts are focused on the smooth flow of this process. Pain and fear can slow down and even stop the progress of labor. Therapeutic touch is especially useful for alleviating the painful sensations of labor contractions and enhancing relaxation. I usually perform a total assessment in between contractions, and work with the field according to my findings. Often the kidney and adrenal area may have a "drawing" sensation, indicating the need for an input of energy here. This is a frequently used site for stimulating the body's energy reserves. It is important to assure that there is a good flow of energy throughout the entire body down the legs and out through the feet. When therapeutic touch is performed early in labor it can help the woman to relax and better integrate the sensations she is having during contractions. I sweep my hand down the abdomen and at the cervical area I move my hands away from the body, brushing the sensation that I feel in my hands outward. I am often now using the color blue, which is said to be both pain relieving and calming. A woman recently wrote to me that when I used therapeutic touch during her labor she felt "instantly relaxed," and during the contractions the "pain dissipated but I could still feel the complete sensation of the contractions." Another woman reported that therapeutic touch changed the sensations from pain to pressure during contractions and she felt then able to "yield the pain" to me. A number of clients have remarked to me that their babies felt and responded to therapeutic touch by relaxing. Perhaps because therapeutic touch is such a conscious attempt to align with the energy flow and the particular rhythms of birth, it is very successful in helping women relax and respond to their bodies and the process of labor.

If the father has learned therapeutic touch and is interested, I encourage him to use it now. When the couple work well together, the father will have a natural attunement to the mother and can use therapeutic touch very effectively because he will be such a good energy channel. Energy can also be imparted indirectly from the midwife to the father who is supporting the laboring woman. This helps to keep the main labor support relationship within the couple and continues to strengthen their bond to one another. There are times when I will just sit quietly and envelop the couple in a sense of deep calm and blue light. This interchange gives them support and quiets them emotionally.

Throughout the labor, there is the attempt to incorporate levels other than just the physical, to keep the woman from experiencing only the intense physical sensations. Too narrow a focus on the physical can inhibit the progressive flow of energy, as the physical sensations can at times be overwhelming. The use of verbal affirmations by the woman gives acknowledgment from the mental level and thus reaches a field other than the physical. Similarly, by bringing in other senses and having the woman focus on them, the woman can move out of the physical and into the mental field. For example using visualization by having the woman focus on the image of her cervix opening, or using sound by having the woman listen to her breathing and its rhythm, can attune her to the rhythms of her body and the birth process, which may have been getting lost amidst a flood of physical sensations.

The general focus of the midwife in labor is to help the woman flow with, or surrender to, the enormous energy of birth. She must help the woman accept the pain and work with it by maintaining the energy flow through all levels.

Some women experience a type of "psychedelic" feeling in labor. They may lose touch with their bodies and may need to be "grounded." Physically touching the woman allows your energy field to enter hers and can give her a sense of relating. Sometimes holding or massaging her feet can assist in "grounding" her. Rhythmic breathing that synchronizes the rhythms of breath to the rhythms of the contractions can help to maximize the energy and efficiency of the contractions. Eye contact can promote good energy flow between the woman and her support person and keeps the woman's energy outwardly focused, again preventing her from being overwhelmed by her own internal sensations and subsequently shutting down the continuous input and output of energy.

When performing therapeutic touch during labor I have found it most helpful to women when I use the earlier mentioned downward stroking gesture over the abdomen, in a very even and rhythmic manner. If the strokes are smooth and timed to the rhythm of her breathing, the practitioner can most effectively attune to, and reflect, the energy she is expressing, and in a sense complete the circuit. It is important to establish a slow and steady rhythm of sending energy. I have been told on a number of occasions by people observing me performing therapeutic touch that the motions had reminded them of a dancer's. It is this smooth, graceful, and rhythmic movement that enhances the comfort and relaxation of therapeutic touch recipients. Downward stroking reminds her to keep her energy moving and centered low in her body where it is most needed. Her shoulders, chest, and arms should be loose and yielding, for tension here can block the smooth flow of energy through to the pelvic area down the legs and out through the feet. Therapeutic touch as well as shoulder massage can help prevent tension locking energy high up in her body.

Another way that I have used therapeutic touch effectively has been in facilitating a type of separation process that occurs. In order for the birth to proceed the woman must, on many levels, give up and separate from her pregnancy. This is a state she has grown accustomed to, and is in many ways comfortable with. Now she needs to move on to the unknown and perhaps frightening aspects of labor, delivery, and parenting. For some this may be a difficult step to make. Therapeutic touch can assist in this emotional transition and may help to prevent or alleviate problems that might otherwise be manifested on a physical level.

If complications do develop one must be sensitive to the disturbance, but at the same time be especially careful to project a sense of wholeness, well-being, and integrity that will help to give the woman strength.

In times of crisis, energy field boundaries contract. When they contract the input and outflow of energy are greatly diminished, and there may not be enough energy to fuel the increased demands of labor; this energy deficit can cause a prolonged or painful labor. The woman becomes unable to open up and let the energy flow. When problems arise one needs to be particularly aware of any emotional disturbances that might be contributing to the physical problems. Sometimes by working at the emotional level and helping to eliminate or resolve fears and anxieties one can have powerful effects on the physical level. When confronted with anxiety and/or fears, I work by supporting the solar plexus area, which has been called the seat of emotions, while encouraging the woman to verbalize her fears or to visualize them wherever she feels them. The woman is then able to use her mental energies and is not functioning solely on emotions. Gentle caring support can facilitate an emotional release at these times.

At various stages in labor there are turning points that are often difficult for the woman to integrate. Therapeutic touch during these times can relieve pain and induce better relaxation so integration can occur and the next phase of labor can be approached.

When the flow of energy becomes blocked, therapeutic touch can help to get the flow moving better and can stimulate the woman by directing an input of energy into her system. Quite often what I feel at these times is a blockage of energy in the pelvis, with no energy flow down the legs. On a number of occasions I have perceived a tightness or blocked area around the throat. One such client was unable to progress past 8 cm of dilation. She was a religious woman and was encouraged to talk about her religious beliefs. After a five-minute discussion she suddenly felt an urge to push and successfully delivered her baby. The release in her throat area, afforded her by the talking, enabled the blocked energies to flow once again. The use of sound with the contractions can produce a similar opening of blocked energies in the throat area.

There are many other complications of labor that can be dealt with using similar concepts, but for now I would like to focus on the pushing stage of labor. I have found the squatting position to best encourage the focus on release and descent. I use perineal massage, starting slowly and rhythmically, always being sensitive to the mother's response and always between contractions so as not to interfere with the energy flow. As in much of the labor process, we are attempting to find the mother's birth rhythms and work with them in order to amplify their energy.

Pushing is a phase that demands active participation from the woman to make the contractions efficient. Pushing is unforced—women are encouraged to go at their own pace—unhurried, and in an atmosphere of calm and quiet. I watch her body language carefully. Her shoulders, neck, mouth, and jaw should all be loose, indicating that tensions are not building up, and that she is concentrating her energy low in her body where she needs it to be. Sometimes therapeutic touch can help her to guide her energy downward.

At the moment of crowning, if the mother is encouraged to touch the baby's head an energy connection is made at the physical level. This helps the pelvis and vagina to relax and also helps the mother to realize the reality of a baby and the imminence of the birth. The woman is encouraged to open her mouth and relax her tongue which helps the vagina to also be relaxed. Noise is encouraged with exhale pushing, as this keeps the throat open and loose and consequently helps keep the vagina relaxed and open. After the head and shoulders are delivered I have the woman reach down as I guide and help her to deliver her baby directly onto her abdomen.

As soon as the baby is born, I encourage the mother and father to touch the baby. They are perfect energy channels to help the baby get started. Skin contact with the mother is especially crucial. The energy fields of the mother and baby are so closely bound it is certainly ideal not to disturb this sensitive connection.

If the baby is having difficulty getting started, I project the color yellow through my hands and stimulate the baby physically by rubbing up and down its spine and feet. I also have the mother touch and talk to her baby, as this is the energy the baby has been so deeply connected to, and is most familiar with. Again, yellow is used to help stimulate contractions to facilitate delivery of the placenta.

It is important to encourage some quiet time for the new family to continue with the bonding process. As we know, the mother and baby are in a state of heightened sensitivity and are particularly open to one another. They are also now especially vulnerable to outside influences, which should be kept to a minimum.

In the immediate postpartum period, therapeutic touch is used to rebuild energy in the mother and to maintain a peaceful atmosphere. I encourage them to stay at home without many visitors in order to keep the baby secure in the mother's safe and familiar energy field. For restoring the mother's energy I stimulate the kidneys, adrenals, liver, and spleen areas. Therapeutic touch can be helpful now to induce relaxation and to help the woman to "debrief." The mother is advised to continue with a daily centering exercise to help her meet the demands of motherhood with a perspective of inner calm from which to draw. I have had some success at preventing or ameliorating neonatal jaundice by stimulating the baby's liver area. I first clear out the congestion so the energy can be readily absorbed, then move the energy out through the feet. It is important when using therapeutic touch with newborn babies to be very brief and very gentle.

A very frequent response after this treatment has been the passage of meconium.

It is useful to remember what a good channel for energy the mother can be because she is so well attuned to her baby's energy, and vice versa. I recently did therapeutic touch at a circumcision to soothe the very upset baby. As I did it, I described the process to the mother. That was her only instruction in therapeutic touch. The mother called me the next day to say that she continued the practice on her own and she was amazed at how well it calmed her child and helped him (and the mother) past the trauma.

If there is a point to be emphasized in this chapter, it is that all life energy has a pattern and a rhythm, and that pregnancy and birth have their own particular rhythms and patterns. There are many factors, such as fear, pain, or anxiety that can interfere with this rhythmic process. The object of therapeutic touch is to become sensitive to the pattern and sensitive to the intrusions and work to allow the process to develop unhindered. This is not to say that all pregnancies and births can be uneventful, but even with complications there is a logic and a pattern that one can sensitively approach.

Maintaining an awareness of that pattern allows the midwife and the mother to approach these complications and see them through in their own context, without beginning a chain of possibly irreversible interventions that may overwhelm any natural strengths and rhythms of the birthing process.

For me, therapeutic touch has proven to be an invaluable tool in the pursuit of healthy and successful birthing experiences for the mother, the baby, and the family, and opens the potential for rewarding new dimensions in human interaction. It is hoped that continued scientific documentation and research will increase our understanding of therapeutic touch, and will create greater availability for its practice in all settings.

Discussion: Chapter 15

Peter Gorski: I was struck by the description of channeling energy through yourself. What I thought of was that I chose the profession I did in part because the work is interpersonal. To me, the channeling that was described sounded almost like a defense against using yourself in the healing process. When I think about how a psychiatrist or even I myself work with families, it's to use my own personal reactions to the feelings that I perceive in somebody else to help me understand what they're feeling. So, when I hear about using myself as a conduit for universal energy and about having to depersonalize myself because if I don't I'll block the energy flow, I have a defensive reaction. To me, communication at a personal level is also communication at a therapeutic level. It's the best tool we have.

T. Berry Brazelton: That's an excellent point, Peter. Many people have been trying for a long time to understand the ingredients of a positive therapeutic relationship, and it seems to me that what both the last two chapters have emphasized is the crucial nature of that relationship.

What you said to me, Iris, was that the communication systems that are available around labor and delivery are wide open, and I couldn't agree more. At that time they are open for enhancement, as well as for going awry. There are opportunities to use this open system not only for attachment but for the goal of attachment, which ultimately is an autonomous baby. Offering mothers and family members a chance to participate in the pregnancy and birth by using touch as a modality is another enlightening and very exciting idea. I hope you're going to study this further, and look at it systematically.

16
Therapeutic Touch: A Critical Appraisal

Judith A. Smith, R.N., Ph.D.

Introduction

There is growing popular and professional discontent with orthodox medicine. This discontent is due to many factors, such as physicians' heavy reliance on drugs in treatment and the increasing trend toward new invasive techniques in diagnosis and therapy. Another source of dissatisfaction is caused by the trend toward medical subspecialization. Physicians, in concentrating their attention on particular parts of the body like the heart or the blood, are seen as lacking interest in the whole person. One result of this has been the rise of the so-called holistic health movement, which embraces a wide variety of innovative and unorthodox health practices. Some holistic health practitioners strive to improve services by making them more comprehensive. Thus, nutrition counseling, stress management strategies, and other types of health education have been added to the traditional medical diagnostic and treatment services. Other practitioners, however, offer alternative health practices such as meditation, acupressure, and therapeutic touch. These practices are preferred by their proponents because they are considered noninvasive and natural (Inglis, 1964; Kopelman and Moskop, 1981). They are considered to be in marked contrast to the invasive, high-technological treatments of traditional medicine with its tendency to produce iatrogenic illnesses.

For some time now the technique known as therapeutic touch has received growing attention and has gained a wide following among nurses. During the past decade, attempts have been made to refine and elaborate its techniques and to develop theoretical justifications for its procedures. It should be noted at the outset that although various claims have been made concerning the effectiveness of this therapy, as far as I know, therapeutic touch healers have not claimed that they can accomplish healings that medical science has not accomplished. The claims for therapeutic touch consist in facilitating healing. Its practitioners argue that some patients who may require prolonged treatment and medication may be healed more quickly by therapeutic touch. This seems to be the extent of their claims.

Close attention has been paid to the development of therapeutic touch techniques and procedures. Some programs have been set up for formal training of therapeutic touch healers. The growing practice of this unorthodox medical art provokes some challenging questions, for example:

1. What precisely is therapeutic touch?
2. What is known of its effectiveness and efficacy?
3. What is the theoretical explanation of the procedure which its practitioners believe give it support?
4. What is a major difference between traditional medical treatment and therapeutic touch?

Answers to these questions will require more than this brief chapter. But we might for the present point to some of the theoretical issues implicit in these questions. Advocates of therapeutic touch have developed elaborate theoretical doctrines in an effort to explain how therapeutic touch works. In certain respects, the theories behind the techniques are as unorthodox as the techniques themselves. Of course, in an examination of this new healing art, one has to admit the possibility that while the art itself is effective, its theoretical support may be unsound.

What Is Therapeutic Touch?

Therapeutic touch is said to be concerned with "fields" and "energy flow" in and around a patient's body. Whatever the nature of these fields and energies (and their nature is not made sufficiently clear), the healer is supposed to be sensitive to their presence and, to a certain degree, is supposed to be able to control and modify them (Krieger, Peper, and Ancoli, 1979; Boguslawski, 1980). In proximate healing, where the patient is in close proximity to the healer, this control and modification is achieved by movements and gestures of the healer's hands. The therapeutic touch procedure is employed in four stages:

Stage I:	A subjective procedure of the healer called centering
Stage II:	Appraisal of the range of the patient's fields and energies, called assessment
Stage III:	Diagnosis
Stage IV:	Treatment

In the first stage, centering, the healer tries to develop a sense of deep internal stillness or quietness, along with an intent to heal. In the assessment stage, the healer's hands move three to six inches above the patient's body. During these movements, the healer becomes conscious of sensations like heat, cold, and tingling, and, in the diagnostic stage, interprets these as revealing the condition of the patient. The diagnosis itself is viewed in terms of so-called energy needs, and not in terms of pathophysiologic diagnostic criteria. For example, perception of tingling over specific areas of the patient's body allegedly means that those areas need energy. During the treatment stage, the healer's hands are held over those areas of the body allegedly needing energy and are supposed to transmit energy through the hands into the patient's body. In order to transmit energy, the healer mentally visualizes light or color as flowing through his or her hands and into the patient's body. The entire process is psychological or mental.

Efficacy of the Technique

Does therapeutic touch work? Dependable statistical techniques are available for testing the effectiveness of this healing practice. We can take two groups of people with a condition requiring medication, such as bronchitis. The first group would get traditional medical treatment, and the second group would get therapeutic touch treatment. Then the relative recovery rates among the two groups could be evaluated. But no large-scale clinical trials are on record to differentiate among self-limiting illnesses, those that may be affected by therapeutic touch and those that are not affected at all by therapeutic touch. The proponents of therapeutic touch should consider performing such statistical tests repeatedly with different ailments and in different parts of the world. Unless there is statistical evidence indicating that every time a therapeutic touch treatment is done it is effective, a skeptical attitude toward the practice should be adopted.

If no such tests of efficacy of the therapeutic touch healing art have been done, what does the confidence of the practitioners rest on? At least for the present, their confidence seems to rest partly on subjective reports and partly on hearsay, but not on scientific evidence. In view of this, is one compelled to conclude that the confidence of the practitioners rests on faith?

Theoretical Explanation for Therapeutic Touch

Although there is no proof of the efficacy of therapeutic

touch, the advocates of this healing art have developed elaborate theories of how it works.

According to one theory, therapeutic touch is primarily a communication or transfer of energy from the healer to the patient (Boguslawski, 1979; Krieger, 1979, p. 36). This energy transfer can be described according to (1) the distance between the healer and the patient and (2) the source of the energy transfer. With regard to the distance between the healer and the patient, two kinds of energy transfer can be distinguished. One is over a short distance between the healer and patient, what might be called proximate healing. The healer's hands are held about three to six inches from the patient's body. The second type of energy transfer is over an indefinitely long distance where the patient may be thousands of miles from the healer.

In proximate healing further distinctions are made according to the source of the energy. In Type 1A proximate healing, the energy is supposedly generated within the healer and transmitted to the patient. In Type 1B proximate healing, the healer channels energy from the environment to the patient.

References to the sources of this therapeutic energy in the literature of therapeutic touch give no indication of how to determine whether in any particular case the therapeutic energy is generated by the healer or is derived from the healer's environment. In the absence of such experimental determinations one is compelled to conclude that the distinction is altogether speculative.

Considering the fact that science distinguishes several types of energy, one might ask what type of energy is used in therapeutic touch? If it is different from other physical energies, what are the characteristic traits attributed to it? Does this energy in fact exist?

Authoritative literature on therapeutic touch refers to an energy named *prana* that is characterized as a basic life energy. This is what is said to be transmitted during the healing act (Kunz and Peper, 1982, p. 19). It is allegedly different from other forms of energy and as yet unrecognized by modern science. It is said to be fundamental to animate matter and is viewed as a necessary condition for a state of health or well-being (Kunz and Peper, 1982, p. 395). In healthy persons, it allegedly flows in currents up and down the body and can be replenished at will. Energy flows within the body, from the environment into the body, and from the body to the environment. In the sick, according to this theory, certain blocks can obstruct this free flow of energy. These blocks are said to be physical, emotional, or mental. For example, the tightening of the muscles between the shoulders can allegedly decrease the flow of energy to the rest of the body. Anger, hate, and envy are viewed as negative emotions that also decrease energy flow within the body and between the body and the environment.

This notion of life energy, viewed as different from other forms of energy and peculiar to animate matter, introduces a kind of vitalism into the theory of therapeutic touch. The theory of vitalism holds that living organisms function by virtue of a life energy, or as it has been called—élan vital or entelechy (Driesch, 1905; Bergson, 1907). It is some nonmaterial mind or spirit distinct from physicochemical phenomena. Life, according to vitalism, is a kind of special creation—in the universe so to speak, but not of it. Thus, organisms possess qualities that defy analysis by the methods of mechanistic analysis upon which much of modern science, including medicine, is based. This method postulates that (1) any whole can be analyzed into parts that can be isolated, such that (2) the characteristics of these parts can be investigated in isolation from the whole; and (3) from the characteristics of the parts, the properties of the whole can be inferred (Descartes, 1637). In modern medical science, for example, it is assumed that from knowledge of the anatomy, physiology, and behavior of the numerous parts of a body one can gain a complete and adequate knowledge of the whole person. The contrast is between a mechanistic explanation of life and its manifestations on the one hand, and explanations using the concept of life or life-force as nonmaterial basis of living, adaptive behavior on the other hand.

Such a theory of vitalism seems to fail to take account of modern developments in cybernetics. Modern cybernetics can provide materialistic explanations for functions and phenomena usually associated with living beings. Can we account for the functions of living things in the same terms that we account for the inanimate? Yes, because we do not need the hypothesis of nonmaterial agencies or elements to account for purposeful, adaptive behavior. With the development of cybernetic theory, we can now understand how both organisms and mechanisms can exhibit purposeful behavior. Such behavior exhibits certain patterns. For example, (1) the system, organism or mechanism, is oriented toward some target or goal; (2) environmental changes may obstruct the movement of the system toward its goal; (3) the obstruction is overcome by a modification of the elements in the system; (4) normal movement toward the objective is resumed. Such structure is present in all adaptive behavior whether it is the behavior of a complex robot or a human being.

The current literature of therapeutic touch does not provide a coherent explanation of theoretical concepts such as *prana*, life energy, and energy field. Such concepts can be adequately clarified only by means of experimental or operational definitions, which are notably lacking in the available expositions of therapeutic touch. Such a key term as *therapeutic energy* must be given an operational definition if it is to serve effectively in the theory of healing practices. In an operational definition, the meaning of a concept is seen in the way it is tested or measured (Hempel, 1966, chapter 7). In contrast to this an ordinary definition is verbal. It sets two expressions as equivalents. For example, the word *chair* means a seat, especially for one person, usually having four legs for support and a rest for the back. It often also has a rest for the arms. In this kind of definition the meaning of the word *chair* is equivalent to the meaning of the foregoing definition. In an operational definition, on the other hand, a word is defined by showing the experimental conditions under which the word is used. It usually takes the following form: (1) some experimental conditions are set up at a certain place; (2) if under these conditions and at that place one observes certain traits, one can apply in that context the term in question.

If the concept of therapeutic energy is to be clearly understood, the experimental condition under which it would manifest itself needs to be stipulated. If a body is put in a particular position, for instance, and if certain traits are observed in the body, then it could be said that therapeutic energy is present in the body.

An operational definition defines a concept by showing how it is related to certain testable conditions in the real world. In the absence of operational definitions that meet such specific criteria, the concepts are only speculative. Is there some empirical test to determine when and in what way therapeutic energy goes from the healer to the patient? If so, it can then be studied in the same way that other forms of energy have been studied. Until operational definitions of key terms in the doctrine of therapeutic touch can be provided, the terms cannot be experimentally tested or measured.

The neglect of some specific description of this so-called life energy would suggest that it is a form of energy already clearly accounted for in the natural sciences. This assumption is not altogether justified because theories of therapeutic healing seem to use the term *energy* without specific association with established scientific usage. In modern physics, for example, the term *energy* is used in a specific way. Energy is characteristic of a body if it has the capacity to do work (Marian, 1980, pp. 115–123). Work is a force acting over a distance. A body can possess either kinetic or potential energy; that is, a body does work by virtue of its motion, as falling water and the winds do, or it has position–potential energy. A coiled spring, with its temporarily stored energy, is an example of potential energy.

We can see that great care is needed when using the term *energy*. It is used in mechanics in a limited sense and becomes more complicated, more refined as we proceed from mechanics to thermodynamics to electromagnetism. When we speak of chemical energy, we again have to change our perspective. Chemical energy arises out of the capacity of atoms to evolve heat as they separate or combine (Hunt, 1979, p. 143). Chemical energy is the energy stored in the chemical makeup of material like food, oil, dynamite.

But in all of these contexts—mechanical, thermodynamic, electromagnetic, chemical—what we call energy can be tested and measured. What tests can determine if there is, in fact, a flow of therapeutic energy from the healer to the patient? If energy is transmitted from the healer to the patient, shouldn't that leave less energy in the healer? Why does holding the healer's hands three to six inches from the patient's body transmit energy to the patient? And if the healer is transmitting energy to the patient, is there any reason to doubt that the patient is transmitting energy to the healer? What is the effect of this interaction?

In therapeutic touch, the healer allegedly has a perception of energy flow, but so far there is no way to get intersubjective proof of this flow. Energy flow cannot be studied if it is based only on the healer's perceptions. A supposed rationale for the lack of a clear idea of energy in therapeutic touch is frequently cited. Practitioners of therapeutic touch have said that physicists know how electricity behaves but they don't know what it is. Now, is there anything to be known about something apart from how it behaves? If we want to perceive/feel electrical energy, we can let it pass through our bodies. But feeling/perceiving the energy is not the same as knowing how it behaves. So in addition to the essence, the perception of a phenomenon, there is its behavior, the way it performs. When we know its behavior, we can communicate the knowledge of it. We cannot communicate the flavor of it. Take, for example, salt; we know it consists of an atom of sodium and one of chlorine; that it will dissolve in water; that it will preserve food. We can taste it and get the flavor of salt but this experience is very difficult to communicate. We need to know about the structure of therapeutic energy and how it acts under certain specific conditions.

Another aspect of the theory underlying therapeutic touch needs clarification. The intent of the healer is to direct energy toward a particular part or parts of the body. How are the healer's actions in therapeutic touch to be explained? We can speak of the healer creating an atmosphere; clearing the field; facilitating the natural tendency of the body to strive toward an optimal condition. Is there such a natural tendency of the body? Yes, there is. Homeostasis within certain narrow limits can be viewed as such a natural tendency of the body. For example, in order to maintain optimal body temperature at approximately 37°C, the operation of certain physiologic mechanisms is required. Loss of body heat results in vasoconstriction of surface vessels and erection of bodily hairs. Adrenalin discharge accelerates combustion, producing more heat in the body, and shivering increases heat since it is a form of muscular exercise.

This tendency operates within narrow limits. For example, a wound will heal untreated under some conditions but not under others. If an artery is cut, no self-healing takes place; but if a person is nicked in shaving, self-healing does occur. How exactly can therapeutic touch kill viruses and bacteria? What is the biochemical transaction that brings this about?

There is another theory to explain the healer's actions. We can speak and communicate through language because of neuromuscular and chemical changes within the body and because of the generation and transmission of a sound wave to a listener. That sound wave activates the listener's hearing mechanism, producing nerve impulses in his brain, and the recognition of the speaker's message. Conceivably, a therapeutic touch theory may affirm that thoughts can produce similar neuromuscular and biochemical changes in the body, and that such thoughts can be transmitted from the healer to the patient. Such a theory might then hold that the transmitted thoughts generate biochemical changes of the desired healing effect in the patient. This, however, is speculative.

Distance Healing

The energy exchange postulated as occurring in so-called distance healing, where healer and patient may be miles apart, presents other kinds of difficulties that need to be resolved. In distance healing, the healer makes use of a name or photograph; that is, some representative symbol of the patient which is used to transfer energy to the patient. The healer, by merely becoming conscious of the patient in some way, can exert an influence on the distant patient's body.

Is distance healing a case of propagation of some influence (i.e., action through some medium), or is it action-at-a-distance, interaction without any intervening process? Current theoretical accounts do not answer this question. Is it possible that an event occurs at point P1 in space (the transmission of energy) and another event occurs immediately following at P2 (reception of energy) such that P2 is caused by P1 without any intermediate event?

In the history of science, continuous-action theories have been preferred over the action-at-a-distance theories. In the former, there is always something being propagated, either directly or through some medium, like air. Field theories are examples of this type where the forces exerted in space, the fields, are viewed as constituting a medium (Hesse, 1965, chapters 7 and 8). In therapeutic touch, energy is said to be propagated. In contrast, action-at-a-distance theories hold that an effect is caused without any intervening process or without the propagation of anything. These kinds of theories have not been acceptable in science because of their association with magic, voodoo, telepathy, and so on (Hesse, 1972, pp. 9–15).

Presumably practitioners of therapeutic touch want to avoid association with magic. If the theory underlying therapeutic touch is to be separated from magical practices, practitioners of therapeutic touch need to explain how the alleged transmission of energy in distance healing occurs. In the physical sciences there is an inverse relationship between distance and energy. In other words, energy attenuates with distance. Therapeutic energy allegedly does not attenuate with distance. What kind of energy could account for such a phenomenon? Certainly not energies that are known to the physical sciences. It is possible that such a form of energy exists. But its existence must be demonstrated by scientifically acceptable tests.

Alternative Theoretical Explanations

In the foregoing theories therapeutic touch was conceived as an energy exchange between healer and patient. There are, however, other theories that can account for therapeutic touch healing without any reference to energy exchange or field theory. For example, Jerome Frank (1961, pp. 114–169) in *Persuasion and Healing* argues convincingly that the key ingredient in psychological healing lies in what he calls a sound therapeutic relationship. According to Frank, in successful therapy the therapist combats a sense of demoralization in the patient and increases the feeling the patient has regarding control over his own life. This in turn restores a sense of self-confidence and hope in the patient. The successful therapist is able to convey to the patient a genuine concern for the patient's welfare, which is communicated as caring, warmth, empathy.

Within this context, the expression of attitude becomes the important factor in healing. The significance for healing is what the healer communicates. The effective medium of transaction for the sick person is the expression of love, caring, and the deep desire to help. The patient responds to the healer's activity with a confident hope. Presumably, in this view, the gestures and manipulations of the healer in therapeutic touch function as a way of communicating concern, affection, trust, and acceptance.

Major Difference Between Medicine and Therapeutic Touch

A major difference between traditional medicine and the use of therapeutic touch in clinical practice arises from the lack of specificity between the cause of disease or dysfunction in the patient and the procedures of therapeutic touch. Consider, for example, the treatment of pain by therapeutic touch. The healer uses the same procedure to eliminate the pain of a tension headache as is used to eliminate pain in the ankle caused by a sprained ligament. The treatment thus appears similar to a universal cure, a panacea.

This uniformity of treatment in a great variety of ailments is alien to medical practice. If a patient has bronchitis, there is a specific procedure used to deal with it. There is also a specific procedure used to treat a person with a diagnosis of pericarditis. The medical treatment that cures the bronchitis does not cure the pericarditis.

In order to effect cures, the practitioner of therapeutic touch passes through three phases:

Phase 1: The practitioner has to put him or herself into a certain psychological state which is designated as being centered.

Phase 2: The healer then imagines seeing a cobalt blue color.

Phase 3: The healer is then able to propagate or transmit this cobalt blue color into the patient. When the blue color reaches the locus of pain, it brings relief.

The theory on the one hand affirms that the healer imagines a certain color; on the other hand it then affirms that the color itself is transmitted into the patient's body. How does an imagined color become the source of an actual color? One might analogously say that a healer imagines the nourishment needed by the patient and then from this imagined nourishment transmits the nourishment itself. Other questions arise once the theory is scrutinized. These questions are perhaps not unanswerable but they have to be dealt with if we are to develop any sound theory of therapeutic touch healing.

Conclusion

The foregoing comments are not to be taken as an expression of opposition to the practice of therapeutic touch. Rather, they are made to highlight certain questions and doubts, and to call attention to the absence of proof regarding the effectiveness and the theoretical explanations of the procedure. They are also made to indicate directions for further thought and investigation.

Discussion: Chapter 16

T. Berry Brazelton: Judy, in asking for rigorous research on therapeutic touch I think you are really talking about increasing the confidence and improving the self-image of the nurses who practice it. I know that when the Brazelton Neonatal Assessment Scale (BNAS) was developed, nothing in it was new. The scale just pinned down the clinical or intuitive insights that we'd all been relying on for a long time. Putting it down on paper made it viable, and I think this is what you're asking of therapeutic touch: that it be made into a viable system rather than a religious or mystical one.

Judith Smith: Yes, it should be critically appraised. I tried in my chapter to raise the questions that should be asked at this sort of conference.

T. Berry Brazelton: I think many of us would prefer a rational approach to a mystical one. One thing we've learned from studying attachment and mother–child relationships is that when you start to break things down, the mystery begins to clear.

Allen Gottfried: Eliminating this mystical quality is of the utmost importance if any progress is to be made on therapeutic touch, I think. Finding out how touch works may require a social learning theory framework, because a social transmission of information is going on that is crucially important. We haven't given much attention to that.

Seymour Levine: One of the things that has struck me throughout this conference has been the parameters of touch within the concept of a social system. We've tried to isolate touch from other essential processes, but we've been unable to separate it from its interaction with a social communicative system. Touch as social communication is something I wish we had more time to discuss.

Martin Reite: There are some striking parallels between the current therapeutic touch movement and the early days of the psychoanalytic movement. In both we have healing systems that are alleged to impact favorably upon certain functional disturbances. The psychoanalytic movement was concerned primarily with disturbances in behavior; therapeutic touch is concerned with disturbances that are more medical. Both movements have theoretical systems that are very dependent upon special ideas that are not part of everyday experience; both work from a position of special knowledge. Both make therapeutic claims based predominantly upon case reports from practitioners and not on controlled observations by others.

I think both systems are open to empirical investigation. Psychoanalysis has chosen not to partake of that, and as a result it has tended to languish. Therapeutic touch, if it is going to become anything other than cult, will have to make the other choice. After empirical investigation has established that it does something, then you can worry about how it does it and begin looking at mutually exclusive testable hypotheses and try to get at mechanisms. The first thing you need is evidence that it in fact does something.

Michael Merzenich: We should keep in mind that the technique has potential advantages beyond the medical. Psychosocial consequences may be just as important, maybe more so.

T. Berry Brazelton: The danger of mysticism and cultism is that it devalues what the process really seems to me to be. As you suggested in your chapter, Judy, the interpersonal relationship between therapist and client may be critical to the positive outcome. It intrigues me that with therapeutic touch you use touch as a language, and in the process you're somehow freeing up the communication system between you and the patient.

I like your parallel with psychoanalysis, Marty. It did set itself up as mysticism of a kind, which really kept it out of the mainstream. I use it in my work with pediatricians and parents, though, and there's nothing mystical about that. We do need to understand the ingredients. There are plenty of ingredients that demand that the therapist understand himself. These aren't mystical, but they do take a kind of focus.

Kathryn Barnard: Ned Muller's work on how children develop shared meaning seems relevant here, because what is going on may be a social learning process, as Allen Gottfried said. When children play, they communicate intent to one another even without words. A similar transmission of intent may occur in therapeutic touch.

Renée Weber: I am very much in favor of scientific investigation of therapeutic touch. However, Judy suggested in her chapter that an operational definition of the energy involved in therapeutic touch is an essential early step in this research, which raises a philosophical issue. If you restrict your scientific methods too narrowly to operational definitions, especially where biological or psychological systems are concerned, you're going to rule out much that contemporary scientists accept in practice. Rigidly construed, operationalism says that the meaning of a statement is its method of clarification. This is not acceptable to philosophers of science or to scientists today. Modern physics makes use of a lot of nonsensible objects. If you require operational definitions, I don't know what you're going to do with black holes, the big bang theory, and self-consciousness, for instance.

In other words, operational definitions can be a preemptive kind of methodology. It may be too early to impose a precise definition on the energy involved in therapeutic touch. At the beginning, the best you can do is get some kind of working consensus so that you at least adopt a similar vocabulary. Then you allow data to pile up. Only much later do you interpret them and pin things down. This is what has happened, essentially, in the history of physics.

Therese Connell Meehan: I'm not sure that it's appropriate to do experimental studies of any sort. What you are looking at is individual and unique, a feeling that's going to help people, and experimental designs don't tell us what's unique. They tell us a general kind of thing that's common to everybody. What's going to be most therapeutic depends on the individual person, so I think a phenomenological approach is most appropriate.

T. Berry Brazelton: Sensitive observations can begin to demystify therapeutic touch just as they've helped to demystify mother–infant attachment. When I first heard Mary Ainsworth present her work some fifteen years ago, people literally laughed and got up and walked out—just like the audiences at Mozart's and Bach's concerts. But I stayed, and I thought, this is the first time I've ever heard anyone at the

Society for Research in Child Development talk about anything but stimulus–response systems as if they were clearly and easily defined. Since then, an enormous amount of work has gone on, and we've begun to identify a lot of aspects of attachment and love that aren't mystical. Therapeutic touch needs the same sort of scrutiny.

References

Bergson, H. (1907), *Creative Evolution*, trans. A. Mitchell. New York: Modern Library, 1944.

Boguslawski, M. (1979), The use of therapeutic touch in nursing. *J. Contin. Ed. in Nurs.*, 10:9–15.

———(1980), Therapeutic touch: A facilitator of pain relief. *Topics in Clin. Nurs.*, 2:27–37.

Descartes, R. (1637), *Discourse on Method, Optics, Geometry and Meteorology*, trans. P. J. Olscamp. Indianapolis, IN: Bobbs-Merrill, 1965.

Driesch, H. (1905), *The History and Theory of Vitalism*, trans. C. K. Ogden. London: Macmillan, 1914.

Frank, J. D. (1961), *Persuasion and Healing: A Comparative Study of Psychotherapy*. Baltimore, MD: Johns Hopkins University Press.

Hempel, C. G. (1966), *Philosophy of Natural Science*. Englewood Cliffs, NJ: Prentice-Hall.

Hesse, M. (1972), Action at a distance and field theory. *Encyclopedia of Philosophy*. New York: Macmillan and The Free Press.

Hesse, M. B. (1965), *Forces and Fields*. Totowa, NJ: Littlefield, Adams.

Hunt, V. D. (1979), *Energy Dictionary*. New York: Van Nostrand Reinhold.

Inglis, B. (1964), *Fringe Medicine*. London: Faber & Faber.

Kopelman, L., & Moskop, J. (1981), The holistic health movement: A survey and critique. *J. Med. & Philos.*, 6:209–235.

Krieger, D. (1979), *The Therapeutic Touch*. Englewood Cliffs, NJ: Prentice-Hall.

———Peper, E., & Ancoli, S. (1979), Therapeutic touch: Searching for evidence of physiologic change. *Amer. J. Nurs.*, 76:660–662.

Kunz, D., & Peper, E. (1982), Fields and their clinical implications, part I. *Amer. Theosophist*, 70: 395–401.

Marian, J. B. (1980), *Physics and the Physical Universe*, New York: John Wiley.

Part VI: Aspects of the Importance of Touch in the Life Spectrum

17
Parental Touching: Correlates of a Child's Body Concept and Body Sentiment

Sandra J. Weiss, D.N.Sc.

The theoretical relationship that has been postulated between one's body image and the resulting organization and functioning of the personality provides substantial rationale for better understanding factors which influence development of the body image. A person's entire developing sense of self, although not limited to sensations generated by the body, appears to be rooted in body awareness, body functions, and body activities (Witkin, Dyk, Faterson, Goodenough, and Karp, 1962; Wapner, 1965). This assumption is supported by studies which show a significant correlation between one's feelings and perceptions regarding the body and one's concept of the total self (Secord and Jourard, 1953; Zion, 1965; Fisher and Cleveland, 1970; Cardone and Olson, 1973). Both sentiment for the body and the cognitive model of the body have been identified as fundamental substrata which are necessary in order to build up other response systems; that is, they are primary dimensions in an individual's overall system of standards for interpreting the world (Schilder, 1950; Fisher and Cleveland, 1968; Gorman, 1969; Peto, 1972).

The Influence of Tactile Experience on Development of Body Perception

Evolution of the body image appears to start when an organism first interacts with other objects in the environment. It is postulated that the sensory experience of touch does much to aid the process of separating the "me" from the "not me," encouraging a greater awareness of one's own body (Schilder, 1950; Bosanquet, 1970). Schilder maintained that every touch provokes a mental image of the spot touched, with these images being necessary for localization of the body parts and functions.

To what extent intrauterine tactile experiences contribute to body image is not known, but there is increasing evidence to indicate that the fetus experiences touch in utero (Als, Lester, and Brazelton, 1979; Van Dongen and Goudie, 1980). By thirteen and one half weeks gestation, the fetus has been observed to move in response to a fetoscope on the abdominal wall as well as insertion of an amniocentesis needle (Liley, 1972). Vaughan (1975) has demonstrated that the cortical regions of the fetal brain are able to respond to tactile stimulation by thirty-two weeks gestation. Purpura's (1975) work would support this supposition, indicating that the dendrites and dendrite spines of the cerebral cortex are formed by twenty-eight to thirty-two weeks gestation, and provide the synaptic connections necessary for beginning self-awareness. Thus, intrauterine tactile experiences may provide the rudimentary foundations for perception of boundaries between one's own body and that of another.

By birth, normative infants possess a fairly well-developed faculty within their central nervous system (CNS) for registering and associating sensory impressions received in personal contact with other human beings. The activity of the CNS is determined in large measure by afferent impulses received from receptors located at the surface of the body. The stimulation of receptor organs in the skin causes physiologic excitation of the body surface which is replete with nervous pathways. These pathways possess neurons of different size, degree of myelinization, and synaptic structure, which determine opportunities for accurate reception of stimulation and successful transmission of the nerve impulse to the CNS. Differences in specialization of nervous pathways enable neurons to respond discriminately to external stimulation, with divergent qualities of feedback to the CNS.

There is increasing evidence that the sensory pathways subserving cutaneous sensation are the first to complete myelinization and maturation in the infant, followed by the vestibular, auditory, and visual senses (Kolb, 1959; Gottlieb, 1971; Turkewitz and Kenny, 1982). It is postulated that these earlier developing functions may give an organism a base for higher order operations, determining many of the initial "cell assemblages" or "cognitive maps" which form the roots for future learning (Hebb, 1949; Armstrong, 1962; Burton and Heller, 1964; Gibson, 1966; Sinclair, 1967; Killackey and Belford, 1979; Merzenich and Kaas, 1980). A cell assembly or map may be described as a cortical representation which is formed within each individual by frequently repeated sensory stimulations and neuromuscular excitations of the body. In this way, each separate tactile impression which a person experiences becomes related to the next and is ordered cognitively. The implications of such a process are that initially developed cortical representations may afford the core experiences and resulting meanings which an individual comes to understand. Schopler (1965) labeled the cell assemblies a receptor hierarchy, whereby learning through tactile stimulation is necessary for subsequent learning via other modalities. Following such logic, development of perceptions and conceptions which provide each individual with meaning can depend on the initial tactile stimulations to which one is exposed.

The early years of life offer multiple opportunities for acquisition of meaning regarding one's body because, at this time, body experiences are the primary means for relationship with others. Schopler's (1965) work has indicated that if a human infant is not given the handling necessary for integrating early undifferentiated bodily sensations, the effect could be a basic distortion or lack of perceptual integration of the body image. He also found that bodily contact with autistic children aided symbolic representation and corrected distorted body perceptions (1962). While little other research has been done to examine the specific relationship between touch and body image, some studies on related developmental variables would support the validity of Schopler's investigations. For example, enrichment of the environment with sensory stimulation has been found to produce an accompanying and proportional increment in perceptual and cognitive development (Ball and Edgar, 1967; Delacato, 1971; Kephart, 1971; Cratty, 1974). Brody (1956) and Casler (1965) found that infants who received an extra twenty minutes of handling each day demonstrated a greater visual attention than those not handled an extra twenty minutes. In a similar vein, Ribble (1943) discovered that increased handling of infants aided respiration and blood flow with resultant increase of oxygenation to growing brain cells. Patton and Gardner (1963) and Montagu (1971) have described case and experimental studies where touch has affected metabolism; intestinal motility; and glandular, biochemical, and muscular changes.

In most work examining the effects of tactile stimulation, theorists have attributed the observed effects of touch to the frequency or overall amount of touching which an individual experiences. However, the types of touch which encourage differential development remain unclear. Specifically, differences between expected, healthy tactile correlates which can function to support body image, and variant tactile correlates which may inhibit or damage body image, are not known. In the main, touch has been viewed as essentially all-positive or at best, as some homogeneous, consistent phenomenon that can have either positive or negative effects (Mintz; 1969;

Montagu, 1971; Burnside, 1973; Knable, 1981). There is danger in accepting either of these assumptions; for the meaning of a tactile experience cannot be derived solely from the mere presence or absence of touching (Weiss, 1978, 1979; Alagna, Whitcher, Fisher, and Wicas, 1979). As an organ, the skin is highly complex and versatile, with an immense range of operations and a wide repertoire of responses. It is capable of selectively discriminating one physiologic stimulus from another, with the form or quality of a touch decidedly changing the resulting perception of the tactile experience. Thus, the therapeutic meaning or value of a touch would seem clearly dependent on its differential or qualitative nature.

Differential Qualities of Touch

In his classic studies on sensory stimulation, Henry Head (1920) differentiated between two cutaneous afferent systems: the protopathic system and the epicritic system. The protopathic or protective system was seen to warn or defend the organism against potential harm; whereas the epicritic or discriminative system was viewed as being concerned with higher perceptual and discriminatory function. Hebb (1949) continued studying these systems and demonstrated that the pattern and locus of sensory stimulation determined the manner in which these two systems of the body came to be utilized. More recent research has concluded that overactivation of the protective system interferes with cortical association responses which are essential to perception (Ayres, 1972). Thus, the individual with an overactive protective system would be limited in his ability to perceive and learn, due either to a distortion in neural representation or a saturation effect (a level beyond which no response is carried to the CNS). In contrast, other investigators suggest that a stimulus may be so insignificant in its effect that it registers no impact with the discriminatory system, resulting in a lack of information to the CNS (DeReuch and Knight, 1966; Zubek, 1969).

Accompanying experiences of pain, disgust, fear, or tension, in contrast to feelings of closeness, comfort, relaxation, or yielding which take place during a particular touch, give the tactile act further meaning as it is carried to the CNS (Schilder, 1950). If an organism is so engaged in protecting itself from what it interprets as potential harm, or is not perceiving adequate stimulation to experience the touch, the discriminative system will not adequately function to contribute input for a mental picture of the body. Clearly then, the quality of the cutaneous stimulation influences the meaning of the tactile message to the body.

Diverse qualities of touch may be viewed as symbols in a language of touch, just as word symbols create a verbal and written language for communication and shared meaning. A tactile quality then is a visible modifier of a tactile interaction which signifies something less visible or less tangible and gives the touch its meaning. These qualities in no way attempt to define the circumstances surrounding the occurrence of touching, such as other concomitant communication, but rather define the act of touching itself as an independent channel of communication.

Considering the two cutaneous systems just discussed, the significance of tactile qualities lies in their power to affect an individual's perceptual ability for sensory discrimination of the body, and body cathexis resulting from experiences of pleasure or pain. Four major tactile qualities emerge from review of neurophysiologic and sociopsychologic literature: duration, location, intensity, and sensation.

Duration of Touch

The duration of a touch is the temporal length of the touch from initiation of interbody contact by one individual to cessation of contact by either individual. Physiologic literature dealing with mechanical stimulation has indicated that shorter durations are more likely to occur below the level of identification, not allowing adequate time for integration of the touch (Rosenblith, 1961; Kenshalo, 1968). On the other hand, longer contact appears to allow the body time to experience the sensory stimulation provided by another human being, encouraging awareness of one's own body as separate from that being touched.

Location of Touch

Location refers to the areas of the body contacted by the persons who are touching. The place where an individual is touched supplies information regarding specific body parts as well as the integrated body whole. The importance of location lies in its three dimensions: threshold, extent, and centripetality.

THRESHOLD

Threshold denotes the degree of innervation within a body area and that body area's resulting sensitivity to touch. The thresholds of different body areas function to report contact with an external object to different degrees, with regions of maximal sensitivity to touch resulting from specialization of the nervous pathway structure in different areas. Body areas that have the most cerebral representation are richly endowed with afferent sensory fibers that cause high sensory acuity and fine discrimination; whereas, body areas of lesser innervation yield dull, vaguely localized impressions such as in the back or arm. Highly innervated body areas such as the face and hand yield bright, discrete, sharply localized impressions (Haber, 1956; Ruesch, 1957; Kolb, 1959; Sinclair, 1967; Geldard, 1972).

EXTENT

The extent of location essentially describes the amount of a person's body which is actually being touched, that is, the number of areas of one's body which are touched in relation to the number of areas available to be touched over the entire body surface. Some individuals may touch or be touched only on their hands and arms, with other body parts rarely being in contact with another human being. In contrast, other persons may regularly experience interbody contact over their entire body.

Jourard (1966) demonstrated that a person's perception of how much of the body is touched by others appears distinctly related to that person's positive evaluation of self. Studies have indicated that an individual who receives body contact from others over most body areas, in contrast to only a few areas, generally feels more attractive, feels closer to other persons, possesses an accurate perception of the form and shape of his body, and has a positive liking for himself as a person (Jourard, 1966; Morris, 1967).

CENTRIPETALITY

Centripetality refers to the degree to which the trunk of the body is touched rather than the limbs. The trunk of the body includes all but the arms and legs, representing the core of the person, that aspect of the body where primary perception of self is concentrated. Both Rubin (1963) and Jourard (1966) maintain that trunk versus limb contact between persons may carry some strikingly different meanings to individuals concerning the closeness or degree of intimacy experienced with others.

The locational dimensions of threshold, extent, and centripetality may all be affected by taboo and stigma because different parts of the body carry different sociocultural meanings, depending on the riskiness of touching them. For example, if a part of the body carries stigma as a result of a physical defect, the degree of contact with that body part by others can be grossly influenced. Sexual taboos placed upon certain parts of the body may also affect how these parts are touched. Murray (1972) and Watson (1970) have shown that the more sensitive areas of the body (those areas with the greatest innervation) often acquire overtones of disgust or fear in an individual because of the nature or actual lack of physical contact which they receive.

Intensity of Touch

Intensity indicates the extent of indentation applied to the body surface by the pressure of the touch. Intensity is strong, moderate, or weak, depending on whether the degree of skin indentation caused by the touch is deep, shallow, or barely perceptible. Different degrees of intensity in a touch can result in different states of hyperexcitability in the cortex. Previous research would indicate that consistently weak and exceptionally strong intensities of touch appear to be the least therapeutic qualities in that they cause distortion, saturation, or are too minimally perceived to elicit a response (DeReuch and Knight, 1966; Zubek, 1969; Geldard, 1972). In contrast, moderate intensity is usually described as having the most potential for furthering accurate perception of the characteristics of the body.

Sensation of Touch

Sensation is the immediate comfort or discomfort reaction of the skin to a touch, with specialized reception and transmission of these sensory impressions to the brain. Sensation defines the tactile interaction as pleasurable or painful to the body surface. When the sensation of touch is too painful, perceptual discrimination is inhibited because the protective response of somatic discomfort interferes with cortical association necessary for accurate interpretation. In other words, the degree to which the touch is painful or pleasurable appears to determine whether the protective or the discriminative system is in operation. Schilder (1950) and Tyler (1972) have attested that painful tactile stimuli (discomfort sensations) distort the body image by preventing adequate functioning of the body's perceptual system. Additionally, Brody (1956) indicates that pleasurable tactile interaction (the comfort quality of sensation) allows for maximal discrimination, providing vital information for development of a positive and stable cathexis of one's body as a worthwhile and valuable part of the self.

A Study to Examine the Effects of Parental Touch

In an attempt to better understand these diverse qualities of touch and their relationship to body image, a study was undertaken to examine differential aspects of parental touch and their correlation with children's body concept and body sentiment. Under normal conditions, parents are the most significant people in the development of the child's body image, for the interaction with parents imparts an indelible impression on the child (Blaesing and Brockhaus, 1972). From the initial tactile interaction with mother to those with father, children's perceptions of their bodies as meaningful objects begin to form. While acknowledging that tactile interactions with other important individuals (siblings, grandparents, peers) also occur during this time, parents endure as those individuals whose touching offers the most available, consistent, and influential source of qualitative information (Cratty, 1970). The body image develops against a background of differences in the qualities present in these tactile interactions between the child and the parents, an image that becomes integrated over time into a personal frame of reference for the child.

Sample

The sample consisted of forty families with children of eight, nine, or ten years of age, including an equal number of male and female children, and both natural parents of each child. Children of eight to ten years were chosen specifically because of (1) their cognitive ability for accurate discrimination regarding their bodies (Witkin et al., 1962; Cratty, 1970); and (2) their retention of a primary bond to the nuclear family, a bond that begins to disseminate in preadolescence as the child reaches increasingly toward peers for developmental input. All children were physically, cognitively, and emotionally healthy; and capable of functioning in their family, peer, and school system.

Families volunteered to participate in the study, in response to flyers distributed at both public and private schools in San Francisco. Flyers described the family's participation as an opportunity to engage in an interesting nonverbal activity which would be videotaped, and to see and discuss the videotape as a family group. The goal of the study was couched as increased understanding of nonverbal communication in normal healthy families. Thirty-one of the families were obtained through private schools and nine through public schools. In general, they were Caucasian, middle-class families with two or three children. The parents were fairly well educated, with the majority of the sample having gone to college, and one parent, usually the father, having completed graduate school. Most parents were in their thirties or early forties and had been married for ten to fifteen years.

Measures

THE TACTILE INTERACTION INDICATOR

The instrument used to measure parental touch was the Tactile Interaction Indicator (TII), a coding system which is applied independently by judges as they observe touching between parents and child. It was created specifically for use with videotaped or filmed tactile interactions. The TII provides indicators for analysis of location, intensity, sensation, and duration of touch. Each indicator is coded and scored somewhat differently.

The location indicator allows for coding of the part of the child's body touched by the parent. Judges may choose from fifteen body parts to code: breast, face, feet, genitalia, hands, head, neck, abdomen, arms, back, buttocks, chest, lower leg, shoulder, and thigh. While judges only code actual body part touched, three scores can be developed from this record for three separate tactile qualities. The first is threshold, with a parent receiving a score based on the percent of locations touched which were high rather than low innervation areas. The second quality is extent, with a score based on the percent of available parts of the child's body actually touched by the parent. Centripetality, the third quality of location, receives a score consisting of the percentage of the time the trunk of the child's body is touched by the parent during the course of all touching.

The intensity indicator enables rating of the touch as strong, moderate, or weak according to the observed pressure of the tactile indentation on the skin as deep, shallow, or not perceptible. Each strong touch receives three points, each moderate touch, two points, and each weak touch, one point. The resulting sum of these points is then divided by the total points possible, based on the number of times the particular parent touches a child. This process yields a score reflecting the degree to which touches are more rather than less intense. Scores are derived from cumulative points for the observed tactile qualities, divided by the actual number of points any one particular parent can receive based upon the frequency with which he or she touches the child. This percentage approach keeps the intensity score from being contaminated by the variations in frequency of touching observed across parents.

The sensation indicator enables rating of the touch as a comfort or discomfort experience to the surface of the body. The judgment is made in terms of the appearance of the touch itself, with disregard for facial and body cues of the child being touched. Parents receive a score for the percent of their touches which are discomfort versus comfort in nature.

Duration is rated by direct temporal measurement of each touch, with codings for five specific units of time: (1) one second or less in length; (2) one and one half to five seconds in length; (3) five and one half to ten seconds in length; (4) ten and one half to twenty seconds in length; and (5) over twenty seconds in length. By pressing a button for the length of each touch used by a parent, an electrographic reading is recorded on paper signifying the exact time involved in each touch. Points from one to five are then given each touch based on its length. For example, touches over twenty seconds receive five points, touches from ten and one half to twenty seconds receive four points, while touches of one second or less receive one point. The summation of points and assignment of a score are handled in the same fashion as for the intensity indicator since more than two scalar dimensions of the quality can be coded and a direct percentage score is not possible.

For all indicators, those qualities of touch which are identified from existing data in the literature as conducive to CNS activity receive higher scores. This arbitrary scoring method is an attempt to achieve consistency of scoring philosophy across indicators of the TII.

Validity

The validity of the TII was based upon the independent evaluations of five doctorally prepared nurses who were asked to define the rating categories of the TII. These individuals were given no theoretical paradigm or definitions regarding touch. Rather, applying their own experiences with touch, they used the TII to rate seventeen videotapes of different types of touch, coding each touch on various aspects of location, intensity, and sensation. The videotape examples which received 100 percent agreement across the five individuals as to the qualities they reflected were chosen as visual definitions of the different aspects of each quality of touch to be rated on the respective indicators. Five examples of touch, which best represented the nature of touching to be rated, were then selected for each indicator; that is, comfort versus discomfort sensation; strong, moderate, or weak intensity; and parameters to clarify different areas of the body being touched. The duration indicator was not included in the validity testing because coding for duration was based on objective measure of time rather than subjective ratings of judges.

Reliability

Reliability of the measure was examined with a set of three multidisciplinary judges who were selected from a group of postgraduate applicants. All judges underwent a training session which included: (1) an introduction to the study; (2) a description of the role of the judges; (3) discussion of the indicators with (a) definition of terms, (b) discrimination of different qualities within indicators, (c) videotaped examples of different qualities of touch, and (d) practice use of the coding system with discussion of any discrepancies in ratings among judges.

Having completed the training, judges tested the interrater reliability of their judgments with fifteen-minute videotape segments of two pilot families. They first observed all touching of one parent in one family, rating each quality of touch during four separate viewings of the videotape segment. They then viewed the videotape four more times, coding the second parent for location, duration, intensity, and sensation. The order in which sex of parent and indicators of the instrument were coded for each family was systematically alternated to control for the effect of numerous viewings of the same tactile interactions on any one quality of touch or parental role.

Interrater reliability for ratings on various qualities of touch ranged from 77 percent agreement for weak intensity to 98 percent for comfort sensation. All qualities had agreement within the 80 and 90 percent range except for weak intensity. It seemed difficult for judges to rate a touch which made an imperceptible indentation on the skin.

Test–retest reliability was also examined by having judges rate the touching of the same pilot families again two weeks later. Comparison of mean ratings across judges on test and retest showed Spearman correlations ranging from $r = 0.90$ to 0.99 ($p<0.01$) for each indicator on each parent. Indicators showed a maximum of seven points in change from Time 1 to Time 2, indicating that qualities of touching were being consistently rated.

THE SOPHISTICATION-OF-BODY-CONCEPT SCALE

The Sophistication-of-Body-Concept Scale (Witkin et al., 1962) is a five-point rating scale designed to assess the degree of primitivity or sophistication of the drawings of human figures. The rating scale is used by a psychologist to interpret actual figures of persons drawn by the children as part of the Draw-a-Person Test. The scale yields a single cumulative global score and three distinct scores based on specific, clearly interpretable criteria: (1) form; (2) identity and sex differentiation; and (3) detail. Higher scores represent greater sophistication of body concept. Concurrent validity for the Sophistication-of-Body-Concept Scale is positive and significant with a correlation of 0.74 @ $p<0.01$ (Witkin et al., 1962). Interjudge reliability produced a correlation of 0.84 @ $p<0.01$ (Witkin et al., 1962). No data on test–retest reliability were available although reliability of the Draw-a-Person test has proven satisfactory (Roback, 1968).

THE BODY SENTIMENT INDEX

The Body Sentiment Index (BSI) was constructed to indicate the strength and direction of feeling that a child has about his or her body (Weiss, 1975). The index operates on the same principle as the human figure drawing test, whereby the child projects an image of his own body onto the figure with which he is working (Roback, 1968). The BSI utilizes a cardboard diagram of the body in the form of a puzzle, with various parts being easily removable from the total diagram. Male or female body diagrams can be given to children depending upon their sex. The models are bare of all clothing or other ornamentation, with no color and a neutral facial expression, reducing the effect of the model's appearance on the child's like or dislike for the body parts.

Utilizing diagrams of both front and back, a child sorts the parts of the body into two separate, identical boxes placed in front of him, which bear labels of different directions of feeling—like or dislike for the body. A child's score is based on the percent of body parts identified as being liked versus disliked. Concurrent validity of the index is significant and test–retest reliability has yielded a correlation of 0.96 at $p<0.01$, with percent of agreement between distribution of body parts on initial test and retest being 91 percent (Weiss, 1975).

Procedures

Initial contact with families was made through home visit to all families who had responded to flyers at their school by expressing a desire to hear more about the research. The visit included all three family members who would potentially be involved in the study, and provided an introduction to the research, a description of each facet of the family's participation, information concerning the family's consent to participate in a research project, and the measures which would be taken to preserve confidentiality. Each family who then agreed to participate in the study made an appointment to come to the laboratory–playroom at their convenience.

Upon arrival at the playroom, parents completed a demographic questionnaire while the child was taken to a separate room where the Draw-a-Person test and the Body Sentiment Index were administered. This period took approximately fifteen minutes, after which the child was taken to join the parents. The parents and child then received instructions regarding the fifteen-minute nonverbal activity in which they would be participating next.

During the activity, parents were asked to function as guides and teachers to the child in his or her learning about the environment within the playroom. The child was blindfolded and all family members were instructed not to speak; but otherwise, the parents could utilize the objects and space within the playroom in their own unique way. Children were blindfolded in order to prevent the family from using primarily gesture or facial expression as communicative modalities, and rather to encourage the use of touch. The objects in the playroom which were available for use by families included the following: a mattress, chair, stool, blanket, pillow, table, pail of water, cotton swabs, bubble blowing liquid, cotton balls, stuffed animal, sandpaper, soap, towel, bowl, ice, heating pad, lotion, piece of fur, deep-heat medication, throw rug, clock, bicycle, wagon, and bandage. No items possessing a specific relationship to any part of the body were used; instead, item selection attempted to maximize the probability of equally occurring use across the body's parts. Identical items were utilized for each family, and located in the same position within the room.

The family's freeform participation during this time in the playroom was videotaped, in order to collect data about the tactile interactions between the parents and the child which were then analyzed at a later date. The open-ended structure of the task was an attempt to exemplify through parents' choice and use of the available learning objects in the room, the interactive experiences of each child within his particular family.

To examine reliability of the touching, which occurred during the nonverbal activity, two families who had participated in the pilot testing were asked to undergo the videotaped nonverbal activity twice. The purpose of this testing was to determine whether the types of touching during the second videotape would be consistent with those used during the first. Each family came into the laboratory–playroom in the morning to participate the first time. Upon completing the nonverbal activity, the parents and child of each family were directed from the room without removing the child's blindfold. By not allowing the child to see the room or the objects within the room, the experience was more similar on retest to the initial experience of the child. The family then went to lunch with instructions not to talk about the activity until after participation the second time. Following lunch, each family came into the lab again and participated in the nonverbal activity exactly as before.

Mean scores across judges on each indicator were correlated for the two activities for each family. No correlation was lower than 0.88 across any indicator ($p<0.01$), suggesting substantial consistency in family touching patterns.

Three trained judges met biweekly for three-hour sessions to watch the videotapes of the forty families who participated in the nonverbal activity. The observational sessions took place on evenings convenient to the judges, because the videotapes could be viewed at any time. A short break occurred every hour to maintain the alertness of the judges. All judges simultaneously watched the videotapes, each of them using the TII to independently rate each touch they observed. The videotapes ran straight through without stopping unless one of the judges asked to see a segment repeated. When a segment was repeated, all three judges watched the segment again so that observational time was consistent across judges.

Results

In examining the mean scores of all parents on the various qualities of location, duration, intensity, and sensation, three qualities of parental touch were found to be significantly correlated with body image in children. As shown in Table 17.1, these qualities were: use of strong intensity in touching, use of discomfort sensation, and contact with a large extent of the child's body parts. While strong intensity was correlated with both body concept and body sentiment, discomfort sensation was correlated only with body sentiment, and large extent of contact was correlated only with body concept.

TABLE 17.1

Significant Spearman Correlations Between Tactile Qualities Used by All Parents[a] and Body Image of All Children[b]

Body Image Measures	Tactile Qualities		
	Strong Intensity	Discomfort Sensation	Location: Large Extent
Body Concept	0.360*	0.194	0.492**
Body Sentiment	0.413**	0.385*	0.233

[a]n = 80. * p<0.01.
[b]n = 40. ** p<0.005.

Breaking the data down to examine differences in touch between mothers and fathers as well as for sex of child produced even more interesting findings. As shown in Table 17.2, diverse qualities of parental touch did not appear to be significant factors influencing the status of girls' body concept. The exception to this norm can be seen in the relationship between location of touch and the form component of girls' body concept. The extent to which many different parts of a girl's body were touched by both mothers and fathers was correlated with the girl's accurate perception of her body's form. In addition, greater touching of the trunk of the body by fathers (centripetality) was correlated with perception of body form.

In contrast, many qualities of touch were significantly correlated with boys' body concept, with very different relationships apparent for mothers' versus fathers' touching. The location and duration of touch seemed the most important qualities of maternal touch. The degree to which mothers touched highly innervated areas of their sons' bodies was correlated with both the form and detail components of body

TABLE 17.2

Spearman Correlations Between Tactile Qualities Used by Mothers[a] or Fathers and the Body Concept of Girls or Boys[b]

Tactile Qualities	Body Concept					
	Girls			Boys		
	Form	Sex & Identity	Detail	Form	Sex & Identity	Detail
Mothers						
Duration	-0.13	-0.30	-0.27	-0.45*	-0.56**	-0.51**
Intensity	0.06	0.14	0.09	-0.21	-0.45*	0.06
Sensation	0.03	0.20	0.23	-0.41*	-0.15	-0.44*
Location						
Threshold	0.27	0.06	0.09	0.52**	0.29	0.58***
Extent	0.40*	0.08	0.15	-0.21	-0.20	-0.34
Centripetality	0.19	0.20	-0.04	-0.21	-0.37	-0.33
Fathers						
Duration	-0.18	-0.21	-0.26	0.31	0.27	0.41*
Intensity	0.11	0.17	0.07	0.55**	0.72****	0.46*
Sensation	-0.13	0.15	0.06	0.58***	0.68****	0.49*
Location						
Threshold	-0.32	-0.01	-0.19	-0.40	-0.29	-0.30
Extent	0.66****	0.31	0.31	0.43*	0.34	0.27
Centripetality	0.55**	0.19	0.18	0.14	0.16	0.16

Note: All correlations are based on tactile scores of a continuous nature, with higher correlations indicating relationships to qualities of touch which are more conducive to CNS arousal (e.g., stronger intensity, longer duration, more discomfort sensation, contact with areas of higher innervation).

[a] n = 40 mothers; 40 fathers.
[b] n = 20 girls; 20 boys.
* $p < 0.05$.
** $p < 0.01$.
*** $p < 0.005$.
**** $p < 0.001$.

concept, while the use of longer durations rather than short was negatively correlated with all components of body concept in boys. Additionally, stronger intensity of maternal touch was negatively correlated with accurate conception of sex and identity characteristics in boys, while touching of a comfort rather than discomfort sensation was correlated with form and detail of boys' body concept.

Paternal touch showed the most significant relationship to a child's body concept in the use of intensity and sensation. Stronger intensity touching by fathers was correlated with all components of boys' body concept as were the more discomfort types of sensation in touching. In addition, longer duration of paternal touch was correlated with accurate conception of the body's detail, and greater touching of many body parts (extent) was correlated with conception of body form in boys, the only significant finding which was identical across both boys and girls.

As displayed in Table 17.3, boys and girls showed quite disparate findings in regard to body sentiment. Only two qualities of touch seemed significant for positive body sentiment in girls. These were strong intensity and discomfort sensation of mothers' touch. In contrast, numerous effects were observed for boys; however, most of these were related to fathers' touch. Only the location of maternal touch seemed important to boy's body sentiment, with touching of highly innervated body areas and minimal use of both a large extent of the body and the trunk being significantly correlated with positive body sentiment.

Correlations between paternal touch and boys' body sentiment were almost the antithesis of those for maternal touching. Touching of highly innervated areas of the boys' body was very negatively correlated with positive body sentiment, while touching of a large extent of body parts was positively correlated. Long duration, strong intensity, and discomfort sensation of touch were also correlated with boys' positive body sentiment.

TABLE 17.3

Spearman Correlations Between Tactile Qualities Used by Mothers or Fathers and the Body Sentiment of Girls or Boys

Tactile Qualities	Body Sentiment	
	Girls	Boys
Mothers		
Duration	0.20	-0.30
Intensity	0.56**	-0.33
Sensation	0.44*	-0.22
Location		
Threshold	-0.33	0.61***
Extent	-0.21	-0.39*
Centripetality	0.04	-0.48*
Fathers		
Duration	-0.12	0.70****
Intensity	0.10	0.62***
Sensation	0.28	0.63***
Location		
Threshold	0.06	-0.64****
Extent	0.08	0.60***
Centripetality	-0.07	0.20

* $p<0.05$. *** $p<0.005$.
** $p<0.01$. **** $p<0.001$.

Because the occurrence of touching per se has been so valued throughout the literature, that is, the frequency rather than quality of touching, Spearman correlations were also employed to test the relationship between body image and the amount of touch received from parents. As seen in Tables 17.4 and 17.5, frequency of maternal touch was not positively correlated with either body concept or body sentiment for boys or girls. In fact, it was negatively correlated with the sex and identity characteristics of girls' body concepts. In contrast, frequency of paternal touch was significantly correlated with body concept and sentiment in both boys and girls.

Exceptions to the significant paternal effects observed were a lack of relationship with either accuracy of boys' detail regarding their bodies or sex and identity characteristics of girls' body concept.

TABLE 17.4

Spearman Correlations Between Frequency of Mother or Father Touching and Body Concept of Girls or Boys

Frequency of Parental Touch	Body Concept					
	Girls			Boys		
	Form	Sex & Identity	Detail	Form	Sex & Identity	Detail
Mothers	-0.02	-0.52**	-0.23	-0.05	0.02	0.08
Fathers	0.56**	0.14	0.50**	0.50**	0.48*	0.30

* $p < 0.05$.
** $p < 0.01$.

TABLE 17.5

Spearman Correlations Between Frequency of Mother or Father Touching and Body Sentiment in Girls or Boys

Frequency of Parental Touch	Body Sentiment	
	Girls	Boys
Mothers	-0.03	-0.38
Fathers	0.39*	0.77****

* $p < 0.05$.
**** $p < 0.001$.

Because of the differences in the relationships of maternal and paternal touch to body image, the differences between patterns of mother and father touching were also examined; that is, to what extent mothers and fathers actually used the various qualities in their touching as well as how frequently they touched their child. Table 17.6 displays the means, standard deviations, and results of t tests comparing parent groups. The only significant differences were in extent of the child's body parts touched by mothers and fathers, and in the frequency of their touch. Mothers were significantly higher than fathers in both frequency of their touch and the extent of the child's body which they touched. However, other than these differences, the nature of touch used by mothers and fathers was similar.

TABLE 17.6

Differences in Quality and Frequency of Mothers' versus Fathers' Touching

Nature of Touching	Mothers		Fathers		
	x	*SD*	*x*	*SD*	*t*
Quality					
Intensity	184	7.73	186	8.57	1.51
Sensation	193	5.97	194	6.58	0.52
Duration	44	4.63	43	4.58	0.58
Location					
Threshold	132	10.80	134	10.15	0.74
Extent	61	15.82	53	19.24	1.87*
Centripetality	27	10.86	24	11.82	1.11
Frequency	81	33.19	66	25.76	1.98*

* $p < 0.05$.

Discussion

DIFFERENTIATION OF TACTILE CORRELATES FOR BOYS AND GIRLS

In general, differential qualities of parental touch seemed more strongly correlated with body image in boys than in girls. The few qualities of touch which were associated with girls' body image were those that the literature indicates afford heightened stimulation to the body, increasing sensory input to the somesthetic cortex (i.e., extent and centripetality of location for body concept, strong intensity and discomfort sensation for body sentiment). In contrast, the numerous qualities of parental touch which were correlated with boys' body image appear to be functioning in a complex and variable fashion to sometimes heighten stimulation and other times not. Most qualities of maternal touch that were correlated with boys' body image seemed to reduce sensory input; for example, comfort sensation, weak intensity, short durations, and minimal trunk contact. Maternal contact with highly innervated areas of a boy's body was the only quality of a more arousing nature which was associated with positive body sentiment and accurate form and detail of the body.

Conversely, fathers' contact with highly innervated areas was negatively correlated with positive body sentiment in boys. This was the only quality of paternal touch correlated with any aspect of children's body image that did not appear to heighten stimulation. Rather fathers' contact with a large extent of the body, use of long durations, strong intensity, and discomfort sensation were all correlated with positive body sentiment and sophistication of body concept.

Distinctions in the character of tactile qualities which correlate with boys' versus girls' body image suggest that a child's sex may determine his or her threshold of responsiveness, whereby the nature of stimuli required to evoke perception of the body is different. Research at various stages of the life cycle has shown females to have higher degrees of tactile sensitivity than males (Bell and Costello, 1964; Tanner, 1974; Thornbury and Mistretta, 1981), a difference which could result in less dependence on parental touch by girls if they more readily integrate ongoing tactile sensations received through other types of contact. Previous research also suggests that, in general, females perceive touch more positively than males (Nguyen, Heslin, and Nguyen, 1975; Fisher, Rytting, and Heslin, 1976; Maier and Ernest, 1978; Whitcher and Fisher, 1979). A more critical, less positive appraisal of touch could result in a more intense impact of the tactile experience and more clearly differential effects upon the males' developing body image.

TACTILE AROUSAL AS A BASIS FOR BODY PERCEPTION

The results clearly indicate that for boys and girls alike, the majority of tactile qualities associated with a sophisticated body concept and positive body sentiment were of a somewhat vehement, instrumental, or dynamic nature. These findings suggest that a substantial level of tactile arousal may indeed be necessary for adequate cognitive and affective awareness of the body to occur. The body's experience of this state of arousal may lie on a continuum, bordered on alternate sides by tactile deprivation and tactile satiation. While deprivation would yield a reduction in the overall level of tactile sensory input and inadequate information to the cortex, satiation implies an excess or overload in the level of input, resulting in a defensive blockage of information to the brain. In contrast to both extremes, tactile arousal may function to enliven or catalyze cognitive and affective perception of the body.

While existing literature might explain the potential value of long duration, strong intensity, or contact with highly innervated body areas, the effect of discomfort sensation is not as easily understood. It should be noted here that what exactly has been measured under the rubric of comfort or discomfort sensation is unclear. Discomfort sensation as a truly painful sensory experience was most likely not observed in the context of this study. What the judges rated as discomfort was their subjective perception that the touch looked uncomfortable. The extent to which such tactile acts could have brought pain (such as that felt during child abuse or invasive health care procedures) is probably minimal.

It is more likely that what has been measured is a combination of the action being observed (e.g., squeezing, grabbing, or pulling the child) and some contamination with the quality of strong intensity; for the qualities of intensity and sensation were consistently correlated with one another. In future studies, it would seem more advantageous to measure discomfort by self-report, physiological response, or perhaps, if observation is necessary, through evaluation of other body cues (although such cues are influenced by a myriad of external factors).

DIFFERENCES IN MATERNAL AND PATERNAL TOUCH

Also of interest in the findings is the fact that frequency of touch did prove to be a significant correlate of body concept and sentiment, but only for father's touching. Frequency of maternal touch was not related to body image, except to girls' sex and identity differentiation where it was negatively correlated. Since comparison of mothers' and fathers' patterns of touching showed maternal touch to be significantly more frequent (perhaps resulting from a longstanding status as primary child rearer), one could hypothesize that children may habituate over time in their response to the frequency of maternal touch, selectively rejecting some of the maternal tactile stimuli as they interpret and evaluate their bodies. The separation–individuation process between mothers and children, which emerges from their historical symbiosis during gestation, may enhance the potential for habituation.

On the other hand, this finding may have nothing to do with a habituation response. Perhaps the results merely indicate differential needs that children may have regarding tactile interaction with one parent versus another. However, it is total speculation as to whether such needs would be socioculturally acquired, whereby mothers and fathers are expected to behave in certain ways, or whether differential needs might be biologically determined. From a sociocultural perspective, one could contrast the more consistently instrumental, arousing nature of paternal touch with the arousal management nature of maternal touch, wherein mothers sometimes heightened stimulation and sometimes reduced it. This comparison is in synchrony with the classic differentiation in parental functions described by many family researchers (Parsons, 1964; Turner, 1970; Friedman, 1981). In their frame of reference, one of a mother's prime functions in the family is tension management, so that her use of touching to both arouse and reduce stimulation would work to create the balance necessary in the touching a child receives.

It is interesting to note that emerging data from primate research would support this conception, indicating that infants use maternal contact as a primary mechanism for modulating and reducing their level of arousal. Studies have shown that physical contact with the mother eliminates certain behavioral and endocrine responses of the infant to arousal–inducing stimuli (Vogt and Levine, 1980; Levine, 1983).

Some theorists would consider all of these interpretations lacking, and simply argue that fathers have a stronger impact on children's evaluation of themselves and on their personality adjustment than do mothers (Parsons and Bates, 1955; Gecas, 1971). The crucial role which fathers may play in child rearing has only begun to receive any substantial attention. Much research is still needed to examine the varying effects of maternal and paternal touch, in relation to its potentially significant impact on male development, and in light of the rapidly changing nature of paternal roles.

IMPLICATIONS

It must be recognized that lack of randomization and small sample size severely limit generalizability of these data. In addition, the results pertain strictly to children of eight to ten years old from white, middle-class, fairly traditional family units. Thus, while implications for child development can be hypothesized, no specific application to the developmental span or across cultural groups can be assumed. Likewise, the experience of being in the laboratory–playroom and being videotaped may have evoked very different types of parental touch than would occur in a natural home environment, where other siblings were present, where a structured activity was not taking place, and most importantly, where the family was not being observed.

In addition, this study has considered the phenomenon of parental touch as a potential predictor of a child's body image. However, the data could indicate a reverse relationship, whereby the behavioral or affective characteristics of children with low-level body image might elicit certain types of touch from parents which would not otherwise emerge. The reciprocal or transactional nature of the variables being examined clearly deserves equal attention in future investigations.

Regardless of these limitations, the study's findings do justify the hypothesis that touch is a complex and variable phenomenon which needs further research. Research to study the relationship between touch and body image among different age groups, different cultural groups, and different settings is essential. Use of a mobile videopac over extended periods of time could offer a fruitful methodological approach to examine variations in tactile patterns of families. Once specific types of touch can be more reliably accepted as potential resources to body image development, experimental application of appropriate tactile qualities would be in order, testing the effects of these qualities on body image through a series of well-controlled clinical trials. If certain qualities of touch consistently show therapeutic effects, only then can we begin to consider their usefulness as a resource for either parental counseling or our own health care interventions. While still distant at this stage of investigation, the future potential within this field of study is most exciting.

Discussion: Chapter 17

T. Berry Brazelton: You've given us an elegant methodology, Sandra, and a beautiful way of looking at sex differences. A mother makes her contribution, and a father makes his, to the total body image of the child. It would be important if we could examine these contributions in more detail, particularly for single-parent families. We need to know how to back up single parents in ways that we can't right now.

Sandra Weiss: Gender differences in regard to touch are an exciting area for continued investigation. Research to date suggests that the two most consistent predictors of tactile differences are age and sex. I recommend that all investigators examine gender distinctions as part of their ongoing touch research.

William Greenough: These differences seem to be critical in modalities other than touch as well.

Seymour Levine: There are many gender differences in sensory processing—a tremendous difference in taste thresholds, for instance.

William Greenough: Do you think the contrived situation of being observed in the laboratory affected parents' behavior? As you know, people sometimes do things differently when the TV cameras are running.

Sandra Weiss: There's little evidence available right now to help us resolve the question of how laboratory behavior differs from "natural" behavior outside the laboratory. However, many methodologists in the field of nonverbal behavior are of the opinion that the pressure of observation provokes the emergence of existing patterns of behavior rather than foreign behavior.

T. Berry Brazelton: Sandra, your data on gender differences in parental touching of infants are similar to our data on parents and small infants. Mothers and fathers touch their infants in different ways, and by the age of six weeks the infant has clearly different expectations concerning each parent. The original differences may have to do with sex-typed behavior, but that in turn creates an expectancy in the infant or child that lends itself to the creation of body image.

Sandra Weiss: You're reminding me of a point Steve Suomi made earlier. He said that male monkeys assumed a distinct role in infant development in that they spontaneously reinforced different behaviors in female and male infants. For example, young female monkeys weren't allowed to play in a rough-and-tumble fashion, whereas such play was encouraged for young males. That fascinates me, because it suggests potential biological underpinnings for human sex-role stereotypes.

William Greenough: The biological influence is definitely present. The appearance of rough-and-tumble play in humans, in nonhuman primates, and even in rodents is governed largely by whether they were exposed to testosterone during a sensitive period (prenatal or postnatal, depending on the species). If they were exposed, they will exhibit more rough-and-tumble play.

T. Berry Brazelton: Dr. Spock was the first person to point out to me that there are subtle motoric and attentional differences between boy and girl babies at birth. For instance, they seem to look at you differently. Using just these little things that he'd observed, Spock could pick out girls and boys in the nursery with about 80 percent accuracy. Many parents are probably aware of these subtle differences, too, and of course that's going to confirm sex stereotyping.

Seymour Levine: You're into a marvelously interesting area. Those of us who study hormones are very aware of a whole variety of sex differences in response systems. For example, when a distressed squirrel monkey infant signals, the males don't respond. The females respond, both hormonally and behaviorally, whether they're mothers or not. They respond because they're females. There is a very profound set of sex differences in terms of responsivity.

References

Alagna, F. J., Whitcher, S. J., Fisher, J. D., & Wicas, E. A. (1979), Evaluative reaction to interpersonal touch in a counseling interview. *J. Counsel. Psychol.*, 26/6:465–472.

Als, H., Lester, B., & Brazelton, T. B. (1979), Dynamics of the behavioral organization of the premature infant: A theoretical perspective. In: *Infants Born at Risk*, eds. T. Field, A. Sostek, S. Goldberg, & H. Shuman. New York: Spectrum Press.

Armstrong, D. M. (1962), *Bodily Sensation*. New York: Humanities Press.

Ayres, J. (1972), Tactile functions: Their relation to hyperactive perceptual motor behavior. *Amer. J. Occupat. Ther.*, 26:6–11.

Ball, T., & Edgar, C. (1967), The effectiveness of sensorimotor training in promoting generalized body image development. *J. Spec. Ed.*, 1:387–395.

Bell, R., & Costello, N. (1964), Three tests for sex differences in tactile sensitivity in the newborn. *Biolog. Neonat.*, 7:335–347.

Blaesing, S., & Brockhaus, J. (1972), The development of body image in the child. *Nurs. Clin. N. Amer.*, 7/4:597–607.

Bosanquet, C. (1970), Getting in touch. *J. Analyt. Psychol.*, 15:42–58.

Brody, S. (1956), *Patterns of Mothering*. New York: International Universities Press.

Burnside, I. M. (1973), Caring for the aged: Touching is talking. *Amer. J. Nurs.*, 73:2060–2063.

Burton, A., & Heller, L. G. (1964), Touching of the body. *Psychoanal. Rev.*, 51:127–133.

Cardone, S., & Olson, R. (1973), Intercorrelations between some body image measures. *J. Personal. Assess.*, 37:122–129.

Casler, L. (1965), Effects of extra tactile stimulation on a group of institutionalized infants. *Genet. Psychol. Mono.*, 71:137–175.

Cratty, B. J. (1970), *Perceptual Motor Development in Infants and Children*. London: Macmillan.

———(1974), *Motor Activity and the Education of Retardates*, 2nd ed. Philadelphia: Lea & Febiger.

Delacato, C. (1971), *The Treatment and Prevention of Reading Problems: The Neuro-Psychological Approach*. Springfied, IL: Charles C. Thomas.

DeReuch, A., & Knight, J. (1966), *Touch, Heat, and Pain*. London: Churchill.

Fisher, J. D., Rytting, M., & Heslin, R. (1976), Hands touching hands: Affective and evaluative effects of an interpersonal touch. *Sociom.*, 39/4:416–421.

Fisher, S., & Cleveland, S. F. (1968), *Body Image and Personality*, 2nd ed. New York: Dover Publications.

——— ———(1970), *Body Experience in Fantasy Behavior*. New York: Appleton-Century-Crofts.

Friedman, M. (1981), *Family Nursing*. New York: Appleton-Century-Crofts.
Gecas, V. (1971), Parental behavior and dimensions of adolescent self-evaluation. *Sociom.* 34/4:466–482.
Geldard, F. (1972), *The Human Senses,* 2nd ed., New York: John Wiley.
Gibson, J. (1966), *The Senses Considered as Perceptual Systems*. Boston: Houghton Mifflin.
Gorman, W. (1969), *Body Image and the Image of the Brain.* St. Louis, MO: Warren Green.
Gottlieb, G. (1971), Ontogenesis of sensory function in birds and mammals. In: *The Biopsychology of Development*, eds. E. Tobach, L. Aronson, & E. Show. New York: Academic Press, pp. 67–128.
Haber, W. B. (1956), Observations on phantom-limb phenomena. *Arch. Neurolog. Psychiat.*, 75:624–636.
Head, H. (1920), *Studies in Neurology*. London: Hodder & Stoughton.
Hebb, D. O. (1949), *Organization of Behavior: A Neuropsychological Theory*. New York: John Wiley.
Jourard, S. (1966), Experimenter, subject distance and self disclosure. *Brit. J. Soc. Clinic. Psychol.*, 5:221–231.
Kenshalo, D. (1968), Intensive and extensive aspects of tactile sensitivity as a function of body part, sex and laterality. In: *Skin Senses*, ed. D. Kenshalo. Proceedings of the first International Symposium on the Skin Senses held at Florida State University. Springfield, IL: Charles C Thomas Publishers.
Kephart, N. (1971), *Slow Learner in the Classroom*, 2nd ed. Columbus, OH: Charles E. Merrill.
Killackey, H., & Belford, G. (1979), The formation of afferent patterns in the somatosensory cortex of the neonatal rat. *J. Comparat. Neurol.*, 183:285–304.
Knable, J. (1981), Handholding: One means of transcending barriers of communication. *Heart & Lung*, 10/6:1106–1110.
Kolb, L. (1959), Disturbances of the body image. In: *American Handbook of Psychiatry,* Vol. 1, ed. S. Arieti. New York: Basic Books, pp. 749–767.
Levine, S. (1983), A psychobiological approach to the ontogeny of coping. In: *Stress, Coping and Development in Children*, eds. N. Garmezy & M. Rutter. New York: McGraw-Hill, pp. 107–131.
Liley, A. W. (1972), The fetus as a personality. *Austral. & New Zeal. J. Psychiat.*, 6:99–105.
Maier, R. A., & Ernest, R. C. (1978), Sex differences in the perception of touching. *Percept. & Motor Skills*, 46:577–578.
Merzenich, M., & Kaas, J. (1980). Principles of organization of sensory-perceptual systems in mammals. *Progr. in Psychobiol. & Physiolog. Psychol.*, 9:1–42.
Mintz, E. (1969), On the rationale of touch in psychotherapy. *Psychother. Theory Res. Pract.*, 6/4:232–234.

Montagu, A. (1971), *Touching: The Human Significance of the Skin*. New York: Columbia University Press.
Morris, D. (1967), *The Naked Ape*. New York: Dell Publishing.
Murray, R. (1972), Principles of nursing intervention for the adult patient with body image changes. *Nurs. Clin. N. Amer.*, 7:697–707.
Nguyen, J., Heslin, R., & Nguyen, M. (1975), The meaning of touch: Sex differences. *J. Communicat.*, 25:92–103.
Parsons, T. (1964), *Social Structure and Personality*. London: Free Press.
———Bates, R. (1955), *Family, Socialization, and Interaction Process*. Glencoe, IL: Free Press.
Patton, R. G., & Gardner, L. I. (1963), *Growth Failure in Maternal Deprivation*. Springfield, IL: Charles C Thomas.
Peto, A. (1972), Body image and depression. *Internat. J. Psychoanal.*, 53/2:259–263.
Purpura, D. (1975), Dendrite differentiation in human cerebral cortex: Normal and aberrant developmental patterns. *Adv. in Neurol.*, 12:91–116.
Ribble, M. A. (1943), *The Rights of Infants*. New York: Columbia University Press.
Roback, H. (1968), Human figure drawings: Their utility in the clinical psychologist's armamentarium for personality assessment. *Psycholog. Bull.*, 70/1:1–19.
Rosenblith, W. A. (1961), *Sensory Communication: Symposium on Principles of Sensory Communication*. New York: John Wiley.
Rubin, R. (1963), Maternal touch. *Nurs. Outlook*, 2:828–831.
Ruesch, J. (1957), *Disturbed Communication*. New York: W. W. Norton.
Schilder, P. (1950), *Image and Appearance of the Human Body*. New York: International Universities Press.
Schopler, E. (1962), The development of body image and symbol formation through body contact with an autistic child. *J. Child Psychol.*, 3:191–202.
———(1965), Early infantile autism and receptor processes. *Arch. Gen. Psychiat.*, 13:327–335.
Secord, P., & Jourard, S. (1953), The appraisal of body cathexis: Body cathexis of the self. *J. Consult. Psychol.*, 17/5:343–347.
Sinclair, D. C. (1967), *Cutaneous Sensation*. New York: Oxford University Press.
Tanner, J. (1974), Variability of growth and maturity in newborn infants. In: *The Effect of the Infant on its Caregiver*, eds. M. Lewis & L. Rosenblum. New York: John Wiley.
Thornbury, J. M., & Mistretta, C. M. (1981), Tactile sensitivity as a function of age. *J. Gerontol.*, 36/1:34–39.
Turkewitz, G., & Kenny, P. (1982), Limitations on input as a basis for neural organization and perceptual development: A preliminary theoretical statement. *Development. Psychobiol.*, 15:357–368.
Turner, R. (1970), *Family Interactions*. New York: John Wiley.

Tyler, N. (1972), A stereognostic test for screening tactile sensation. *Amer. J. Occupat. Ther.*, 26:256–260.
Van Dongen, L. G., & Goudie, E. G. (1980), Fetal movement patterns in the first trimester of pregnancy. *Brit. J. Obstet. & Gynecol.*, 87:191–193.
Vaughan, H. G. (1975), Electrophysiological analysis of regional cortical maturation. *Biolog. Psychiat.*, 10:513–526.
Vogt, J., & Levine, S. (1980), Response of mother and infant squirrel monkeys to separation disturbance. *Physiol. & Behav.*, 24:829–832.
Wapner, S. (1965), *The Body Percept.* New York: Random House.
Watson, W. (1970), Body image and staff-to-resident deportment in a home for the aged. *Aging & Hum. Develop.*, 1/4:345–359.
Weiss, S. (1975), *Familial Tactile Correlates of Body Image in Children.* Unpublished doctoral dissertation. University of California, San Francisco.
———(1978), The language of touch: A resource to body image. *Iss. in Ment. Health Nurs.*, 1:17–29.
———(1979), The language of touch. *Nurs. Res.*, 28/2:76–80.
Whitcher, S., & Fisher, J. (1979), Multidimensional reaction to therapeutic touch in a hospital setting. *J. Personal. & Soc. Psychol.*, 37:87–96.
Witkin, H., Dyk, R., Faterson, H., Goodenough, D., & Karp, S. (1962), *Psychological Differentiation.* New York: John Wiley.
Zion, L. (1965), Body concept as it relates to self-concept. *Res. Quart.*, 36:490–495.
Zubek, J. P. (1969), *Sensory Deprivation: Fifteen Years of Research.* New York: Appleton-Century-Crofts.

18

Parental Aversion to Infant-Initiated Contact Is Correlated with the Parent's Own Rejection During Childhood: The Effects of Experience on Signals of Security with Respect to Attachment

Mary Main, Ph.D.

I am not concerned in this chapter with differences in the amount of time that parents and infants spend in contact. Some parents hold their infants for long periods for feeding, but are nonetheless rejecting of infant-initiated contact, while some parents characteristically hold their infants relatively little, and yet gladly accept the infant whenever actively approached or signaled. Ainsworth's extensive Baltimore home observation study showed that the amount of time the

Acknowledgments: This article is based upon research which was supported by grants to the author from the William T. Grant Foundation (1978–1979); from the Small Grants program of NIMH (MH 32089–01); from the Institute of Human Development at the University of California, Berkeley; and from the Society for Research in Child Development. I am grateful to Sharon Slaton, Stewart Wakeling, Donna Weston, and Marya Hass for their analyses of the infant data, and to Ruth Goldwyn for her analysis of the Adult Attachment Interview. Finally, I wish to thank Mary D. S. Ainsworth for the discussions which prompted a part of this research, and for generously making her extensive Baltimore records available.

mother spent holding the infant had no observed consequences for infant behavior, although the manner in which she held the infant (e.g., affectionately vs. awkwardly) did have consequences (Ainsworth, Blehar, Waters and Wall, 1978). Both the manner in which the infant was held, and overall ratings for mother's observed aversion to physical contact with the infant were found to be predictive of infant behavior in other circumstances (Ainsworth et al., 1978; Main, 1981; Main and Stadtman, 1981).

According to Darwin (1872), touch is the means by which the mother expresses her love to the infant, a sentiment which has long been echoed by theorists such as Winnicott (1960) and Balint (1949). The rationale for the set of research investigations reported here is, however, based upon the ethological–evolutionary theory of attachment developed by John Bowlby. Bowlby (1969) postulates the development of an "attachment behavioral system" in all ground-living primates, a system which continuously assesses the physical and psychological accessibility of one or several "attachment figures," those persons who serve the protective and parental function of seeing to the infant's survival. Whenever surrounding circumstances are alarming, therefore, the attachment behavioral system is highly activated. Bowlby (1969) argues that physical (tactual) contact with an attachment figure is then required to reassure the infant of its safety. Physical contact with an attachment figure is thus the ultimate signal that the infant is in safe (secure) circumstances.

Because in achieving contact with the attachment figure the frightened and relatively helpless primate infant has done all that it may do to further its survival, and because, correspondingly, the infant's survival furthers the parent's reproductive success, the ethological–evolutionary understanding of parent–infant contact suggests that such contact should be evaluated as "pleasant" by both parties. However, experience has been shown to alter this response to contact. Toddlers subjected to stressful separations from parents for several weeks or months become avoidant of contact with their parents (Robertson and Bowlby, 1952; Heinicke and Westheimer, 1966). In addition, some nonseparated one-year-olds avoid physical contact with their parents when under stress (Ainsworth, Bell, and Stayton, 1971), and our own studies of Ainsworth's Baltimore records have demonstrated in turn that the parents of these infants have shown strong aversion to physical contact with their infants in the home environment as early as the first quarter of the first year of life (Ainsworth, et al, 1978; Main, 1981). The overall objective of this chapter is therefore to examine the ways in which parent–infant contact can come to be evaluated negatively, rather positively, by both parties; that is, the ways in which it can come to be felt to be aversive.

In earlier papers (Main, 1981; Main and Stadtman, 1981) I suggested that the rejected, attached infant must experience an increased "attraction" to the mother, which is the result of the positive feedback loop created by rejection. The frustration of the system should lead to aggression, while the difficulty of resolution through either approach or avoidance should lead to conflict. In these papers, I also suggested that, while all physically rejected infants would show some aggressive behavior and some conflict behavior, many would still be able to shift their attention from the immediately "irresolvable" situation of rejection; that is, some would be able to avoid it. For infants capable of shifting their attention from this situation, conflict behavior should be relatively limited in its expression.

Recently, we have found that some infants show strikingly conflicted behaviors in response to the Ainsworth Strange Situation (i.e., they become "disorganized/disoriented"; Main and Solomon [1986]. We have suggested that in the home, the experience of these infants often involves actively frightening behavior or frightened behavior on the part of the parent (Main and Hesse, in press). I now believe that the most striking conflict behavior probably appears as a result of infants experiencing frightening or frightened behavior on the part of the, therefore, unapproachable parent, rather than, or in addition to, simply experiencing a parent who is quietly aversive to contact.

Parent–Infant Contact as the Ultimate Signal of Security For the Infant's Attachment Behavioral System: Expectations and an Observed Anomaly

My interest in parental aversion to contact grew out of the theoretical work of John Bowlby (1969), who describes the development of an "attachment behavioral system" in ground-living primates and humans raised in all but extremely abnormal rearing conditions. The attachment behavioral system is conceived of as a control system which develops gradually throughout infancy and finally focuses attention upon one or a few "attachment figures," individuals who are likely, but need not necessarily be, the infant's parents. The biological function of the attachment behavioral system is presumed to be the protection and care of the infant, and attachment behavior is presumed to have been incorporated within the behavioral repertoire to serve this purpose. Once the system has developed to the point of focusing on one or a few figures, the physical and psychological accessibility of these attachment figures is continually monitored, because maintaining proximity to these figures (or being assured of their accessibility) is the key to infant primate survival within the environment of evolutionary adaptedness.

Maintaining proximity to an attachment figure is the sine qua non of infant primate survival (Main, 1981). In the case of the ground-living primate infant, the attachment figure supplies protection from predation, threatening conspecifics, and threatening changes in the immediate environment, as well as providing nourishment and assuring that the infant keeps up with movements of the troop.

Although in the case of human infants raised in protected circumstances the presence of attachment figures may not actually be necessary to survival, the attachment behavioral system is nonetheless presumed to develop and be operative. Indeed, the system is presumed to remain present throughout the human lifetime, although persons other than the parents may later serve as attachment figures, and attachment behavior may be much less easily activated.

In the case of the human infant, threatening or frightening environmental conditions are presumed to activate the attachment behavioral system, leading to one of two results: infant signaling to bring the attachment figure into increased proximity (e.g., crying), or direct efforts to approach. According to Bowlby (1969), when the system is only slightly activated (as, for example, by the appearance of a stranger in a familiar environment), the infant may merely need increased proximity to attachment figures for reassurance, while in conditions of stronger activation (the sudden appearance of a threatening stranger in an unfamiliar environment), only physical contact with an attachment figure will serve as reassurance.

It is the theoretical import of physical contact as the final signal of security which provides the basis for the research investigations reported in this chapter. Because physical contact with the attachment figure is the ultimate signal of security for the attached individual, it is expected that parent–infant contact will generally arouse pleasant feelings for both individuals, and for dyads living in undisturbed circumstances it is certainly unexpected that either member of the dyad should experience aversion to physical contact with the other. Bowlby's (1969) analysis of feelings and emotions as evaluations suggests that circumstances closely associated with survival and reproductive success should evoke particularly strong responses. Infant–parent contact should therefore generally be evaluated as "good" (or pleasant) by both parties, because of its close association with the infant's survival, on the one hand, and the parent's reproductive success on the other. Unusual rearing conditions or immediate circumstances can, of course, alter an individual's evaluation of such events.

I became interested in parental aversion to tactual contact with the infant because of what seemed to be an anomaly in Ainsworth's studies of interactions between normal, nonseparated infants and mothers. Ainsworth studied twenty-six infant–mother pairs throughout the first year of life, collecting approximately eighty hours of observational data for each dyad, which was recorded in the form of narrative records. At the end of the first year, twenty-three of these dyads were seen in a brief laboratory observation now known as the Ainsworth Strange Situation (Ainsworth et al., 1971), involving the infant in two brief separations from, and reunions with, the mother in the laboratory environment. As expected, following the second separation, the majority of the infants in this unfamiliar setting approached the mother and clung to her, or actively signaled her for contact. This response is, of course, the expected one because of the alarming circumstances.

The anomaly consisted in the fact that, under the stress of separation and reunion in the unfamiliar laboratory environment, some infants failed to approach the mother, and indeed, six out of twenty-three actively avoided almost all forms of contact (Ainsworth et al., 1978). While this behavior had been observed in toddlers long separated from their parents (Robertson and Bowlby, 1952; Heinicke and Westheimer, 1966; Bowlby, 1973), these infants had never undergone major separations from the mother. The six most avoidant infants were termed *insecure–avoidant:* they showed little or no distress upon separation, then actively turned away and moved away upon reunion, indicating that they wished to be put down if mother picked them up. Under these stressful circumstances, then, these infants unexpectedly showed aversion to tactual contact with the mother. Infants who showed little or no avoidance were categorized either as secure (the infant seeks contact on reunion and then easily returns to play) or insecure–resistant (the infant seeks contact but the parent is unable to settle the infant in its distress, which often includes indices of anger).

Avoidance was scored for each infant on a seven-point scale ranging from a brief look away immediately upon reunion, to active ignoring and moving away as mother approached, and signaling to be put down when picked up (Ainsworth et al., 1978). Later, investigators working with middle-class samples found that avoidance of the mother was stable across the second year in successive Strange Situations, and that avoidance at twelve months predicted avoidance at six years (Main and Cassidy, in press).

Avoidance of proximity and contact in stress situations was unexpectable in infants who had not undergone major separations from the parent. Each of the six most strongly avoidant infants had proven to be attached to the mother during home observations, and many had anxiously pursued the mother from room to room in the familiar home environment. Later studies showed that, when infants were seen independently with each parent in the Strange Situation, there was no relationship between avoidance of the mother and of the father (Main and Weston, 1981). A given infant could be strongly avoidant of mother, but not at all avoidant of the father. This suggested an interactive basis for the development of avoidance.

Our search through the Ainsworth records of infant–mother interaction throughout the first year of life suggested that this interactive basis consisted at least in part in the *mother's own aversion to physical contact with the infant*. Using a nine-point rating scale for maternal aversion to physical contact with the infant (described below), Ainsworth found that the mothers of the six infants who were most avoidant of contact under stress at one year of age (the infants classified as insecure–avoidant) had a mean score of 7.3 for aversion to contact with their infants during the first three months of life, while mothers of infants classified as secure or insecure–resistant on the basis of their response to this separation-and-reunion observation were not aversive to contact, having mean scores of 2.28 and 1.73 respectively (Ainsworth et al., 1978).

That a mother should be averse to physical contact with her own infant is, of course, as much an anomaly as is the infant's aversion to contact with its mother. Having now established the link between mother's aversion to contact with the infant and the infant's avoidance of contact with the mother in a stress situation, we can begin to examine a set of succeeding questions. We must ask first whether parental aversion to contact is a stable characteristic, and then discuss the nature of its consequences for the infant.

Parental Aversion to Physical Contact with the Infant: Stable, and Correlated with Infant Aggression and Conflict

STABILITY OF AVERSION TO CONTACT OVER THE FIRST YEAR OF LIFE

A first question regarding almost any behavioral characteristic under examination is whether, in the absence of major changes of circumstance, it is stable. Mary Ainsworth loaned her Baltimore narrative records of mother-infant interaction throughout the first year of life to Jackolyn Stadtman and the author for a first analysis concerning stability (Main and Stadtman, 1981). As noted earlier, Ainsworth, together with a small team of observers, had visited twenty-six infant–mother dyads at three- and four-week intervals throughout the first year, for approximately four hours of observation per visit. During each visit, the observers took extensive notes on interaction. The notes were dictated and transcribed into narrative records.

Using these narrative records, research assistants working with Main and Stadtman (1981) rated each mother in the sample during *each* visit for apparent aversion to physical contact with the infant. Because each visit lasted approximately four hours, the records included observations of the mother holding, bathing, feeding, and transporting the infant. In these situations, a substantial range of attitudes could be observed. Some mothers, for example, were described as carrying their infants "tenderly, and close to mother's chest," while others were described as indicating aversion to contact during transport, "holding the infant at some distance, with arms stiff and straight in front of her, as though the infant is being transported on a platter."

Mother's statements to the observer and the infant were also taken into account. One mother stated that she had always had an aversion to physical contact with people; others made comments to the infant such as, "you know I hate to have you crawling over me!" and, very simply, "don't touch me!". Mothers who made statements such as these, or showed a strong aversion to holding or contacting the baby, received a high rating for aversion to contact, whereas mothers who habitually stiffened while holding the baby, made milder statements, and/or showed mild examples of aversion, received a middle rating. Three assistants read and rated each visit. Interrater reliability was very high (>0.85 for each set of raters). Each visit was assigned the mean rating for the three raters, and the mothers were then assigned the mean ratings for all visits made during each quarter of the year.

During the fourth quarter of the year (9–12 months), we not only rated mother's apparent overall aversion to physical contact with the infant, but also tabulated each instance of active rejection of physical contact by the mother, such as pushing the baby away, or angrily shouting at the baby when he or she was making a bid for contact. The assistant coding these events had no knowledge of the more "holistic" ratings made for overall aversion to physical contact.

We found that aversion to close body contact was a stable maternal characteristic in the first year of life (Main and Stadtman, 1981). Thus, for example, the mother's rating for aversion to physical contact during the first quarter predicted her aversion to contact during the third quarter [r (26) = 0.67, p < 0.001)], and during the fourth quarter [r (26) = 0.51, p < 0.001]. Moreover, the mother's rated aversion to contact with the infant in the first quarter was highly related to coded instances of actual, active rejection of bids for contact in the fourth quarter [r (23) = 0.72, p < 0.001]. So, aversion shown at a general level before the baby could actively approach and initiate contact was highly predictive of later responsiveness to bids for contact made by the more competant and mobile baby.

One possible interpretation of these results would be that mothers were simply respondants to relatively stable indices of *infant* aversion to physical contact. Some of the mothers interviewed by Schaffer and Emerson (1964) recalled that their infants had been uncuddly from the first weeks, and that they continued to show some aversion to physical contact over the first year of life. Ainsworth made extensive observations of infant responsiveness to cuddling during the first six weeks of life, so that we were able to devise a rating system to represent the infant's apparent "cuddliness" in this time period. We found ratings for early cuddliness unrelated to mother's observed aversion to contact during any of the four quarters of the first year of life. Thus, early infant differences did not appear to account for differences in mothers.

INFANT CORRELATES OF MATERNAL AVERSION TO PHYSICAL CONTACT: AGGRESSIVENESS AND CONFLICT BEHAVIOR

On the basis of a theoretically based rationale described in the succeeding subsection, we expected that mother's aversion to physical contact with the infant would be related to infant aggressiveness (seen as a response to the frustration of attachment) and infant conflict behavior (seen as the result of a relatively "unsolvable" conflict situation involving simultaneous activation of approach and withdrawal tendencies). We used Ainsworth's records of infant behavior during the fourth quarter (9 to 12 months of age) to assess infant aggressiveness and anger. First, an assistant blind to both our hypotheses and all ratings for maternal aversion to contact made a simple tabulation of instances of aggressive behavior or threatened aggressive behavior toward the mother, such as baby hitting the mother, hitting at the mother, or threatening to hit the mother. Working with these twenty-six mother–infant dyads, we found a 0.44 correlation ($p < 0.025$) between this simple tabulation of aggressive displays and mother's aversion to physical contact with the infant during the first quarter of the year. In addition, a second assistant, again blind to hypotheses and all other ratings, rated each infant for the extent to which anger seemed to dominate the infant's mood and activities (whether or not the infant was observed actually striking at the mother). There was a 0.65 correlation ($p < 0.005$) between mother's aversion to physical contact with the infant in the first year of life and the infant's angry mood between nine and twelve months of age.

We next examined the relationship between maternal aversion to physical contact with the infant and infant conflict behavior. In general, conflict behavior included any behavior that seemed odd or disturbing in itself (such as stereotypies, hand-flapping, hair-pulling, echoing speech, periods of frozen, trancelike stance or expression) and any behavior that seemed odd or disturbing simply because it occurred out of context, or in the wrong context (as when the infant showed sudden, inexplicable fear of a familiar object). Although the coder was instructed to tabulate any behavior that seemed "odd" in itself, a review of the behavior actually noted in this study (and in the two studies described directly below) showed that most could be described as *conflict* behaviors (see Hinde, [1966], for a description of behaviors considered to be conflict behaviors by ethologists). In the Ainsworth sample of twenty-six dyads, we found a 0.55 correlation between mother's aversion to physical contact with the infant in the early months, and instances of infant conflict behavior between nine and twelve months of age.

The Ainsworth home observation records were the only records extensive enough to permit us reliable observations of infant aggression and angry behavior. However, we also had available two sets of relatively brief observations of infant and mother behavior in the laboratory setting, and these provided us with opportunity to assess both infant conflict behavior and maternal aversion to contact. In a first study involving mothers and toddlers at twenty-one months of age, we found a significant correlation between mother's aversion to physical contact with her toddler while directed to play actively with him or her for ten minutes, and toddler conflict behavior as observed in another ten minute session in which mother was present but requested not to direct the child's activities [r (38) = 0.40]. In this study, a seven-point rating scale was utilized.

Our final study utilized dyads participating in the Berkeley Social Development Project (the characteristics of this sample are described more fully in Main and Weston [1981]). For this study involving mothers and their twelve-month-olds in the presence of a friendly interactive stranger (an eleven-minute "Clown Session"), we undertook a final revision of our rating scale, emphasizing especially the parent's apparent attitude to ventral–ventral contact. The correlation between the mother's aversion to physical contact with the infant and infant conflict behavior [r (30) = 0.63] for this latter study is higher than for the preceding two studies, very likely because maternal and infant behavior is assessed within the same session (Main and Stadtman, 1981). I have included a copy of the scale devised for this final study in appendix 1 to this chapter.

CONSEQUENCES OF THE REJECTION OF BODILY CONTACT BY ATTACHMENT FIGURES: SOME THEORETICAL CONSIDERATIONS

Earlier, I offered a brief review of the concept of the attachment behavioral system as developed by John Bowlby (1969). The system is conceived of as being as vital to survival and reproduction as is the sexual behavioral system. Infant nonhuman primates would not survive if they did not keep in relative proximity to protective adults during their helpless immaturity, fleeing to those protective adults when threatened by predators, by conspecifics, or by malignant changes in the environment.

Let us now derive some consequences of this theory of attachment. As we normally conceive of the working of the attachment behavioral system, the child who is alarmed—by thunder, by threats of predators, or threats by conspecifics—inevitably seeks his primary attachment figures as a haven of safety. But if alarm stemming from *any* source leads to strong activation of the attachment behavioral system (a system designed to bring the infant and attachment figure into proximity in time of danger), then these systems will be activated even when the attachment figure herself is the source of the alarm (Bowlby, 1969; Main, 1981; Main and Stadtman, 1981).

Therefore, the child whose mother pushes him away will experience a desire to approach her. How much this desire is experienced will turn on the circumstances, including whether mother's action is calm, on the one hand, or rough and frightening, on the other. At the same time the child will experience some fear of the mother and some desire to withdraw from her—again, dependent upon the immediate form taken by mother's actions. What is peculiar to the situation in which the "attack" comes from the "haven of safety" is the arousal of conflicting tendencies. From this single threat or signal at least two conflicting messages are received: to withdraw from, and to approach, the attachment figure.

While this argument may appear theoretical, there is substantiation within the nonhuman primate literature, where workers have long noted that acts of physical rejection by the primate mother often lead to a peculiar response on the part of nonhuman primates (Harlow, 1958; Kaufman and

Rosenblum, 1969; Sackett, Griffin, Pratt, Joslyn, and Ruppertal, 1967). Rather than withdrawing from a mother who attempts to push the infant away, the primate infant again attempts to approach the mother or clings to her all the harder. The immediate effect of the primate mother's rejection of her primate infant is then to draw the infant toward her. By repelling her infant, the mother at some level simultaneously "attracts" him. If mother is aversive to contact, however, the attracted infant cannot approach her, and the situation is then theoretically irresolvable.

If this is true, then rejection of physical contact by an attachment figure should lead to conflict behaviors. The degree and timing of the conflict behavior shown should depend upon many factors, including whether the experience of rejection is sudden and frightening (more conflict behaviors) or calm and consistent (fewer conflict behaviors, and more avoidant shifts of attention). The frustration to the attachment system should frequently result in angry behavior as well. Here again, I would expect more or less of this behavior depending upon circumstances, with the attachment figure who consistently rejects approach behavior having an infant who exhibits angry behavior more often.

There are still other ways in which the results of this situation will turn on circumstances. If a mother rebuffs her infant's approach but shortly thereafter permits access—as is certainly common—no lasting conflict situation is created. However, as we have seen already, some mothers seem to find close body contact with their infants consistently distasteful (i.e., some show aversion from the earliest months of the infant's life). When a mother with a consistently expressed aversion to physical contact with her infant rebuffs her infant (so that he or she "must" experience a desire to approach her as a haven of safety), she obviously will not permit the infant access immediately thereafter.

The subjective experience of conflict for the latter infant will be repeated and nonverbal. A single movement on the part of the mother intended to lead her child away from her, at least initially brings the child anxiously toward her. Yet, he or she cannot contact her, even though only contact would terminate the anxious search for safety. The renewed recognition of the mother's inaccessibility should further activate the system and conflict behaviors should be expected to appear in the infant. In addition, when the attachment behavioral system is activated without termination, angry behavior is observed in infants (Bowlby, 1969). In the situation described above, the infant is in a state of continual activation without termination with respect to his mother. Strong anger should be expected, as well as signs of conflict. These are, of course, the sequelae we have reported.

The conflict described is self-perpetuating. Once an infant is rejected by an attachment figure who is continually aversive to contact, the attachment behavioral systems are activated, necessarily frustrated, and therefore still more strongly activated, to meet again with more frustrations. This is positive feedback. At the same time, withdrawal tendencies conflict with approach tendencies, and the impossibility of approach arouses an anger which can probably no more safely be expressed than can attachment. Eventually the physically rejected child may feel fearful and angry in every situation which normally arouses love and longing.

Positive feedback cannot, however, continue indefinitely. Eventually there must be a qualitative shift which permits the attached infant to escape from this theoretically irresolvable situation. If there are alternative and accepting attachment figures available within the environment, the infant can escape the field of conflict and probably ultimately escape the most damaging effects of repeated experiences of rejection. The alternative attachment figure may be the infant's other parent, or a grandparent, a favored baby-sitter, or an older sibling. A second means of escape from the arousal implicit in the experience of continual conflict is through an organized shift of attention from the attachment figure, and perhaps eventually from most situational cues to the arousal of feelings of attachment. This is the means of "escape" shown by infants and children who are classified as insecure–avoidant.

As noted earlier, I believe this attention-shifting "avoidant" solution to parental rejection is available only when the parent is not pervasively frightening. When the parent is either frightening or frightened, I believe the infant is less likely to be able to successfully shift its attention. In this case, the conflict situation is less escapable, and conflict behaviors may be expected to be so well marked in form that the infant can be considered somewhat disorganized and disoriented (Main and Solomon, 1986; Main and Hesse, in press). (The "disorganized/disoriented" infant attachment classification is a recent addition to the Ainsworth classification system, and is used in conjuction with the secure, insecure–avoidant, and insecure–resistant classifications as alternatives.)

The Role of Experience in the Development of Aversion to Physical Contact With an Infant or Caregiver: Findings, and Suggestions From Other Studies

PARENTAL AVERSION TO CONTACT WITH THE INFANT IS RELATED TO THE PARENT'S OWN REJECTION DURING CHILDHOOD

To this point I have described what I see as an important dimension of the infant's experience of its parent—the parent's relative aversion to, versus acceptance of, physical, and especially ventral–ventral, contact with the infant. Parental aversion to contact with the infant has been described as stable, and as predictive of the infant's subsequent aggression and conflict. We have found that maternal aversion to contact with the infant exhibited in the first quarter of the first year of life predicts the infant's avoidance of contact with the mother at the end of the first year in a stress situation. By the end of the year, then, the infant has taken on the maternal pattern.

This latter finding parallels another set of reports from

our laboratory, in which we studied the behavior of battered toddlers in their day-care settings (George and Main, 1979; Main and George, 1985). These studies were undertaken in response to reports of an abused–abusing intergenerational cycle in child maltreatment, and indeed, we uncovered some supportive evidence. As compared to a set of well-matched controls (children matched to the battered toddlers not only in terms of age, sex, and economic status, but also in being from stressed families), we found battered toddlers more aggressive to both peers and caregivers (George and Main, 1979). In addition, they responded with fear or anger to distress in other toddlers, rather than responding (like the control toddlers) merely with interest or concern (Main and George, 1985).

Given these suggestions of cross-generational continuity, it seemed natural to search for the sources of individual differences in parental aversion to contact within the parent's own attachment history. The simple hypothesis to be examined was whether a parent's observed physical rejection of his/her infant might be connected to a history of the parent's own rejection by parents.

As part of a more general "move to the level of representation" in the study of attachment (Main, Kaplan and Cassidy, 1985), we conducted an Adult Attachment Interview with the parents of 40 of the children studied in the Berkeley Social Development Project sample (see Main and Weston, 1981, for a full description of sample characteristics). This interview was conducted when the children in the sample had reached six years of age, i.e., approximately five years following the infancy observation. The interview (designed by George, Kaplan, and Main, 1985) lasted approximately an hour and ranged over many topics of concern to attachment. The interview opened with a request that the parent describe his/her relationship to each parent in childhood, beginning with a list of five adjectives for each parent. For each adjective chosen, the parent was queried regarding memory for specific episodes supporting the choice of this adjective. Parents were also asked which parent had they been closest to (and why), whether there had been any changes in relationships with parents over childhood, whether they had ever felt rejected during childhood, and what they had done when hurt or upset in childhood. We also examined experiences of separation and loss, threats of separation, and the ways in which the parent felt early attachment relationships and experiences had affected them as adults and as parents.

Transcripts of the Adult Attachment Interview were rated for the adult's experiences of rejection by each parent (mother and father separately). Rejection was defined as the turning back or away of the child or the child's attachment. Each transcript was considered as a whole, so that a mother who stated that she had had an accepting mother—but who contradicted this in her recounting of specific episodes relevant to attachment—could be considered to have been rejected by her mother. The rater for the Adult Attachment Interview had no knowledge of the parent's behavior in any other assessment, including of course the assessment for aversion to physical contact. Interrater reliability for rejection was high ($r = 0.82$), and a copy of the rating scale for rejection is included in Appendix 2 to this chapter.

Altogether there are 25 mothers and 17 fathers for whom we have available both ratings for observed aversion to physical contact with the infant in the Clown Session (Main and Weston, 1981), and ratings for probable rejection by the parent's own mother during childhood. We find a substantial relationship [$r (42) = 0.56$, $p < 0.001$)] between apparent rejection by the parent's own mother during childhood and observed aversion to physical contact with the infant during the Clown Session. Impressively, the relationship holds when mothers and fathers are treated as separate samples: for mother, $r (25) = 0.56$, $p < 0.002$; for fathers, $r (17) = 0.63$, $p < 0.003$. Thus, rejection by mother in childhood is related to aversion to contact with one's own infant for men as well as for women. Considering that we are comparing an estimate of rejection based upon an hour's interview with the parent with a ten-minute observation of parental behavior with the infant five years previously, this is a striking degree of relationship.

So far as I know, this is the first report of a cross-generational effect in human response to physical contact. It is flawed in that we deal with retrospective data rather than direct observation, but the dynamic at work is nonetheless of interest. The parent who shows aversion to the attachment behavior of the infant in the manner specified within this study is a parent who appears to have felt rejection from his or her own mother many years previously.

SOME STUDIES SUGGESTING PATHWAYS TO INTERVENTION

Perhaps the most interesting and well established of all literatures dealing with parent–infant contact is the primate literature concerning the effects of abuse or isolation upon primate mothering in macaque species. A review of much of this literature (Erwin, 1983) reminds us that most isolated monkey mothers are abusive or neglectful toward their first offspring, but that behavior toward later-born offspring is often much improved. In other words, the first-born infant of the isolated monkey mother is often pushed away from her body harshly, or is physically ignored, and may even be killed. Later-born infants, however, are often reared adequately. This altered responsiveness to the infant may conceivably be a function of the length of time that the mother has had physical contact, and perhaps even specifically ventral–ventral contact, with her first-born (a hypothesis which will soon be under investigation by Stephen Suomi). Thus, a "priming" effect of ventral–ventral contact is suggested for the macaque.

Something very like a "priming" effect has been reported for our own species in a report emerging from the Department of Pediatrics at Columbia University (Anisfeld et al.,

1987). The Anisfeld study was intended to investigate, in an experimental rather than an observational fashion, the effect of close body contact on infant–mother attachment. It was hypothesized that infants who had more close physical contact with their mothers through being carried ventrally in a soft baby carrier would be more likely to be securely attached to their mothers than infants who had less such contact.

The sample consisted of low-income women with initially neutral attitudes to soft baby carriers. Shortly after birth, the women were randomly assigned to an experimental group (N = 23) or a control group (N = 26). Experimental group mothers received soft baby carriers and control group mothers were given plastic infant seats. Both groups were encouraged to use the item daily, and it was determined that the two groups did indeed differ on the amount of physical contact during the early months of infant life. At thirteen months of age, security of attachment to mother was assessed by means of the Ainsworth Strange Situation. Eighty-three percent of infants in the soft-carrier group were found securely attached to their mothers, while only 38 percent of the infants in the control group were securely attached to their mothers. These differences were shown to be statistically significant.

The import of this study for the continued study of the parent–infant contact relationship can hardly be overestimated. Of course, for our own purpose, it would be important to know the mean scores for avoidance of mother shown by infants in the two experimental groups (perhaps there were the usual proportion of insecure–avoidant infants in the experimental group, with only other types of attachment insecurity being affected), and whether some of the secure experimental infants showed the newly recognized "disorganized/disoriented" Strange Situation response pattern (Main and Solomon, 1986) in addition to approaching mother and attempting to maintain contact. Even so, it appears that this contact-related experimental manipulation had an important effect in preventing the development of the most obviously insecure patterns of infant–parent attachment. In other words, infants who had been carried close to mother's chest in the early months were more likely to approach her following separation, then settle and return to play than infants who had not enjoyed close contact. These differences may be in part explained by the infant's response to its experience of continued close contact with mother's ventral surface, but must also be explained by the mother's response to extended experiences of ventral–ventral contact with her infant.

The Anisfeld study (Anisfeld et al., 1987) is, again, a study in prevention. But what can be done for dyads in which mother *has* shown extremely strong aversion to physical contact with the infant in the early months, dyads in which the offspring has developed distinctive emotional and behavioral difficulties in early childhood?

Impressed with the import of the early contact relationship to child clinical problems, a child psychotherapist recently reviewed three cases of children who had been extremely physically rejected by mother in infancy (Hopkins, 1987). All three children came from well-intentioned, intact families in which there was no hint of child maltreatment. One child was three-and-one-half, one was six, and one was sixteen at the time of entrance into therapy. Only the younger children will be discussed here. The cases are of interest both because of the constellation of symptoms presented, and because of the success of therapy.

Clare, a six-year-old girl, was referred on account of night terrors. Her mother reported that she had found her physically repellent as a baby. She had propped her infant bottle, and kept her in a playpen until the start of nursery school.

Although Clare was too old for study within the Ainsworth Strange Situation, she presented with the repertoire of behaviors which I have come to associate with the insecure–avoidant attachment pattern. She walked away from her mother and was likely to get lost; she was described as stoically independent and unlikely to ask for help; she was "accident prone"; but even when she hurt herself she did not cry.

Clare often talked about "lepers," which gave her bad dreams. She said that lepers were contagious, and could kill others through touching them. She thought that lepers themselves could be cured by the laying on of hands. As therapy proceeded she began to describe herself as a leper whom no-one wanted to touch because it would kill them, and her therapeutic sessions began to be filled with discussions of her wish to be touched and her fear of it. After a year of therapy, Clare fell heavily from the therapist's desk onto the floor. As she lay on the floor, she raised her arms "beseechingly" and burst into tears. The therapist picked her up and she sobbed for several minutes on the therapist's lap, while keeping her head averted.

Clare's mother reported that the day after this event Clare came to her to be comforted in distress for the first time. The mother, having had successful therapy herself, readily responded to Clare and thereafter Clare continued to turn to her mother when upset. She became cuddly, and before very long, clinging and demanding and no longer accident prone.

Paddy, three-and-a-half years, was referred for psychiatric assessment by a pediatrician. His mother was described as a chronically depressed and very anxious woman who had made several attempts at suicide in her teens. She suffered from severe eczema and explained that she had always avoided touching and cuddling Paddy for fear that his germs would infect her skin.

Paddy showed both a pattern of extremely avoidant attachment, and highly conflicted patterns of behavior which are associated with the new "disorganized–disoriented" attachment category (Main and Solomon, 1986). With respect to the insecure–avoidant pattern of attachment: (1) his parents reported that he had never shown signs of preferring them to anyone else, neither greeting them nor protesting their departure; (2) he wandered off and got lost unless locked indoors; (3) he rejected cuddling; (4) when injured, even severely, he appeared to feel no pain. With respect to the disorganized–disoriented attachment pattern (which may appear in conjunction with insecure–avoidant attachment): (1) Paddy engaged in tense mannerisms such as pulling his ears and rocking; (2) when pleased and happy he avoided eye contact by closing his eyes while grasping his nose and mouth; (3) he would lie for long periods under the therapist's couch; and (4) at times his eyes were described as "glazing over," at which times he became inaccessible.

As therapy progressed, Paddy began tentatively to approach the therapist when distressed. On the first occasion he bumped into her backwards, and then sat down and held onto her shoe. In later months, he began to jump into the therapist's arms, although with clenched teeth and fisted hands, and soon afterwards he began to greet her and protest at parting. These latter responses were not yet exhibited to the parents.

In his final term of therapy, Paddy began to whimper when he hurt himself, and one day when he had injured his thumb he climbed into the therapist's lap, crying loudly. After this, he sought the therapist's lap whenever hurt, but also took better care not to injure himself. During the summer holiday, he caught measles, and mother nursed him. He then sought comfort in mother's arms for the first time, and soon afterwards became affectionate, and sometimes clinging, to both his parents.

Case studies have the virtue of showing us what can happen, and of providing material for the development of new hypotheses. The two histories reported above indicate that the dyadic syndrome of parental aversion and infant avoidance can be altered, even when work begins relatively late. In addition, in both cases (1) the therapist waited for the child patient to initiate contact, and (2) following the initiation of full contact with the therapist in a distress situation, the pattern of avoidance of the parent was replaced by approach and clinging. Thus, once physical contact with one attachment figure (or substitute attachment figure) was seen as a signal of security or safety, the system was reorganized so that the parents themselves were approached in similar situations. The expected evaluation of contact with an attachment figure under stress as good, comforting, or pleasant had returned.

Summary

I will summarize this chapter in terms of its potential usefulness to persons interested in the consequences of early individual differences in touch-related experiences. In raising evolutionary attachment theory as an issue, I hope that I have succeeded in setting aside any notion that "touch" exclusively as a sensory phenomenon, that is, as an "experience" apart from questions of who and when and how, can have much meaning for infants who have reached the stage of forming attachments to caregivers. From that time forward, the physical and hence tactual accessibility of certain persons (including, of course, familiar day-care caregivers) is continually monitored by the infant, while in normal circumstances the tactual accessibility of other persons is a matter of relative indifference. The relative ease or difficulty involved in physically reaching attachment figures in times of stress, or simply as a support for exploration of a novel environment, now becomes an organizing principle in infant behavior. Rejection of physical contact by attachment figures has specific consequences: it leads initially to increased approach efforts and, as I have shown, eventually to anger and to conflict. Rejection of physical contact by persons who are not attachment figures leads neither to increased efforts to approach, nor (usually) to anger, nor (certainly) to conflict. The infant rejected tactually by relative strangers does not experience an increased desire to approach them as a consequence. "Touch" by this age has meaning chiefly in terms of physical contact with attachment figures, and even in the case of attachment figures, I believe that it is mostly meaningful in terms of the accessibility of the individual in response to infant initiative.

I have ended this chapter with a report concerning an apparent cross-generational transmission of behavior indicative of rejection. This work represents a very different line of endeavor from that connecting "observed behavior" to "observed behavior" (e.g., observed early rejection of contact by mother to number of observed infant attacks upon mother several months later). Here we are tying the individual's current mental representations of experiences as a child to the individual's overt behavior as a parent. Study of our interview transcripts showed that where the judge found strong evidence of early rejection by the mother, both men and women were likely to show aversion to physical contact with their children. However, it is my informal impression that where early rejection was clearly and consciously described by the individual, rather than inferred by the rater, parents were less likely to show aversion to contact with their infants (Main and Goldwyn, 1984).

Under stressful circumstances, the ultimate signal of safety and security within the attachment behavioral system is the acquisition of physical contact with an attachment figure. The principle aim of this chapter has been to investigate ways in which this normally comforting signal may become aversive. It is important to recognize, however, that the experience of tactual contact with an attachment figure can be favorably reevaluated in at least some cases, following experiences of obtaining contact under stress conditions (Hopkins, 1987). Because the individual's felt appraisal of this event appears to have such a large effect on the remainder of experience, continued investigation of this phenomenon should be encouraged.

Appendix 1: Parental Avoidance of Tactual Contact with the Infant: Directions for Coding from Videotape

Loretta Townsend and Mary Main

This rating scale was designed for use with videotaped observations of parent and infant made during a session involving a friendly interactive stranger (the "Clown," see Main and Weston [1981]). Throughout this eleven-minute observation, the parent is seated on the floor directly across from the videocamera, while the infant, twelve to eighteen months, is free to move about the room. At the beginning of the session, a masked Clown appears silently in the doorway for one minute: removing the mask, the clown then becomes a friendly, interactive stranger who plays a game of ball with the infant, and finally cries in an effort to elicit sympathy. The Clown session was deliberately designed as a situation which, in its initial minutes, provides mild stress which the presence of the parent should alleviate. Seating the parent on the floor makes the parent available for infant approaches and potentially available for ventral–ventral contact at all times. The parent cannot avoid approaches except through signals indicating that approaches are unwelcome, and cannot avoid tactual contact or even ventral–ventral contact except through active movements of avoidance or refusal. Parents are informed ahead of time that they will be seated on the floor, so that styles of dress which might make this uncomfortable can be avoided.

The directions which follow should be appropriate for use in any similar situation, in which a parent is seated on the floor in the presence of a mobile infant who, because of the brief presence of mild stressors, might be expected to approach the parent or at least to orient toward her. The position of the camera relative to infant and parent is most important in this observation. The parent should be seated with his or her back to the wall opposite the camera, and the camera should have a zoom lens permitting a wide enough angle to include both parent and infant when the infant is at a distance from the parent, but close-ups when parent and infant are in contact.

INDICES OF AVERSION TO INFANT APPROACH AND CONTACT

Our rating scale is based upon observations of nonverbal behavior—on posture, orientation, and subtle movement. Even when the child is at a distance, some parents seem physically available for tactual contact, while others seem aloof, closed, and unapproachable. Some indices of aversion are as follows:

1. Keeping the head at a different level from the infant's, or making no effort to align the head with the infant's, when this would be appropriate.
2. Keeping the body midline angled away from the infant.
3. Keeping the shoulders back rather than curved toward the infant.
4. Keeping the knees up or in some other position so that there is no opportunity for the infant to reach the lap/chest/stomach.
5. Failing to shift posture to "follow" the infant's movements.
6. Arching back or away at the infant's approach.
7. Moving the neck and head back uncomfortably while holding the infant.
8. Moving into or remaining in uncomfortable postures, the relaxation of which would bring the parent into contact with the infant.
9. Folding the arms across the stomach as though to prevent the child's body from touching the parent's

ventral surface, especially when the child is seated upon the parent's lap.

10. Wincing or flinching as the child moves into closer contact.

Ratings are assigned on the following nine-point scale. Any rating between one and nine can be given (e.g., 4.5).

1. Physically Approachable:

The parent responds to the infant physically. The parent follows the infant's movements and gives the impression that the infant is welcome to approach physically (whether or not the infant actually approaches). If the infant does approach, the parent remains physically open.

This parent may seem either highly sensitive and appropriate in behavior toward the infant, insensitive and inappropriate, or somewhere in between. In other words, the parent may be physically *and* psychologically (emotionally) accessible, or only physically accessible. All that is necessary for the "1" rating is that the parent be *physically* accessible.

3. Somewhat Unapproachable, or Slightly Aloof While in Contact:

The parent is largely approachable or welcoming to the infant. Perhaps the parent is a little reserved, staying a little bit upright, and perhaps slightly back from the infant. If the infant does comes to the parent, perhaps the parent accepts contact and gives comfort, but without giving complete ventral–ventral contact, or without being tender in movements.

5. Definite Unapproachability, or Marked Physical "Aloofness" While in Contact:

The parent may behave in a fashion which suggests that he or she believes that the infant does not *want* contact, that at present there is no occasion for contact. This includes assuming a position such that the infant couldn't approach if he or she wanted—the parent may assume a closed or "barred off" posture, not rounded toward the infant, nor oriented to him, with a kind of ignoring of potential approach movements which is discouraging. Often in this case the infant does not approach, so that the parent cannot be rated higher. The impression is only, however, that the parent *might* not like contact even if the infant required it. If parental movements and posture make this seem a certainty rather than a possibility, rate somewhat higher.

A parent whose infant comes into contact, and who allows himself some tactual response (by holding the infant in a businesslike way, etc.) may still be rated a five if he or she fails to align the body with the infant's movements, or keeps hands away from the infant when they could more comfortably (for the parent) be placed closer. The parent rated a five is physically aloof and businesslike, even when the infant is on his or her body. However, the judge cannot be certain the parent is *averse* to contact with the infant: the parent may simply be being reserved, or hoping to keep the infant focused upon the activities of the friendly stranger.

Ratings of four or below are given when a parent seems initially unapproachable, then "melts" later in the session and takes the infant into close bodily contact.

7. Definite Aversion Without Actual Movements of Avoidance:

The parent definitely seems to dislike physical contact with the infant, but does not necessarily "flinch" or show real movements of physical avoidance at the infant's approach. Perhaps the parent indicates to the infant from a distance that contact is undesirable, and then, when contact is nonetheless made, handles the infant gingerly or limply, or is extremely unresponsive. At the approach of the infant, the parent may hold his or her body stiffly without aligning it to the infant's, or may avoid looking at the infant or returning the infant's gaze when it seems that this might lead to contact. The parent may permit the infant to sit upon her lap, but carefully fold her arms across the ventral surface, as though to guard against the infant's body touching her stomach. For this rating, ventral–ventral contact with the infant must be definitely prevented throughout the session.

This rating should not be given unless the rater's judgment (taken from all indices) is that there is more than an aloof or preoccupied "businesslike" attitude at work. In other words, where this rating is given, it must be obvious that the adult's prevention of contact is not merely the result of the parent thinking the infant "ought" to be attending to the interactive stranger (in our sessions, the "Clown") instead; rather, something more personal is at work. There is an attitude about contact with the infant which is actively negative, even though it is not shown in sharp movements of avoidance.

9. *Physical Avoidance Indicative of Aversion:*

Distaste for physical interaction is evident, and physical closeness may be discouraged. When the infant approaches, the parent may pull away, or sit back, or hold the infant's hands away to prevent further contact—or even push the infant away, or flinch at being touched. For this highest rating, real physical movements of avoidance must be shown.

Appendix 2: Rejection: Aversion to, Avoidance of, the Child or the Child's Attachment

Mary Main and Ruth Goldwyn

This scale is designed for use with the Adult Attachment Interview (George, Kaplan, and Main, 1985), a structured, hour-long interview in which the subject is asked to describe his or her relationships to parents during childhood, and evaluate the effects of those relationships upon adult personality. The interview is transcribed in full, and ratings are based upon assessment of the full transcript. While subjects are asked whether they felt rejected during childhood, ratings are based upon the judge's best estimate of the subject's actual experiences, whether or not these agree with the subject's own apparent estimate.

This scale assesses the extent to which the subject's parent appears to have rejected, turned away, and/or avoided the child's attachment behavior, or even avoided or rejected the child entirely. Rejection need not involve abuse in behavior or in language. The quality being assessed is the "turning back or away" (from the Latin *re-jacio*) of the child and the child's affection and attachment.

At the low end of the scale, the parent may simply have placed a somewhat early or inappropriate stress upon independence, perhaps urging the child not to cling and not to express distress, and discouraging physical affection. At the midpoint of the scale is the parent who is reserved, business-like, cool, stern, or even inexpressive, but not beyond the limits of what would be expected for some cultures at some times (e.g., Puritan New England). At the high end of the scale, the parent's behavior is indicative of a real and pervasive turning away of this child. The parent seems not to have wanted the child: there is an implication that the parent would have preferred not to have the child, and would now actively like to be rid of her.

The following are signs of rejection of attachment:

- There are no voluntary remarks during the interview on expressions of physical affection from the parent, although the subject may answer "Yes, of course" to "Did your (parent) hold you?" But these remarks are unconvincing in the context of the interview as a whole, or they are contradicted.
- The subject responds that when upset, she kept to herself, or went away.
- The subject avoids discussing the relationship with the

parent, although she may repeatedly state that "it was a fine relationship."

- The subject begins to recount an incident of being hurt or upset, or an incident intended to demonstrate parental supportiveness, but the incident has an odd ending, or no ending, and does not demonstrate support.
- The subject remembers active rejection by the parent—degrading or abusive treatment, being told to leave, etc.—or else recalls a childhood which was empty of affection.
- The subject remembers rejection of siblings, directly or by implication, without showing convincingly that the self was an exception.
- The subject recalls serious threats of abandonment.
- The subject recalls being picked at, criticized, nagged (this is not necessarily strong rejection—the critical parent may be pushing or picking at the child, but not really turning her away).
- The parent was angry when the subject hurt himself (be sure to distinguish this from "upset" or "panicked," which suggests role-reversal rather than rejection).

Ratings are assigned on the following nine-point scale. Any rating may be given (e.g., 4.5).

1. Not at All Rejecting:

There is no indication of rejection of the subject during childhood. The subject may recall disagreements or "spats," but these do not seem associated with rejection. The parent may have been entirely supportive of the child and extremely loving. Alternately, there may have been some difficulty in the relationship such as strong role reversal, with the parent actively utilizing rather than turning back the child's dependence.

3. *Slightly Rejecting:*

Either a brief period of rejection or a slight sense of rejection (as in an early push to independence or achievement) seems to have been experienced by the subject, but rejection does not seem to have played an important role within the relationship.

5. *Moderately Rejecting:*

Perhaps the child is seldom given any encouragement, or told that the parent is glad to have her around, or proud of her. The parent may be reserved, removed, or physically cold or "stern." This parental "remove" does not go beyond culturally accepted limits, however, and might not be uncommon in essentially supportive parents living within some cultural settings. The rejection goes beyond early stressing of independence, push to achievement, or single brief periods of childhood. The parent's affectional response to the child is consistently somewhat limited.

7. *Rejecting:*

This parent is more than reserved, aloof, or removed and businesslike. Rejection is personal and not merely a matter of culturally approved reserve. Absence of tie or closeness between subject and parent is an impressive quality of the transcript, and rejection of the child has become a pervasive quality of the relationship. Rejection is definite. However, there is no indication that the parent would have preferred to be rid of the child entirely.

9. *Very Rejecting:*

There seems to have been no emotional tie at all between this child and parent. There is no indication of support, and there may be indications of emotional abandonment. The reader may have the impression that there was an active dislike of this child, or that there were quiet emotional cruelties. The reader may infer that throughout the child's life the parent desired/preferred her absence. The child and the child's affection were turned away entirely. Again, this may have been accomplished without any signs of either verbal abuse or violence.

References

Ainsworth, M. D. S., Bell, S. M., & Stayton, D. J. (1971), Individual differences in strange situation behavior of one-year-olds. In: *The Origins of Human Social Relations*, ed. H. R. Schaffer. London & New York: Academic Press.

———Blehar, M. C., Waters, E., & Wall, S. (1978), *Patterns of Attachment: A Psychological Study of the Strange Situation*. Hillsdale, NJ: Erlbaum Associates.

Anisfeld, E., Casper, V., & Cunningham, N. (1987), Cache or carry? Experimental evidence for positive effects of early infant carrying. Paper presented at the meeting of the Society for Research in Child Development, Baltimore, Maryland.

Balint, A. (1949), Love for the mother and mother-love. *Internat. J. Psycho-Anal.*, 30:251–259.

Bowlby, J. (1969), *Attachment and Loss*, Vol. 1. New York: Basic Books.

———(1973), *Attachment and Loss*, Vol. 2. New York: Basic Books.

———(1980), *Attachment and Loss*, Vol. 3. New York: Basic Books.

Darwin, C. (1872), *The Expression of the Emotions in Man and Animals*. London: John Murray.

Erwin, J. (1983), Primate infant abuse: Communication and conflict. In: *Child Abuse: The Nonhuman Primate Data*, eds. M. Reite & N. G. Caine. *Monogr. in Primat.*, 1:79–102.

George, C., & Main, M. (1979), Social interactions of young abused children: Approach, avoidance and aggression. *Child Develop.*, 50:306–318.

———Kaplan, N., & Main, M. (1985), *The Adult Attachment Interview: Interview protocol*. Unpublished manuscript, Department of Psychology, University of California at Berkeley.

Harlow, H. (1958), The nature of love. *Amer. Psychol.*, 13:673–685.

Heinicke, C., & Westheimer, I. (1966), *Brief Separations*. New York: International Universities Press.

Hinde, R. A. (1966), *Animal Behavior*. New York: McGraw-Hill.

Hopkins, J. (1987), Failure of the holding relationship: Some effects of physical rejection on the child's attachment and on his inner experience. *J. Child Psychother.*, 13:5–17.

Kaufman, I. C., & Rosenblum, L. A. (1969), The waning of the mother–infant bond in two species of macaques. In: *Determinants of Infant Behavior*, Vol. 4, ed. B. Foss. London: Methuen, pp. 37–59.

Main, M. (1981), Avoidance in the service of proximity. In: *Behavioral Development: The Bielefeld Project*, eds. K. Immelmann, G. Barlow, L. Petrinovitch, & M. Main. New York: Cambridge University Press.

———Cassidy, J. (in press), Categories of response to reunion with the parent at age six: Predictable from infant attachment classifications and stable over a one-month period. *Develop. Psychol.*

———George, C. (1985), Responses of abused and disadvantaged toddlers to distress in agemates: A study in the day care setting. *Develop. Psychol.*, 21:3, 407–412.

———Goldwyn, R. (1984), Predicting rejection of her infant from mother's representation of her own experience: Implications for the abused-abusing intergenerational cycle. *Child Abuse & Neglect*, 8:203–217.

———Hesse, E. (in press), Lack of resolution of mourning in adulthood and its relationship to infant disorganization: Some speculations regarding causal mechanisms. In: *Attachment in the Preschool Years*, ed. M. Greenberg, D. Cichetti, & M. Cummings. Chicago: University of Chicago Press.

———Kaplan, N., & Cassidy, J. (1985), Security in infancy, childhood and adulthood: A move to the level of representation, In: *Growing Points in Attachment Theory and Research*. eds. I. Bretherton & E. Waters. *Monogr. Soc. Res. Child Develop.*, Serial #209, 50:1–2, 66–104.

———Solomon, J. (1986), Discovery of a new, insecure-disorganized/disoriented attachment pattern, In: *Affective Development in Infancy*, ed M. Yogman & T. B. Brazelton. Norwood, NJ: Ablex Press.

———Stadtman, J. (1981), Infant response to rejection of physical contact by the mother: Aggression, avoidance and conflict. *J. Amer. Acad. Child. Psychiat.*, 20:292–307.

———Weston, D. (1981), The quality of the toddler's relationship to mother and father: Related to conflict behavior and the readiness to establish new relationships. *Child Develop.*, 52:932–940.

Robertson, J., & Bowlby, J. (1952), Responses of young children to separation from their mothers. *Cour. Cent. Internat. Enf.*, 2:131–142.

Sackett, G., Griffin, G. A., Pratt, C., Joslyn, W. D., & Ruppertal, G. (1967), Mother–infant and adult female choice behavior in rhesus monkeys after various rearing experiences. *J. Compar. Physiol. Psychol.*, 63:376–381.

Schaffer, H. R., & Emerson, P. E. (1964), The development of social attachments in infancy. *Monogr. Soc. Res. Child Develop.*, Serial #94, 29.

Winnicott, D. W. (1960), The theory of the parent–infant relationship. *Internat. J. Psycho-Anal.*, 34:1–9.

19
Adolescents and Touch

Elizabeth R. McAnarney, M.D.

Adolescent pregnancy is considered a major health problem in the United States. Approximately 1 million young people younger than twenty years of age become pregnant annually, of whom approximately 560,000 bear live-born children. Fifteen percent of infants of women younger than fifteen—compared to 6.5% of infants of women twenty to twenty-nine years of age—weigh less than 2500 g. Prevention of adolescent pregnancy is the ideal. Preventive strategies include:

1. Encouragement of adolescents, particularly those younger than fifteen years old, to delay the initiation of coitus. The understanding of why adolescents initiate coitus may help us to define effective preventive strategies. This chapter will address why some early adolescents may initiate coitus.
2. Encouragement of adolescents who are contemplating or who have initiated coital activity to utilize contraception.

It is against this background of interest in the prevention of adolescent pregnancy that this chapter has been developed.

> As children grow older, physical contact (by parents) becomes more restrained, and by adolescence is completely terminated [Montagu, 1971, p. 147].

> If there is a diminution in tactual sensitivity and experiences in middle childhood, the so-called latency period, it abruptly ceases at puberty when the pubertal boy and girl usually become avid for tactual contacts, seeking to touch and be touched [Frank, 1957, p. 233].

In examining these two quotations, one notes the potential for a major dilemma for adolescents: (1) Their parents touch them less during adolescence than they did during infancy and childhood, and (2) adolescents' need for touching may increase during this period. As touching of adolescents is decreasing, adolescents are gradually becoming capable of physically relating intimately to heterosexual partners. The adolescent's basic need may be to be in close physical proximity to another human being, to be touched and/or cuddled; they may use their newly acquired physical, genital capability and coitus to meet this basic need.

The purpose of this chapter is to examine the question of whether coitus during early adolescence (10–14 years of age) represents the use of sexual behavior for nonsexual purposes and whether early adolescents who engage in coitus prematurely are seeking closeness to another human being rather than sexual pleasure.

The Importance of Touching in the Well-Being of Animals and Humans

Touching and contact are important for optimal animal survival (Frank, 1957). Gentled rats were able to metabolize food better and were less susceptible to the ill-effects of surgical shock than nongentled rats. Gentle handling of rats also produced gentle, unexcitable animals and lack of gentling produced excitable, fearful animals.

Harlow (1958) reported that a baby monkey raised on a bare wire-mesh cage floor survived with difficulty, if at all, during the first five days of life. When a wire-mesh cone was introduced, the baby monkey did better. If the wire-mesh cone was covered with terry cloth, where contact comfort was an important variable, the monkey babies thrived and were healthy and husky. Harlow's data indicated that "contact comfort is a variable of overwhelming importance in the development of affectional responses . . ." (Harlow, 1958, p. 676). "The manner in which the young of all mammals struggle and cuddle against the body of the mother . . . strongly suggests that cutaneous stimulation is an important biological *need* for both their physical and their behavioral development. Almost every animal enjoys being stroked or otherwise having the skin pleasurably stimulated" (Montagu, 1971, p. 28).

Human infants also need close parental contact to survive. "The behavior and motivations of all mammalian infants are directed toward maintaining contact with the mother. Contact seeking is the foundation upon which all subsequent behavior develops" (Montagu, 1971, p. 136). Spitz recorded striking observations of anaclitic depression of children who were separated from their mothers. Their severely withdrawn behavior disappeared when their mothers returned (Spitz, 1946). Children who experience failure to thrive on a nonorganic basis improve following hospitalization, caring, and feeding by nurturant adults (Powell, Brasel, and Blizzard, 1967). These studies reflect the importance of the mothering process in humans, of which touching is of critical importance (Klaus, Kennell, Plumb, and Zuchike, 1970).

It is clear at least during infancy that close contact with a mother or a mother-substitute is critical to the infant's optimum development. As a child matures, mothers (and fathers) spend less time in physical proximity and contact with their children.

Differences in Touching Between Children and Parents by the Child's Age and Other Variables

A major thesis of this chapter is that parental touching of children decreases as the child matures so that by adolescence, in most American families, touching between adolescents and their parents is minimal. Other factors affect touching behaviors between children and their parents such as socioeconomic status, the child's sex, and ethnicity. As is true of other developmental phenomena, the age of the child is only one sociodemographic characteristic of importance, but the major one for this chapter.

Figure 19.1 is a schematic representation of touching, (1) by the age of the child and (2) the persons who are most likely to touch the child. These data are based partially on empirical data which will be presented below, but are based mostly on clinical observation and clinical history. Data presented on the vertical axis represent an approximation of a quantitative measure of touching which is hypothesized, and thus, is not exact. The horizontal axis represents the child's age. The person or persons doing the touching are represented schematically.

During infancy, parents (or caretakers) are the individuals who cuddle and touch the child, and the amount of touching by adults is maximal during this stage. Human mothers exhibit a species-specific characteristic pattern of tactile contact with their newborn infant beginning with fingertip touching of the infants' extremities and progressing to palmar touching of the trunk (Rubin, 1963; Klaus, et al., 1970). Other authors (Trevathan, 1981) believe that tactile contact of mothers and their infants does not follow a species-specific pattern. Despite this debate about the nature of touching between human mothers and their infants, infants, partially because of their helpless state, are in close tactile contact with their parents or caretakers.

As early as infancy, there are differences in touching

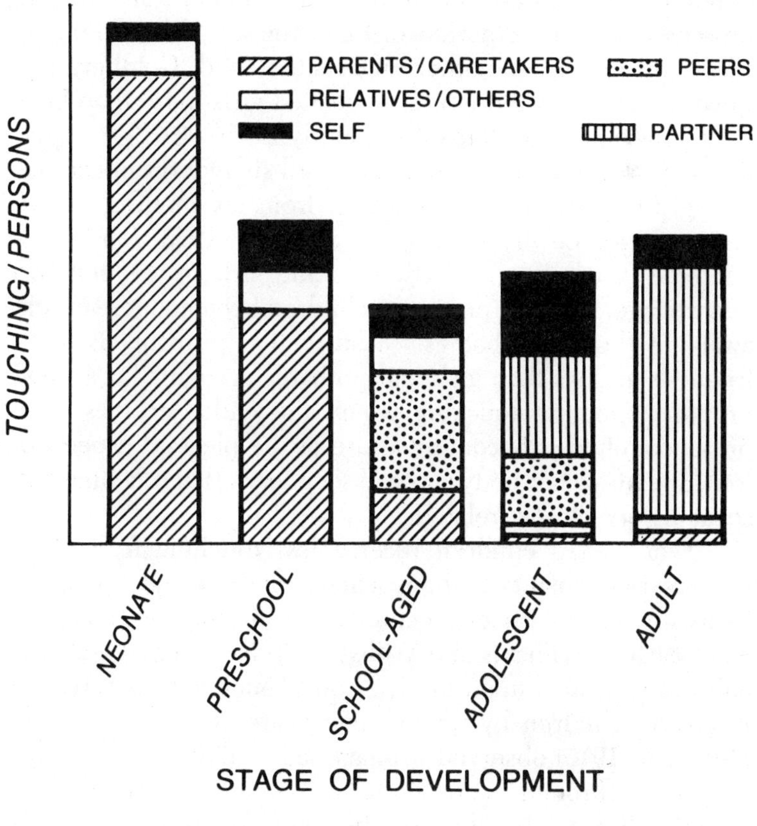

FIGURE 19.1
Touching by stage of development and persons.

behaviors among mothers of different socioeconomic status. Lewis and Wilson (1972) reported an increase in the frequency of maternal touch as socioeconomic status decreased. Lower socioeconomic status mothers touched their infants twice as much as middle-class mothers.

Preschool children are ambulatory and can move physically away from their parents. Thus, the amount of touching between preschool children and their parents decreases. Other factors also are important in the amount of touching preschool children experience. First, the sex of the child may affect how much the mother touches the child. Goldberg and Lewis (1969) reported mothers touched girls more than boys at six months of age, but subsequently Lewis (1972) reported that boys received more touching until six months of age but that girls received more touching from six months to two years of age. Lewis, Weintraub, and Ban (1972) reported a decrease in touching in both boys and girls in the first two years of age. Second, preschool children become increasingly aware of their own bodies. Masturbation probably is more frequent in boys than girls and probably accounts for a small proportion of the touching which the child receives. The preschool child is becoming aware of the pleasant aspects of touching his or her body and will soon learn that touching and sexuality are closely related.

School-aged children receive less touching from their parents than infants and preschool children and are more likely to engage in peer touching and self-touching than they were earlier. Williams and Willis (1978) have concluded that cultural restraints upon interpersonal touch are operative in American children by four or five years of age. Willis and Hofmann (1975) observed primary school children from kindergarten through sixth grade and found a reduction in touching for white children but not for black children. Touching was more frequent in same-sex peers in inside play areas. Touching was highest in frequency between black children and least likely from whites to blacks.

Adolescents (12–18) receive even less parental touching than younger children. They also touch their peers less than is the case amongst younger children. Willis and Reeves (1976) reported a study of 1028 junior high school students in the greater Kansas City area. Their data were similar to their data from children in the primary schools. Touching for black-black and white-black children was about half as much as that observed in the younger children. The junior high students were more likely to touch shoulder to shoulder or elbow to elbow in what appeared to be almost inadvertent contacts. Aggressive touching among junior high students was manifested by fist-fighting by females and play fighting among males.

Willis, Reeves, and Buchanan (1976) replicated their study of junior high students with 1154 pairs of students enrolled in grades 10 through 12 in six public high schools in greater Kansas City. The probability of touching was almost identical to that observed in the junior high population.

There are few quantitative observations of adolescents' interaction with heterosexual peers. Adolescents begin to move gradually away from parental and same-sexed peer touching to heterosexual peer touching (for the majority of adolescents) which may result in coitus.

Physical Growth and Development During Adolescence Which Prepares Adolescents to Engage in Physically Intimate Sexual Behaviors

We still do not understand why puberty begins in humans. The hypothalamic–pituitary gonadal circuit matures and episodic secretion of the gonadotrophins occurs. Following puberty, adolescents are physically capable of adult genital behavior. Some of the pubertal changes which occur during adolescence are:

1. Males and females acquire adult somatic proportions (height, weight, organ size).

2. The central nervous system (hypothalamus and pituitary gland) matures. The hypothalamus secretes luteinizing hormone-releasing factor (LHRF), corticotrophin-releasing factor (CRF), thyrotrophin-releasing hormone (TRH), growth hormone-releasing factor (GHRF), gonadotrophin-releasing hormone (GnRH), and prolactin-releasing factor (PRF). Inhibitory hypophysiotrophic hormones are also secreted and include: prolactin inhibitory factor (PIF) and somatostatin (SRIF, somatrophin release-inhibiting factor). The pituitary gland secretes luteinizing hormone (LH), follicle-stimulating hormone (FSH), thyroid-stimulating hormone (TSH), adrenocortical hormone (ACTH) and growth hormone (GH).
3. The pituitary hormones (LH, FSH) stimulate the maturation of the ovaries and testes, which in turn, secrete estrogen, progesterone, and testosterone which are the hormones responsible for feminization and masculinization of adults.

During adolescence, young people begin to experience adult sexual urges and become physically capable of coitus. Most males reach a peak of sexual drive before twenty years of age and females experience increasing sexual responsiveness until the thirties which then levels of until they are fifty years of age or older. The peak physiologic sex drive of male adolescents often occurs before they are psychologically capable of truly intimate sexual behaviors.

Psychological Growth and Development During Adolescence Which May Negate the Adolescents' Ability to Engage in Truly Intimate Sexual Behavior

According to psychoanalytic theory (Freud, 1940), sexual impulses reemerge at adolescence marking the onset of the genital stage. The adolescent begins to recognize that the opposite-sexed parent cannot be the adult love object. During adolescence, the young person surrenders the opposite-sexed parent as a love object. The emotional distancing which occurs between an adolescent's parent and his or her opposite-sexed adolescent may be one of the reasons there is a decrease in touching between parents and their opposite-sexed adolescents.

The incest taboo disallows the adolescent and the opposite-sexed parent from becoming emotionally or physically too close. The combination of the emotional distancing between an adolescent's parent and his or her opposite-sexed adolescent and the incest taboo may be the major theoretical reasons why adolescents and their parents do not engage in touching behaviors. Independence from the parents, emotionally and physically, is a major task of adolescence.

PSYCHOSOCIAL THEORY

Psychosocial theory (Erikson, 1950, 1960) focuses on the definition of identity during adolescence. Initially, the "who am I?" is directed toward the definition of the physical self or "who am I in this changing physical body?" This usually occurs between ages ten to fourteen years. The next step is the global question of "who am I as a person, the same or different from others around me?" This usually occurs at fifteen to sixteen years of age. The final step is "who shall I be in the future as a sexual being, as a vocational being, and as an integrated member of society?" This usually occurs between seventeen to twenty-one years of age.

Adolescents who have not yet established their own identities are incapable of engaging in sexually intimate behaviors which require that the individual knows who he is as a separate person before he then can merge that identity with a heterosexual partner.

The psychosocial stage which follows that of adolescence, namely young adulthood, is intimacy: "the young adult, emerging from the search for and the insistence on identity, is eager and willing to lose his identity with that of others: He is ready for intimacy . . ." (Erikson, 1950, p. 263). Most young adolescents are not capable of true psychological intimacy.

The adolescent is often egocentric and unable to separate his own needs from those of others. His inability to think of others ahead of self may negate his ability to engage in truly intimate sexual behaviors in which one must relate to another's needs as well as one's own.

The powerful effects of adult physical sexual capacity in psychologically immature adolescents whose parents and same-sex peers are less likely to engage in touching behaviors sets the stage for the use of sexuality for nonsexual purposes—the use of coitus in order to be touched and to be closely held by another person.

Figure 19.2 represents a summary of the dilemma which the adolescent faces. The physically mature adolescent receives less parental touching than at earlier stages of development, because of the psychological developmental task of distancing from the opposite-sex parent and because of the incest taboo. His newly developed biologic urges, secondary to hormonal secretion, and his physically mature genitalia provide another means through which he can obtain touch by peer heterosexual contact and coitus. As Montagu has stated: "Touching may take the form of caressing, cuddling, holding, stroking, or patting with the fingers to the whole hand, or vary from simple body contact to the massive tactile stimulation involved in sexual intercourse" (Montagu, 1971, p. 290).

Thus, some adolescents will turn to heterosexual partners for close human contact, perhaps, to substitute for the loss of parental touching, and so young people not yet capable of truly intimate sexual behavior may be using their sexuality for nonsexual purposes; that is, to be touched.

The Incidence of Coitus Among Adolescents

More adolescents were coitally active in the mid- to late 1970s than in the early 1970s. Twenty-eight percent of a

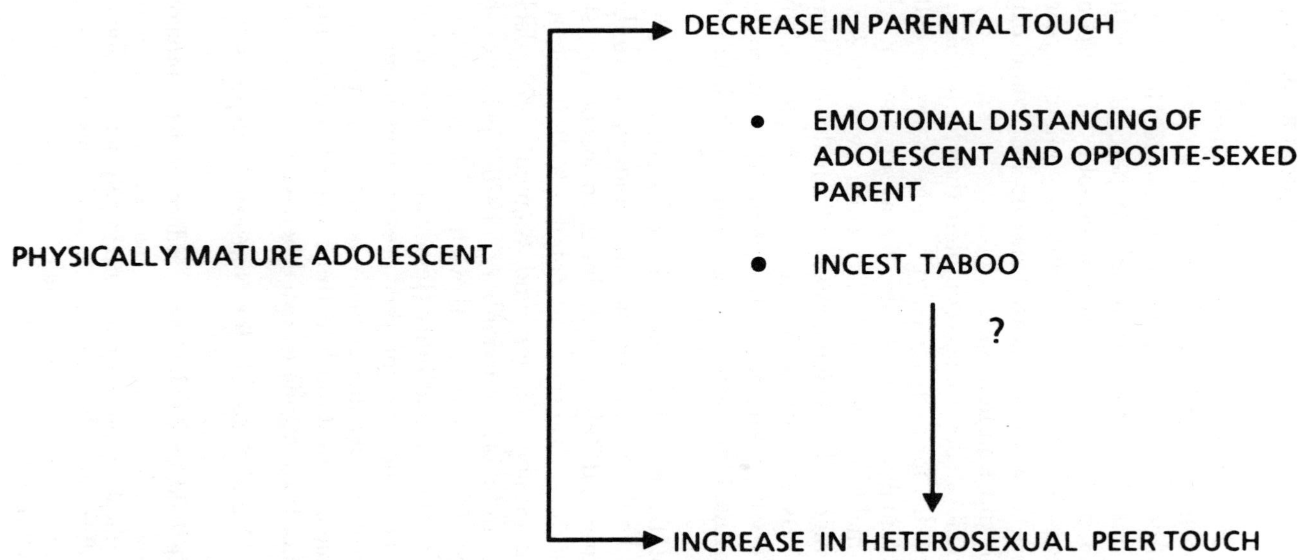

FIGURE 19.2
The dilemma of adolescents.

population of "never-married" fifteen to nineteen-year-old females reported coitus in 1971 compared to 46% of "never-married" fifteen to nineteen-year-old females in 1979. In 1979, 22 percent of fifteen-year-old, 38 percent of sixteen-year-old, 48 percent of seventeen-year-old, 57 percent of eighteen-year-old, and 69 percent of nineteen-year-old "never married" women reported having had coital experience (Zelnik and Kantner, 1980).

The data for males are less complete than for females, but it is believed that for each age cohort, more males are coitally active than females. In one study, the average age at which adolescent males experienced first coitus was 15.7 years and the average age at which adolescent females experienced first coitus was 16.2 years. Young men were less likely to have coitus with someone with whom they were going steady or engaged than were young women (Zelnik and Shah, 1983).

Several factors which have been associated with the increasing likelihood of coitus during adolescence are: being older (Kantner and Zelnik 1972); lower socioeconomic status and black heritage (Kantner and Zelnik, 1972); frequent and early dating (Simon, Berger, and Gagnon, 1972); lack of educational ambition (Furstenberg, 1976); pressure from peers and sexual partners (Cvetkovich and Grote, 1980) and low parent–friend compatibility (Jessor and Jessor, 1975).

The major question for this presentation is why very young adolescents become sexually active when psychologically they have not established their own identities and are not capable of truly intimate sexual behavior.

The Use of Sexuality for Nonsexual Purposes

> "Being held or cuddled may reduce anxiety, promote relaxation and a feeling of security, and provide a distinctive type of gratification. Since women are usually held or cuddled before or after coitus, they can use sex as a means of obtaining this type of body contact" [Hollender, Luborsky, and Scaramella, 1969, p. 188].

Hollender and colleagues studied thirty-nine patients, admitted to the psychiatric services of the University of Pennsylvania for the treatment of relatively acute psychiatric disorders, the most common of which was neurotic depression. The study population consisted of women between the ages of eighteen and fifty-nine years who had finished at least eleven grades in school and who were or had been married.

Of the entire study group, twenty-one (53%) had used sex to persuade a mate to hold them. A response by one of these adults was as follows: "I want somebody just to hold me . . . And it just seems to me . . . one thing goes with another—if I do go to bed with someone . . . they would hold me for a little while anyhow" (p. 189).

Malmquist, Kiresuk, and Spano (1966) reported on twenty women who had three or more illegitimate pregnancies. The sexual life of these women began early, as thirteen of the twenty (63%) reported initiation of coitus before twelve years of age. Sexual pleasure was reportedly quite restricted. Eight of the twenty (40%) reported they were aware at a conscious level that coital activity was the price to be paid for being cuddled.

The very young adolescents (10–14 years of age) who engage in early coitus may be a population similar to those individuals whom Hollender and colleagues and Malmquist and colleagues were reporting on as adults.

Hollender (1970) described factors which might influence the wish to be held: (the interpretation is slightly modified)

1. *Depression*: A depressed person may seek closeness at one point and then may withdraw from close contact at other times. Some depressed individuals desire physical closeness to another person; others do not.
2. *Anxiety*: Some individuals feel less anxious and feel more secure when they are being cuddled; that is, the

boundaries of an embrace may provide structure and security for a person who is experiencing lack of structure and insecurity.

3. *Anger*: Hollender reports that anger was more likely to evoke a reaction of drawing away from body contact than of moving toward body contact. For some individuals, however, anger may be a means of propelling two individuals together, especially when making up after an angry interaction.
4. *Misuse of self*: This factor applies particularly to individuals whose validation of self and self-worth is based upon the demonstration of affection by another.

Hollender further suggested that some women think the wish to be held is childish. Thus, the use of adult sexuality as a means to being held and cuddled may make the wish to be held an "adult" and therefore, an acceptable activity. Thus, "body contact commonly provides feelings of being loved, protected, and comforted" (Hollender, 1970, p. 453).

There are no empirical data known to this author about the use of sexuality for nonsexual purposes by adolescents. Cohen and Friedman (1975) described this phenomenon among adolescents. One could speculate that young adolescents are using their heterosexual capability to acquire closeness to another human being.

Areas for Future Investigation of Touching During Adolescence

1. Documentation of touching behaviors of adolescents by age of adolescence: early adolescents (10–14 years of age); middle adolescents (15–16 years of age); late adolescents (17–20 years of age).
2. What percentage of touching of adolescents is done by parents, by the self, by heterosexual partners, by homosexual partners, according to the substage of adolescence?

3. Why do early adolescents (10–14 years of age) engage in coitus? These data should be examined by socioeconomic status, sex, ethnicity, religious background, and educational background of the family.
4. How do adolescents of various ages view touching of themselves by their parents? These data should separate maternal and paternal touching.
5. How do parents view touching their adolescents by the age and sex of their adolescent? These data should separate maternal and paternal data.

We know little about parental touching of adolescents. What we do know about coitus in early adolescents is discouraging: these young people are physically capable of coitus, but not psychologically capable of adult intimacy. Some adult females openly have stated they have used coitus to fulfill a need to be touched, held, and cuddled. Would substitution of parental touch of early adolescents decrease the incidence of premature coitus? This question is worthy of serious consideration in our effort to understand why very young adolescents engage in coitus and often suffer the consequences of unplanned pregnancies and sexually transmitted diseases.

Discussion: Chapter 19

T. Berry Brazelton: Elizabeth, I like the way you've presented the concept of the changing meaning of touch over time. Touch as a substitute for intimacy is another idea I like.

Elizabeth McAnarney: We've asked our pregnant adolescents about their early sexual experiences, and we've found, too, that by and large they are not pleasurable. The girls often say things were done in a very hurried way, and they are not exactly sure why it all happened. There's a lot of ambivalence on the part of both males and females.

Judy Smith: Have you looked at homosexual behavior in adolescents?

Elizabeth McAnarney: We recognize clinically that some homosexual experience is common during early adolescence—exploratory touching, often. This phase might best be called a period of undifferentiated sexuality. We haven't investigated homosexuality as an established pattern at later ages, partly because it is beyond our capability to predict what a young person's choices will be down the line.

William Greenough: Is it a problem getting accurate information from adolescents about their sexual experiences?

Elizabeth McAnarney: Yes, but as you get to know them, they're easy to work with. They're quite egocentric, and if you give them some attention they become more open and often give you very good data.

T. Berry Brazelton: Do they let you touch them?

Elizabeth McAnarney: Yes. Even if a young person is referred for depression and suicidal tendencies, we always start with the physical examination. It seems to communicate our concern to the young person, to show that we want to look at everything totally. Even adolescents you've been told are very hostile and angry usually relax if you start talking with them and perform a physical examination. The awareness that their symptoms are being taken seriously seems to increase their sense of self-worth.

I will tell you though, Berry, that I find it easier to work with adolescents as I get older. Touch is less likely to be misinterpreted as a sexual message from someone of my age and stage. There's a sort of an incest taboo in clinical settings as well as in the family, I think.

Seymour Levine: I wonder about your assumption that the parents and adolescents in virtually all families observe that incest taboo. As the issue of incest has begun to emerge more publicly, the incidence of reported cases has risen a lot, and I suspect that these are only the tip of the iceberg. For every rape reported, many others occur that are not reported. Don't you think this is also true of incest?

Elizabeth McAnarney: Yes, I do. In clinical work, we become concerned when a very young pregnant adolescent won't give a good history as to who the father is, for example. That happens quite frequently. When the youngster's eyes go directly toward the ground, you know you're getting into something that she doesn't want to talk about. Often these pregnancies can be traced to an incestuous relationship. There are good data on that.

Still, in the majority of families the taboo does hold. I think that most parents in the American culture feel a need to move away from their pubertal youngsters physically, and that this is related to the fact that coital activity between parent and child is seen as unacceptable by the culture.

T. Berry Brazelton: As we learn more about incest and it's made more and more of a public issue, I think parental touching is going to go down and not stay stable, unless we do something to counteract it.

This may seem irrelevant at first, but I'd like to mention a statistic that I've been using to talk to Congress. The national average for infant mortality is 12.8 per thousand. In Washington, DC, it's 23.8, and if you break that down into black and white it becomes about 29 per thousand blacks and 8 per thousand whites. If you break the black group down further, you find that the two groups having babies who die in the first year are girls under fifteen and women over thirty-five, and girls under fifteen are the larger group. The point I'm trying to make is that these young girls never get any sort of reaching out of touch from the medical community, and at one level or another all of us are paying the price. The example you're setting, Elizabeth, with your research and your fine clinical work, helps show us all some ways to get in there and begin to play a role.

Elizabeth McAnarney: Infant mortality and morbidity discourage us sometimes, but one advantage of having done something over time is that I see major gains in our thinking. There are now good data to show that prenatal intervention can reduce, at least, the incidence of prematurity in this age group.

Another encouraging thing is that, as Tiffany Field and her colleagues (1982) at the Hailman Center and others have shown, you can actually teach adolescents about child development. Young women are quite interested in and involved with their babies. Although we would certainly like to reduce the adolescent birth rate, particularly during the early teens, it's heartening to know that young mothers have so much potential for becoming good parents.

References

Cohen, M. W., & Friedman, S. B. (1975), Nonsexual motivation of adolescent sexual behavior. *Med. Asp. Hum. Sexual.*, 9:8–31.

Cvetkovich, G., & Grote, B. (1980), Psychosocial development and the social problem of teenage illegitimacy. In: *Adolescent Pregnancy and Childbearing: Findings from Research*, ed. C. Chilman. Washington, DC: U.S. Department of Health and Human Services, NIH Publication No. 81–2077, pp. 15–41.

Erikson, E. (1950), *Childhood and Society*. New York: W. W. Norton.

———(1960), *Identity and the Life Cycle*. New York: International Universities Press.

Field, T., Wildmayer, S., et al. (1982), Effects of parent training on teenage mothers and their infants. *Ped.*, 69:703–707.

Frank, L. K. (1957), Tactile communication. *Genet. Psychol. Monogr.*, 56:209–257.

Freud, S. (1940), The development of the sexual function. In: *An Outline of Psychoanalysis*, ed. S. Freud. New York: W. W. Norton.

Furstenberg, F. (1976), *Unplanned Parenthood: The Social Consequences of Teenage Childbearing*. New York: Free Press.

Goldberg, S., & Lewis, M. (1969), Play behavior in the year-old infant: Early sex differences. *Child Develop.*, 40:21–31.

Harlow, H. (1958), The nature of love. *Amer. Psychol.*, 13:673–685.

Hollender, M. (1970), The need or wish to be held. *Arch. Gen. Psychiat.*, 22:445–453.

———Luborsky, L., & Scaramella, T. (1969), Body contact and sexual enticement. *Arch. Gen. Psychiat.*, 20:188–191.

Jessor, S. L., & Jessor, R. (1975), Transition from virginity to non-virginity among youth: A social-psychological study over time. *Develop. Psychol.*, 11:473–484.

Kantner, J., & Zelnik, M. (1972), Sexual experience of young unmarried women in the United States. *Fam. Plan. Perspect.*, 4:9–18.

Klaus, M. H., Kennell, J. H., Plumb, N., & Zuchike, S. (1970), Human maternal behavior at the first contact with the young. *Ped.*, 46:187–192.

Lewis, M. (1972), Parents and children: Sex-role development. *School Rev.*, 80:229–240.

———Weintraub, M., & Ban, P. (1972), *Mothers and Fathers, Girls and Boys: Attachment Behaviors in the First Two Years of Life*. Princeton, NJ: Educational Testing Service.

———Wilson, C. D. (1972), Infant development in lower class American families. *Hum. Develop.*, 15:112–127.

Malmquist, C., Kiresuk, T., & Spano, R. (1966), Personality characteristics of women with repeated illegitimacies: Descriptive aspects. *Amer. J. Orthospsychiat.*, 36:476–484.

Montagu, A. (1971), *Touching: The Human Significance of the Skin.* New York: Columbia University Press.

Powell, G. F., Brasel, J. A., & Blizzard, R. M. (1967), Emotional deprivation and growth retardation simulating idiopathic hypopituitarism. 1. Clinical evaluation of the syndrome. *New Eng. J. Med.*, 276:1271–1278.

Rubin, R. (1963), Maternal touch. *Nurs. Outlook*, 11:328–331.

Simon, W., Berger, A. S., & Gagnon, J. H. (1972), Beyond anxiety and fantasy: The coital experiences of college youth. *J. Youth & Adol.*, 1:203–222.

Spitz, R. A. (1946), Anaclitic depression: An inquiry into the genesis of psychiatric conditions in early childhood. *The Psychoanalytic Study of the Child*, 2:313–342. New York: International Universities Press.

Trevathan, W. R. (1981), Maternal touch at first contact with the newborn infant. *Development. Psychobiol.*, 14:549–558.

Williams, S. J., & Willis, F. N. (1978), Interpersonal touch among preschool children at play. *Psychol. Rec.*, 28:501–508.

Willis, F. N., & Hofmann, G. (1975), Development of tactile patterns in relation to age, sex, and race. *Development. Psychol.*, 11:866.

———Reeves, D. L., & Buchanan, D. R. (1976), Interpersonal touch in high school relative to sex and race. *Percep. & Motor Skills.*, 43:843–847.

——— ———(1976), Touch interactions in junior high students in relation to sex and race. *Develop. Psychol.*, 12:91–92.

Zelnik, M., & Kantner, J. (1980), Sexual activity, contraceptive use, and pregnancy among metropolitan-area teenagers. *Fam. Plan. Perspect.*, 12:230–237.

Zelnik, M., & Shah, F. K. (1983), First intercourse among young Americans. *Fam. Plan. Perspect.*, 15:64–70.

20
Touch and the Acutely Ill

Ruth McCorkle, R.N., Ph.D
Margaret Hollenbach, Ph.D.

Introduction

In nursing practice we usually assume that touching the patient is a good thing: we assume that touching expresses nurturing and that sick people need to feel nurtured at the same time as they feel they are receiving competent health care. Clinical experience almost continually reinforces this assumption. However, when we scientifically examine the importance or usefulness of touching in patient care, this assumption becomes a question. How do we know that touching is a good thing—and when and how and to whom is it most likely to be therapeutically effective?

The senior author became interested in this area of research early in her graduate education and designed a master's thesis to investigate the effects of touching on nurse–patient interaction. That study is still one of no more than a handful concerned with touch and the acutely ill (McCorkle, 1974). We believe that one of the reasons for this lack of research is cultural; touching is relatively inhibited in public social life in North America, hence it does not occur as a variable for research.

Furthermore, modern medicine has become more specialized and impersonal as technology has advanced. Hence touch may have seemed insignificant compared to the impact of major advances in diagnosis and treatment of disease. Health care has been shaped by the tremendous technological advances of our times; but Naisbitt (1982) has described eloquently in his best-selling book, *Megatrends*, the tendency for high technology to be balanced by "high touch." The human needs for contact and touching reassert themselves against impersonal, high tech activities; and this is nowhere more evident than in the new consumer demands being placed on medicine. "High touch" is a megatrend of importance to health care. But we need more knowledge of touch based on solid research.

Review of the Literature

Mainstream, white, North American culture certainly inhibits touching, or at least restricts it. Perhaps the most dramatic and simplest demonstration that touching is embedded in culture is provided by Sidney Jourard's pilot exercise for his 1966 study of "body accessibility." Jourard simply counted how many times one person touched another while engaged in conversation at a table in a coffee shop in four cities—San Juan, Puerto Rico, London, Paris, and Gainesville, Florida. The score was 180 San Juan; 110 Paris; 0 London; and 2 Gainesville. Jourard then drew up a chart of the body divided into areas somewhat along the lines of the butcher's meat charts; he asked unmarried undergraduates which areas of their bodies had been seen or touched by parents, friends of the same sex, and friends of the opposite sex. He discovered that unmarried people without a close friend of the opposite sex are hardly touched at all, even by family members, except occasionally on hands, forearms, shoulders, and head.

In short, in this culture extensive touching is confined to sex partners. But this is not a universal human norm;

cross-cultural comparison reveals wide variation in the amount, kinds, and contexts of touching allowed in normal daily life. Our society varies, too, from family to family and along ethnic and class lines. In addition, there is some controversy about the importance of touching and some impetus to social and cultural change. Such a heterogeneous environment makes a complex situation in which to establish therapeutic guidelines with respect to touching the acutely ill patient.

Most of the research on touching pertains to infants, children, nonhuman primates, or other animals. Research on nonhuman primates and studies of infants suggest that body contact and cutaneous stimulation by touching is essential to growth and development. Clinical evidence indicates that being touched is also important for adult human health (Frank, 1957; Montagu, 1971). Exhortations to integrate more "affective touching" of patients—particularly the acutely ill, elderly, or psychiatric patients—are common in the literature of nursing (De Thomaso, 1971; Leung, 1981; Seaman, 1982). But studies demonstrating the effects of touching, the appropriate contexts for touching, and whom, how, when, where, and by whom—well-designed studies to illuminate the territory and support what seems to be common sense—are very few. Well-designed studies specifically involving acutely ill patients in hospital settings can be counted on the fingers of one hand (Lynch, Flaherty, Emrich, Mills, and Katcher, 1974; McCorkle, 1974; Whitcher and Fisher, 1979; Knable, 1981; Lorensen, 1983).

Social psychological studies on adults in North American society reveal a few general patterns. First, as already mentioned, most touching occurs in a sexual context; nonerotic touching mostly consists of handshakes and light touches or pats on hand, forearm, shoulder, head, neck, or face (Jourard, 1966). Second, in some contexts touch conveys a message about social status. Higher status persons touch or initiate touch toward lower status persons, and not the reverse

(Henley, 1973; Juni and Brannon, 1981). Third, women are touched more than men and, in many social contexts, respond more positively to touch than men, who are apparently more likely to interpret touch in terms of dominance, dependence, or intrusion than simple contact or nurturing (Sussman and Rosenfeld, 1978; Whitcher and Fisher, 1979). In some contexts both sexes respond more positively to touch when it comes from a person of the opposite sex, even when the touch is unmistakably nonerotic (Alagna, Whitcher, Fisher, and Wices, 1979).

Efforts to apply these findings to specific therapeutic problems in psychotherapy and medicine have run into difficulty due to the fact that the meaning of touching is open to multiple interpretations. Touching as a therapeutic event is not so simple as a mechanical procedure or a drug, because it is, above all, an act of communication. As in all embodied communication, the message being sent is not necessarily the same as the message received. Touch, as a nonverbal message, can be conditioned by other nonverbal messages which are virtually impossible to analyze, much less control, in the experimental situation.

For example, Alagna et al. (1979) found that counseling clients who were touched lightly on the forearm and given a handshake at the beginning and end of a counseling interview "evaluated the counseling experience more positively than no-touch control subjects" (p. 465). Jourard and Rubin (1968) found that contextually appropriate touching of client by counselor produced greater self-disclosure by the client in the interview. On the other hand, Stockwell and Dye (1980) attempted to replicate these studies (with some variation) and found that counselor touch did *not* have a significant effect on the client's evaluation of counselor effectiveness, nor on the depth of his self-exploration.

In addition to the problem of standardizing touch events for study, naturalistic observation can be intrusive to the point of altering the behavior observed. In a carefully designed but extremely brief observational study of touch interactions between nurses and patients on a psychiatric ward, De Augustinus, Isani, and Kumler (1963) found that nurses and patients gave the same interpretation to the touch that had occurred only 50 percent of the time. They concluded that "specific touch gestures do not have universal meaning," and that nurses should be aware of the possibility that their touch gestures might be misinterpreted or might increase rather than decrease the anxiety of the patients. The most interesting contribution of this study, however, is the painstaking description it provides of the effects of the observers' presence on the interaction in the ward.

> It was noted that personnel who were interviewed during the initial observation and interview periods seemed to alter their attitude toward the use of touch gestures . . . related to what they thought was the positive or negative attitude of the researchers. After the initial interview, some of the personnel began touching almost every patient with whom they communicated verbally. Other personnel, after the initial interview, were observed to begin the initiation of a touch gesture and suddenly stop just before physical contact with the patient. Frequently, patients who appeared guarded and hesitant during the initial part of the interview changed their answers in the latter part . . . from such replies as "No, I don't know," "I didn't notice," and "No meaning" to "Oh, yes, she always does that. We're friends" or "She likes me" [p. 291].

Sussman and Rosenfeld (1978) suggest that lack of attention to cultural justification for touch may have produced some inconsistent research—in other words, some experimental touch situations might have seemed less justified or appropriate than others. They constructed situations in which subjects were touched or approached closely by others, varying the verbal justification of the touch or spatial intrusion. They found, as they expected, that females responded much more positively to touch or intrusion, whether justified or not, than males, and that unjustified or unexplained physical contact was much more aversive to males than the same contact verbally justified.

Whitcher and Fisher's 1979 study, "Multidimensional Reaction to Therapeutic Touch in a Hospital Setting," explored sex differences in interpreting touch in the more complex natural environment of the hospital. They were interested in the effect of the dependency experienced by a hospital patient on the patient's interpretation of a nurse's touching. The experimental situation was a brief presentation by a nurse of information about surgery to preoperative patients. The independent variable was the nurse's gentle touch on the patient's hand and then forearm during her verbal presentation. Dependent variables measured were the patient's anxiety about surgery, the unpleasantness they anticipated in hospitalization, their vital signs before and after surgery, and how extensively they read the booklet about surgery left by the nurse. Female patients were less anxious about the surgery and anticipated less unpleasantness in hospitalization when they had been touched. Male patients were more anxious. Physiologic readings showed trends not reaching a high level of significance toward higher blood pressure both before and after surgery for the touched males and lower blood pressure before and after surgery for the touched females. "The findings on a variety of measures suggested that in this context, touch led to positive effects primarily for females" (Whitcher and Fisher, 1979, pp. 93–94).

These findings relate well to Jourard's suggestion that being willing to be touched is a personality trait. "Presumably there are people who freely exchange touches with others, and another population which sharply restricts the points of physical contact" (1966, p. 228). In our culture, men are more likely to be in the latter category and women in the former.

While the above studies concentrated on variations in how the receiver would interpret touch, other investigators have explored the caregivers' perceptions of touching. In this category is Burton and Heller's classic paper (1964) on the taboo of touching the patient in psychoanalytic psychotherapy, and studies by Aguilera (1967), Barnett (1972), Schaefer (1981), and Tobiason (1981) involving nurses and nursing students. Schaefer found a significant positive correlation between nurses' self-reported use of touch with patients and the nurses' self-esteem; the nurses' use of touch also correlated positively with the frequency of use of touch in the nurses' past and present families. However, Schaefer found no correlation between the self-reported use of touch and a number of other demographic or educational variables.

Aguilera (1967) found that touching increased verbal interaction between psychiatric nurses and patients; however, she noted that nurses felt more comfortable about touching schizophrenic patients than depressive patients, and more comfortable touching younger than older patients. A reluctance or hesitance about touching the elderly was found by Tobiason (1981), who asked nursing students to choose words describing the sensations of touching both newborn babies and elderly patients. She found that they used more positive words about newborn than elderly, with contrasts such as "warm" versus "dry," and that they became even more positive about the babies after actually touching them, but not about the elderly. Similarly, Barnett (1972) found that nurses touched acutely ill patients significantly less than those in fair or good condition, and speculated that the nurses' own fear of death and illness might affect their motivation toward touching. Burton and Heller (1964) suggested that physicians and psychotherapists as occupational groups particularly dislike being reminded of their own mortality, and "dislike their bodies at an unconscious level (because) the body is what is born and what dies, and this is disturbing. . . ." (1964, p. 130).

Regardless of the possible negative interpretations of touching by male patients or the possible distaste on the side of the healthy physician or nurse, what of the evidence that affective touching does indeed have positive effects for the acutely ill patient?

First, there is ample evidence that touching has a physiological effect—even when the patient is unconscious. Lynch et al. (1974) found "significant heart rate changes" during pulse taking or handholding of curarized patients in a shock-trauma unit. These patients couldn't move and may or may not have been conscious; nevertheless they showed significant physiologic response to being touched. Whitcher and Fisher (1979), as previously cited, found changes in vital signs after touching of preoperative patients but no significant trends in the direction of changes. Knable (1981) found changes in blood pressure, heart rate, and respiratory rate produced in acutely ill patients whose hands had been held by nurses for up to three minutes. (How to interpret the changes was another matter.) Nonverbal gestures observed in this study were "the majority positive." The nurses' impressions of patients' responses also were positive.

McCorkle (1974) hypothesized that a nurse's touching seriously ill patients while talking with them in the hospital setting would produce more positive responses than a similar interaction without touching. The purpose of the intervention (talk with or without touch) was to convey to patients the idea that the nurse cared about them and that they were not alone at a time when their outlook or prognosis was very poor. Sixty patients age twenty to sixty-four years were randomly assigned to two groups. The nurse asked each patient how he felt, what had been happening to him, and what he was thinking about as he lay in bed. As the nurse talked, she touched thirty of the patients on the wrist, increasing pressure with each question. The other thirty patients in the experiment served as untouched controls.

Watching for positive, neutral, and negative responses, two assistants dressed in laboratory coats stood at the foot of the bed recording the patient's responses—facial expressions, body movements, eye contact, and overall response. At the completion of the interaction, one of the assistants stayed behind to get the patient's opinion about whether or not the nurse had been interested in him and how she showed it. Counting smiling, laughing, crying, and nodding of the head as positive responses; blank looks and raised eyebrows as neutral; and yawns, sighs, frowns, moans, and moving the head from side to side as negative, McCorkle determined that more patients in the experimental group had shown positive facial expressions while the controls had balanced more toward the negative. In the body movement, those who had been touched lay still (neutral) more often and turned away less frequently (negative) than the controls. These findings suggest it may be more realistic to expect a seriously ill patient simply to be less negative than more positive when touched.

During the postinterview, twenty-seven of the experimental patients and twenty-six of the controls said they felt the nurse was interested in them. Many of those who had been touched readily reached out to make physical contact with the assistant, although none had tried to touch the nurse. They all seemed to want the assistant to stay, indicating that their need for human warmth and contact was greater than their need for rest and privacy. Only two patients described the nurse's interest in terms of her having touched them, but most said that she was attentive and kind. The controls were more likely to mention that the nurse asked questions about them personally rather than their disease or symptoms.

Whitcher and Fisher's summary statement from their research and their review of the literature was that "whether touch is experienced positively or negatively depends on the meaning and evaluation inferred by the recipient . . . a touch will be experienced as positive to the extent that it (a) is appropriate to the situation, (b) does not impose a greater level of intimacy than the recipient desires, or (c) does not communicate a negative message (e.g., is not perceived as condescending)" (1979, p. 88). As we have seen, cultural, situational, personal, and interpersonal factors all contribute to the context in which the meaning of touching is inferred. However, it appears from the above studies concerned specifically with the acutely ill that the nature of the hospital setting has a dominant effect on the responses to touch.

Characteristics of the Hospital Environment

Cousins (1979) observed in his book *Anatomy of an Illness* that a hospital is no place for a person who is seriously ill. As a patient he felt that hospital routine regularly took precedence over the human aspects of care, thus negatively affecting his own recovery. There is increasing concern among health professionals that the environment plays a significant role in the etiology of disease, the ill person's adaptation to illness, and his recovery. However, environment as a concept has been almost ignored by the scientific community. Generally research has been directed at studying the individual and developing methods for dealing with "person" problems. Much less systematic research has been directed to understanding the impact of the environment on illness, although there are certain questions in which environment has been included, such as research on the effects of noise and density in hospitals (Minckley, 1968; Haslam, 1970; Falk and Woods, 1973; Cohen, Glass, and Phillips, 1979); the influence of the psychosocial environment on health status (Nuckolls, Cassel, and Kaplan, 1972; McFarlane, Norman, Streinei, Roy, and Scott, 1980); and personal space preferences of hospitalized adults (Tolor and Donnon, 1969; Allekian, 1973; Geden and Begeman, 1981).

Studies of hospital noise have suggested acoustic modifications in the structure of the hospital and have documented broad sources of noise and ambient noise levels. Noise is a factor capable of enhancing pain perception in the recovery room (Minckley, 1968), disrupting sleep patterns, and effecting hearing loss (Kryter, 1972). However, there is no quantitative evidence that sleep loss caused by environmental disturbances leads to medical or physical disability.

Kaplan, Cassel, and Gore (1977) have identified two types of psychosocial processes of importance in disease etiology: the stress factors that enhance disease susceptibility and the protective factors that buffer the individual against the effects of stress. A characteristic of most stress situations is the person's uncertainty that his actions will produce certain desired outcomes. Adequate social support systems are thought to be the major protective factors related to incidence and severity of disease (Cassel, 1976). A number of studies have produced reasonably convincing evidence implicating lack of social support in disease genesis (Nuckolls et al., 1972; McFarlane et al., 1980). Clearly, institutionalization and particularly hospitalization may modify the quality and quantity of support a patient can receive from his social system.

Hospitalization has the potential of being very invasive of a patient's personal space (Geden and Begeman, 1981). Research in this area has focused primarily on comparative studies of patients with mental health diagnoses. Tolor and Donnon (1969) found that the longer patients are hospitalized the smaller their personal space preferences. Unwitting intrusions within a person's space may inhibit the formation of a helping relationship; conversely, maintenance of, and respect for, another's personal space may facilitate a helping relationship (Garfinkel, 1964).

Today's hospitals are structurally organized and designed from the standpoint of the work that needs to be done, which in turn has been shaped by advances in medical technology and the trend toward increasing medical specialization. A patient, from the point of view of hospital staff, is not assigned a territory. He is the temporary occupant of a specified area within the hospital, to which all authorized personnel appropriately have access. Psychologically, of course, the ill person brings his own personal space with him; and an individual's concept of his personal space can be drastically altered by the experience of confinement to a hospital. Complaints about lack of privacy refer more to the feeling that personal space is violated than to an invasion of a larger territory (Sommer and Dewar, 1963).

Health care professionals appear to have no reluctance about intruding into a patient's personal space. The ill person must stay in bed and permit a host of strangers to observe, move, and monitor his body and disease. Nowhere does this intrusion occur more than in areas that are designated as critical care units such as coronary care units, burn units, and trauma centers. Patients in these units are continuously monitored. The patient quickly learns he has little or no control over his immediate physical environment, not even over the inside of his own body. The person must adapt to the hospital; the hospital will not change to suit the needs of the patient (Roberts, 1976).

The Nature of Illness

In addition to the enviromental effects of hospitalization on a patient's receptiveness to, or need for touch, the nature of the illness is an important factor to consider. As a young medical student, Selye (1956) observed that physicians were concentrating their efforts on recognizing individual diseases and finding specific remedies for them, without giving any attention to what he called "the syndrome of being sick." Yet the syndrome of being sick, he argued, is an important component of all diseases. Today we find it useful to distinguish the illness, or the person's experience of disvalued changes in states of being and social function, from the disease, or abnormalities in the structure and function of body organs and systems (see Fabrega, 1979; Eisenberg, 1979). Traditionally, physicians have diagnosed and treated diseases; but patients universally suffer illnesses. The person's perception of his illness may be affected by the limitations and disabilities which are imposed on him as a result of his disease; how it will affect what he is able to do and what he wants to do?

While this distinction is maintained in the scientific literature in certain fields, such as medical anthropology and research on primary care, in general medical practice the term *illness* still refers to aspects of both bodily changes and personal states. "Acutely ill" patients are in crisis states from both the medical and personal point of view.

Acute and *chronic* are terms that have been used to describe both the severity and duration of an illness. In the past, "acute" did not refer to the seriousness of the illness per se, but to the rapid nature of onset and progress. Today, acute illness implies life-threatening conditions and has been associated with critical care units such as intensive care, coronary care, isolation, burn units, respiratory care, or hemodialysis. Smith and Gips (1963) suggested defining an acute condition as one in which there is a rapid state of change, indicating the need for close observation and monitoring.

Illness is a stressful event for most people, especially if it occurs suddenly and threatens the future. In addition, modern medical response to acute illness involves removing the ill person from his social support system and placing him in the unfamiliar surroundings of a hospital. In a sense, the person is placed in a vulnerable, isolated, and stressful situation just by being admitted to the hospital. His vulnerability is increased if his alertness has been compromised by his condition. His immediate environment is filled with the electronic mechanical equipment of modern medical technology, allowing little opportunity for human contact. The patient is seen more as an extension of the equipment surrounding him than as a person.

During the acute phase of an illness, the person temporarily withdraws from adult responsibility and is limited in his ability to participate in his own care. He is dependent upon the people caring for him. At times such as these, the patient has a tendency to return to a more satisfying communication mode used during the earlier periods in his life when he obtained some degree of success in communicating with others under similar feelings of stress. The use of touch and physical closeness may be the most important way to communicate to an acutely ill person that he is important as a human being and that his recovery is related to his desire to improve. And yet, most acutely ill patients are placed in critical care units where their emotional needs are subordinated to the rigorous demands of the equipment. Nurses touch patients routinely as part of their work responsibilities, monitoring vital functions, and managing apparatus such as IV tubes and urinary catheters; but patients in critical care units are seldom touched in nontechnical ways—and not even the inside of the body is treated as personal space.

An important question to be answered is under what conditions do patients' needs for human contact take precedence over their needs for privacy and their own personal space. The male patients in Whitcher and Fisher's (1979) study were apparently more threatened than soothed by being touched in the context of their hospital rooms before surgery; how would they have responded to a similar touch if they were patients in critical care? Would differences between male and female responses to touch in the context of acute illness disappear or be exacerbated? Should specific structured touching interventions be developed for patients in critical care environments? And if so, what effect would such interventions have on recovery? These are the directions for future research indicated by our observations.

A Special Case

For the last several years, the senior author has been a consultant to the nursing staff at the Fred Hutchinson Cancer Comprehensive Research Center. Both adults and children are treated at the center for bone marrow transplantation, which is a procedure to replace diseased marrow cells with the bone marrow stem cells from a normal donor, free of disease. In order to replace the diseased bone marrow with healthy stem cells, total body irradiation, cytotoxic drugs, and antilymphocystic globulins are used with the goal of destroying as many as possible of the diseased cells and creating "living space" for transplanted cells. Because of the nature of the treatment for these patients, the work is often stressful. The staff recognized their need for assistance in managing their day-to-day stress. They reported not having enough personal time to interact with patients and a lack of opportunities to get to know patients. They were finding that they spent increasing amounts of time monitoring the equipment, administering medications, and performing procedures.

The great danger in bone marrow transplantation is that the patient will die from infection if the transplant is not successful. Extraordinary measures are taken to prevent infection; as consultant, McCorkle recommended structured touching experiences between nurse and patient to mitigate the stressful effects of the unusual conditions of treatment.

Patients are randomly assigned to either a laminar flow room or private hospital room. In the laminar flow room all materials brought into the room must be sterilized and both staff and family members must wear protective clothing including gowns, boots, caps, and gloves. There is no skin-to-skin contact with the patient for thirty-five to forty days. Extensive precaution must be taken to minimize the chance of infection during the stages when the recipient has little or no immune response capacity. As the engrafted bone marrow cells home to the bone marrow of the recipient, the recipient begins to regain immunological competency by means of the donor cells, which then have the potential to differentiate into immunologically competent cells.

A successful transplant takes at least one hundred days. Patients come from all over the world and from various cultural backgrounds. During that time patients experience multiple procedures in which their bodies are directly touched in invasive and nontherapeutic ways. Some of these procedures include multiple bone marrow aspirations, cleansing of their interarterial lines, and routine douches. Patients report that there are times when they are extremely fatigued and have little energy to interact with others, especially if the transplanted bone marrow is not accepted and the patient's condition deteriorates, with death as the obvious outcome. Often these patients feel confused, alone, and isolated. They may have no contact with their family except for the person who accompanies them to donate his or her bone marrow. The patient is ambivalent about his needs. He wants human contact but he retreats as someone touches him because his memory is filled only with the pain and not the pleasure associated with touching.

We have found that structured experiences in which the nurse establishes a relationship with the patient based on a time and distance ratio may enhance the patient's quality of living during the transplant process. The formula may differ between men and women and adults and children. An example of an experience for a man forty-three years old and a nurse who is twenty-six years old would be:

1. Day 1 to 2 — Nurse remains approximately five feet from patient to interact.
2. Day 2 to 3 — Nurse moves within three feet to interact.
3. Day 3 to 4 — Nurse moves within one foot of patient.
4. Day 5 — Nurse interacts with patient using touch in some systematic and nonprocedural way.

The type of touch includes hand holding, stroking the patient's arm, or sitting next to him. It is recommended that not every nurse who is responsible for the patient's care participate in this structured experience, but that only one or two nurses do it, preferably a nurse who has limited responsibility for the procedural aspects of care. Clinically, we have observed that these steps are especially important in establishing a relationship with children and their tolerance of the invasive procedures. The outcomes observed have been improved self-concept, less depressive responses, and a shorter overall hospital stay. Clearly, these recommended experiences need to be formalized into protocols that are pilot tested and revised.

These patients have a 50 percent chance of survival. Death primarily results from infection. The body's defense against infection depends in large part on the mechanisms of humoral and cellular immunity, but these mechanisms themselves are influenced by a person's mental state. There is good reason to believe that the patient's state of mind can affect the course of all pathological processes that involve immunological reactions. Mobilizing the natural defense mechanisms of the patient may be indispensable for recovery (Cousins, 1979). This process may be activated and enhanced by the recognition conveyed by the nurse through her presence and through consistent touching. Nurses have been taught not to become involved with their patients, and yet nurses do become involved. Few nurses have adequate preparation to cope successfully with their involvement, and consequently retreat. We need to study how to become involved with one another and how to enhance our involvement for the patient's recovery and the nurse's mental health and job satisfaction.

Directions for Future Research

This chapter has emphasized that there is little known about the use of touch with acutely ill patients. Acutely ill patients are usually hospitalized in critical care units and health care professionals pay little attention to patients' needs for privacy or personal space. Patients are touched only as they are monitored and worked upon. Research is needed to determine if touching acutely ill patients in noninvasive ways over time will affect their sense of who they are and eventually their recovery. There is no question that there is a shift of emphasis from the knowledge of disease to the knowledge of human beings in whom the disease exists; but the knowledge we have gained about human beings and their responses is minimal in relation to what is needed.

Discussion: Chapter 20

Seymour Levine: The importance of a strong social support system has been demonstrated repeatedly, in animal studies as well as human studies. We have some marvelous data showing that if you subject animals in a social group to environmental stress, they do not show a physiological response. They do show a response when they're alone. Other recent work shows more immunological incompetence. There are also data relating social support or the lack of it to complications of pregnancy, and to the behavior of combat personnel during the Vietnam war. It's a very profound variable.

Elizabeth McAnarney: Is there a television set in the laminar flow room?

Ruth McCorkle: Yes. As a matter of fact, one of the biggest and most important things that has happened to these patients is videogames. The amount of physical touching that goes on between family members and patients sitting on the bed together playing videogames is a most rewarding thing to see.

William Greenough: One of the issues that your work raises, Ruth, which should be empirically decided, is whether touch is "magic" in some way or whether it's not particularly special, as long as you communicate concern. The wave of this meeting seems to be that touch is special, but it may not be.

T. Berry Brazelton: I don't think we can ignore in the medical professions the need to use symbolic modalities like touch to convey the fact that we are going to take over what control we can and try to help. Even if we can't save somebody, we certainly can do that.

However, touch is not the only modality that can be used. We've been looking at immunological failures in children at Boston Children's Hospital, and we've been trying to reach these children in other ways, too—through eye contact, for instance. At first, when they've been isolated for a long time, the children give us a defensive smile, sort of a grimace. Later, when they are really smiling and accepting interpersonal communication via visual, auditory, and other modalities, then we think we're on the right wavelength with them.

Susan Rose: I agree that we should question the idea that touch has unique effects. Certainly in all the work that we've done with preterm infants, if we find deficits in responses to tactile stimuli, we also find deficits in responses to visual stimuli, and in the ability to integrate information from various sense systems.

William Greenough: There is probably nothing "magic" and possibly nothing very special about cutaneous activation per se. The important consideration from the clinical perspective is to find the optimal conditions for treating patients, ranging from premature infants to older patients and those likely to die. Touch may be a value in many cases, but so may anything that mitigates the inhospitable environment of the hospital. Many types of intervention have potential value.

Anneliese Korner: In many hospitals, particularly university hospitals, if you come up with a good, commonsense, and humane proposition and you ask for permission to implement it, the answer usually is: Show me the evidence that it does any good. One can play the game and look for evidence in order to get it done, but there is something very wrong with this attitude.

From a humanistic point of view, it should not be necessary to have to do research on touch to prove its effectiveness. It seems amply clear that touch gives comfort to patients, and that is reason enough to provide it.

Kathryn Barnard: In American institutions, particularly hospitals, it's important to show that you've accomplished things. A humanistic approach runs counter to being efficient. One of the reasons we need supporting data is so that the medical and nursing staff can take time to be human.

Paul Satz: I might prefer just to do what seems right, but I think we have to be somewhat hard-nosed about it. An experimental design that can't demonstrate an effect is a poor experimental design, unless nothing is happening. I have to disagree with the implication that humanism is incompatible with science.

Ruth McCorkle: I think there can be a combination of the two. We just haven't looked at all the right variables. In other words, there are certain types of patients for whom one thing is good and others for whom another thing is good. We need to define subgroups of patients, using individual factors of personality and temperament—human qualities. But that doesn't mean these factors can't be part of an experimental design. In fact, I think they have to be if we're to make any valid generalizations.

T. Berry Brazelton: In our work with immunological patients, we found that when we and the staff became convinced we could reach these children, the whole ambience of the floor changed. It was very powerful.

Elizabeth McAnarney: There's a tremendous contrast between the environment of our adolescent inpatient unit and the environment of the adult unit. In our unit, patients who are not critically ill wear their own clothes, and they can have friends in any time they want. We have a room where no medical procedures are done, a teen canteen. The unit works very well. In the adult unit, the patients wear nightgowns all day and the window shades are sometimes pulled down. The atmosphere is oppressive, and illness behavior is reinforced.

But I don't think you need data to change this kind of thing. It's very obvious, and I think most hospitals will agree to change the routine if you make a serious effort to show them a better way. Research is helpful, of course, but it doesn't necessarily need to come first.

T. Berry Brazelton: Nurses seem to have fewer problems with burnout if you give them some back-up for what they're doing and free up this humanism on their part. In our premie nursery, we got rid of burnout almost completely by giving the nurses some intellectual back-up for what they would like to do anyway.

William Greenough: Another reason for collecting data is that if you don't, you may miss some very important things. For example, data could show that touch is a less important therapeutic intervention than we think. But the studies have to be done. You really have to investigate these things and see what works and what doesn't.

Kathryn Barnard: Well, we're trying to. In order to establish a better research base in nursing, we need financial support, and support from all of you. You must realize that as a scientific endeavor, nursing is very young. We've only been dealing in science for the last fifty years at most. So we haven't had as much experience as some of you here—but we're getting it.

Cathleen Fanslow: Although I am perhaps more a practitioner than a scientist, I would be happy for the marriage of the scientist and the practitioner. I would welcome it.

References

Aguilera, D. C. (1967), Relationship between physical contact and verbal interaction between nurses and patients. *J. Psychiat. Nurs.*, Jan.–Feb.: 5–21.

Alagna, F. J., Whitcher, S. J., Fisher, J. D., & Wices, E. A. (1979), Evaluative reaction to interpersonal touch in a counseling interview. *J. Counsel. Psychol.*, 26/6:465–472.

Allekian, C. (1973), Intrusion of territory and personal space. An anxiety-inducing factor for hospitalized persons: An exploratory study. *Nurs. Res.*, 22:236–241.

Barnett, K. E. (1972), The development of a theoretical construct of the concepts of touch as they relate to nursing. Final Report to U.S. Dept. of Health, Education and Welfare, Project No. O-G-027.

Burton, A. & Heller, L. G. (1964), The touching of the body. *Psychoanal. Rev.*, 51:122–134.

Cassel, J. (1976), The contribution of the social environment to host resistance. *Amer. J. Epidemiol.*, 104:107–122.

Cohen, S., Glass, D., & Phillips, S. (1979), Environment and health. In: *Handbook of Medical Sociology*, 3rd ed., eds. H. E. Freeman, S. Levine, & L. G. Reeder. Englewood Cliffs, NJ: Prentice-Hall, pp. 134–149.

Cousins, N. (1979), *Anatomy of an Illness as Perceived by the Patient*. New York: W. W. Norton.

De Augustinus, J., Isani, R. S., & Kumler, F. R. (1963), Ward study: The meaning of touch in interpersonal communication. In: *Some Clinical Approaches to Psychiatric Nursing*, eds. S. Burd & M. Marshall. New York: Macmillan, pp. 271–306.

De Thomaso, M. T. (1971), "Touch power" and the screen of loneliness. *Perspect. in Psychiat. Care*, 9/3:112–118.

Eisenberg, L. (1979), Disease and illness. *Cult., Med. & Psychiat.*, 1:9–23.

Fabrega, H. (1979), The ethnography of illness. *Soc. Sci. & Med.*, 13:565–576.

Falk, S. A., & Woods, N. F. (1973), Hospital noise—levels of potential health hazards. *New Eng. J. Med.*, 289/15:774–781.

Frank, L. K, (1957), Tactile communication, *Gen. Psychol. Monogr.*, 56:209–225.

Garfinkel, H. (1964), Studies of the routine grounds of everyday activities. *Soc. Prob.*, 11:225–250.

Geden, E., & Begeman, A. (1981), Personal space preferences of hospitalized adults. *Res. Nurs. & Health*, 4:237–241.

Haslam, P. (1970), Noise in hospitals: Its effects on the patient. *Nurs. Clin. N. Amer.*, 5/4:715–724.

Henley, N. M. (1973), Status and sex: Some touching observations. *Bull. Psychoanal. Soc.*, 2:91–93.

Jourard, S. M. (1966), An exploratory study of body-accessibility. *Brit. J. Soc. & Clin. Psychol.*, 5:221–231.

———Rubin, J. E. (1968), Self-disclosure and touching: A study of two modes of interpersonal encounter and their interrelation. *J. Hum. Psychol.*, 8:39–48.

Juni, S., & Brannon, R. (1981), Interpersonal touching as a function of status and sex. *J. Soc. Psychol.*, 114:135–136.

Kaplan, B., Cassel, J., & Gore, S. (1977), Social support and health. *Med. Care*, 15:47–58.

Knable, J. (1981), Handholding: One means of transcending barriers of communication. *Heart & Lung*, 10/6:1106–1110.

Kryter, K. (1972), Non-auditory effects of environmental noise. *Amer. J. Pub. Health*, 62/3:389–398.

Leung, J. K. C. (1981), A touching moment . . . *Nurs. Mirror*, 153/12:36–37.

Lorensen, M. (1983), Effects of touch in patients during a crisis situation in hospitals. In: *Nursing Research*, ed. J. Wilson-Barnett. New York: John Wiley, pp. 179–194.

Lynch, J. J., Flaherty, L., Emrich, C., Mills, M. E., & Katcher, A. (1974), Effects of human contact on the heart activity of curarized patients in a shock-trauma unit. *Amer. Heart J.*, 88:160–169.

McCorkle, R. (1974), The effects of touch on seriously ill patients. *Nurs. Res.*, 23:125–132.

McFarlane, A., Norman, G., Streinei, D., Roy, R., & Scott, D. (1980), A longitudinal study of the influence of the psychosocial environment on health status: A preliminary report. *J. Health & Soc. Behav.*, 21:124–133.

Minckley, B. (1968), A study of noise and its relationship to patient discomfort in the recovery room. *Nurs. Res.*, 17/3:247–250.

Montagu, A. (1971), *Touching: The Human Significance of the Skin.* New York: Harper & Row.

Naisbitt, J. (1982), *Megatrends*. New York: Warner Books.

Nuckolls, K., Cassel, J., & Kaplan, B. (1972), Psychosocial assets, life crisis, and the prognosis of pregnancy. *Amer. J. Epidemiol.*, 95:431–441.

Roberts, S. (1976), *Behavioral Concepts and the Critically Ill Patient*. Englewood Cliffs, NJ: Prentice-Hall.

Schaefer, J. L. (1981), *The Relationship Between Attributes of Nurses and Their Use of Affective Touch.* Unpublished Master's thesis. University of Washington, Seattle.

Seaman, L. (1982), Affective nursing touch. *Geriatr. Nurs.*, 3/3:162–164.

Selye, H. (1956), *The Stress of Life.* New York: McGraw-Hill.

Smith, D. W., & Gips, C. D. (1963), *Care of the Adult Patient.* Philadelphia: J. B. Lippincott.

Sommer, R., & Dewar, R. (1963), The physical environment of the ward. In: *The Hospital in Modern Society*, ed. E. Friedson. London: The Free Press, pp. 319–342.

Stockwell, S. R., & Dye, A. (1980), Effects of counselor touch on counseling outcome. *J. Counsel. Psychol.*, 27/5:443–446.

Sussman, N. M., & Rosenfeld, H. M. (1978), Touch, justification, and sex: Influences on the aversiveness of spatial violations. *J. Soc. Psychol.*, 106:215–225.

Tobiason, S. J. B. (1981), Touching is for everyone. *Amer. J. Nurs.*, 81/4:728–730.

Tolor, A., & Donnon, M. S. (1969), Psychological distance as a function of length of hospitalization. *Psycholog. Rep.*, 25:851–855.

Whitcher, S. J., & Fisher, J. D. (1979), Multidimensional reaction to therapeutic touch in a hospital setting. *J. Personal. & Soc. Psychol.*, 36/1:87–96.

21
Touch and the Elderly

Cathleen A. Fanslow, R.N., M.A.

In our American society, the process of aging is not as pleasant or respected as it is in many other parts of the world. In the United States, we view the changes that accompany the aging process as losses over which we have no control. What seems to happen is that in a sense we become what these changes appear to be. In our minds, greatly formed and affected by a death- and age-denying society, an elder is a person changed and lessened by the aging process. A different view is offered by Martha E. Rogers (1971) in her book, *An Introduction to the Theoretical Basis of Nursing*. Dr. Rogers describes man and the aging process as follows:

> The life process evolves unidirectionally along the space–time continuum and is bound in the four dimensional space–time matrix . . . the life process is a becoming. . . . At each point in space–time, man is what he has been becoming but he is not what he has been. Moreover, he cannot go back to what he had been. Life proceeds unidirectionally and is inextricably bound within the space–time dimension [p. 88].

Many contributors to this volume have centered on the need for touch of those at the beginning of the journey of life.

It is equally important to address the needs for touch of those at the end of life. It has always fascinated me that the two senses that are myelinized earliest in fetal development are touch and pain. We should also be aware that these two senses enable us to stay in contact with life until life ends. The changes that occur in the developing fetus are imperceptible to it on a conscious level; yet the fetus is indeed changed. We call this process growth and development. We can also say that maturation causes intrinsic changes: This process we call aging.

The road to healthy and normal growth and development contains a variety of life experiences that "touch" us and make us whole. The landmarks on the journey of life take place on three levels. The *physical or tactile level* of touch plays a crucial role in helping us define our own body view. The infant's exploration of his tiny fingers and toes gives him his first sense of self and of the world of his own body. The physical touch, caress, and contact comfort of mother, father, and loving grandparents give the infant the identity and security he needs to go beyond the boundaries of his own world.

Psychological "touch" helps us form the internal self-image that enables us to face the world, participate in life, and evolve from within. Our internal self-image needs loving care and feeding even more than our external physical self because our own inner or deeper self does not change or diminish as our external, physical, more tangible body image eventually does. Rather, our internal self-image continues to expand and grow. Finally, *emotional "touch"* is possibly more expansive and penetrating than either physical or psychological touch. Emotional touches interlace and interconnect with the other life touches to form the intrinsic life matrix that contains deep patterns of love, anger, fear, trust, anxiety, and rejection.

The human need for touch on all these levels does not lessen as we grow, develop, and age. Rather, the need for touch on all levels increases with age and wisdom. Physical, psychological, and emotional touches are all essential for the proper establishment of internal sources of security, self-image, trust, and interdependence. They are needed for normal growth and development and are essential for a healthy aging process.

The empathetic physical touch, hand clasp, or hug assures the elder that in fact he or she is in safe hands. The myriad meanings of touch have a special place in our interaction with the elderly, who have in so many ways become the untouched, the forgotten. To be acceptable to the aging, physical touch must be gentle, cognizant of thin skin and frail tissue. The need for tactile, safe, and secure touch is seen clearly in agitated and confused, as well as in withdrawn or regressed, patients. Actual physical touch seems to ground or quiet them so that we are able to relate to them differently.

Many elderly people require assistive devices such as walkers, wheelchairs, geri-chairs, and side rails on beds to make their environments safe and secure. These devices are necessary for safety, but they can also become "fences," creating a barrier between us and the elderly, particularly the frail elderly. The presence of this physical equipment may interfere with our ability to touch them in the way they need to be touched at this most critical part of life's journey. How difficult it is to touch old people we have so carefully, and carelessly, fenced in! We must make an effort to include consciously directed, caring touches during transfer activities, and to go beyond the fences to touch them, particularly those confined to bed behind bed rails, the worst fences of all.

Those working with the elderly must be acutely aware that infants and growing children are not alone in their need for physical touch and contact comfort to help provide the safety and security necessary for growth and development. So too, our elders need the actual physical touch of a warm handclasp, hug, or arm about the shoulder or waist. This touch requires the caregiver to overcome physical barriers and reassures the elderly of their continuity and existence.

The external self-image changes with age, whether gradually in the course of the normal physiological aging process or acutely, as a result of trauma, progressive arthritic changes, chronic illness, or neurological problems and/or deficits. The nurturing and maintenance of an internal self-image, which is established and maintained by psychological touch, therefore takes on even greater importance in the elderly. The availability of affective, compassionate, and self-affirming touch is what makes the difference for elderly people between truly living out life or merely existing. Although physical touch is the way in which we actually make contact with the elderly, it is the affective, intangible, yet deeply sensed touch representing caring, empathy, compassion, and acceptance that sustains the internal self-image. This enables the elderly to continue their growth and development throughout this crucial period.

Lastly, emotional touch is essential for our aged population because it makes them feel more alive and connected with the world. As a result of illness as well as of the aging process, the elderly often experience sensory deficits; impaired hearing and lack of visual acuity head the list. Decreased mobility and vitality can make older people feel helpless and vulnerable. All such impairments contribute to feelings of fear, distrust, and anxiety characteristic of physical and social isolation. The emotional component of touch can reach through isolation and help the elderly relate to us on the feeling, affective level. The love, trust, affection, and warmth that are expressed through emotional interaction transcend the mode of expression.

I have attempted to reemphasize the need for physical, psychological, and emotional touches for the elderly and would now like to discuss the concept and application of a touch-centered approach called therapeutic touch, which has great ramifications in the care of the elderly. Therapeutic touch, which has been called the imprimatur of nursing by its discoverer (Krieger, 1975), is gaining a well-deserved place in our modern-day health care system. Touch has always been the special mark of the nursing profession, its way of making its presence felt by those in need of comfort and care. Indeed, one might say that the art of nursing the elderly is made manifest through the touch of the nurse as a primary caregiver.

Therapeutic touch is actually an energy transfer. The caregiver becomes centered, or quiet within, by stilling the chattering mind, and then transfers a portion of his or her life energy to the person in need. The energy lack, or need, evidenced by disease, disorder, or disrhythmia or, in the case of the elderly, all the above factors plus the normal aging process, calls forth the energy through the helper. The nurse, helper, or caregiver makes energy available to the other by acting as a conduit through which the energy flows. However, it is the person himself that absorbs this life energy and, with the help of the energy infusion, restores his own inner balance and harmony. The manner and application of therapeutic touch respond to the need of elderly patients for touch on all the levels I have described and in a most particular way to their energy level need. Decreased energy on the physical level is very apparent in the need for frequent rest periods and profound exhaustion after even mild physical exertion. The decrease in psychological and emotional energy levels is shown by an inability to maintain deep relationships or intense emotion for any length of time. The distraction, withdrawal, and regression evident in this population are indications of their diminished energy reserves.

My experience as a therapeutic touch practitioner with the elderly for the past ten years has demonstrated that although actual physical contact is generally not necessary for therapeutic touch to be effective, physical contact during therapeutic touch is more likely to be necessary for the elderly (Krieger, 1979).

Two essential components of therapeutic touch respond to the other touch needs in our elderly populations. The first is intentionality, the intent to help or heal. This component is what actually initiates the healing process. A major part of the focus of intentionality is to see the person in need as whole and well and image him or her in that way before and during the act of therapeutic touch. Since so much of disease, distortion, or dysrhythmia is in the image the individual has of himself (i.e., "I feel sick," or "I am old"), seeing the person as whole and well while directing energy can facilitate the absorption of energy at a deep level. The energy interchange thus responds to the special self-image sustenance needs of our elders. Such interaction actually appears to reduce depression in the elderly that stems from decreased self-image. It can help prevent the aged from more deeply imprinting a sick, diminished image, which then contributes to their becoming more depressed and withdrawn.

Compassion is the second essential component of therapeutic touch and can help fulfill the emotional touch need of the elderly client (Fanslow, 1983). This compassion is a pure form of love; it is love without hooks, a love that gives freely to the one in need with no expectations of return. Compassion conveys to the other a warmth, respect, acceptance, and a willingness to be present without asking anything in return. This approach creates a climate that allows for the establishment and maintenance of a trusting relationship. Such an approach offers respect for the hopes of the individual and greatly decreases the insecurity, fear, and anxiety that plague the aged.

The physical body changes that we note in the aging person all indicate a lessening of strength, endurance, and vitality. Muscles and flesh once firm and solid are now weakened and atrophied. Tall, straight backs and spines with excellent posture and head held high, now bow to the aging process and shrink in our eyes and arms. Although their spirit is willing, the flesh has become weaker. Since man is indeed an open system, continuously changing and interacting on all levels with his environment, and since there are energy exchanges on all the intangible levels we have already discussed, let me describe the particular energy field we draw on in the practice of therapeutic touch.

There is an energy body or field that is an exact duplicate of the physical but much less dense. This energy field or body is adherent and interpenetrates the physical body and is called the bioenergetic field. Both fields are needed for human life. Some have called the bioenergetic field the first energy field of the human aura. It extends approximately three-fourths to one and one-half inches above the physical body. It is tightly interwoven in the healthy person and in the younger person. The presence of ill-health as well as the normal aging process changes or alters this field. The bioenergetic field of the elderly, by reason of the normal aging process, is more open and fragile, replicating the physical energy of the physical body. This energy field, interpenetrating and forming the human life matrix, is less interconnected and more open and diffuse than it is earlier in life. The openness, diffusion, and fragility of the field increase and become even more apparent the older or sicker the person becomes, and as death approaches.

Decreased energy levels are manifested in the elderly by loss of vitality, by fatigue, and by intermittent weakness. Therapeutic touch is extremely effective with the elderly population because their field is so friable. This openness facilitates the transfer of energy and its absorption by the elder. Because the influx of life energy is so easily absorbed, it penetrates deeply into the fragile matrix of the elder, causing deeper and more profound changes than tend to occur with others whose field is not so open. This phenomenon of fragility also, however, permits life energy to ebb more quickly. Thus, shorter, more frequent therapeutic touch sessions are the treatment of choice for the elderly.

Since therapeutic touch is able to reach and affect all levels of the elderly person, it becomes an extremely effective and holistic therapeutic tool (Fanslow, 1981). In fact, I know of no other treatment modality that is so integrative for the human person. Since the elder in our society fears his decline and is made to think he is disintegrating, it has special application to this population.

Therapeutic touch is becoming accepted by the scientific world through Dr. Delores Krieger's research, which demonstrated that therapeutic touch with intent to help or heal raised hemoglobin and hematocrit ratios in ill persons. These hypotheses were supported by statistical analysis at the 0.001 level of significance (Krieger, 1975). In additional to raising the hemoglobin level and hematocrit ratio, which makes more oxygen available to the organs and tissues of elderly individuals, therapeutic touch responds to two additional areas of need that have definite and far-reaching implications for the geriatric population.

Therapeutic touch is noticeably useful for eliciting a rather profound, generalized relaxation response in the patient and for relieving pain (Krieger, 1979, p. 17). The profound relaxation response occurs very rapidly in the elderly. Particular effects are noted in the cardiovascular system, which is greatly changed in both normal and pathological aging. Decreased heart and respiratory rate, as well as peripheral flush, occur quickly and aged arteriosclerotic vessels are relaxed. This process gives the elderly a profound physical sense of well-being, as well as increased blood supply to their whole body. Many symptoms of impaired cardiac output and vascular disease, particularly edema of the sacral area and the lower extremities, respond beautifully to frequent, regular, brief sessions with therapeutic touch.

Over a five-year period I have used therapeutic touch as a primary modality in several pilot studies with the elderly. In the first study, previous history and treatments for increasing and maintaining ambulation as well as treatment of affected sites were used as baseline measures. Involved in the study were six seventy- to eighty-year-old patients who had cardiovascular and respiratory difficulties with resultant limitations in ambulation. This study lasted over a period of two years, during which time all significant intervening factors were controlled and the only treatment in addition to medication was therapeutic touch.

As a result of continuous, repetitive, therapeutic touch treatments, the ambulation and mobility of all six patients were increased from baseline data, the degree depending on the severity of their preexisting conditions (Fanslow, 1979). As a result of increased mobility and ambulation skills, one elder (in a nursing home) was transferred back to a more "independent" floor and reunited with his wife! In three subjects with severe pitting edema of both lower extremities (3+−4+) with probable skin breakdown, stasis leg ulcers were prevented. Another two patients of comparable age and disability already had skin breakdown and stasis leg ulcers at the time of the study. The subject treated with therapeutic touch and conventional treatment (i.e., Dakins solution followed by swabbing with Gentian violet) healed four weeks sooner than the subject treated only with conventional treatment.

In the second year, due to degenerative disease progression, arteriosclerotic heart disease, and congestive heart failure, three subjects of this sample became bed bound. Continued use of therapeutic touch treatment for two of the subjects, whose skin was in a very fragile condition, contributed to the prevention of decubitus ulcer formation: none occurred even though the two subjects were bedridden for a six-month period. However, the third subject of this sample group was transferred to another floor in the same institution where no therapeutic touch practitioner was available. This patient developed decubitus ulcers after one month in bed. Upon the patient's return to the original unit, therapeutic touch treatments were resumed, and the decubitus ulcers were healed in four weeks. Although the sample in this pilot study was extremely small, the positive responses in such a high-risk group are indeed indications for further research.

The second study concerned itself with four sixty-eight- to seventy-seven-year-old patients with arthritis. Three subjects suffered from long-standing osteoarthritis and one from traumatic stress-related rheumatoid arthritis. When therapeutic touch was used for one year as the primary therapy, the symptoms of pain, inflammation, and joint swelling associated with arthritis decreased, as demonstrated by repeated measurements with a standardized tape measure. One year after therapeutic touch treatments, cessation of these symptoms continued to be maintained in all four patients.

A treatment regime instituted by Fanslow (1979) for patients with arthritis was carried out over a two-year period in the following sequence. The regimen begins with therapeutic touch treatment two to three times every week for one-half hour to forty-five minutes, depending on the duration of the condition. The longer the disease has been present, the more deeply the pain and disability pattern of the individual with arthritis appears to be imprinted into his or her very being. The longer duration and deeper pattern requires more consistent and continuous intervention in the beginning of the regime. This enables the healing energy to penetrate into the bioenergetic matrix, thus reaching deeply into the pain pattern so that additional energy is made available for the person to change.

Once the area is energized and the blocks released, treatments may be reduced to one each week and, in time, even less frequently. This decrease in frequency of treatment can occur because the energy transfer is cumulative, and the effect is sustained for longer periods after each treatment. The response to treatment seems slower with the elderly who have chronic illness than with younger persons with the same pathology. This may be due to the permeability of their field. Interfacing therapeutic touch with imagery, visualization, and meditation with two of the younger sample appeared to hasten the cessation of symptoms; they were symptom-free for several weeks prior to the two other treatments.

A concomitant of therapeutic touch treatments for these patients was the reduction of corticosteroid levels from 60 mgm daily to 10 mgm daily. Two are now completely free of this medication. Clinical studies over the past twelve years appear to indicate that therapeutic touch directed to the adrenal glands energizes and stimulates the adrenal cortex and appears to decrease the suppressive effects of steroid therapy.

There are indications that some mild forms of confusion in the elderly that I and others treated during this time have been positively affected by continued therapeutic touch treatments. This appears to be due to the relaxation of the cerebral vessels and increased hemoglobin levels, which may have increased oxygenation to the brain. Relaxation of the vessels of the kidney and the eye with therapeutic touch, which are similar in size to those of the brain, have helped some very minor visual and kidney problems, thus increasing the comfort and function of the elderly people with whom we worked.

A third small study involved eight stroke veterans, five right hemiplegics and three left hemiplegics, who had all completed a regular physical therapy and occupational therapy program at a small private hospital. They were all white males, aged sixty-eight to seventy-two and of mixed ethnic background, who were treated with therapeutic touch twice weekly with family followup daily in most cases for a six-month period. The most noticeable observed responses to the treatment were marked reduction in spasticity of the affected upper extremity and dramatic lessening in pain. These phenomena occurred more quickly and were more lasting in the right hemiplegics than in the left hemiplegics. After several therapeutic touch treatments, eight of the stroke veterans, even those with aphasia, began to verbalize or indicate by gesture that they felt a sensation of flow, current of electricity, or movement in the affected extremity. This sensation, coupled with a decrease in pain and spasticity greatly lessened some of the fear and anxiety commonly seen with stroke victims. Families, home health aides, and now many physical therapists and occupational therapists are utilizing therapeutic touch effectively with this patient population (Fanslow, 1981).

In using therapeutic touch with stroke patients, I have been greatly impressed by the change in their way of seeing and relating to themselves. The energy made available to them appears to facilitate greatly a new harmony and balance within them, and to eliminate some of the disequilibrium and body distortion they usually manifest in the poststroke periods. When these patients become able to see themselves as two-sided again, their increased sense of integrity and wholeness creates a profound effect on their self-image. This self-image shift has also helped their family members and caregivers to see them again as whole. Families also are helped to reintegrate and adjust to the person with disabilities and are not simply reacting to the disability itself.

My work persuades me that further application and investigation of therapeutic touch with poststroke patients can do a great deal to improve the quality of their lives as well as help them feel and reengage on the mental image level. The consistency of the therapeutic touch treatment is most essential with this patient population due to the profound cerebral insult. Teaching therapeutic touch to nurses and aides in stroke units and rehabilitation hospitals, as well as to families of poststroke veterans is important for both patient and family.

An eight-month study on two Parkinson's disease patients showed a response of a gradual decrease in tremors and gait improvements on a therapeutic touch regime. In a one-year study four patients with multiple sclerosis were treated with therapeutic touch, primarily through the spinal column, in an attempt to actually stimulate and revitalize the myelin sheath. In the patients treated in this manner, eye problems decreased markedly, and balance and gait problems improved with regular treatments over the one-year period.

One cannot conclude a chapter dealing with the elderly without including a discussion of death and dying. Therapeutic touch can be used as a primary modality to assist the dying process and death transition of our elders (Fanslow, 1981). I stated earlier in this chapter that touch needs increase with the aging process and seem to take on an even greater intensity as the elderly near the end of the life continuum. I am drawn to place my hands on or near the heart area of the dying elder, since this is the area of relationship and fear. It requires a tremendous amount of life energy to make amends, say goodbye, I'm sorry, or I love you, before death occurs. As I hold my hand on or near the heart area, I am consciously sending thoughts of peace, love, and wholeness to the dying. This sensitive and profound interaction makes energy available to them to finish their business with those who will remain here, to decrease some of the predeath anxiety, and to enable them to separate.

The elders treated feel a deep warmth and a feeling of peace and calm filling the entire heart area. In addition to placing my hands in the heart area, I use other hand movements in the therapeutic touch interactions, following the human life flow from head to foot, and from body center point out the upper and lower extremities in a gentle rhythmic manner. This special energy transduction gives the elder a sense of total body calming and relief. Feeling more nearly total and whole, the elder is able to let go on this level.

I have taught countless nurses and family members this technique as a primary modality to facilitate the predeath separation phase, to assist the dying person in the transition we call death, and to help the family adjust to the reality of the imminent transition. The inner balance and harmony that are effected by this kind of interaction release the dying person to begin the last leg of his or her personal life journey.

Like our entrance into life, this final journey must be embarked upon, and finally accomplished, essentially alone, despite the helping hands and presence of others during the process. As the family members, caregivers, and nurse practitioners realize that they can facilitate the separation in this unique, exquisitely human interaction, they are able to begin their own separation and deeper letting go, which is initiated by the sudden, yet clear recognition of the reality of the impending death. Therapeutic touch can therefore assist the dying person, the family, and the helper to ease the difficulties surrounding and influencing the "holding on and letting go" which is the resolution of the life–death conflict within all of us (Fanslow, 1983).

I have become convinced that therapeutic touch, more than any other helping modality, responds on a very deep level to the most basic needs of the elders. First, it addresses their need for actual, tangible physical touch, creating a sense of safety and security. Second, the energy made available to support them at the self-image level addresses psychological, affective need. The therapeutic touch interaction is able to decrease the fear, anxiety, and insecurity experienced by elders, with the result that they begin really to live each day rather than just exist. The functional and affective quality of their life is greatly improved by cumulative energy interchange that restores balance and harmony to their life. Therapeutic touching of the elderly is indeed an essential element during perhaps the most critical period of life.

From my work with the elderly, I have come to realize how great is the significance of touch for those at the end of life. Through the medium of therapeutic touch, the nurse's intentionality, desire to help, and compassion for the elder are actualized, expressed, and made manifest to and for those who are waiting and longing to be touched on so many levels.

Discussion: Chapter 21

Paul Satz: It's interesting that you got better results with right hemiplegics than with left in working with stroke patients. There is evidence now that right hemiplegics tend to go into rehabilitation feeling anguished, often aphasic, with comprehension impaired and unable to communicate. These people feel frustrated, and they suffer. Left hemiplegics come in with benign indifference to their problems, by and large. A year later we find that the right hemiplegics have made a great recovery and the left hemiplegics have not, by virtue of being somewhat neglectful of the diseased side or extremity.

Cathleen Fanslow: My observations fall right in line with what you're saying, Paul.

William Greenough: With the brain-injured, the way you treat the person has to vary somewhat depending on the injury. One form of therapy is not going to be good for all.

Paul Satz: Absolutely. For example, a person with left hemiplegia tends to deny or neglect what happens on the left side of space. If you don't understand this—if you approach these people from the left and perhaps try to lay hands on them—this could do them a disservice. It could make them very paranoid.

T. Berry Brazelton: Couldn't you pick up on that behaviorally?

Paul Satz: Probably not. They would smile at you. Even though they're devastated, they might seem unresponsive. There's a basic lack of affect.

T. Berry Brazelton: Cathy, Renée Weber described three models for an approach to touch: the physical–sensory, which we are more or less stuck with in this culture; the psychological–humanistic, which I trust we're reaching for; and the field model, which has been tough for some of us here to take. I'd like to thank you for showing us what clinical work based on the field model can do. The idea that safe-and-secure touches can overcome the barriers of age is a beautiful image for all of us.

Sandra Weiss: I'd like to add that I believe the multidisciplinary nature of this work has been extremely valuable. The diversity of our perspectives will expand the ways that all of us conceptualize our work in the future. It should increase both the validity of our research efforts and the effectiveness of our therapeutic interventions.

Seymour Levine: One thing that's come out of it for me is a whole new appreciation of the nursing profession. I don't think I really had any notion of the nature of the different roles and how they can be defined.

Kathryn Barnard: I have a great deal of respect for the descriptive work you've done, Cathy. It's helped us become ready to move from a descriptive level to one that gives us more ability to infer general phenomena. The elderly and the dying have, until very recently, been abandoned by most of us in health care, so my hat is off to you. They need touch very badly.

Cathleen Fanslow: And the world needs it. The world needs it very, very much. What's come through to me here is that there's always a risk, but we have to act anyway. It's hard to give people the courage to try even though we don't know everything. But we must try—the more knowledgeably, the better, of course. We have to take the risk, and not to wait.

References

Fanslow, C. (1979), Role of the clinical nursing specialist in rehabilitation in the general hospital. In: *Current Perspectives in Rehabilitation Nursing*, eds. R. Murray & J. Kijeh. St. Louis: C. V. Mosby.

———(1981), Death: A natural facet of the life continuum. In: *Foundations for Holistic Health Nursing Practices, The Renaissance Nurse*, ed. D. Krieger. Philadelphia: J. B. Lippincott, pp. 249–271.

———(1983), Therapeutic touch: A healing modality throughout life. *Topics in Clin. Nurs.*, 3:72–79.

Krieger, D. (1975), Therapeutic touch: The imprimatur of nursing. *Amer. J. Nurs.*, 75:784–787.

———(1979), *The Therapeutic Touch: How to Use Your Hands to Help or Heal*. Englewood Cliffs, NJ: Prentice-Hall.

———(1981), *Foundations of Holistic Health Nursing Practices: The Renaissance Nurse*. Philadelphia: J. B. Lippincott.
Rogers, M. (1971), *An Introduction to the Theoretical Basis of Nursing*. Philadelphia: F. A. Davis.

Part VII: Touch as a Touchstone

22
Touch as a Touchstone: Summary of the Round Table

T. Berry Brazelton, M. D.

In this concluding chapter, I would like to relate some of the aspects of touch we have examined to my own work with neonates; to highlight the diverse perspectives of the contributors to this volume; and to suggest directions for further work.

Touch, as we have seen, functions on many levels of adaptation, first to make survival possible and then to make life meaningful. Many of the ideas discussed in this volume are extremely relevant to my own work with neonates. The notions of passive and active touch, for example, can be looked at in relation to the concept of state, a critical issue for newborns. The fragile infant on the waterbed, as Anneliese Korner has shown us, settles down and begins to learn how to use inner control to manage his state. In the process, the infant becomes more effective, gaining mastery over state and motor responses. Touch acts as an alerter, helping the infant reach a receptive alert state in which he can process information. Touch represents, in itself, an important source of information for the infant: it tells the neonate, whose vision is still not good, that the caregiver is present. Touch keeps the infant in contact with the human world.

We should also remember, as we consider the relation between touch and the newborn's state, that we need to be sure that the infant's experience of touch is a positive one. For touch can overexcite and overload, as well as soothe and control. Michael Merzenich reminds us of the importance of respecting the individual's needs and hypersensitivities. A baby who has experienced a central nervous system (CNS) insult is hypersensitive to the very experiences around which he needs to organize his nervous system. Unless we respect that hypersensitivity, the information we convey, through touch and other modalities, will overload the infant. Unless we are aware of the baby's threshold for receiving information, our best-intentioned therapeutic efforts may go awry.

In addition to state, mother–infant interaction has been a major focus of my own work, and here again touch plays a crucial role in that most fundamental of social systems. Seymour Levine has pointed out that touch is a form of social communication which transcends almost all culture. It is in the mother–infant relationship that the infant begins the process of using the elements of his environment to become a socialized organism. As the baby learns about himself, learns about the mother, and learns that he can be effective in his universe, touching and being touched are vital.

When Renée Weber distinguished the intent and expectations involved in the touch of an "I–it" interaction from those in an "I–thou" relationship, I realized that with this distinction, applied to mother–infant interaction, one could almost differentiate between mothers who are going to "make it" with their babies and mothers who will have difficulty. Intent is another concept useful in thinking about mother–infant interaction. Mary Main, as we have seen, could discern the smallest nuance of an interaction between mothers and their children. "Touch accessibility" is an elegant idea—I can see it in the rhythms, in the imitation between adult and infant that I observe so often. I found myself particularly intrigued by the idea of touch regulating the mother's response as much as it does the baby's. It is fascinating to learn from Seymour Levine's work that the mother's cortisol is affected if she has the opportunity to touch and to be with her infant. I am concerned that if our society allows mothers to go on being pulled apart from their babies too early, before their learning process has gone on, then no matter what kind of surrogate care we provide for the babies, *mothers* are likely to suffer in terms of their own maturation.

Of course many of the contributions in this volume have particular relevance to my own interest in fragile babies. Several authors have described the ways in which touch can comfort these infants, help them control their state, and enhance their physiological functioning. Other authors remind us that we need constantly to attend to the babies as monitors of our own interventions: Peter Gorski notes that by exercising support for CNS maturation in our care for fragile newborns, we will at the same time create healthier lungs, digestive systems, and other organ systems, all ultimately reliant on the CNS. Since I am always looking for ways to support parents, Patricia Rausch's study of tactile and kinesthetic programs aimed not only at improving the status and control systems within the baby but also at reproducing something that could be passed on to parents, was particularly meaningful. Susan Rose observes the difference in organization between preterms and full terms, suggests common mechanisms that may underlie effective interventions to improve state organization, and reminds us of the careful research designs that are needed to increase our understanding.

Thinking about preterm infant's efforts to overcome persistent effects of disorganization leads me to mention another theme of this volume—deprivation or insult, and repair. Michael Merzenich's work on the potential for recovery even after sensory deprivation or trauma to the CNS helps us get beyond the "fixed deficit" model of the central nervous system.

Martin Reite tells us about the kind of control and peripheral mechanisms in mother and infant primates that are affected by deprivation of touch and by grief, and which seem strikingly similar to problems I encounter regularly in my pediatric practice among mothers and infants attempting to adjust to separation. Stephen Suomi has observed that, for primates, the effects of tactile deprivation can be reversed in a social situation, leading us to wonder how we can help human mothers from deprived backgrounds to nurture their infants adequately and sensitively. Marian Diamond's findings about the increased size of the female rat's cortex during pregnancy and possibly during nurturing may lead to interesting avenues for exploration. These themes resonate further as we think about the brain-injured and about individuals near the end of life. Cathleen Fanslow reminds us that people with specific kinds of deficits have different needs. Paul Satz notes advances from past years when the brain-injured languished with no help whatsoever, but cautions that the remediation of the brain is now in its infancy, perhaps with "more help than evidence" at present.

The search for evidence to bolster our hope and direct our energies is the final theme I wish to emphasize. That contributors to this volume come from a broad range of intellectual disciplines, research traditions, and clinical settings has encouraged, I believe, a particularly rich exchange of questions that need to be investigated and methodological approaches that may be useful as we seek to document observations, test hypotheses, and increase our understanding of still mysterious phenomena. Allen Gottfried observed that just a few years ago we had no knowledge about the environment of hospitalized premature newborns. The discussions between interventionists and other researchers led to the accumulation of a considerable body of evidence on the physical and social environment of these infants, evidence which has laid the foundation for more sophisticated interventions and for further research on infant neurology.

Careful observation must underlie all of our investigations, as well as meticulous efforts to put our observations in proper context. Thus, Susan Rose and Anneliese Korner, in intervention studies, have suggested not only that preterm infants be compared to full-term babies as well as to each other, but also that thought be given to the appropriate age for full-term control. Paul Satz has pointed out the difficulties of many current follow-up studies of children that start too late, use samples that are too small, and look only at academic performance. Given the costliness of prospective studies, we may need to develop new research designs to address these problems. In the area of therapeutic touch, we see special opportunities for systematic observation of phenomena and documentation of what is being done. The work of Therese Connell Meehan, Judith Smith, and Iris Wolfson remind us that people need to study and document what they are doing in order for others to believe in it and to use it. Such a process of study also increases the confidence of the therapist. This process certainly occurred in the development of my neonatal scale: nothing in it was new; rather the scale put down on paper clinical or intuitive insights that many of us had been relying on for a long time. Yet putting the items on paper made them into a viable system.

Challenging concepts and new ways of framing questions also suggest promising paths for investigation. William Greenough reminds us that we know very little about touch because we can deprive an animal of most sound and all vision, but not of touch. What kinds of experiments, other than deprivation experiments, then, can we devise to yield more information? The concept of state organization and the evidence accumulated by intervention programs spur our interest in discovering a common mechanism providing the "fuel for organization" in many modalities. Mary Main's conceptualizations of an "attachment figure in my space" and of "tactile accessibility" provide a focus for observations that are critical to our understanding of the nurturing process, whether between mother and infant or nurse and patient. Sandra Weiss urges us to continue investigation of gender differences in regard to touch, an approach which complements Ruth McCorkle's thinking about touch in relation to cultural differences and social status, as well as to gender. Elizabeth McAnarney's concept of the changing meaning of touch over time gives us another window on the importance of touch and a direction for further research.

The image of the touchstone may be a fitting one with which to conclude this volume. A touchstone is a black, salacious rock that in ancient times was used to test the purity of gold and silver. One rubbed the object to be tested against the stone; gold or silver would each produce a streak of a characteristic color. I like to think of the contributors to this book as rubbing their research methodologies, their observations, their hypotheses, and their explanations against the touchstone of touch. As we have seen, a treasury of precious ideas has already been discovered, and I feel confident that as we continue our conscientious prospecting, we will unearth an even richer vein of understanding about touch, the foundation of experience.

Name Index

Subject Index